Believers Church Bible Commentary

Elmer A. Martens and Willard M. Swartley, Editors

Believers Church
Bible Commentary

Hosea, Amos

Allen R. Guenther

HERALD PRESS
Scottdale, Pennsylvania
Waterloo, Ontario

Library of Congress Cataloging-in-Publication Data
Guenther, Allen R., 1938-
    Hosea, Amos / Allen R. Guenther.
      p. cm. — (Believers church Bible commentary)
    Includes bibliographical references and index.
    ISBN 0-8361-9072-6 (alk. paper)
      1. Bible. O.T. Hosea—Commentaries. 2. Bible. O.T. Amos—
Commentaries. I. Title. II. Series.
    BS1565.3.G84 1997
    224'.607—dc21   97-37901

Canadian Cataloguing-in-Publication Data
Guenther, Allen Robert, 1938-
    Hosea, Amos
(Believers church Bible commentary)
Includes bibliographical references and index.
ISBN 0-8361-9072-6
1. Bible. O.T. Hosea—Commentaries. 2. Bible. O.T. Amos—
    Commentaries. I. Title. II. Title: Amos. III. Series.
BS1563.3.G83 1997   224'.607   C97-932020-8

The paper used in this publication is recycled and meets the minimum requirements of American National Standard for Information Sciences—Permanence of Paper for Printed Library Materials, ANSI Z39.48-1984.
Bible quotations are used by permission, all rights reserved, and are from the author or from the NRSV: *New Revised Standard Version Bible,* copyright 1989, by the Division of Christian Education of the National Council of the Churches of Christ in the USA. Other versions are used briefly in making comparisons: NIV: *New International Version;* NEB, *New English Bible;* RSV: *Revised Standard Version.*

BELIEVERS CHURCH BIBLE COMMENTARY: HOSEA, AMOS
Copyright © 1998 by Herald Press, Scottdale, Pa. 15683
    Published simultaneously in Canada by Herald Press,
    Waterloo, Ont. N2L 6H7. All rights reserved
Library of Congress Catalog Number: 97-37901
Canadiana Entry Number: C97-932020-8
International Standard Book Number: 0-8361-9072-6
Printed in the United States of America
Charts by Robert C. Tylka
Cover by Merrill R. Miller

07 06 05 04 03 02 01 00 99 98 10 9 8 7 6 5 4 3 2 1

To Anne, Ron,
Barry, and Michael

BELIEVERS CHURCH BIBLE COMMENTARY

Old Testament

Genesis, by Eugene F. Roop
Jeremiah, by Elmer A. Martens
Ezekiel, by Millard C. Lind
Daniel, by Paul M. Lederach
Hosea, Amos, by Allen R. Guenther

New Testament

Matthew, by Richard B. Gardner
Acts, by Chalmer E. Faw
2 Corinthians, by V. George Shillington
Colossians, Philemon, by Ernest D. Martin
1 and 2 Thessalonians, by Jacob W. Elias

Contents

HOSEA

Introduction to Hosea

Part 1: Biography of a Marriage Failure, 1:2—3:5

Part 2: Trial Transcript: God Versus the Heirs, 4:1—14:9

AMOS

Abbreviations and Cross-References

ANE   ancient Near East(ern)
(*ANEP*), (*ANET*), or (author's name)   See Bibliography
ca.   *circa*, approximately
cent.   century
cf.   *conferre*, compare
[*Covenant, p. 379*]   Sample cross-reference to Essays
e.g.   for example
et par.   and parallel(s), as in Matthew, Mark, and Luke
Heb.   Hebrew language or text of OT
(Hillers: 58-60)   Sample reference to source listed in Bibliography
lit.   literally
NEB, NIV, NRSV, RSV   Versions; see copyright page (p. 4)
notes   Explanatory Notes for each section
NT   New Testament
OT   Old Testament
pl./s.   plural/singular
TBC or *   The Text in Biblical Context
TLC or +   The Text in the Life of the Church

Series Foreword

The Believers Church Bible Commentary Series makes available a new tool for basic Bible study. It is published for all who seek more fully to understand the original message of Scripture and its meaning for today—Sunday school teachers, members of Bible study groups, students, pastors, and other seekers. The series is based on the conviction that God is still speaking to all who will listen, and that the Holy Spirit makes the Word a living and authoritative guide for all who want to know and do God's will.

The desire to help as wide a range of readers as possible has determined the approach of the writers. Since no blocks of biblical text are provided, readers may continue to use the translation with which they are most familiar. The writers of the series use the *New Revised Standard Version*, the *Revised Standard Version*, the *New International Version*, and the *New American Standard Bible* on a comparative basis. They indicate which text they follow most closely, as well as where they make their own translations. The writers have not worked alone, but in consultation with select counselors, the series' editors, and the Editorial Council.

Every volume illuminates the Scriptures; provides necessary theological, sociological, and ethical meanings; and in general, makes "the rough places plain." Critical issues are not avoided, but neither are they moved into the foreground as debates among scholars. Each section offers explanatory notes, followed by focused articles, "The Text in Biblical Context" and "The Text in the Life of the Church."

The writers have done the basic work for each commentary, but not operating alone, since "no . . . Scripture is a matter of one's own interpretation" (2 Pet. 1:20; cf. 1 Cor. 14:29). They have consulted with select counselors during the writing process, worked with the editors for the series, and received feedback from another biblical scholar. In addition, the Editorial Council, representing six believers church denominations, reads the manuscripts carefully, gives church-ly responses, and makes suggestions for changes. The writer considers all this counsel and processes it into the manuscript, which the Editorial Council finally approves for publication. Thus these commentaries combine the individual writers' own good work and the church's voice. As such, they represent a hermeneutical community's efforts in interpreting the biblical text, as led by the Spirit.

The term *believers church* has often been used in the history of the church. Since the sixteenth century, it has frequently been applied to the Anabaptists and later the Mennonites, as well as to the Church of the Brethren and similar groups. As a descriptive term, it includes more than Mennonites and Brethren. *Believers church* now represents specific theological understandings, such as believers baptism, commitment to the Rule of Christ in Matthew 18:15-20 as crucial for church membership, belief in the power of love in all relationships, and willingness to follow Christ in the way of the cross. The writers chosen for the series stand in this tradition.

Believers church people have always been known for their emphasis on obedience to the simple meaning of Scripture. Because of this, they do not have a long history of deep historical-critical biblical scholarship. This series attempts to be faithful to the Scriptures while also taking archaeology and current biblical studies seriously. Doing this means that at many points the writers will not differ greatly from interpretations which can be found in many other good commentaries. Yet these writers share basic convictions about Christ, the church and its mission, God and history, human nature, the Christian life, and other doctrines. These presuppositions do shape a writer's interpretation of Scripture. Thus this series, like all other commentaries, stands within a specific historical church tradition.

Many in this stream of the church have expressed a need for help in Bible study. This is justification enough to produce the Believers Church Bible Commentary. Nevertheless, the Holy Spirit is not bound to any tradition. May this series be an instrument in breaking down walls between Christians in North America and around the world, bringing new joy in obedience through a fuller understanding of the Word.

—The Editorial Council

Author's Preface

This commentary is my invitation for you to learn to know and love two personal friends, Hosea and Amos, and the message that came through them for God's people in a critical time in Israel's history.

This friendship has grown to maturity over the past ten years. I am told that I spend some of my sleeping hours interpreting their words. We even laugh together in those night hours. They are pleasant company, though they speak strong words in times of crisis. Still, I have only begun to feel their passion for God and his people, their zest for life.

I am indebted to the many who have nurtured this friendship. Foremost among these is my wife, Anne, who has supported me with humor and affection. The sabbatical policies and generosity of the seminary board of directors provided three six-month sabbaticals. Without them, I could not have finished this commentary. I have been both buoyed and challenged by my friend, colleague, and editor, Professor Elmer A. Martens. Readers Dave Durksen, Malinda Nikkel, Joby Dupuis, and Phyllis Martens were immensely encouraging. Hebrew exegesis students stimulated my thinking, questioned my assumptions, debated my exegesis, challenged my understanding of biblical Hebrew, and offered many constructive counterproposals.

Teaching assistant Cal Bergen and my son Michael absorbed much of the tedium by entering revisions on the keyboard. Special appreciation is due to the many who have listened to parts of earlier versions and who energized me by comments from "Uh-huh" to "What difference does that make?" and "When will it be available?" Finally, I acknowledge the patience of the publisher, who interpreted my annual unrealistic projections of progress with grace.

No other venture has been as intellectually and spiritually stimulating for me as this in-depth reading of the words of Amos and Hosea, first spoken to Israel (the Northern Kingdom), written to Judah (the Southern Kingdom), and preserved for us "on whom the fulfillment of the ages has come" (1 Cor. 10:11, NIV).

Thanks and praise be to God, the Father of our Lord Jesus Christ.

—*Allen R. Guenther*
Mennonite Brethren Biblical Seminary
Fresno, California
Spring 1996

Hosea

Introduction to Hosea

Hosea, the Man

Nothing is known of the prophet Hosea beyond what his prophecies yield concerning him. Even that is sparse. By God's command, Hosea married Gomer, a prostitute. Their family eventually consisted of three children: two sons, Jezreel and Lo-ammi; and a daughter, Lo-ruhamah. Husband and wife were divorced, but then Hosea bought her back. Hosea's life experiences became a backdrop for the Lord's message to his people.

The name *Hosea* means "[God] delivers." God saves his people. Hosea lived through the closing chapter of the Northern Kingdom. His ministry bridged the collapse of the North and continued in the South after the death of Jeroboam II.

The Times

Assyria and Egypt appear repeatedly in these prophecies of the eighth century B.C. Assyria poses a threat to the people; Egypt acts as a refuge for those seeking escape from the coming judgment. The historical background is identical to that of Amos *[Historical Summary, p. 384]*.

Unlike Amos, Hosea appears to be a citizen of the Northern Kingdom, Israel. The evidence is circumstantial rather than definite.

Hosea as Literature

Its Source

The book of Hosea appears to be a collection of sermons preached over a lifetime of ministry. We can only speculate who might have compiled and edited them. Was it Hosea himself as he reflected on life in the joy of restored love? Was it a student in one of the prophetic schools which dotted the Northern Kingdom (cf. 2 Kings 1-6)? Could it have been one or more persons who attached themselves to the man of God as his disciples (cf. Isa. 8:16-18)? Or might it have been a Judean or group of Judeans for whom the Assyrian destruction of Samaria was the test of truth for the man and his message?

Its Beauty and Power

Hosea is the stuff of artists' daydreams and translators' nightmares. The author compresses ideas into compact, image-filled prophetic pronouncements. Figures of speech tumble over one another, inviting the reader into a complex world of multilevel relationships and meaning. Thoughts cascade in fits and starts. The emotional intensity varies only slightly through recurring cycles of disappointment, anger, and hope, for in Hosea we are encountering a prophet still raw from the wounds of offended love.

Hosea is a master of the diatribe, satirical criticism. He turns the people's words against them with the thrust and parry of an expert swordsman. He quotes their everyday speech; he knows their practices (4:15; 13:2), proverbs (9:7), prayers (2:16; 8:2; 11:7), and pride (12:8). Hosea writes as an insider, one intimately familiar with the people's ways of thinking and speaking.

Its Design

Metaphor and story merge to form a collage capturing the agony and the ecstasy of Hosea and Gomer's relationship. Simultaneously it depicts the rocky marriage of God and Israel (Hos. 1-3). Chapters 4-14 are not easily fused to the opening story—unless the second large block of text is intended to elaborate in concrete form, under the metaphor of the children, what is initially depicted in the story of Hosea and Gomer.

The book follows a design in its parts as well as in its larger whole. Hosea's entire ministry and message bear the stamp of his marital and family experience. Indeed, the language of the divorced wife and mother occurs in both parts (2:4; 4:5), as do references to the children, whom he denounces along with their mother. Those same children later become special objects of unreserved love (2:21-23; 11:1-11).

Hosea!

The pages of the book remain at the level of drama until we hear every accusation, every thundering judgment, and every invitation to unfold the meaning of that name. Hosea! "He saves."

Numerous catchwords and themes tie the two major sections closely together. The author forms the redemptive story unifying the book by using the language of prostitution, lovers, shame, sacred stones, idols, lawsuit, fertility, wilderness, drought, wild animals, covenant breaking, and covenant renewal [Covenant, p. 379].

The prophecies move the reader through a number of dimensions of thought, space, and time simultaneously. The stories of Yahweh (the Lord) and Israel also tell us of Hosea and Gomer. The prophet's words lead us through different strata of society, occasionally within the same pericope (section), past king and princes, the religious hierarchy, and commoners. They portray Israel as mother and at the same time as three children of their mother. They reflect at least two levels of religious life coexisting amicably but under divine censure: the official religion of the nation and the people's everyday faith [Israelite Religion, p. 385]. The prophecies transport us through time, linking past and present, anticipating the future.

Yes, the future. The future itself consists of judgment and salvation, sometimes intermingled, sometimes held apart by Israel's inertia and God's holiness. Finally, the prophetic announcements insert Hosea's words into the flow of the text. On occasion he dialogues with God (9:10-17), at other times he gives voice to divinely informed judgments of Israel's condition and fate (9:1-9; 10:1-8; 12:2-8; 12:11—13:3). One has the impression that God and prophet have been in conversation about Israel: some of it Hosea conveys verbatim, some he records as dialogue generated in the recesses of his heart. Indeed, the book may contain as few as twenty-two verses in which God addresses Israel directly (2:16, 19-20; 4:5-6, 13b-14a, 15a; 5:1-3; 6:4-6; 9:10a; 10:9a; 11:8-9; 12:9-10; 13:4-5, 9-11).

Nor is Israel silent. Her words, like Gomer's, are sparse; but they indicate the condition of her heart. The hollow formula of the appeal to God's sovereignty, As surely as Yahweh (the Lord) lives (4:15), later becomes, Come, let us return to Yahweh (6:1). Her distraught My

God! We know you! It's Israel here! (8:2) leads on to depression and despair: *We have no king because we do not fear Yahweh, and, as for a king, what can he do for us?* (10:3). The final step in that progression is the death wish spoken to the mountains, *Cover us!* and to the hills, *Fall on us!* (10:8c). In the end we hear Israel's boast, *I have become rich! I have become powerful! In all my accumulated wealth they will not find any sin of which I am guilty* (12:8); and her blatant acceptance of Baal worship: *Those who offer human sacrifices kiss calf-idols* (13:2) *[Ba'al, p. 373]*. These statements must be replaced by the only words which can please God: *Forgive our iniquity completely . . .* (14:2b-3).

Chapters 1–3 prefigure the structure and themes of the body of the book of Hosea. Gomer, the wife, is Israel. Jezreel, Lo-ruhamah, and Lo-ammi, the children, are also Israel. The Northern Kingdom is Israel and Jacob, Ephraim and Samaria *[Jacob and Isaac, p. 389]*. Israel is also the prostitute, a cow in heat *[Bovine Imagery, p. 374]*, the land, and a bride. Hence, the language shifts rapidly and sometimes unaccountably from "you" (singular) to "you" (plural), to "he" and "she" and "they" (masculine). The names identify the sins of God's people, convey the consequent judgment, and sow seeds of hope in the divine saving initiative.

Accusation, judgment, salvation: this is the pattern of speeches on each of the three themes in the second part of the book.

There is more to the book than meets the eye. The language of chapters 1-3 springs from everyday life: from marriage, home, family, and from the law court, with its technical terminology of divorce proceedings, renunciation of paternity, and disinheritance. The vocabulary and phraseology, as well as the order of events and the rituals involved, can be compared with those of marriage, divorce, and other family documents from Hammurabi's Babylon to the Aramaic and Greek-speaking Jewish communities in Egypt down to 300 B.C. *[Marriage, p. 393]*. These chapters are set in the family life and divorce courts of Hosea's day. Comparisons and details will appear, frame by frame, as we explore the text.

The Story

Chapters 1-3 trace the tragedy of Hosea and Gomer's marriage through the birth of three children. God's touch appears in the command to *go, take for yourself a wife* (1:2), as well as in the names of the three children. The attention given to the birth and naming of the children signals their importance.

The wife's first child, *Jezreel*, meaning *God-will-sow*, was fathered by Hosea (*she . . . bore him a son*, 1:3). The second and third children were probably not fathered by the prophet. We deduce this from the details and omissions of the story.

Lo-ruhamah literally means *Not-loved* or *Not-pitied* (1:6). In the legal language of Babylon, Lo-ruhamah describes a child who is disinherited. The name of the third child, *Lo-ammi*, signifies rejection: *Not-my-people*. In Babylonian legal documents it means *Disowned*. *Lo-ammi* represents, at one and the same time, a statement of non-paternity and the third stage of parental distancing.

Gomer's unfaithfulness shreds the fabric of their marriage. We wonder, How much pain and rejection love can endure? When will Hosea leave well enough alone? "Let it be!" "Your marriage is dead!" we call out across the centuries.

When Hosea cannot endure the pain any longer, the story erupts in a pathos-filled divorce-court scene. Their children act as witnesses to Gomer's unfaithfulness (2:2). The details receive close attention. In corresponding Babylonian divorce proceedings, guilt or innocence determine whether the wife forfeits or retains her dowry. Adultery can occasion the death penalty in Babylon as well as in Israel. Hosea apparently chooses to send Gomer away empty-handed rather than subject her to a trial for a capital crime. The divorce, however, does not end the relationship. Hosea's goal is Gomer's restoration.

Though their names are weighted with meaning, Hosea's children disappear after the pronouncement of divorce: *Plead with your mother, plead—for she is not my wife, and I am not her husband* (2:2). Across the ancient Near East, the marriage laws and practices declare that the children belong to the husband. When Hosea buys back his wife, Gomer, from her pimp, the children are not mentioned. Where have all the children gone?

The Story Around the Story

Hosea's family, in name and reality, is Israel written small. The Lord chooses Hosea to represent him as a living message to the Northern Kingdom. At Sinai, God committed himself in a covenant to Israel. Since marriage is also a covenant, Hosea's marriage to Gomer fittingly pictures the intimacy and unfaithfulness of Israel *[Covenant, p. 379]*.

Each of Hosea and Gomer's children initially represents a distinctive aspect of the nation. *Jezreel* is associated with the *kingdom of the house of Israel* (1:4), the rule or the authority to rule over this people and their territory. *Lo-ruhamah* is connected with the *house of Israel* (1:6), those who by right lay claim to that territory. *Lo-ammi*, on the other hand, is addressed to the people as a whole (1:8).

At the birth of the third child, the words of hope spoken to Hosea indicate that the firstborn, *Jezreel*, will alone remain in the land. One day Jezreel will welcome back the other children, renamed *Ammi* (*my people*) and *Ruhamah* (*chosen heir*, 1:8—2:1).

When the Lord interprets his experience with his people, he implies that Israel was a foundling daughter who was reared and later betrothed by her gracious Lord *[Marriage, p. 393]*. The scenario is realistic in that world. Israel had no dowry; she came to marriage destitute, with the social status of a concubine. If the marriage patterns serve as background to the metaphor, the Lord's bride had just passed puberty. In contrast with her mature Husband (the Lord), Israel was a young adolescent wife.

Israel's Benefactor and Husband lavished on her gifts of wool and linen clothing, food in abundance, and a secure land. Immature Israel gathered the gifts to herself and flaunted them to attract other lovers. With patient and persistent love, the Husband was calling the wife, Israel, back as he endured a series of Israel's adulterous relationships. But when the wife persisted in pursuing one liaison after the next, God initiated divorce proceedings, recovered his gifts from her hand, and expelled her from his land (Hos. 2).

At this point Gomer and the three children merge fully with the figure of Israel. Her restoration (2:14-22) goes hand in hand with an invitation for the children to be reconciled to one another and to their Father (2:23). The promise of reconciliation with Lo-ruhamah and Lo-ammi, already spoken at their name-giving, becomes reality. God affirms its fulfillment in Hosea 2. Thereafter the children appear as aspects and attitudes of Israel (Hos. 4–14).

The dominant themes in the second major part of the book grow out of the three children's characters. The three themes are identified in 4:1c: *no faithfulness (integrity), no loyalty (covenant love), and no knowledge of God in the land.* In typical Hebrew fashion, these topics are explored in reverse order in the remainder of the book. Each of these themes is represented by one of the children, as shown in the following chart:

Order and Relationship of the Parts of Hosea

	A	Jezreel (1:4-5) = No integrity (4:1b)
Part		
	B	Lo-Ruhamah (1:6-7) = No family affection (4:1b)
One		
	C	Lo-Ammi (1:8-11) = No knowledge of God (4:1b)
	C'	No knowledge of God (4:4—6:3)
Part		
	B'	No family affection (6:4—11:11)
Two		
	A'	No integrity (11:12—14:8)

Lo-ammi (*Not-my-people*) corresponds at the national level to *no knowledge of God*. In Hosea 4:1, the designation (*my/your*) *people* introduces the first section of part two (4:4—6:3) and is concentrated there in vocabulary and concept.

Lo-ruhamah is the *Not-loved* child. The language of love, compassion, and covenant affection are concentrated in the central section of the second part of Hosea (6:4—11:11).

Jezreel, the eldest child, symbolizes the occasion of Jehu's deceit and violence (2 Kings 9-10), as well as the productivity of the Valley of Jezreel, the breadbasket of the Northern Kingdom. The language of death and fertility; of conception, womb, and childbirth; or of violence and deception—such terms color virtually every verse of this closing section (11:12—14:8) [*Canaanite Fertility Myth, p. 376*].

Each of these names represents an aspect of Israel. Yet each also stands for a part of the whole. Hosea, Gomer, and the three children recede into the background. More accurately stated, they become absorbed by the larger drama of which they are a part. Now God and Israel occupy the main stage.

One should not conceive of these themes as distinct and unique treatments of Israel's history or moral condition. Just as the children's names represent facets of Israel's life, so the themes represent related perspectives from which to appraise the faith of this people. Visualize them as the nodes and sides of a triangle, as in the following chart:

Hosea 1-3: Gomer and Her Children

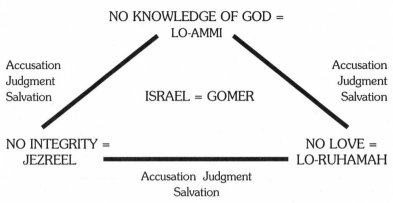

NO KNOWLEDGE OF GOD =
LO-AMMI

Accusation   Accusation
Judgment   Judgment
Salvation   ISRAEL = GOMER   Salvation

NO INTEGRITY =   NO LOVE =
JEZREEL   LO-RUHAMAH
Accusation Judgment
Salvation

Accusation, judgment, and salvation are not rigid categories; they follow Hebrew literary convention *[Accusation-Judgment-Salvation Oracles, p. 372]*. In general, accusation oracles describe in graphic form the sins of Israel—past and present—for which this people is held accountable. Occasionally the accusation oracle paints the sin of Israel against the backdrop of the Lord's love, gifts, or faithfulness. On other occasions the readers are ushered into the city gate and invited to observe the legal proceedings in which God is the Plaintiff and Judge and Gomer-Israel the accused. With the exception of the two accusation oracles in 7:1-7, all prophecies of this type end in brief statements of judgment.

The judgment oracles contain a measure of accusation and move quickly to the divinely appointed consequences of the sin. Initially (Hos. 5; 9:1—10:8) the judgment speeches contain no ray of hope. Beginning with the last judgment speech from the second perspective (No-love), words of impending destruction are inlaid with invitations to repentance (10:12). There is a reminder that the Lord is their Savior (13:4, 14a-b) *[Accusation-Judgment-Salvation Oracles, p. 372]*.

The children, Lo-ruhamah (Not-loved) and Lo-ammi (Not-my-people), receive their just reward. The natural consequences of broken relationships and distorted worship translate into the judgments of rejection, abandonment, prostitution, moral blindness and decay, internal strife, sickness, ravaging beasts, famine, and war. These rip the national will to shreds. The end result is exile (4:19; 5:14; 7:16;

8:10; 9:3, 15, 17; 10:5-7, 10; 11:5, 10-11). *Disinherited* and *Disowned* picture the nation in its eventual scattering among the peoples of the world.

In the concluding section (11:12—14:8, about Jezreel, God-sows), Israel comes under judgment, but the language of exile is absent. Israel fails to hear even the reminders of how God rescued them from Egypt. How then will they take warning of the consequences of making alliances with Egypt and Assyria? The east wind (Assyria) will sweep through the country. Israel serves as prey to the savage beasts. God abandons her to the slayer of pregnant women and infants. Jezreel, the firstborn, represents the remnant left in Palestine. The story of Hosea's family comes full circle only in the restoration of God's people.

Three salvation oracles bring hope to a disobedient family and nation. They consist of a song of repentance (6:1-3); a pathos-filled inner dialogue of God, the loving parent (11:1-11); and a joint appeal by Hosea and the Lord for genuine repentance. Repentance is the fitting way to prepare for God's restoration (14:1-8) *[Accusation-Judgment-Salvation Oracles, p. 372]*.

God and Hosea both raise their voices in protest, complaint, anger, and invitation. The sorry condition of Jacob's family and the prophet's family fuel their mutual anguish. The prophet is not unaware of the double message. Were it not for the plight of Israel, his family would have been intact. Hosea's words, whether raised in warning cry or in announcing the judgment, echo from his own home down through the centuries.

Character and Emphases of This Commentary

This commentary series is designed for the nonspecialist. It will serve the Christian community of laypersons, teachers, and pastors who are not necessarily fluent in the currents of Hosea studies, the fine points of Hebrew grammar, or the details of Near Eastern history and culture. Those are resources the commentator brings to the study of the text. The intended audience and limited space bring restraints. Frequently a debate with other commentators lies hidden in a turn of phrase, a specific scriptural reference, a surprisingly strongly stated point, or a brief word study. The primary concern is with truth and clarity.

I wish, however, to be explicit about the major features which characterize this interpretation and to some degree distinguish it from other studies in Hosea. Each student of any literature (sacred or common) develops a perspective from which the material is read and explained. To help the readers orient themselves to this commentary, I offer a summary of what I regard as the primary assumptions, distinctive features, perspectives, and insights of this commentary.

First, the book of Hosea falls naturally into two parts, chapters 1–3 and 4–14. The outline of the second part is my own, as is the correlation between the children and the three sections of part two.

Second, I view the recurring cycles of accusation (sins named and described), judgment (punishments identified), and salvation (hope in God's future work) as essential elements of the book's design. They characterize each of the six subsections.

Third, I see the sermons or sermon summaries as deliberately and carefully arranged to present a larger whole. On a first reading, the prophetic pronouncements reflecting the author's meditations, emotions, personal experiences, and public experiences may appear to be a random collection. The larger, sustained argument emerges only as we follow the primary images and themes of the individual sermons, cued by the occasional integrative editorial comment (cf. 4:1-3).

Fourth, I read the metaphor of marriage and family as running through both parts. Hosea's marriage experience was real (historical). It corresponds to what we know about marriage, family, sexual morality, sacred prostitution, divorce, inheritance, and remarriage from laws and family documents across the ancient Near East, from Hammurabi to the Christian era. Yet it is more accurate to say that the marriage of the Lord and Israel is the base form, the historical reality to which the book is addressed. That marriage is described in the language of Near Eastern societies. Hosea's marriage and family experiences then serve as the real metaphor, pointing to the covenant relationship between the Lord and Israel.

Fifth, I observe that the Yahwism (worship of Yahweh, the Lord) of the Northern Kingdom (Israel) developed differently than it did in Judah (the Southern Kingdom). Hosea validates the historical role of the exodus, conquest, and the Davidic monarchy. The distinctive Israelite emphases of the wilderness years and the Feast of Booths are prominent. Hosea also acknowledges, without criticism, Israel's worship at several centers of Yahwism [Israelite Religion, p. 385].

Sixth, I approach Hosea with the conviction that one cannot separate religious values and practices from other features of personal, community, civil, and national life. We should not be surprised to see what appears to be a hodgepodge of issues in the prophetic message.

Each culture creates a synthesis out of the stuff of life with its own glue. It is the interpreter's task to uncover the complex interactions of the core values, institutions, history, and practices of the people whose literature one is examining.

Thus, at one and the same time, "prostitution" may represent a socially accepted occupation, a religious ritual, adultery, a disapproving description of practical politics, the act of negotiating an international treaty, and honoring Baal for the produce of the soil. Westerners wish it to be one or the other [Prostitution, p. 393]. The reader of Hosea rarely has the luxury of choosing a single dimension of reality. That is not to make the text mean "anything you choose." Texts, like cut gems, are multifaceted and contain multiple dimensions of meaning. As each face turns to the light, it exposes the gem's hidden beauty. I hope the comments on the text will alert the reader to this complexity and brilliance.

Seventh, the book of Hosea is *written* for the people of Judah, inasmuch as its sermons bridge the trauma of the Assyrian exile (cf. 1:1). The fulfillment of Hosea's original message to the Northern Kingdom validated the rest of his words. In its written form, the book is intended first as a word of warning for the Judeans, and only secondarily as a message of repentance and hope to the scattered exiles of Israel. In its original spoken form, the reverse was true: the people of the North were the primary recipients, and the Judeans were a secondary audience.

Eighth, the book of Hosea comes to us with layers of accumulated meaning. This meaning has been gathered up within the biblical record itself. Occasionally we recognize distinctive strands as they emerge in other texts. But studies in intertextuality (comparing texts) based primarily on verbal cues capture only surface features of a much larger mass of truth-in-ferment. The reflections entitled "The Text in Biblical Context" are an attempt to uncover a few of the strains which recur elsewhere in the grand redemptive orchestral masterpiece. To those we must add our personal histories, our denominational and collective Western religious tradition and experience, and Christianity's deep Jewish rootage. All these have significantly shaped and colored our reading of the text. Some may regard the comments under "The Text in the Life of the Church" as out of place in a serious commentary; yet for those who stand in the evangelical Anabaptist tradition, the test of relevance is whether it reaches into other times and places. If the text has been so explained that it gracefully carries its meaning forward to our world, God be praised!

Much of the time in Hosea and Amos, I supply my own translation of the Hebrew text. Otherwise, of the many good versions of the Bible, I have chosen to follow the New Revised Standard Version. It is contemporary in its language, faithful to the biblical text, and inclusive of both genders. The prophet and this commentary refer to *Judah, Israel,* or *the nation* with a variety of pronouns, such as *you/your, he/his/him, she/hers/her, it/its, they/their.* This is due to the layers of characters and meanings and the unfolding drama and imagery, as introduced above. The context makes the meaning clear.

Hosea 1:1

Heading

PREVIEW

These opening words read like the data heading a memo:

From: *The Lord*
To: *Hosea, son of Beeri*
Date: *In the days of Uzziah*

EXPLANATORY NOTES

The Subject 1:1a

The superscriptions or headings of the prophetic books may be similar, but they are hardly slavishly identical. The phrase, *the word* (Heb.: *dabar) of the Lord* is common in the prophets (cf. Joel 1:1; Jonah 1:1; Micah 1:1; et al.) but refers to more than spoken words, though it includes them. When the term *word (dabar)* is connected to a person, it consistently refers to someone in authority or power, whether the Lord, Samuel (1 Sam. 4:1), David (2 Sam. 14:17), Elijah (1 Kings 17:1), or the king of Assyria (2 Kings 18:28-29). The contents of this book, therefore, are authoritatively given. They may be ignored only at considerable risk.

Dabar may also imply *affair, matter, business, thing,* as in *the mat-*

30

ter (dabar) concerning Uriah (1 Kings 15:5). Hence, while God is communicating with Hosea by means of words, he is not conveying speeches to be regurgitated. God is disclosing his intentions, his business with Israel. In the process of receiving the word of the Lord, the prophet becomes a member of the heavenly council, to whom God reveals his secret plans (Amos 3:7; cf. Jer. 23:18). Therefore, when Hosea interacts with God or offers a prophecy from his own lips, that word is to be regarded as coming from the counsel of the Lord; it consists of the purposes of God as fully as if he had quoted a first-person speech from the Almighty.

The phrase the word of the Lord that came is unique to the prophetic literature. The verb translated came/became to/belong to suggests an action which transcends speech. God's counsel fills the prophet's soul and consciousness. The words he speaks are an outpouring of those divine purposes. The word both possesses Hosea and is possessed by him. Yet it is not intended for private ownership, for the prophet is God's agent in this world.

The Prophet 1:1b

Hosea son of Beeri. The designation prophet is unnecessary, since God's word comes to prophets in this unique way.

Hosea is a relatively common name. The OT (Old Testament) identifies five people by this name. It was also common in the fifth-century B.C. Jewish community in the southern Egyptian city of Elephantine. The name comes from the Hebrew word yasaʿ, meaning to save, and thus means "salvation" or "deliverance." Nothing is known about Hosea's father, Beeri. Perhaps the father's name is given to follow convention. Since the name Hosea is commonplace, the prophet needs to be distinguished from others by that name.

The Date 1:1c

The dating formula attracts attention at three points. First, the contents of the book grow out of a ministry spanning the reigns of a number of kings. Five are identified. Thiele (see Bibliography) calculates that Jeroboam II's reign over Israel ends in 753 B.C., and Hezekiah's reign over Judah begins in 716 B.C. If so, Hosea's ministry extended from about 755 B.C. to at least 715 B.C., for forty years.

Second, it is unusual to have Hosea, a prophet of the Northern Kingdom, locate the dates of his ministry with reference to the kings of Judah before mentioning the king of his own country. Is this due to a bias on the part of Judean compilers of these prophecies? If so, why would these compilers include so few prophecies from Hosea's early Northern ministry, prophecies first *spoken* to Judah?

I suggest that following the Assyrian destruction of Samaria, Hosea turned to Judah with the earlier message originally given to the Northern Kingdom. These messages contained a sprinkling of references to Judah, showing he recognized that God's words through him were intended for all God's people *[Judah and David, p. 389]*. Israel rejected Hosea's messages. But the prophet continued to address the remnant of Israel which populated the countryside after the deportation of the leading citizens (2 Kings 17:5-6). Apart from the specific references to Judah, the contents of the book fit the period of time *before* the exile of Israel. None of the prophecies other than the calls to repentance naturally fit the situation of the exiles.

The most likely reason for using the kings of Judah as the primary chronological reference point is that the *book* is intended largely for the people of Judah. The degeneration of the Northern monarchy revived hope that Israel might again be reunited by a descendant of David (3:4-5). Using the kings of Judah as the primary reference point strongly accents the message of hope and reinforces Hosea's indictments against the rival king in the North (7:7; 8:4; 13:10-11).

The dating formula using the kings of Judah points even further toward the function of the book. The devastating earthquake predicted in Amos (8:8; 9:1-10) validated his message for future generations. Therefore it was recorded for posterity when that earthquake struck (1:1). Similarly, the sweeping victory of Assyrian armies predicted by Hosea in his ministry to the Northern Kingdom validates the rest of his words (1:4-5; 10:5-15; 13:14-16). Those words include messages of warning specifically addressed to Judah. So Hosea's earlier prophecies become the proof of his genuineness.

Every allusion to the word of God given through Hosea, every reminder of the message given to him before the fall of Samaria, stands as a call for Judah to repent. The prophecies which compare Judah's condition to Israel's alert the Judeans to their spiritual condition. God had fulfilled his earlier word against Israel; Judah faces mortal danger on its present course. Additional words are unnecessary.

While there is no known connection between the composition of Hosea and the reforms of Hezekiah, the description of the religious perversions which Hezekiah addresses in Judah are amazingly similar to those denounced in Hosea. Could it be that Hosea's message (together with the prophetic word of Isaiah) contributed to the spiritual renewal and the national reforms in Judah (cf. 2 Kings 18-20; 2 Chron. 29-32)? That would help to explain why Hezekiah's reforms were deliberately extended into the territory of the Northern Kingdom. Hezekiah may even have seen himself as the new David (Hosea 3:5) under whom the descendants of Abraham, Isaac, and Jacob would be reunited and reestablished in the land.

The third unusual feature in the dating formula concerns the last six kings of Israel. They are conspicuous by their absence. This omission should not be read as a sign that God has turned his back on Ephraim even before the end has come. Though the language of judgment is severe, Hosea continues to invite the nation to repentance (12:6). God's grace has not become exhausted, though their rebellion has wearied and grieved him deeply. Perhaps the rapid succession of four usurpers to the throne in the last five reigns raised the question of the legitimacy of these kings in the eyes of Hosea and his scribes.

What are we to make of these unusual features in the heading of the book of Hosea? They point to the essential, the theological unity of the people of God. The divided monarchy was a deviation. It did not represent God's intention, though he permitted it. The message of the unity of God's people fits well with the destruction of Samaria and the end of the monarchy in the North. Hezekiah seems to have captured that theological perspective when he invited Israel, *from Beersheba to Dan* (the order is significant) to return to the Lord and join in keeping the Passover in Jerusalem (2 Chron. 30:1-12). In devotion to the Lord, the worshipers at that time spread out through Judah, Benjamin, Ephraim, and Manasseh to destroy sacred stones, Asherah poles, high places, and altars—to purge the nation of the pervasive symbols of false worship [Asherah, p. 372].

Judah and Ephraim (Israel) are kin. The message addressed to the Northern Kingdom applies equally to Judah, particularly since the religious conditions of the South so closely resembled those in the North. They deteriorated in parallel. The focus, then, is on the character of the message rather than on the particular occasion of each prophetic speech. Indeed, the historical events surrounding the individual prophecies in their written form are incidental.

The book of Hosea addresses the prevailing sins and precarious condition of the Southern nation while still speaking to the remnant in the North who had survived the tidal wave of judgment.

Part 1

Biography of a Marriage Failure

Hosea 1:2—3:5

OVERVIEW

This prophecy may begin like a memo but it proceeds like a modern novel. The first three chapters introduce the characters and develop the plot. The remainder of the book (Hos. 4-14) analyzes the situation in depth, exploring the relationship between God and Israel from three perspectives.

The book of Hosea is a sung love story, actually two love stories of rejected, spurned, defiled love. The Hebrew opera develops a complex plot in echo form. Or one may think of it as performed on a bi-level stage. The upper level develops the romance of God and Israel; the lower level, that of Hosea, Gomer, and the children. Male voices predominate, though female characters are on stage and vividly active. At times God's voice carries the plot alone, at other times Hosea's love song dominates. Occasionally their voices blend into a common line. It is a drama of passion and pathos, of ecstasy and of excruciating pain.

Israel's love has gone cold. Yet the Lord will not let her go. Cut to the quick by her unfaithfulness, God is torn between the need to show his bride the error of her ways and the desire to restore the intimacy that once was theirs. Intimacy can flourish only when the lovers are knit together by integrity, commitment, and love. Intimacy blossoms by choice, not coercion. God's patience offers Israel that choice.

What better way than a human love story to display the heart of God and to stir his people to repentance? That solution brings Hosea and Gomer and their three children on stage. Through the tragedy of this marriage, Israel can glimpse the wounds the nation has inflicted on her Husband, the Lord, and be alerted to the reconciliation needed to bring healing to the people.

If Hosea's marriage is to evoke an "O Lord, forgive!" from Israel, they will have to see the depths of God's hurt. Normal marital stresses will not awaken Israel to recognize her Husband's pain.

What pain could be more throbbing than the one induced by adultery? Here we see a spouse lusting after lovers while living under her husband's roof, a spouse given to prostitution *[Prostitution, p. 393]*, the agony of divorce, and the rejection of one's children. In the depths of Hosea's agony lies hope. Perhaps Israel will see herself in Gomer and return to her God. Hosea has become a suffering servant, bearing five hundred years of Israel's covenant violations condensed into one life span *[Covenant, p. 379]*.

In outline, these first three chapters appear as follows:

God in Covenant with Israel

Covenant breaking	Judgment	Restoration
Past (1:2—2:1)	Present (2:2-13)	Future (2:14—3:5)
Marriage and Family	Divorce	Remarriage

Hosea in Covenant with Gomer

The English chapter and verse divisions (Hos. 1–2, 14) differ from that in the Hebrew. We will follow the English divisions, assuming that those who read the Hebrew text can easily make the adjustment.

Hosea 1:2—2:1

Hosea and Gomer: Marriage Metaphor in Four Dimensions

PREVIEW

No other human experiences bear so much potential for pain and pleasure as those of family life. Hosea's prophetic role begins with God's instructions for his marriage and the promise of children. These form the foundation and are built into the major symbols of his ministry to Israel. Both are bittersweet, with a surplus of agony over ecstasy.

Five to eight years of marriage and child rearing are condensed into a few short verses. The power of this event impacts us when we release our imaginations and unfetter our feelings.

Yet what begins as tragedy ends as triumph. Hard words become destructive unless tempered by love. Chastisement leads to rage and despair unless accompanied by words of hope. God offers that hope. Indeed, every major section of denunciation and judgment is followed by the inbreaking of God the Savior. Hosea/Hoshea means "God saves/delivers." Chapter one is no exception.

OUTLINE

Narrator: Introducing the Actors, 1:2a

A Marriage Made in Heaven, 1:2b-3a
1:2b	Go Marry!
1:3a	Yes, Lord!

Jezreel, 1:3b-5
1:3b	It's a Boy!
1:4-5	God Explains: The End of the Line

Lo-ruhamah, 1:6-7
1:6a	A Daughter!
1:6b	God Explains: The End of Israel
1:7	. . . And Promises: But Judah . . .

Lo-ammi, 1:8—2:1
1:8	Another Son!
1:9	God Explains: You Are Not My People
1:10—2:1	. . . And Promises: But You Will Become . . .

EXPLANATORY NOTES

Narrator: Introducing the Actors   1:2a

Hosea's ministry began when the Lord first instructed him to marry and have a family. The prepositional phrase *through Hosea* could also be read as *by* or *with Hosea*. Grammatically, it is impossible to determine which is intended. In any case, the conversations between God and Hosea were not intended solely for his personal edification. They may have been private and personal, but they were always tied to his prophetic calling.

The sparse phrase *The Lord said to Hosea* stirs questions in us. Did God speak audibly? Did the message come in the form of a vision or in a dream? Perhaps after his marriage went awry, Hosea recognized the message of God in that marriage. This third option can probably be discounted, since the instructions to give the children unusual and negative names suggests that the marriage and family experiences were not the result of later interpretations, but of specific, divine direction.

A Marriage Made in Heaven   1:2b-3a

1:2b   Go Marry!

In ancient Israel, marriage was the norm *[Marriage, p. 393]*. The instructions to go and take a wife are necessary because this part of Hosea's life is to embody his ministry. To *take* a wife usually means to marry (Deut. 24:1, RSV; Num. 12:1), though it may also refer to a more specific part of the act of marrying, such as the consummation (Deut. 20:7). The issue is marriage, not concubinage.

The command to *take* includes children as well as a wife, suggesting a more general meaning for *take* than the marriage ceremony or the consummation. Gomer brought no children with her into the marriage. The instructions and description which follow identify the children as born after the marriage.

Hosea's wife and children are all characterized as *promiscuous* (NRSV: *of whoredoms.*) The word is related to *prostitute/prostitution* and refers to sexual activity outside of marriage. It seems to describe the *character* of Gomer and the children, though the remainder of the book indicates promiscuous *actions*. In the biblical view of persons, character and actions are not held as distinct from each other. Gomer and the children she bears reflect the sexual standards and activities of the society (cf. 4:12). There is no suggestion that Gomer was a known prostitute at the time of marriage or that she showed character flaws which would lead Hosea to believe that she would be unfaithful to him. Nor can children of prostitution by itself mean children born of extramarital sexual activity, since the first child is explicitly said to be born to Hosea (1:3). The explanation lies elsewhere. Gomer comes to violate the marriage covenant and thus symbolizes Israel's unfaithfulness to the Lord.

Canaanite religious practices had infiltrated Israelite worship and daily life, especially with King Ahab's marriage to Jezebel, the daughter of Ethbaal, king of Sidon. Jezebel induced Ahab to follow Baal (1 Kings 16:29-34). Her influence released a flood of Baal worship, a religion characterized by extramarital sexual activity, idolatry, and magical practices. Israel had been warned not to follow the ways of the nations whom they were to dispossess (Deut. 7:1-6; 18:9-14). Yet under Jezebel's influence and active promotion of Baalism, the nation opened itself to this fertility religion *[Canaanite Fertility Myth, p. 376]*. In 2 Kings 9:22, Jezebel's sins are identified as idolatry and witchcraft, a combination characteristic of the other nations whom Israel strained to imitate (cf. Lev. 20:6; Micah 5:11-13; Isa. 47:9; Hos. 4:12; Mal. 3:5).

Hosea was not alone in referring to the worship of other gods as prostitution or promiscuity. The account of the renewal of covenant following the making of the golden calf (Exod. 32–34) describes the act of pagan worship as *prostituting themselves to their gods* (34:15; cf. Deut. 31:16). The language and concept appear prominently from Judges to the literature dating from the Babylonian exile. Prostitution symbolizes the sexual license associated with Baal worship. Likewise, it signifies the covenantal relationships between Israel and pagan nations, in violation of Israel's covenant with the Lord *[Prostitution, p. 393]*.

Israel's wisdom tradition shares that language and concept (Prov. 1–10). The immoral woman embodies foolishness. She is a foreigner who casts spells on those who visit her. Dalliance with her leads to death.

Prostitution is also the language of covenant infidelity *[Covenant, p. 379]*. Covenant curses in treaty documents of the ancient Near East show that prostitution represents one of the punishments imposed on one who breaks a solemn oath, such as the oath made in covenants (Hillers: 58-60). Pursuing another covenant lord violates the existing covenant. It is adultery. Therefore, in pursuit of Baal, Israel is appropriately described as an adulterous wife. Gomer will display the same disdain for the marriage covenant that Israel has shown for the Lord's covenant made at Sinai. Gomer comes to symbolize the entire people and their practices in the land (Hos. 2:2-4). *The land commits great whoredom by forsaking the Lord.* The clause reinforces the idea of covenant disloyalty.

1:3a Yes, Lord

Hosea marries Gomer. No word is said about whether it is a marriage arranged by his parents or whether he chooses the bride. The latter would be the case if his parents have died. Nor is the name, Gomer, of any special significance. The narrative contains no unnecessary details. God speaks; Hosea acts. The sequence of instructions and responses points to unhesitating obedience on Hosea's part.

Jezreel 1:3b-5
1:3b It's a Boy!

The marriage is blessed with a child, Jezreel, a son to ensure a future to the family line. The fact that God names all three children suggests their symbolic significance; their names are of crucial importance in the ministry of Hosea.

God explains: *Jezreel* transports Israel back to the massacre conducted by Jehu in Jezreel some four generations previously *[Historical Summary, p. 384]*. Jehu was anointed by God to succeed Ahab on the throne of Israel. Through him, God promised to "avenge on Jezebel the blood of my servants the prophets, and the blood of all the servants of the Lord. For the whole house of Ahab shall perish" (2 Kings 9:7-8). His reward was that he and his descendants should rule in Samaria for four generations (2 Kings 10:30). Yet his excessive zeal in killing Ahaziah, king of Judah (9:27-28), and Ahaziah's relatives (10:12-14) seems to come under divine disapproval. Likely his act of destroying the house of Ahab was vengefully motivated in part. Though Jehu described his massacre of Ahab's family as *zeal for the Lord* (2 Kings 10:16), he did not purge Israel of the idolatrous images which led Israel to defect from God in the first place (2 Kings 10:29, 31). His acts rid him of contenders to the throne and of the political impact of Baal worship, but this did not represent a thorough turning to God.

Jezreel, the site of the massacre, is the name of a city located at the northern foot of Mt. Gilboa. Invading and defending armies fought for control of the city, which guarded the main commercial and military route to the southern part of Palestine. Jezreel is also the name of a fertile valley extending westward from the city of Jezreel; Megiddo overlooks this valley from the south. The rich soil and abundant water supply accent the literal meaning of the name: *God will sow*. Implicit in the name is the assurance that God continues to extend salvation to his people. Jezreel, then, conjures up images of decisive battles, a capital city, fertility, and salvation.

1:4-5 God Explains: The End of the Line

The significance of the child's name, Jezreel, is explained by the Lord. *In the valley of Jezreel*, God will direct his judgment against Jehu's dynastic successors. The royal line of Jehu-Jehoahaz-Jehoash-Jeroboam is about to come to an end. Jeroboam's son, Zechariah, was assassinated after a mere six-month reign (2 Kings 15:8). The fulfillment of this prediction is near but not imminent.

Such a political message, spoken in all likelihood during the closing years of Jeroboam's reign, would not have been popular, though it would have attracted attention. The reprieve from foreign domination was coming to an end (cf. 2 Kings 14:25-27). Confirmation of the message giving this first name came early in Hosea's ministry and added weight to the remainder of his words.

The prophecy is directed at the house of Jehu as well as at the *kingship* or *kingdom of the house of Israel*. The term *bow of Israel* symbolizes heroism and strength (cf. Jer. 49:35; Ezek. 39:3; Job 29:20), pointing to the military leadership of the nation. To *break the bow* appears elsewhere in covenant contexts to denote the god's curse and destruction of the covenant-breaker (Hillers: 60).

Those who read the signs of the times would recognize the threat this child's name represents to Israel's internal and international stability. The child Jezreel points toward political upheaval. His existence marks a visitation of God, not merely a shift of power. Bloodshed gives birth to bloodshed. Assassinations and pogroms follow one another in rapid succession. Jezreel leads to Jezreel.

Jehu's family line ended in 752 B.C.

Lo-ruhamah 1:6-7

1:6a A Daughter!

One child follows another. Was the daughter Hosea's child or the child of Gomer's unfaithfulness? The omission of the statement *bore to him* may suggest that the child was not Hosea's. Hebrew scholars correctly note that linked parallel accounts tend to become increasingly shorter, as happens here with the omission of *the Lord* in the second birth narrative. There are, however, four arguments which heighten the possibility that Lo-ruhamah and Lo-ammi are Gomer's children but not fathered by Hosea.

First, since the accusation is that of unfaithfulness, the phrase *to him* becomes critical to the very essence of the message. It is unlikely that the author would have omitted a phrase for economy of expression if that phrase determined the interpretation of the narrative. Second, the names of the second (Not-pitied) and third child (Not-my-people) reinforce the interpretation that Hosea is not their father. Third, the statements of 2:4-5 connect the mother's shameless promiscuity with their conception. Fourth, the judgment speech of 5:1-7 accuses Israel in the metaphor of unfaithfulness and prostitution: *They have dealt faithlessly with the Lord; for they have borne illegitimate children.*

An alternative interpretation of the children's parentage draws on a reconstruction of Israel's religion *[Israelite Religion, p. 385]*. While the children may all be the offspring of Hosea and Gomer, they are appropriately designated children of promiscuity because Gomer was going to the Baal shrine to ensure her fertility. She may have engaged in sacred prostitution to guarantee conception, or she may simply have brought an offering and a prayer to request this blessing. The phrase *children of whoredom* is applied to all three children (2:4), including Jezreel, who was born *to* Hosea.

Hosea is aware of Gomer's infidelity, just as the Lord is conscious of Israel's disloyalty. Both "husbands" display a long-suffering spirit. Each attempts to recall the covenant partner by pointedly exposing her unfaithfulness. The children's names represent that confrontation through the prophetic word.

Lo-ruhamah. Not-pitied. Not-shown-compassion. The choice of words at this point is crucial to the message of Hosea. The root verb, *raham*, expresses the love, compassion, and pity a mother feels for her children. It is warm and intense. It carries no sexual overtones. When *raham* describes God's love, it is always a love which stretches out to the wounded, the alienated, the obstinate, and willfully disobedient child. It restores God's people from under judgment. It is not love in a neutral context. This is not love at first sight.

For example, God says: "I will restore their fortunes, and will have mercy on them" (Jer. 33:26). "In overflowing wrath for a moment I hid my face from you, but with everlasting love I will have compassion on you" (Isa. 54:8). *Raham* appears in parallel with *mercy* and *restore the fortunes of*, pointing to its unique emphasis as love that restores. As such, it always describes God's concern for his people, and never expresses his love for the nations generally.

1:6b-7 God Explains: The End of Israel

The meaning of this child's name becomes plain: *I will no longer have pity on the house of Israel.* The phrase *no longer* recalls the implicit message of salvation in the earlier announcement of judgment (1:4). *Lo-ruhamah*, however, indicates that Israel has reached a point of no return. God will no longer restrain or deflect his judgments with compassion.

The name Lo-ruhamah carries two distinct, yet related connotations. The full consequences of covenant disloyalty are about to come crashing down on the Northern Kingdom, the house of Israel. *Lo-ruhamah* implies that the covenant curses are descending on Israel in all their fury to drag the nation off into exile *[Covenant, p. 379]*.

Second, the root *rhm* appears in fifth-century Jewish Aramaic marriage contracts from Egypt in connection with the rights of inheritance. The noun there appears to refer to the one designated principal heir. To say that a person is Lo-ruhamah is to call her "Disinherited." Since Israel was promised the land as a gift, when God calls his offspring, Lo-ruhamah, he indicates thereby that they will not continue to possess the Lord's property. The two life settings of the language of compassion and inheritance, then, converge to point toward Israel's destiny as an exiled people.

Translators and expositors struggle with these two verses. Is God distinguishing his actions against the Northern Kingdom from those against Judah *[Judah and David, p. 389]*? Andersen and Freedman say no. They translate the text:

> Call her name Lo-ruhamah, because I—as Yahweh their God—never again shall I show pity for the state of Israel, or forgive them at all; nor for the state of Judah will I show pity, or save them. I will not save them from bow. (142-143)

Others suggest that the word *forgive* should be read as *withdraw*. Stuart has argued for another translation of the end of verse six: *since I have been utterly betrayed by them* (23, 31). The NIV reads, *For I will no longer show love to the house of Israel, that I should at all forgive them*. Each of these solutions requires changing the Hebrew or invokes problematic grammatical constructions.

There is a rather straightforward translation which resolves both the grammatical and theological problems:

> *Name her Not-pitied (Lo-ruhamah), because I will no longer continue to love (raham) the house of Israel, though I will forgive them. The house of Judah, however, I will love (raham), and I will rescue them by means of Yahweh their God.*

At least two other Hebrew clauses in the OT have the grammatical construction which is said to represent a problem in the clause *I will forgive them* (as in Isa. 2:9), confirming the grammatical foundation of this interpretation.

1:7 . . . And Promises: But Judah . . .

When we recognize that *raham* represents restorative love, we can distinguish the divine action toward Judah from that of God toward Israel. God *will no longer love (raham)* the Northern Kingdom.

That means that the Northern Kingdom will not be restored from exile as a separate entity. It will not inherit the land apart from Judah. God will forgive them for their sins but will not reestablish them as a separate kingdom (cf. 3:5).

Judah, however, is not yet subject to the full outpouring of the covenant curses (cf. Lev. 26:46; Deut. 28:15-68). Even if it were, God's restoring love would reach out to them in exile (Deut. 30:3) to reconstitute them in the land.

Judah's deliverance will occur through an act of God (Hos. 1:7). No human or military might will serve as God's weapon to defeat the foe. God will not even draw on the cavalry or chariot corps. There will be no misinterpreting the hand of God in Judah's rescue.

Hosea is probably predicting the miraculous deliverance which Jerusalem (Judah) experienced from the army of Sennacherib (2 Kings 18-19). The Lord sent his angel to decimate the Assyrian army besieging the city and occupying the land. That act was a tangible expression of the Lord's restorative love.

Lo-ammi 1:8—2:1

1:8 Another Son!

The third child is conceived after Gomer weaned Lo-ruhamah. Weaning normally occurred when the child was about three years old (2 Macc. 7:27). One can imagine the impact on the family and on the community when they hear the name *Not-my-people*. The modern English equivalent *bastard* does not capture the effect of this child's name on the community, though it does approximate the impact on the family's life.

1:9 God Explains: You Are Not My People

The Lord's interpretation, *You are not my people, and I am not your God*, resembles the divorce formula of the day (cf. 2:2). God has disowned his people.

The expression "You are not my son" occurs in Old Babylonian marriage documents to disown the son(s) of a wife who is being divorced (Westbrook: 129, from PBS 8/2 155; PRAK I B 17). The child is sent away from the father's home and has no rights of inheritance. Normally this happens only when the child is conceived by the mother and begotten by some man other than her divorcing husband.

The explanation of the child's name takes us back to Exodus 3:14

[Exodus Tradition, p. 384]. In the powerful act of rescuing Israel from Egypt, the Lord declared himself to be their God (cf. Exod. 6:7). In affirming the terms of the covenant (Exod. 19:7-8; 24:3), Israel announced her acceptance of her calling as the people of God (Exod. 19:5-6) *[Yahweh-Baal Conflict, p. 398]*. The strong ties between Hosea 1:9 and Exodus 3:14 are apparent in the fact that both use the common verb form *'ehyeh* (*I will be*) as a personal name for the God of the patriarchs. The NRSV and NIV interpret the phrase differently by supplying the word *God* to make it read *and I am not your God*. Instead, the Hebrew reads *and I am Not-your-ehyeh* (*Not-your-I-will-be*). The unique construction rivets attention on the God who rescued his people from Egyptian bondage.

The child *Lo-ammi* signals that God, at least temporarily, is abandoning his people. The covenant people have become like all the other nations, a *Not-people* (see TBC, below). In that name the Lord announces that the privileges of the special ties between them have been suspended. Rejection and abandonment, however, can quickly lead to despair. To prevent that from happening, God immediately announces the word of promise which shall follow the time of rejection. *Lo-ammi* is not God's last word, even for an exiled people.

1:10—2:1 . . . And Promises: But You Will Become . . .

A fivefold promise reverses the judgments symbolized in the three children's names (1:10-11). The language of these promises embraces both kingdoms, adding to the emphasis on the restoration of *all* Israel, the larger community of faith. Jeroboam I's secession had separated and weakened Israel. God's restoration will reverse that process and renew the integrity of the nation.

A decimated, exiled people shall be restored in large numbers. God promised Abraham (Gen. 22:17) and Jacob (32:12) that their descendants would increase to countless numbers, like the sand on the seashore *[Jacob and Isaac, p. 389]*. That growth in descendants was fulfilled in Egypt (Exod. 1:1-8). It was fulfilled in new measure in Solomon's day (1 Kings 4:20), even though the actual population of the nation at that time was probably less than two-thirds of a million (Stuart: 38-39). Sargon II (King of Assyria, 722-705 B.C.) records the deportation of 27,290 inhabitants of Samaria (*ANET:* 284). Probably the major portion of the population of the Northern Kingdom was killed in the war with the Assyrians. Yet the descendants of *Not-pitied* and *Not-my-people* will become *Not-measured* and *Not-counted*

(1:10a). The reversal of fortunes is dramatic. God, though unmentioned, is the Guarantor of this promise made to the patriarchs.

The second promise reverses the effect and power of the name Lo-ammi. But what is *the place* referred to in this promise? We can only speculate, though *the place* seems to be associated with the naming of a child. If that is the case, it might mean: the child's name announcing judgment was proclaimed in the public square (or city gate); the word of salvation shall also be shouted from the rooftops.

The new name, *Ammi, My-people,* signals God's acceptance. The covenant people were repeatedly challenged to choose life over death, obedience over defection, blessings over curses (cf. Deut. 30:13-20). This people was known as God's "firstborn son" (Exod. 4:22-23), as the "children of the Lord" (Deut. 14:1-2) and his inheritance, his "very own possession" or "portion" (Deut. 4:20; 32:9). In other nations, the gods had land as an inheritance; the Lord's concern was and is first and foremost with his people (see Block). This God is living, in contrast to idols (Hos. 4:12; 8:4-6; cf. Isa. 44:9-20). He was the Originator of life (Hos. 14:5-8; cf. Gen. 1–3) and the One who revived the sick and the dying (Hos. 6:1-3).

The first promise fulfills God's covenant with the patriarchs: *like the sand of the sea.* The second promise renews the blessings of the Sinaitic covenant: *My-people.* The remaining three promises restore the blessings of the Davidic covenant: the people will be *gathered together, appoint one leader,* and *come up out of the land [Judah and David, p. 389].* Dispersed Israelites and Judeans will, in the days to come, be reassembled and rejoined into a new community of faith. Their long-standing divisions and animosities will disappear. The bonds that shaped them into one will reemerge.

Just as David drew together the North and South and welded them into one great nation under God, so the fourth promise marks their reunion under the new Davidic ruler (Hos. 3:5). While the term for *head* does not commonly refer to kings, it represents a king in Psalm 18:43 and Job 29:25, and probably here.

The final promise is puzzling and may intentionally have several meanings. The Hebrew reads *they will come up from the land* (NRSV: *they will take possession of the land*). Does this refer to the way Israel will be regathered, indicating that there will be a new exodus of the scattered exiles (cf. Hos. 8:13; Exod. 1:10; 3:8)? Or does the term *the land* here represent the underworld, the world of the dead (cf. Hos. 6:1-3; 13:14; cf. Ezek. 37)? Or could this promise be referring to the reconquest of surrounding nations and the reestablishment of the larger Davidic empire? That empire included Edom, Moab, Ammon, Amalek, Syria, and part of Philistia (2 Sam. 8). All are possible; all may be intended.

In further support of this latter suggestion, we note that the verb "go up" is frequently used to refer to a military campaign or invasion. Furthermore, that day will be a day of magnificent victory: How *great shall be the day of Jezreel!* (Hos. 1:11). The earlier use of the name *Jezreel* was also associated with the royal house but denoted a major military catastrophe (1:4-5); this day of Jezreel marks victory for the restored people. In confirmation of this perspective, Amos 9:11-12 links the reestablishment of the Davidic monarchy and the restoration of the nation with a conquest of the surrounding nations. That tradition appears to be reflected in this salvation oracle *[Accusation-Judgment-Salvation Oracles, p. 372].*

Hosea 1:10-11 assures us that the purposes of God remain intact. God is not hamstrung by the unfaithfulness of his people. He can take even a nonpeople and recreate Israel from its scattered remnants. It is a people's sin that triggers judgment. Cause and effect in this process are readily understood. But what motivates such promises as those found in verses 10-11? Nothing of merit within a people is sufficient cause for an act of restoration. The only possible and sufficient cause lies in the character of this Deity: God is gracious. The sharp side-by-side presentation of judgment speech and salvation oracle poignantly emphasize God's grace as the wellspring of restoration.

Hosea 2:1 advances the metaphor another step. Jezreel is pictured as the remnant which continues in the land, and Lo-ruhamah and Lo-ammi represent the exiles. Previously the nation (*house*) was referred to as *Not-pitied* and *Not-my-people*. Now the restoration God is bringing about will require all Israelites to acknowledge that they serve a common God and have experienced restorative love. The plurals, *your brothers* and *your sisters* (NRSV note), are important in that they direct the command, "[You, Jezreel,] *say, to the restored Israelites.*"

Lo-ammi and Lo-ruhamah of the original metaphor are being fleshed out in every Israelite. None need be excluded. But to be included, they must acknowledge one another as *Pitied* (*Ruhamah*) and *Belonging-to-God* (*Ammi, My-people*). The imperative is important. While God acts sovereignly, he calls for genuine repentance in those through whom he will fulfill his promises. The people of God will recognize and acknowledge one another. The wedges which separated them will be removed. Jezreel is to welcome back his sisters and brothers as full-fledged family members.

THE TEXT IN BIBLICAL CONTEXT
Hosea as Suffering Servant

The prophet has become a message. Hosea's marriage and family life carry a distinctive word to Israel. Hosea's story is metaphor, but it is also reality. It symbolizes God's relation to Israel, but it also participates in the shattered relationships to which it points.

One can identify three levels of symbolic message through the prophets. God's messengers occasionally use symbolic actions to convey their message. Jeremiah presents the object lessons of the linen belt (13:1-11), the wineskins (13:12-14), the potter and the wheel (18:1-18), the breaking of a clay jar (19:1-15), and an ox yoke (28:1-17). These are acted illustrations. The prophet himself is not central to the symbol.

God used other prophets to convey a message via the metaphor of life experiences. At the Lord's command, Isaiah walked about naked and barefoot for three years. This ordinarily shameful behavior was a sign against Egypt and Cush, symbolizing their destruction and captivity (Isa. 20) and signifying the futility of relying on Egypt. Hosea is like his older Northern Kingdom contemporary, Isaiah, who with his children became a message to Judah. The children's names, "A-remnant-shall-return" (Isa. 7:3), "Quick-to-the-plunder—swift-to-the-spoil" (8:1), speak of hope as well as judgment. Isaiah recognized that he and his children were "signs and portents in Israel from the Lord of hosts" (8:18).

Jeremiah's life, like Hosea's, was itself a message. Jeremiah was to embody the coming judgment by remaining single and childless, and by refusing to mourn the dead or to celebrate marriages (Jer. 16:1-18). His life would anticipate the experiences of the nation in the days ahead. On another occasion Jeremiah bought back a family field at Anathoth, even as the city of Jerusalem was besieged by the Babylonians (32:1-44). The purchase was a sign that life would return to normal after the coming judgment.

Similarly, Ezekiel's mouth was sealed by God and he was placed under house arrest, preventing him from making all but specially authorized public announcements of impending judgment (Ezek. 3:24-27). He was instructed to symbolize the coming siege of Jerusalem by lying on his left side for 390 days, to represent the years of punishment imposed on the Northern Kingdom; and then he was to lie on his right side for forty days, to represent the time of Judah's punishment (4:1-17). When the siege of Jerusalem began, his wife died, a symbol of the nation's loss. Ezekiel was forbidden to mourn her or make any prophetic pronouncements until Jerusalem fell to the Babylonians (24:15-27; 33:21-22).

There is a third way in which the prophets bring a message to God's people. They are, in their own person and character, God's personal representatives. As ambassadors of the Lord (Jer. 7:25), they are privy to the most intimate plans of the Holy One of Israel (cf. Gen. 18:17-33; Num. 12:6-8; Amos 3:7). They represent God before the nation. Samuel, Elisha, Jeremiah, and Amos were among the prophets who served in this way.

The NT (New Testament) also presents the apostles and ministers of the Word as a message. They are not merely the medium; they are also the content. The apostle Paul speaks of those who proclaim the good news as "the aroma of Christ to God among those who are being saved and among those who are perishing" (2 Cor. 2:15). Therefore, he tells the Corinthian Christians, "You yourselves are our letter" (2 Cor. 3:1-5). For that reason, it seems fitting for Paul to exhort Christians to imitate him as he follows God (1 Cor. 4:16; 11:1; Phil. 3:17; 1 Thess. 1:6).

When people reject the message, Jesus warned, they will also feel a need to discredit or destroy the messenger (John 15:18-25). The bearer of the good news becomes a vital part of the message. Those who receive the messenger are said to have received the message. Therefore, people's response to "the least of these who are members of my family" can be described as the basis on which God will approve or condemn them in the final judgment (Matt. 25:31-46; cf. 10:40-42). Those who reject the message will reject the messenger also. Israel responded to Elijah, Jeremiah, and Micaiah ben Imlah by rejecting their ministry.

Sometimes God's servant(s) identify so totally with the message, its Sender, and the people whom they serve, that they become vehicles for the salvation of God's people (cf. Isa. 52:13—53:12). Jesus and Paul saw their ministries in that light (cf. Matt. 16:21-28; Col. 1:24; 2 Cor. 2:12—6:13). Moses and Paul interceded on behalf of their people with such intensity and total identification that they were ready to forfeit their lives and eternal destinies for the salvation of their fellow Jews (Exod. 32:32; Rom. 9:2). In so doing, they suffered intensely on behalf of those they loved and tried to serve. Hosea acted on behalf of God in the noble and trying tradition of the suffering servant.

Reaching Back, Leaning Forward: Hosea 1:10

A *Not-my-people* will become *Children-of-the-living-God*. Hosea reaches back to the Song of Moses (Deut. 32:21) for words to describe Israel's rebellion and its consequences:

Words and Ideas	Hosea	Deuteronomy
Not-my-people	1:10	32:19-21
no one *shall rescue*	2:10	32:29, 39
heal, revive	6:1-3; 7:1	32:36, 39
fed, satisfied, forgot	13:5-6	32:10, 13-18
silly, without sense	7:11	32:6, 28
the *wise understand*	14:9	32:29
They *store* up *sin*, evil	13:12	32:18

To these correspondences and similarities, we may add the promise that Israel will sing (answer, testify) a new song when the Lord next invites her into the wilderness for a second honeymoon experience (2:15; cf. Deut. 31:19-20, 30; 32:44-47) *[Tabernacles, p. 396]*.

Hosea draws heavily on the covenant curse tradition to point to the fulfillment of the covenant sanctions against disobedience *[Covenant, p. 379]*. He also draws on these words and concepts to point toward the day when the curse will be replaced by a deluge of blessings (2:14-23; 6:1-3; 11:8-11; 14:1-8).

The rabbi, Saul-Paul of Tarsus, reaches back into Hosea to find evidence that the conversion of the Gentiles was not a new idea, original to Paul (Hos. 1:10; 2:23; cf. Rom. 9:19-33). Peter speaks to his readers as once not a people, but now the people of God (1 Pet. 2:9-10). This intimate connection between the covenants focuses the larger purpose of God and accents the unique role given to Israel, to be a light and blessing to all the nations of the earth (Gen. 12:1-3; Exod. 19:5-6; Isa. 42:6-9; 49:5-13).

TEXT IN THE LIFE OF THE CHURCH

The Purposes of God

All Scripture converges on the divine purpose: that the world might be saved, freed, delivered, rescued. Much of church history is a record of those who devoted themselves not only to enjoying the state of being saved but also to declaring the good news that all are invited to the celebrations of life.

When the sense of purpose grows dim, the energy of the church is redirected toward maintenance and survival: organizational stream-lining, rooting out heresies, defining fine points of doctrine, building cathedrals and social halls.

Which of the most troubling problems of the church would disap-pear altogether, and which would recede into the background, if the church put its best people and most vital energies into announcing the good news from the living God?

Models of Faithfulness in the Power of a Deep Affection

Throughout its history the church has affirmed the representative and exemplary role of its leaders. Hosea, unassuming as we may imagine him, is remarkable for his ready compliance with God's di-rectives. Few leaders wish to speak with Paul's boldness in inviting believers to "follow me as I follow Christ." Yet leaders are models, whether they wish it or not. Positive flesh-and-blood examples are vi-tal to developing a deeper spirituality and a more consistent faith life in the community (cf. Amos 2:9-16).

The Catholic Church has encouraged younger Christians to search out and attach themselves to spiritual directors. Protestants speak of leaders as engaging in discipling or mentoring for personal growth and leadership training. Underlying such deliberate modeling is the awareness that the messenger is an integral aspect of the mes-sage. Word and practice reinforce one another.

Healthy Christian modeling begins with a deep devotion to Christ. An intense preoccupation with the person of Christ inevitably creates a more humble and gentle disciple. It results in openness to the truth, in love for people, and in compassion for the poor, the disadvan-taged, the sick, and the suffering. The grasp of love is both strong and tender.

Godly persons model by their faithfulness. The positive influence of a Mother Teresa or Billy Graham flows out of their consistent faith. Their lives are powerful not because they deliberately set out to be models, but because they have had a deep experience of the living God. As they pursue God, others are drawn to follow their pattern of faith.

Spiritual directors are formed by the purifying and refining work of the Spirit. Spiritual giants are sensitive to their own imperfections, weaknesses, and sins. They are sensitive to correction from the Spirit of God directly, as well as from within the body of Christ. Conviction and humility are not at all mutually exclusive. The greatest spiritual directors are unconscious of the extent to which the graces of the Spirit have matured in them. They continue to lay aside even the good and the better in pursuit of the best.

Yet there are dangers. Public religious figures who attract followers may be of another sort, manipulative or unscrupulous. Any form of modeling by leaders who long for personal power makes for situations particularly susceptible to abuse. Powerful charismatic leaders like Thomas Müntzer and Jim Jones may be rightly accused of exercising a form of mind control. When disciples become unthinking imitators of their leaders, the potential for harm is as great as it might have been for good.

The saints throughout the ages have been conscious of the seduction and the exercise of power. True saints dedicate their power to the welfare of others. Healthy disciple making is voluntary on the part of both mentor and disciple.

Hosea 2:2-23

The Death of a Marriage: Rebirth of Hope

PREVIEW

Two colored strands are tightly interwoven in this literary unit. Sometimes one is exposed, sometimes the other. At other times both appear together. One strand is flesh-toned. It is the story of Hosea and Gomer, distanced from one another. Infidelity has torn them apart, and Hosea proceeds with divorce.

The other is the scarlet strand of divine redemption offered to a rebellious and obstinate covenant-breaking people. Restoring love prevails. God persists in love until unfaithful Israel faces the reality and significance of her sin.

Five life situations shape this literary painting: a court of law and divorce proceedings; a heifer in heat; the fertility cult and its prostitution; courtship, betrothal, and remarriage; and a covenant-making ceremony. The rapid, unannounced, and frequent shifts in imagery can be confusing. Israel is described as a Baal devotee [Ba'al, p. 373], a prostitute and adulteress, the land, and the children. These symbolic referents should be understood as roughly synonymous.

In chapter one the Israelites were punished because of past unfaithfulness. Chapter two paints the central part of the mural in scenes of lust and disgust, adultery and forgiveness, promise and

55

hope. It depicts a brazen, selfish, lustful, and pragmatic adulterous woman—Gomer. Israel is her historical counterpart.

OUTLINE

The Divorce Proceedings, 2:2-5

The Divorce: A Separation to Reconcile, 2:6-13

It's a Long Way Back, Even on Love's Initiative, 2:14-23

EXPLANATORY NOTES

The dominant interpretive issue of the larger text unit is this: Did God divorce Israel? How one settles this question is based largely on what one already believes. Can we imagine God using a sinful act (divorce) to represent this relationship with his people? When does a covenant end? Does God indeed dissolve the covenant with Israel *[Covenant, p. 379]*? One's conclusion is further shaped by a series of choices faced while interpreting the passage. These will be addressed in the essays *[Marriage, p. 393]*.

The Divorce Proceedings 2:2-5

2:2a-b The Children as Witnesses

The court is in session. God functions as plaintiff, judge, and bailiff. But Hosea, Gomer, and their children are also present—as though two cases were being heard in the same room, one in an upper chamber, the other in the lower. At times they merge.

The command to the children is unusual. Translations vary from *rebuke* (NIV) to *plead with* (KJV, NRSV). The Hebrew construction found here appears elsewhere only in Genesis 31:36 and Judges 6:32. One might appropriately translate the command:

> *Confirm the charge against your mother!*
> *Confirm that she is not my wife, and I am not her husband!*

As hostile witnesses, the children corroborate Hosea's claim that Gomer has deserted him. Her desertion amounts to divorce, and Hosea is "making it legal." Had Hosea sent Gomer out of his house, by law he would have been obligated to give her a "writ of divorce" for her protection (cf. Deut. 24:1). Isaiah 50:1 implies that in case of desertion by the wife, no such legal document is required. But apparently the court requires evidence that Hosea is not forcing his wife out of his home. The children testify to that.

There is little question that a divorce is taking place (Friedman: 199). Marriage and divorce documents spanning two thousand years confirm that statements such as "She is my wife" and "You are my husband" represent the heart of the marriage declaration. The marriage is dissolved when the spouses publicly negate those words:

> "She shall not be wife to me";
> "You are not my husband." (Kalluveetil: 110-111)

Why else would God again court (2:14-15) and betroth (2:19-20) Israel to himself? Why else would Israel repeat the marriage formula, *"My husband"* (1:16) [Marriage, p. 393]?

The divorce documents identify specific grounds for divorce. Just cause, such as adultery or slander, permit the husband to retain his wife's dowry and take back gifts he has showered upon her. Two grounds on which the husband is justified in keeping or repossessing the goods given to his wife are *adultery* and *deliberately damaging her husband's reputation* [Marriage, p. 393].

2:2c-d Adultery Can Be Forgiven

God and Hosea proceed to prove their spouses' infidelity. In the same breath, they appeal for their return.

Israelite court proceedings differed greatly from ours. The Israelite judge appealed for repentance and confession. In the Lord's lawsuits against his rebellious people, the appeal for repentance may be part of the legal procedure (Isa. 1:5-6, 16-20; cf. Hos. 2:2-4).

The implicit call to repentance is signaled by the Hebrew conjunction which in this grammatical structure should be translated *Rebuke your mother . . . so that she might remove the marks of prostitution* [Prostitution, p. 393]. The purpose of this divorce is not for the aggrieved husband legally to rid himself of an unfaithful wife. The testimony of the witnesses and the husband's subsequent actions are intended to draw the unfaithful spouse back to himself. If it is possible to convince Gomer/Israel to renounce her adulteries in the course of the legal proceedings, the action can still be stayed. The goal is restoration rather than retribution. Love, not revenge, is the driving force in this lawsuit.

If only she can be convinced to repudiate her lovers and refocus her passion on her husband! The NRSV translates the Hebrew quite literally: *that she put away her whoring from her face and her adultery from between her breasts.* Verse 13 helps us to understand this statement. Apparently the unfaithful wife bejeweled herself with a nose ring (before her face) and a necklace or pendant (between her breasts) before committing adultery. Were these a prostitute's symbols (cf. Jer. 4:30; Ezek. 23:40) or were they distinctive jewelry used in the worship of Baal? We lack the data to decide.

2:3-5 Deep Pain, Angry Threats

A sixfold threat follows, five directed at the spouse and one at the children. The threats pulsate with intensity and pain. The first ones are against Gomer (2:3), and then the children are included (2:4-5).

According to Deuteronomy, adultery was punishable by death if the parties were caught in the act (22:22). Hosea (and God) are determined on a less severe course of action. Unless the faithless wife repents, she will be stripped naked for public display and shame, exiled from her home, and left exposed to the harsh elements. In typical poetic Hebrew, the first five threats come in parallel statements:

I will strip her naked
  and expose her as in the day she was born,
and make her like a wilderness,
  and turn her into a parched land,
and slay her with thirst.

The imagery is rich. Hillers (1964a:58-60) argues that to be "stripped like a prostitute" is covenant-curse language *[Covenant, p. 379]*. Conquered peoples were sometimes led into exile, naked and bound (*ANEP*: 305, 323, 358, 365). Israel persistently and brazenly violated the covenant with God and will be sent into exile.

The text may also reflect a custom in which the husband publicly shames his adulterous wife by stripping her naked, symbolizing her persistent self-exposure to lovers; after she has been publicly shamed, the lovers are no longer attracted to her (Jer. 13:26-27; Ezek. 16:35-42; 23:10, 28-29).

The act of stripping and exposing her to public shame may also be a way for the husband to announce that he is no longer legally obligated to provide food, clothing, and conjugal rights (Exod. 21:10). The remainder of the chapter explains how her food, clothing, and fertility are withdrawn (Hos. 2:5-13) and then later restored in a new marriage relationship (2:14-23).

Israel brought nothing to her marriage. She was destitute. She left Egypt as a slave people. God showered the wealth of the Egyptians on his bride, claimed from slavery (Exod. 12:25-26). He gave her the land of promise, the equivalent of a dowry at marriage *[Marriage, p. 393]*. In case of divorce for just cause, the goods received by the wife are to be returned to her husband. Israel will be sent from the land.

Her public exposure *as in the day she was born* brings to mind the act of displaying the newborn infant to onlookers to signify the health and sex of the child. It also evokes the image, developed by Ezekiel, of an abandoned newborn, left by its mother to die of exposure, but cared for, reared, and finally wed by God, the gracious Stranger (Ezek. 16).

To be made *like a wilderness* and be turned *into a parched land* is full of meaning. Gomer and Israel are still depicted as persons, though the language begins to shift toward depicting Israel as the land. The wilderness and desert are hostile, threatening territory. The desert speaks of the sterility, impotence, or death of Baal (cf. 1 Kings 17-18). There Baal, the God of rain and fertility, cannot sustain life *[Canaanite Fertility Myth, p. 376]*. God *will slay her with thirst* as proof of his sovereignty in the wilderness. In contrast, the ideal bride is described in the Song of Solomon as a garden and a spring, a lover's delight (4:12-15). But the barren and arid wilderness invites no lovers—until God again woos his bride and lures her into that Baal-forsaken territory (Hos. 2:14-17).

The sixth threat (Hos. 2:4) is leveled at Gomer's children. They are responsible persons, not nursing infants. Since they share their mother's inclinations to promiscuity (including idol worship), they share their mother's fate. They walk closely in their mother's footsteps.

The Divorce: A Separation to Reconcile 2:6-13

2:6-7a Building Hedges

The accusation (2:5) is followed by the Lord's announcement of the consequences (2:6-7a). Each accusation consists of actions and words. These reinforce and interpret one another.

The mother has turned to prostitution *[Prostitution, p. 393]*. The language is that of prostitution; the actual sin is adultery. The weight of evidence in this chapter favors the interpretation of unfaithfulness and promiscuity rather than that Gomer turned to common prostitution for a livelihood. Why the use of this language?

It is the language of covenant curse (Hillers: 1964a:58). Amos uses it when he prophesies that Amaziah's wife will be forced to turn to prostitution to survive the day of judgment (7:17).

Gomer/Israel is accused in this first cycle of turning to prostitution (2:5). If the lovers whom she wishes to pursue are the shrine male prostitutes or Baal worshipers, they represent Baal and the other gods from whom she claims to receive her bread and water, wool and flax, oil and drink. If the lovers are casual adulterers, it is difficult to explain the reference to the gifts. The most comprehensive interpretation may be the best. The *lovers* are the baals, masters *[Ba'al, p. 373]*. The *whoredom* refers to all acts of pursuing the Baal religion and the resulting way of life *[Canaanite Fertility Myth, p. 376]*.

Israel claims the local baals provide the daily necessities of life: food and clothing. The omission of meat, shelter, and children would be strange if this were a list of necessities. Marriage documents from other Near Eastern cultures describe the husband's obligations toward his wife to consist of generous provisions of grain, oil, and wool (cf. 2:8). The addition of water (*drink*) and *flax* (linen) suggest luxury (2:5). *Linen* is not everyday cloth. The provision of *water* constitutes a luxury in that the wife does not need to share the daily toil of drawing and carrying water from the local well. The *oil* mentioned here is identified in the marriage documents as cosmetic oil, not cooking oil. Gomer and Israel claim that Baal has truly blessed them.

This accusation cycle ends with the covenant partner's response (2:6-7a). The recording artist now merges two images—a cow and an unsuccessful prostitute. Gomer/Israel is like a cow making her *way* over the hills along well-worn paths. Cattle were fenced in by means of thornbush and thistle fences or by stone walls. God, aware of Israel's lust for good things, has put obstacles in her path to prevent her from pursuing the baals, symbolized by the bull *[Bovine Imagery, p. 374]*.

The second image reinforces the first. Gomer/Israel is like a prostitute pursuing her clients. But God obstructs her way, delaying her so long that she is unable to catch up with them. The scene resembles that described in Proverbs 7. The prostitute or adulteress observes passersby on the street below. When she sees a likely client, she rushes down to advertise her wares and services personally. But the Lord delays her just long enough for her to miss the prospective customer. Running, she searches the nearby streets and alleys to find him (2:7a), but he is gone. Persistent failure to catch her prospective clients frustrates her, so she resolves to return to her husband.

2:7b-8 Recognizing Attitudes

The effect of these connected oracles, each growing out of the preceding one, is to depict God as Judge. Israel's rampant defection leads the offended judge to pronounce the verdict. At first glance, it appears that the judge's threats have brought about repentance (2:7b). But Israel's words contain neither an awareness of guilt nor a confession of sin. Israel's attitude demeans her husband.

This second criticism of Gomer/Israel accuses the spouse of using her husband for her own convenience. Her words—whether spoken or merely thought—and her actions both point to a purely functional relationship. Frustrated by God's actions of blocking her way, the unfaithful spouse decides to return to her husband's home. She returns, not because she loves her husband, nor because she repents of her adulteries, nor because she has come to recognize the enormity of her sin, but because his home offers more comfortable living conditions (2:7b).

Reconciliation between estranged marriage partners is always appropriate. No legal barrier stands in the way of reconciliation since Gomer has not married the baals; they have been *her lovers*.

She did not know that it was I lies at the heart of this oracle (2:8). The list of goods the aggrieved husband may repossess includes everything he has given his wife. Other than wine, the items mentioned here appear in marriage contracts of the ancient Near East under descriptions of dowry. That implies that Gomer came to the marriage without a dowry and was graciously provided one by Hosea.

Israel returned to God (and, presumably, Gomer to Hosea) because of the benefits experienced with him. She has taken the blessings but ignored the relationship. In fact, she does not even recognize the Lord as the source of the blessings. Either she is unthinking or is so committed to the baalistic worldview that she is incapable of seeing life from the Lord's perspective. Is this what occurred during the superficial repentance (return) of Jeroboam I (1 Kings 13:1-6), Ahab (1 Kings 18), and Jehu (2 Kings 9-10); and during the partial repentance of Asa, Jehoshaphat, Joash, Amaziah, and Azariah? Of each of them it was said that he did

> what was right in the sight of the Lord, yet the high places were not taken away, and the people still sacrificed and offered incense on the high places. (1 Kings 22:43; cf. 15:11-14; 2 Kings 12:2-3; 14:3-4; 15:3-4)

Hosea's accusations here seem to reflect the two-tiered and compartmentalized religion which the nation had created *[Israelite Religion, p. 385]*. Yahweh (the Lord), the One who brought them up from Egypt, is the country's national God. His concern and his domain are of cosmic proportions. He rules the nations. The patriarchs knew him in his manifestation and by his name, El Shaddai (cf. Exod. 6:3). El Shaddai was the God of last recourse. The effective symbols of this El and Yahweh deity were the two golden bull calves installed by Jeroboam I at Bethel and Dan (1 Kings 12:28-30) *[Bull Calves, p. 375]*.

The words of their installation by Jeroboam I are instructive: *Here are your gods, O Israel, who brought you up out of the land of Egypt.* Alongside these symbols of the Lord, Jeroboam set up numerous hill shrines on high places (1 Kings 12:31). The Bethel sanctuary is the king's sanctuary, the temple of the kingdom (Amos 7:13). The hill shrines are the places of Baal worship of the common people. The Lord (I Am) regulates national and historic affairs; Baal is thought to regulate the affairs of everyday life. As long as the high places remain intact and in use, returning to the Lord will be perfunctory. God intended a fundamental repentance, a 180-degree turn; Israel thinks a nod in the right direction will do.

Israel/Gomer did not know. . . . Her religion has become so thoroughly perverted that she is not aware that all the gifts she attributes to the Baal actually come from the Lord. Fertility is the Lord's domain. He blessed the world made by his own word and infused it with the ability to reproduce (Gen. 1). Fertility rites, therefore, are acts of unbelief in the providence of the Creator *[Israelite Religion, p. 385].*

Sorcery, frequently associated with idolatry and sexual license, was a popular medium for manipulating the gods (Exod. 22:18; Hosea 4:12; Isa. 47:9; Micah 5:11-13; Nahum 3:4; Mal. 3:5). We lack details as to how sorcery was tied to Baal worship or how it used God's gifts to manipulate the gods.

The gifts in crops, flocks, and herds are God's gracious gifts. National prosperity flourished during the majority of Jeroboam II's long reign. Yet the nation does not attribute her newfound wealth to the Lord. Instead, they use it to honor Baal. The Baal cult prospers through God's bounty. Will God be party to his own demise?

Hardly!

2:9-13 Avoiding Codependency

Israel's cavalier attitude toward her marriage partner demeans the Lord and, unless checked, will escalate into disgust and abuse on her part. God is determined not to encourage that attitude by delaying the consequences of her adulteries any longer. Love knows when to say, "No more!" God will not share in Israel's self-deceit nor be manipulated by false repentance. Decisive actions follow. God's tolerance has reached its limit.

The Lord will withdraw benefits of marriage (2:9). Israel's *return* (Heb: *šub,* 2:7b in NRSV) causes God to *take back (šub,* 2:9a in NRSV) his gifts, introducing a change of fortunes which may bring the nation to its senses (2:9-13). The judge is speaking. The threat spoken at the beginning of this court case (2:3) is now explained in greater detail.

God's response introduces the harvest metaphor. He hopes that an interrupted harvest, major crop failures, and removing the medium of worship may bring Israel to her senses. God determines to *rescue* (2:9b; NRSV: *take away)* his bounty, which the people have attributed to Baal and with which they have served Baal. The Lord himself will harvest their crops of grain and wine, of wool and flax.

The scene is graphic: as Israel is about to harvest the fruit of the fields, God cuts down the corn and tramples the grapes into the wine of his wrath. Since Israel is misusing the harvest gifts, God himself will *rescue* his wool and linen, but no one will be able to *rescue* Israel from his hands. The wordplay stirs the imagination.

The Lord will make a public disclosure (2:10). It is not right for the Lord privately to deny or conceal this attitude of resentment. Publicly, the husband would be labeled a cuckold. Such reality-denying love, patience, and forgiveness would destroy the reputation of any husband, be he Hosea or (figuratively) God.

The solution is for the husband to strip away the gifts he gave his bride and send her away. Let her lovers care for her! No one respects this woman enough to protect her from public shame. The Lord has loved her in comparable circumstances (cf. 2:3a); no other god will identify with such a promiscuous people.

Therefore, the Lord *will put an end to* the parties (2:11). Israel's celebrations will grind to a halt. Festivals marked special occasions in Israel's history and experience. The Scriptures identify three pilgrim festivals in which every male was to participate (Exod. 23:14-17; 34:18-24; Deut. 16:1-17; Passover/Unleavened Bread, Harvest/Weeks/Pentecost, Ingathering/Booths/Tabernacles). The new moon celebrations (Num. 28:11-15) and the Sabbaths (Num. 28:9-10), together with other holiday seasons, were regular reminders of God's historic redemption and ongoing provision for his people. But now they have lost their original meaning and become *days of the Baals* (Hos. 2:13). Only by bringing them to an end might Israel be stirred to reconsider their meaning.

The Lord calls in witnesses from his created order (2:12). It is one thing for the Lord to withdraw benefits, disclose the true state of affairs, and restrain the celebration of evil. It is another for him to call on the world to give witness to what is seen (cf. 4:3; notes on 2:21). Heaven and earth, the covenant witnesses, come to cast the first stone [*Covenant, p. 379*]. The curse falls on unfaithful Israel. The Promised Land reverts to a chaotic state. Vines and fig trees become an impenetrable forest. Their fruit has become food only for animals.

The agricultural metaphor points in two directions. It points to Baal as impotent and to the Lord as sovereign. Israel has failed to honor God in the land, so the land and its produce come to give witness about the degree to which God's people have neglected him. When Israel presumes on God's grace, she eventually claims his gifts as rights and his grant of stewardship as private possession. Sooner or later, neglecting God will show itself in nature's revolt against abuse of every kind.

There are decisive consequences (2:13). God begins by withholding benefits, and he ends by directly punishing his adulterous wife. Hosea does not figure in this sequence of punitive steps. In light of the extended metaphor, however, Hosea is present, imitating God's discipline by letting the consequences fall on his estranged wife. He will not act on her behalf to protect her, now that she has become emotionally abusive. If he protected her, he would become a partner and a codependent in her sordid acts of self-deception.

Some two hundred years earlier, Elijah represented Israel's God in the contest with the prophets of Baal on Mt. Carmel. His lightning victory consumed altar and sacrifice. It also deluged the nation with life-giving rain. Who could doubt the Lord's superiority? But Israel soon reverted to Baal worship. The paths to the high places were too deeply trodden, the patterns of thought and life too deeply entrenched; they could not be altered by a bolt out of the blue or by one, two, or even three crop failures.

God will not be used. Israel has stolen God's possessions by claiming them for her own purposes; God is determined to *rescue* his property. No one, not even the baals, are capable of intervening in God's judgment (cf. Deut. 32:39). Perhaps, the thought goes, they may recognize the hand of God the warrior when he brings a national enemy against Israel—*the wild animals* (Hos. 2:12; cf. 5:14).

The threat (2:12b-13) unites accusation and judgment. As the bounties of God are being removed, Israel bemoans her loss—like a child complaining when its abused toys are removed. Israel seems incapable of seeing the truth. Appeals have fallen on deaf ears; chastisement has gone unheeded.

God himself breaks the pattern. Sandwiched between verses 13 and 14 are the unspoken judgments which will later be announced in sordid and gruesome detail in chapters 4–14 of the book.

At this point in the drama, Hosea and Gomer have receded into the background. Onto center stage tumbles the larger family history, the unfailing divine love rejected by God's people, while God longs for reconciliation. Israel fails to see what might be, so God offers her a vision of what will be—the consequences. Divorce is not the end; it is a step toward recovery of hope. That hope rests in God's initiative.

It's a Long Way Back, Even on Love's Initiative   2:14-23

The plaintiff, God, continues to address the court (2:14-23). He unveils his plans to restore his bride. Divorce does not end his longings for reconciliation. Indeed, the divorce is intended for reconciliation. Three hoped-for results are mentioned.

God will induce new actions (2:14-15a) and new words (2:15b-17) in Israel and initiate a new covenant (2:18-23). Whether or not these three results were originally defined in different prophetic speeches is irrelevant. They form a coherent whole as they stand. They capture the purposes of God as set forth in the Deuteronomic covenant: reconciliation and restoration (Deut. 30). The two-stage return is reflected in these verses. On Israel's behalf, the new covenant will embrace the whole world of creation. Only later will the Lord consummate his renewing work in faithless Israel (2:21-23).

2:14-15a Rediscovering Friendship and Romance

New actions on Israel's part issue from God's initiative. God will seduce, lure, and persuade Israel to return to the wilderness *[Tabernacles, p. 396]*. He will tenderly whisper to her the intimacies and joys of their original desert honeymoon. He will romance her with gentle words and kindnesses (cf. Gen. 34:3; Judg. 19:3).

The wilderness has a dual significance. It refers to the desert Israel crisscrossed on her way out of Egypt. In that inhospitable place, God fed and cared for them. There, Israel became the people of God as they exchanged vows with him at the foot of Mt. Sinai.

But there is more. The barren wilderness points to Baal's geographical limitations and impotence, even though Baal is reputed to be the god of fertility *[Canaanite Fertility Myth, p. 376]*. Any gifts Israel receives in the wilderness can be attributed only to the Lord. The desert stands outside Baal's sphere of influence.

Restoration to favor leads to restoration of the promises. The curses have matured into judgments which exiled Israel from the land of plenty. God's word of promise will restore the land to Israel. It will release the flow of milk and honey, the abundance of olive trees and vineyards (cf. Exod. 3:8, 17; Josh. 24:13), as witnessed by the twelve spies when they traversed the country (Num. 13:23-28). Unfortunately, that initial promise was received only through the pain brought on by disobedience and defeat. Achan and his family were stoned in the Valley of Achor, meaning *trouble* (Josh. 7:24-26). The future fulfillment of the promise will restore Israel without such an experience of *trouble*. The Valley of Achor will open the door into the Judean foothills. Jubilation in victory over their enemies will replace the despair of defeat. Trouble will turn into hope; the restoration will exceed their wildest dreams and their most glorious past experiences.

2:15b-17 Creating New Words of Endearment

In that day, the Lord will also draw forth new words from his bride. Courtship will lead to remarriage in the wilderness. When God first led Israel out of Egypt, the people affirmed the covenant relationship and conditions at Mt. Sinai: *All that the Lord has spoken we will do, and we will be obedient* (Exod. 24:7). They acknowledged him as Lord (cf. Jer. 2:2-3) *[Covenant, p. 379]*. In the redemption to come, the people will repeat their vows but with a new vocabulary. The word *ba'al*—meaning *husband, master, owner, or Baal*—will be erased from Israel's vocabulary. As designation for "husband," *ba'al* applies only to the first marriage, the one that constitutes the husband as a householder and eligible to assume a ruling role within his community *[Ba'al, p. 373]*. Its common meaning (*husband*) as well as its function as a proper noun (*Baal*, a god) will fall into disuse. The exile will achieve its intended purpose; Israel will be purged of idolatry.

The woman has been divorced, so the negotiations for remarriage take place between her and her suitor (her former husband). She, then, becomes what is known as the "loved" wife (cf. Gen. 29:30-31; Deut. 21:15-17; 1 Sam. 1:5), usually so called because she was his choice rather than the bride gained through his family's negotiations.

Gomer/Israel left her husband's home as destitute as on the day she was born. This implies that she has no equity to bring to a new marriage. Her loving husband turned suitor promises to restore her dowry. On her part, she promises never again to use the language of the baals. This implies that she leaves all others to remain faithful to him alone (Hos. 2:16).

2:18-23 A New Marriage Covenant

At the heart of the Lord's response is the initiation of a new covenant (2:18-23). These verses are infused with covenant language and concept *[Covenant, p. 379]*.

The Lord will provide a safe setting (2:18). At the time of restoration, after Israel has repeated her vows (2:15b-17), God promises to ensure her safety. Land and fertility are not enough. Crops, herds, flocks, and children can be decimated by the ravages of wild animals and war. Therefore, God guarantees Israel's security and tranquillity in two ways: by making a covenant with the creatures inhabiting the land, and by promising absence of conflict and war. Nature and nations are now bent to serve God's saving purposes.

The covenant is made with the animals on Israel's behalf. It resembles in measure and echoes the covenant enacted with Noah, humanity, and "with every living creature" (Gen. 9:10). God's preserving care ensures their security; yet this covenant carries additional overtones of meaning. Since the Fall, enmity and competition for survival have existed between humans and animals (Gen. 3:14-21). When God's people disobey his will, the wild animals and other creatures became agents of judgment (Lev. 26:21-22; Deut. 28:26, 42). But the new order will be totally different.

A further implication of the covenant with the creatures of the earth grows out of the misuse of animals and animal representation within the Baal cult. The second commandment prohibited idolatry (Exod. 20:4-6). Baal worship placed the bull on a pedestal for purposes of worship; other deities had *their* animal symbols. The covenant with the creatures of the earth placed them in a subordinate role, for accountable use by humans rather than abuse or worship. God's restoration, therefore, will return creation to its designated order.

War was a curse on disobedience (Lev. 26:25-39; Deut. 28:25, 31-33, 49-52). Restoration to covenant blessings represents the advent of a reign of peace rather than victory in war. God will create security without recourse to military strength or strategies. Violence will be replaced by shalom.

The Lord will help Israel develop qualities that last (Hos. 2:19-20). The threefold *I will take you for my wife* (Heb.: *betroth you*) marks the conclusion of God's covenant with Israel. According to the marriage customs of Israel, courtship resulted in marriage negotiations. When concluded, the payment of the bride-price sealed the betrothal. The betrothal marked the marriage union, even though the marriage might not be consummated for some time (cf. 1 Sam. 18:25; Deut. 22:23-24).

The bride-price is itemized in Hosea 2:19-20. *Righteousness* or rightness consists of the appropriate, normal, equitable relationships between people. It transcends law and appears as a sense of fairness rather than an expression of law. *Justice* applies to conflict of interests and the administration of the welfare of the individual and family in relation to the group. The weak members of society are given power through justice. *Steadfast love* governs the relationship of parties who are in covenant with one another. It speaks of maintaining familylike bonds. *Mercy* denotes strong compassion, especially for those who do not measure up to the norm. *Faithfulness* characterizes a person of integrity. It is observed by others as consistency, trustworthiness, and firmness. These qualities surpass material goods as the greatest gifts of God. When relationships of this type prevailed in Israel, the nation enjoyed an inner cohesion and strength and preserved the essence of the covenant.

Then and only then can that future remarriage be consummated, with the stated result: so that *you shall know the Lord.* The broken marriage has been restored, not through superficial repentance or disregard of sin, but through confrontation, chastisement, confession, healing, a new mutual recommitment, and new gifts creating a new people. This covenant will be permanent, *forever* (2:19), enduring.

The Lord will break the destructive pattern (2:21-22). The eschatological (end-time) blessings of the covenant are associated with two additional processes. The first is that of countermanding the covenant curses (2:21-22). The Hebrew word in question means *to respond to someone,* either in word or song. Under the terms of the Sinaitic covenant, heaven and earth are witnesses to the agreement. When violations occur, the witnesses testify against the unfaithful (Deut. 4:26; 30:19; 31:28) and become the agents of death (17:7).

Hosea 2:21-22 may be describing orders passing along a chain of command, beginning with God and ending with the national model of divine bounty, Jezreel Valley. Each witness to Israel's earlier disobedience is advised that those curses are ended and the blessings are to be restored. Or perhaps the imagery is that of processional choirs responding to one another in question-and-answer form (cf. Ps. 15; 24) or in alternating chorus (cf. Ps. 136; Deut. 27:11—28:6). If that is the underlying imagery, then the divine Cantor starts the song of blessing. Each successive choral group—heaven, earth, and its rich bounties—takes up the song until it is heard in Jezreel. The entire universe celebrates the restoration of God's people.

The Lord will give new names for familiar faces (2:23). The second process leading to full restoration and blessings involves the renaming of the children (2:23). The place of national defeat, *Jezreel* (*yizreʻeʼl*), becomes *God's sowing* (*zrʻ*); *Not-pitied* becomes *Pitied,* and *Not-my-people* becomes *My-people.* Both God's naming and renaming of persons are important. They signal ownership, dominion, or the identification of the true nature of the one being named. Israel has become a new people; the Lord is their God.

THE TEXT IN BIBLICAL CONTEXT
God's Divorce: A Moral Dilemma?

Hosea 2 depicts a divorce proceeding. It occurs simultaneously at two levels: Hosea and Gomer; God and Israel. But would God endorse and perhaps even encourage Hosea to act in a way which he clearly condemns as sinful elsewhere in the Scripture? "For I hate divorce, says the Lord, the God of Israel" (Mal. 2:16). Moses allowed divorce as a concession to hardhearted husbands, Jesus says, but from the beginning God's intention is for marriage to last for life (Mark 10:2-9 et par.; Deut. 24:1-4).

The moral dilemma posed by the divorce language of Hosea 2:2 is real. We cannot deny the divorce on the grounds that it violates our understanding of God. In that respect, the issue resembles God's institution of levirate marriage (Deut. 25:5-10), which required polygamy in those instances where the duty fell on a married brother. A similar moral dilemma is created by the command to annihilate the inhabitants of the land (Deut. 7:17-26) or by commending the wisdom of the unjust steward (Luke 16:1-12).

One might appeal to the nature of metaphorical language. God explains his relationship to Israel by using the metaphor of divorce. Indeed, a later text cites God as saying, *[Judah] saw that for all the adulteries of that faithless one, Israel, I had sent her away with a decree of divorce* (Jer. 3:8). This confirms the metaphor as appropriate to describe God's relationship to his people. That, however, does not justify Hosea's act of divorcing his wife. If both of these relationships are said to be merely described by divorce as a metaphor, then we are pressed in the direction of accepting Hosea's entire marriage experience as a metaphor. The concreteness and specificity of the first chapter, however, militate against that conclusion. The divorce is real, yet God abhors divorce.

The language of love and hatred defines choice and rejection as in the case of Jacob and Esau: *I have loved Jacob but I have hated Esau* (Mal. 1:2-3; cf. Deut. 7:7-8). The language also reflects the normal emotional ties characterizing polygamous marriages. Thus, the "loved" wife is the second wife chosen by the husband rather than the parents (Deut. 21:15-17; 22:13-19; cf. Gen. 29:31-32). Malachi 2:16 is clear and unequivocal: God does not desire divorce as an end for human marriage, and likewise he does not take pleasure in judgment for Israel (cf. Ezek. 18:21-24). Yet the language of divorce is appropriate since it captures God's response to evil and his judgment on those who repudiate the covenant (Hos. 9:10-17). The language of divorce reflects human experience and becomes an appropriate vehicle to communicate the heart of God. It is just as suitable as the language of God as warrior or as ravenous beast when depicting divine holiness in purifying action.

Divine Patience and Persistence

Hosea 2 speaks of judgment on persistent sin. Israel's history consists of one dalliance after the other. It is a story of unfaithfulness to a loving God. We wonder at God's patience; we are amazed at his persistence in calling Israel back to himself. There is no formula which defines the moment of his judgments or the limits of his restoring grace.

At times in Israel's history, specific sins were immediately matched with judgment (Exod. 32; Num. 11; 2 Sam. 24; 1 Kings 14). At other times the sin and its consequences are separated in time and circumstances (Job 27; Ps. 73). The unpredictable time frame warns God's people not to play fast and loose with God; he could bring about the consequences at any time. Humans ought not to presume on God's patience. His delay is unmerited favor, not indifference (cf. Ps. 94; 2 Peter 3:1-13).

The silence of God's patience and recalling grace translates into the suffering of the saints. The faithful remnant calls out, "How long? Vindicate us, O Lord!" There the unpredictable time becomes a test of faith (Ps. 73; Rev. 6:10).

God surely acts to call his people back. He will never desert them (Deut. 30; Jer. 31). That applies both to the Israel of Hosea's day and to the new Israel. But no individual, local congregation, denomination, or any other segment of God's people can lay claim to unconditional blessing (Gen. 17:1-14; Lev. 26; 2 Sam. 7:8-17; Rev. 2-3). Those who disobey God and take a cavalier attitude toward God are on the road to forfeiting their share in that inheritance with God's people. The marvel is that God's love keeps reaching out to all with the invitation to renew our covenant commitments and be restored. Israel's history is recorded as both warning and assurance (1 Cor. 10; Heb. 3-4) [Covenant, p. 379].

TEXT IN THE LIFE OF THE CHURCH
The Witness of Marriage and Family

The first and strongest witness to God's presence and grace occurs in the church family (Mark 3:31-35; et par.; Rom. 8:14-17, 29). The church wants that witness to be reflected in marriages and family units (Eph. 5:21—6:4). It has always struggled with the destructive effects of divorce and the resultant complications of remarriage. Recent research indicates that we have underestimated the long-term disruptive power of severed marriage bonds (Wallerstein). These are symptoms of deeper distortions and disturbances; they are frequently the cause of further irreparable harm.

Withdrawal from the marriage covenant is filled with pain. Hosea registers the anguish of ending an emotionally and morally destructive marriage. At the same time, the church needs to acknowledge that divorces are caused. Most marriages sustain considerable abuse and neglect before they shatter. Indeed, because of their intense intimacy, most marriages are amazingly resilient, often surviving personal immaturity, silence, distance, addictions, third parties, and even physical abuse. Adultery, abuse, and desertion are serious offenses but need not be the last word in this human relationship.

Hosea, the man and the book, also mirror the persistence of God's restoring love. Hosea addresses every age with the invitation for the faith community to call brothers and sisters to renew damaged and even severed marriage ties. Divorce is not the solution. Confession, repentance, confrontation, truth-telling—these are the way toward restoration and a return to marital health. In this eighth-century pre-Christian drama, Hosea and God offer a recovery of hope for fractured homes and society. Restored marriages and reconciled families speak powerfully to the oneness and saving grace of God. These are primary witnesses to Christ.

Christ and the Church: Bridegroom and Bride

The use of marriage imagery to depict the Israel-God covenantal bond of intimacy and faithfulness is not new (cf. Jer. 2:2-3; Ezek. 16:1-14). This interpretive tradition flourished among the rabbis, who applied it to the Song of Solomon. In Judaism, the typology featured Israel as a collective covenant community; it was not used of individuals.

Later Christian interpreters kept a distance from the erotic features of the Song of Solomon by reinterpreting the lovers individually, as Christ and the individual Christian. This approach was common among the Desert Fathers and in the writings of Teresa of Avila. Ecstasy became an appropriate description of a personal love relationship with Christ; it was considered inappropriate as a literal portrayal of human love and intimacy.

The NT carries forward the imagery of Christ the Bridegroom returning for his bride, the church (Eph. 5:22-33; 2 Cor. 11:2). In the final vision of the book of Revelation, the future redemption brings together the imagery of God's people as a metaphor of a metaphor:

> Then I saw a new heaven and a new earth. . . . And I saw the holy city, the new Jerusalem, coming down out of heaven from God, prepared as a bride adorned for her husband. . . . And I heard, . . . "See, the home of God is among mortals. He will dwell with them as their God; they will be his peoples," and God himself will be with them. (Rev. 21:1-3)

The language is intentionally similar to that of the OT prophets. In its consummation, the vision in Revelation fulfills the expectation of Hosea for a restored covenant relationship between God and his people. This happens as Christ the Lamb is united with the church, saints from all nations (Rev. 19:7-9; 7:9-10). The question of historical fulfillment of Hosea remains. Does the return under Ezra (and Nehemiah) represent God's initial act of calling his wife back? That, we believe, is the first step in a two-stage redemption. The final stage is God acting through Christ to renew and restore Israel under the terms of a new covenant that is emphatically open to believers from every nation (Matt. 26:26-29; 28:19; Heb. 8–9).

Hosea 3:1-5

Reconciliation: Born of a Persistent Love

PREVIEW

Hosea's marriage has become the visual aid by which God opens his heart to unfaithful Israel. The divorce and subsequent acts of judgment were designed to be remedial. Expulsion from the Promised Land leads to death in the wilderness (2:3). Yet the Lord's miracles are not ended. God expels Israel into certain death in the barren and arid Baal-less wastes. When Israel looks about her in a state of desperation, the figure of God reappears—beckoning, wooing, and inviting his people to a new marital relationship, welcoming them to new life.

The salvation oracle which concludes chapter two contains the Lord's words of promise to his alienated and separated wife. Those are the dreams of lovers, the promises of an exuberant bridegroom. The actual process by which such dreams translate into reality is frequently much more mundane and trying than those flowery promises suggest. Hosea 3 presents the steps by which the promises become reality in the lives of Hosea and Gomer. Earlier, Hosea's marriage displayed Israel's checkered past (Hos. 1); now Israel's future is anticipated in the life of this family [Accusation-Judgment-Salvation Oracles, p. 372].

OUTLINE

EXPLANATORY NOTES

Love Breaks Deadlocks 3:1-3

3:1 Go, Remarry Your Ex

"*Love a woman.*" Is this Gomer or someone else? The interpretation depends partly on how one reads the opening words of address:

(A) *The Lord said to me again, "Go love . . .";* or
(B) *The Lord said to me, "Go, love . . . a second time."*

The adverb "again" implies continuation. The question is, what is continued? God's speaking or Hosea's going and loving? A study of the underlying Hebrew adverb shows that though it more frequently follows the verb it modifies (as in A, above), on occasion it precedes its verb (as in B; cf. Isa. 56:8; Jer. 2:9; Ezek. 5:4). So the exegetical decision will have to be made on the basis of context.

For Hosea to marry another woman after the divorce is to create a problem with the metaphor. Surely the Lord does not choose a second and different wife because Israel has been unfaithful! Furthermore, the woman is still regarded by God as married, since she is described as *an adulteress,* committing adultery. That matches the very point of the preceding and enticing words spoken by the husband as he leads his divorced wife back into the wilderness (Hos. 2:14). He intends to remarry his wife (Gomer/Israel) and renew their covenant of love. The initiative is entirely the husband's.

The description of the woman is unusual. The NRSV reads: *a woman who has a lover* (3:1). Literally, the wording is: *one beloved by a dearest friend* (Heb.: *rea'*). Until now the wife's love affairs have involved *lovers* (plural: 2:5, 7, 12-13). Why the change? The puzzle deepens when we note that the word translated *buy* (3:2) is unusual as well. The Hebrew verb *karah* is most often translated *to dig* and refers to digging a well (Gen. 26:25), a tomb (Gen. 50:5), or a pit in which to catch animals (Exod. 21:33); or piercing an ear (Ps. 40:6). On other occasions it refers to preparing food (Job 41:6 [Heb.: 40:30]; 2 Kings 6:23). In Deuteronomy 2:6, Moses reviews the directions he gave to the people about passing through Edomite territory:

> You shall purchase (Heb.: *šabar*) food from them for money (silver), so that you may eat; and you shall also buy *(karah)* water from them for money (silver), so that you may drink.

The difference between the two words for *purchase* indicates that the food was a commodity exchanged for silver, whereas the water was purchased in the form of water rights while passing through the country. That would presumably include the right to dig for water or use existing water sources. The sexual overtones are evident in the association of the word with food, water, and digging (cf. Song of Sol. 4:10—5:4); and with the purchase of rights to a service rather than paying for a commodity handed over to another.

Consider how this shapes the meaning of Hosea 3. If Gomer has become a cult prostitute, the use of the term *rea'* (friend) is unusual. Has she sold herself into slavery because she was no longer sufficiently attractive to her lovers? Possibly. In that case, however, to refer to her as *beloved by another* (singular) *and practicing adultery* would be inappropriate. The strongest possibility is that she has become a *kept woman*. If so, she is neither formally a slave, nor is she any longer practicing prostitution. Her lover provides for her keep—her bed and board—in exchange for sexual favors.

The verb *buy (karah)* reinforces the idea that Hosea is purchasing the rights to her sexual favors. She is not a wife, and yet she could become his wife, if he so chose. After Hosea has purchased the rights to her sexual activity, he immediately serves notice that she will not be asked to serve in the role she has come to love—neither for Hosea nor for any other man (3:3).

Such an arrangement probably gives the woman a status halfway between a prostitute and a concubine. She does not have the security of a dowry to bring to the relationship; there is no promise of long-term commitment or being cared for in her old age, and no rights of inheritance for her children. Surely the arrangement is entered into for survival purposes for herself and possibly for her children.

The stories of Gomer and Israel are similar. Gomer's former lust has been reduced to satisfying the sexual drives of one lover, like a husband, yet not in a marriage. Note the parallels in 3:1:

Go, love *a woman*	as the Lord loves *Israel*
(A) *beloved* of a friend	(B')*they* turn to other gods
(B) *an adulteress*	(A')*lovers (plural)* of raisin cakes

God's love is the model and the measure of Hosea's love. He will not irrevocably reject his people. Divorce through exile and decimating judgment is designed to awaken Israel to the enormity of her crime against the Lord's love. In spite of Israel's pursuit of other gods and turning to *love raisin cakes* (NRSV), God's love reaches out to them. The reference to *raisin cakes* parallels the reference to other gods. Such cakes are mentioned elsewhere without negative connotations (2 Sam. 6:19; et par., 1 Chron. 16:3; Song of Sol. 2:5; Isa. 16:7). Yet raisin cakes bearing the image of a goddess were offered to Asherah or Astarte (or Ishtar, goddess of the star Venus, "the queen of heaven" in Jer. 7:18; 44:15-28; Martens, 1986:75, 291) [*Asherah, p. 372*]. What kind of love can be so gentle and yet so confrontative? So chastising and yet so patient in waiting for repentance? So utterly pure and yet so willing to forgive?

Four times the root of the word *'ahab* (*love*) appears in Hosea 3:1, illustrating the breadth of the word. It describes, in turn, Hosea's forgiving love for his unfaithful spouse, the affection and intimacy of illicit lovers, the persistence and unswerving faithfulness of the divine love, and even the desire for the raisin cakes which satisfy the senses in pagan worship. Forgiveness, affection, faithfulness, desire.

3:2-3 Taking the Initiative

Hosea's actions anticipate the Lord's. He pays Gomer's lover to get her back. The price is less than the thirty shekels charged for a female slave (Exod. 21:32), the same amount paid for a woman dedicated by vow to the Lord (Lev. 27:4). The payment, made in *silver* and *barley*, suggests negotiation rather than a fee set by decree. *Fifteen shekels of silver and about seven bushels of barley* were a bargain price. The price reflects negatively on her age, desirability, or physical condition. Gomer is no longer in great demand. She has become a cast-off, attractive only to an inordinate lust or a genuine love.

Hosea buys Gomer back. That gives him the right of ownership. She no longer has the freedom of a spouse; the obligations he imposes on her will be binding. Hosea lays down the following restrictions: he will test her fidelity over a longer period. She is to refrain from prostitution, presumably also from participating in sacred rites at high places. She is not to have intercourse with any other man.

This last phrase, *you shall not be/belong to a man*, has a range of meaning from *marry* to *have sexual intercourse with*. Here it appears to refer to having sexual intercourse (cf. Lev. 21:3; Gen. 24:16; Andersen and Freedman, 1980:302-303).

David had similarly imposed lifelong sexual abstinence on the ten concubines with whom Absalom had had intercourse (2 Sam. 20:3; cf. 16:21-22). Such devotion to abstinence appears to be the subject of the legislation of Leviticus 27:1-8 and may also be present in Paul's advice regarding marriage and singleness (1 Cor. 7:36-38).

The restraints imposed on Gomer are more than matched by Hosea's love commitment: *Nor I with you*. This marriage and love relationship exist for a long time without sexual activity. Hosea does not expect from Gomer something that costs him nothing. This platonic relationship works an emotional hardship on both, but especially on Hosea; he is waiting for Gomer to have a change of heart. Meanwhile, his acts toward her spring from purest love. Such love waits for the spouse's inner renewal, for a rekindling of the deep bonds of affection they once experienced. It refuses to place demands on the other for personal gratification. The marriage bond is fully restored only when love produces repentance and love in return.

What Else Should We Expect? 3:4-5

3:4 Restoring Trust Takes Time

The explanation, the larger reality to which the Hosea-Gomer remarriage points, is now disclosed by the Lord. Hosea demands sexual abstinence of his wife because (*for,* 3:4) God intends the parallel to point to his treatment of Israel. The ensuing relationship will have limitations. The nation will exist for many years without her major political and religious symbols. *Without king nor prince* anticipates national dispersion and subjection. The nation's military and political leaders are gone. Israel will no longer be influenced by her rulers, the majority of whom actively practiced and promoted the worship of other gods (2 Kings 17:21-23). The Northern Kingdom has come to an end. Gone are her rulers who led her astray. The existence of Gomer, however, assures the reader that the nation will not disappear. God has not cast his people away.

The suspension of *sacrifice* (3:4) applies to all sacrifices, whether offered to the Lord or to other gods. During this long period of abstinence, all official sacrifice will cease. The cult itself has been misunderstood and misused. No longer will Israelites seek to manipulate

God by feeding him with their animals. God looks for a new heart rather than a revived frenzy of animal sacrifices.

A *pillar* or *sacred stone* (3:4) was a common feature of Canaanite worship (Deut. 7:5), though originally used without negative connotations [*Canaanite Fertility Myth, p. 376*]. Prior to and even after Israel's entry into the land, such sacred stones were used as personal monuments (2 Sam. 18:18), to mark graves (Gen. 35:20), commemorate covenants (Gen. 31:45-52; Josh. 24:26-27) or divine appearances (Gen. 28:18, 22; 35:14), and were associated with worship at altars (Exod. 24:4). In ways that are unclear, a stone pillar (representing the male deity) became an integral part of the worship of Baal (often near a wooden pole for the female deity [*Asherah, p. 372*]). Therefore, the pillars were forbidden in Israelite worship (Deut. 7:5; 16:22). One test of the king's faithfulness to the Lord was whether he destroyed the sacred stones at the high places (2 Kings 10:26).

During Israel's long chastisement in exile, they will not have access to the high places of the land. This distance from their popular pagan symbol will remove their love for the sacred stones.

Ephod and teraphim are mentioned in tandem. *Ephods* were linen vestments worn by priests. They contained some means of determining the will of God in yes-or-no form by lot, perhaps through drawing a colored stone from a pocket (1 Sam. 23:9-11; 30:7-8). *Teraphim*, on the other hand, were household gods of different sizes (Gen. 31:34; 1 Sam. 19:13), probably in human form. They may have served to legitimate family leadership, guard the household, and perhaps even disclose the will of the gods in family matters. Together, *ephod and teraphim* represent guidance in everyday affairs of life. In exile, these means of searching for direction will be removed until Israel again longs for God and seeks for him in acceptable ways.

3:5 The Result Is Worth It All

Hosea and Gomer have faded into the background. God's restoring love is here at work in Israel. The long period of enforced isolation from paganism and from the full benefits of God's blessings accomplish their goal. Three essentials have been withheld: approved monarchical leadership, the fitting way to approach the Lord, and the signs of his guiding presence. These are the heart of the promised salvation. Israel's faith will be restored to life.

The time frame is indefinite: *afterward*. The many days are indeterminate, not because God is unsure, but because that focuses on

God as One who waits. The primary concern is with the purpose of this span of judgment. Israel will be brought to her senses. Contrition leads to repentance; repentance to a new longing for God; the awareness of God to a deep awe and humility; and that reverence for the Almighty bursts open the storehouse of God's bounty. Israel is foreseen as fully restored.

The word *return* denotes a full turn. It refers to a new direction, one that leads to their Lord. The old way was to follow after other gods, to pursue the baals, to pant after lovers. When the Israelites turn back toward the Lord, they *seek* him. To seek God means to approach him in worship, to passionately long for his presence in one's life, and to live out his righteousness (cf. Matt. 6:33).

But why seek *David their king?* Hosea is addressing the people of the Northern Kingdom. Is that an addition introduced into the text by a Judean? Not likely. The historical literature (Samuel, Kings, Chronicles) recorded God's promises to David as the focused point of the fulfillment of national expectations. The schism between North and South resulted in perversion of the worship and the service of the Lord. Israel cannot expect to receive God's blessings in the future if the nation continues to follow the ways pursued by the other kings. Jeroboam introduced into Israel an alternate worship and priesthood by promoting the use of the bull calves as symbols of the Lord (1 Kings 12:25-33) *[Bull Calves, p. 375].* The hope of the people lies in a return to God's promises as given to David.

The end result is deep reverence for God and a willingness to receive *his goodness* as his bounties. The history of Israel's unfaithfulness has centered in their forgetting the Lord, claiming his promises as unchangeable, and even crediting his gifts to Baal. When Israel repents, they will reencounter God in all his majesty. Their casual attitudes will melt away in awe before his presence. When they receive goodness from the Lord, they will accept it with gratitude as gift.

These restorative events shall occur *in the latter days.* That term is typically prophetic and refers elsewhere to the period of restoration (Deut. 4:30, RSV; Isa. 2:2). In the end, the Lord achieves his original design, in spite of the waywardness of his people.

THE TEXT IN BIBLICAL CONTEXT
The Nature of Love

What kind of love can both punish and heal, withhold and give, promise and demand? The theme of God's love binds the books of

Deuteronomy and Hosea together. The connections can hardly be coincidental.

Deuteronomy portrays God's love as fundamentally rooted in his choice, his election of Israel. He brought them out of Egypt "because he loved your ancestors" (Deut. 4:37; cf. 7:7-9) so that he might give them the land. That love invites or rather demands a return of affection and constancy. It is jealous. God will not share the object of his love with casual lovers, or with any other lovers, for that matter. Israel is to "love the Lord your God with all your heart, and with all your soul, and with all your might" (Deut. 6:5). That means obeying him, serving him, loving those whom God loves, and walking in his ways (Deut. 10:12-22; 11:1-25). As in ancient Near Eastern treaties, to love the sovereign is to obey him (Moran: 78-80).

Obedience may seem too austere a description of demonstrated love. Yet the same equation is found in the writings of John: "If you love me, you will keep my commandments" (John 14:15). "Whoever obeys [God's] word, truly in this person the love of God has reached perfection" (1 John 2:5). The gospel of both Testaments speaks in unison on the theme of love. The element of "newness" in Jesus' command lies in love's measure. The Sinaitic command to love the neighbor set love of one's self as the standard (Lev. 19:34). Jesus offers the higher measure: "Love one another as I have loved you" (John 15:12; 1 John 3:16). Though that new measure was not held up explicitly in the law, it was already present in the metaphor and teaching of Hosea: *Love her as the Lord loves the Israelites* (Hos. 3:1).

The Lord's judgments are often seen as antithetical to his love. The dissonance created in our minds by those two concepts reflects our lack of understanding and appreciation of the divine love. It is as pure and guileless as the driven snow. But it is also boldly confrontive and pointedly corrective. God's love does not hide the truth about the human condition nor about how much God abhors sin. If that disclosure creates guilt in the sinner, it has achieved its initial design. The fuller intent of God's exposure of sin is to bring about reconciliation and restoration. So guilt must be followed by confession, contrition, and forgiveness before renewal can occur. In that way, "Love covers a multitude of sins" (1 Pet. 4:8). Anything less is cheap grace. Those who hate the sin in their lives and in their community, as God hates it, are prepared to enjoy the long, warm embrace of God's love.

TEXT IN THE LIFE OF THE CHURCH
Renewing the Passion

The church, like Israel, has struggled through the centuries with keeping passion in its relationship to her covenant lord. The story of God's people is one of passionate first love giving way to a humdrum sameness and institutionalization. Blessedly, God does not abandon his people when they lose the flush of first love. His restorative love is as vigorous as his electing love. Frequently that love is revived only when his people see how their lukewarm pretenses affect themselves and God.

Rarely has an accommodation to the surrounding culture lifted the people of God to new heights of affection for their bridegroom, Christ. Flirtations with material well-being have usually resulted in increased greed, lust for power, and idolatry of possessions. Close identification with a particular political party leads the people of God away from their prophetic mission to the power structures. Constantine's "conversion" led to a mutual endorsement of church and state and resulted in the emperor's assumption of power over the church.

Paradigm of Restorative Counseling

The action and process by which the Lord brings Israel to a new covenant may be taken as a paradigm for counseling and assisting previously married spouses back into a new marriage with one another. The dynamics of restoring such a relationship differ considerably from those of preparing a divorced person to marry another partner. The former spouses have frequently become enemies and developed destructive ways of relating.

Marriage counselor Bill Talley uses the biblical theme of reconciliation as the way of addressing marriage breakdown. At the heart of the gospel is the message that reconciliation is possible. He writes that "one of the hardest things to get across to a formerly married single is that reconciliation is not an *option* for the Christian intent on obeying God." Talley's highest goal is full reconciliation, remarriage to the former spouse. He recognizes that many "will never achieve the spiritual, emotional, and financial maturity to become good candidates for remarriage." So he sets as his minimal goal their reconciliation to the friendship level of relationships (Talley: 143-148).

After counseling thousands of couples, Talley contends that *reconciliation is possible* and that it begins with the commitment to confess and forgive sins in the spirit of "seventy times seven" (Matt. 18:22, RSV).

TEXT IN THE LIFE OF THE CHURCH
Through Tami's Eyes

Tami grew up in an urban middle-class family. Her memories of early childhood were filled with sadness and tears. Her mother and alcoholic father fought long and often. As the oldest child, Tami came to feel that she was somehow the cause of the bickering and the anger which exploded into yelling, cursing, name-calling, pushing, and the occasional beating. When her father came home drunk on his weekend binges, she cringed with fear, wanting to protect her mother and knowing at the same time that she would become the object of his anger as well.

Most such weekends, her father would find a time alone with Tami, since her mother worked on weekends. "You can make up for being bad—and for your mother," he would say as he abused her sexually. Then he swore her to secrecy. "If you tell your mother, you'll break up our family. She won't understand."

Tami's mother found out about the secret when Tami was twelve. She sued for divorce and obtained custody of the children. Her mother assured her, "What your father did to you was terribly wrong." Yet Tami could not rid herself of the feeling that she was responsible for the divorce and the hardships that followed.

They moved into an apartment in another part of the city. That meant changing schools and making new friends. Tami was desperate for friendship and affection and felt lonely. She thought, "I don't know anyone here. Nobody loves me. I'm not worth anything." She found it harder to concentrate on schoolwork. Her grades dropped.

Tami began hanging around with a group of fringe students. They accepted her. When her dates began asking for sexual favors after an evening out, she complied, hoping to find the acceptance she was looking for. But instead of feeling loved, she felt used. They just reminded her of her father. "Men are all the same!" she thought.

Except for Steve. He was a good student and helped her with her homework, saving her from public embarrassment. Through him, Tami got to know another group of students—clean living, drug-free, many of them members of a Christian campus club. Tami struggled with loyalty to her friends, who seemed to represent two different worlds. In her junior year, she became a Christian. It was difficult to leave her partying friends, but she was committed to a new way.

Steve and Tami attended the same Christian college and were married soon after graduation. They had received counseling which addressed Tami's dysfunctional family relationships and her personal abuse by her father and many dates. Steve and Tami were determined to have a Christian marriage and family. They identified with a local church, nurtured their spiritual life together, and were blessed by the arrival of a son.

Tami, however, developed a severe case of postpartum depression. She was again overcome by feelings of worthlessness. She refused the help of their friends and counselors. Steve and Tami agreed not to have any more children until she recovered emotionally. The pregnancy was an accident. They talked about abortion but ruled it out. When the daughter was born, Steve found it hard not to think of her as "Accident."

Tami's depression deepened, and she began a pattern of unfaithfulness. Steve was as understanding as he knew how to be, but he could no longer get through to Tami. Their third child, a son, was not fathered by Steve. As much as Steve tried to rid himself of the thought, the more persistent it became: "This child is a bastard!"

Tami, distraught, left Steve and the children. She moved in with an old high school friend for a while, prompting Steve to file for divorce and the custody of the children. Both were granted.

Years went by. Steve remained single; Tami remarried, divorced, and then lived with another man—an abuser—until she developed hepatitis. Steve heard that Tami had been admitted to the local hospital and went to visit her. The illness seemed to have had a powerful impact on Tami, restoring her to her Christian commitment. The medical and hospital bills mounted, and she felt that there was no way she could ever pay them. But when Steve came to visit, he paid her bill in full. He offered to cover her counseling costs if she would return to the Christian counselor who had helped them so much before. It was years before she was ready to accept a new offer of marriage from Steve, a marriage they did not consummate until she was able to reach down to the roots of her alienation and depression.

This contemporary portrayal of Gomer and Hosea may help to change the emotional tone with which we read their history. It may reshape the theological posture from which we appreciate the grace of God and the history of salvation.

Part 2

Trial Transcript: God Versus the Heirs

Hosea 4:1—14:9

OVERVIEW
Connections to Part 1

The book of Hosea divides naturally into two parts. Chapter four begins the second part. Here the personal family experiences of Hosea
recede into the background and the nation of Israel takes center
stage.

Hosea's descendants form a threefold warning against idolatry.
Their mother's stage performance discloses the seamy side of Israel's
lusting, relentless pursuit of the baals. The children themselves became the words of condemnation—Jezreel (defeat), Not-loved, Not-
my-people.

The drama on the human plane takes an intermediate step in the
form of divorce (2:2). The Hebrew word meaning *contend* or *indictment* marks the beginning of the divorce proceedings. It stands at the
head of part 2 of the book (4:1). Hosea 4:1—14:7 fits chronologically
and dramatically into Hosea 2:2. Part 1 has provided the narrative
framework; part 2 fills in the details of Israel's tragedy.

The three children now become three themes. They develop in
reverse order to which they stepped on stage in part 1:

Not-my-people ——> No Knowledge of God (4:4—6:3)
Not-loved ————> No Covenant Affection (6:4—11:11)
Jezreel ————> No Integrity (11:12—14:7)

Hosea's collected sermons come retrofitted to these three larger themes. Under each of these major themes, the sermons and sermon excerpts are further arranged as oracles:

Accusation Oracles
Judgment Oracles
Salvation Oracles.

This ordering of materials helps us to follow the author's flow of thought. There are no clues as to their original preached order [Accusation-Judgment-Salvation Oracles, p. 372].

Parallels and Contrasts

The two parts of the book (Hos. 1-3 and 4-14) contain parallels and contrasts beyond that of structure. Covenant language and imagery run through the book. The marriage covenant is only one of the sources which feeds this rich concept. Part 1 alludes to the covenants of God with Noah, Abraham and the other patriarchs, Sinai, and David. It also draws on those covenants. Part 2 swells our understanding of the complexity and depth of covenant love and of covenant unfaithfulness.

The language of marital infidelity is prominent throughout. Adultery, unfaithfulness, prostitution/prostitute, lovers—these dance together on stage and off.

Public ethics, politics, and foreign relations occupy most of Hosea's attention. Unfaithfulness in the lives of individuals and families only mirrors the values and relationships at the national level.

There are significant differences between the two major parts of the book. In part 1, people's names are important. Their names carry the weight of the message. But in part 2, Hosea names only the patriarch Jacob and the king Shalman (10:14). God treats his people very personally, but he also addresses them corporately. To isolate particular kings or priests for reproof might tempt others to excuse themselves. Hosea directs this word to everyone.

In part 1, Jezreel is the only place name, but geographical references fill part 2. Place names become moral, historical, and redemptive reference points. Shechem, Gilgal, Beth Aven (Bethel), and Samaria represent perverted worship. Baal Peor characterizes Canaanite worship as practiced in Israel (9:10) [Canaanite Fertility Myth, p. 376]. Gibeah, Ramah, and Beth-aven mark the assault of Judah against a family member, Israel (5:8). Gibeah doubles as a refer-

ence point for the decay of the monarchy (10:9). Gilead speaks of violence within the nation itself (6:8).

Egypt and its major city Memphis both point to the grace of God
the Savior, as well as to a time of slavery and oppression from which
they were rescued and to which they will return. Assyria becomes the
contemporary equivalent of Egypt. Judgments spring to life in the
names Beth-arbel (10:14) and Aram (Mesopotamia, 12:12). Closer
to home, Admah and Zeboiim, the small cities destroyed with Sodom
and Gomorrah, mark a boundary which God's judgments will not
allow people to cross. Beyond the judgment lie Tyre (9:13) and Lebanon (14:5-6), snapshots of a new planting.

Hosea 4:1-3

Preface to the Trial

PREVIEW
The rest of the book will unpack these three compact verses.

OUTLINE
The Case: God Versus North Israel, 4:1a-b
    4:1a   Hear Ye! Hear Ye!
    4:1b   The Case Described: Heirs Claim Squatter's Right

The Charges, 4:1c-2
    4:1c   Found Missing: Variations on a Theme
          No Integrity: Jezreel
          No Family Affection: Lo-ruhamah
          No Knowledge of God: Lo-ammi
    4:2   A Litany of Evil: Violations of the Law
          Cursing: Atheism in Action
          Deception: Destroying Trust
          Murder: Premeditated Violence
          Theft: Threat to Livelihood
          Adultery: Violations of Family Intimacy
          The Snowball Effect

The Whole World Cries with Them, 4:3

EXPLANATORY NOTES

The Case: God Versus North Israel, 4:1a,b

4:1a Hear Ye! Hear Ye!

The introduction is that of a messenger or a herald: *Hear ye* (cf.
5:1)! The setting is the royal courtyard, a public square, a temple area,
or the gate of a city. Conversation freezes in midsentence. The hustle
and bustle ceases. What has God to say to his people? Prophets tend
to follow their "Listen up!" with something ominous. And ominous it
is.

4:1b The Case Described: Heirs Claim Squatter's Right

The prophet comes as the bailiff of the heavenly court. God has
filed a complaint against the entire population of the land. He is
charging them with one serious crime after another. The noun *indictment* introduces a legal case. Since it is the Lord who is filing these
charges, he will expect the nation to respond to them on his terms
and in the court of his choosing.

The accused are *the inhabitants of the land*. The phrase has both
a feeling of settledness to it, as well as something tenuous. They lived
in it but did not actually own the land. It was God's gift to a homeless
people. God promised Abram, "To your offspring I will give this land"
(Gen. 12:7). Yes, it had been promised to Abraham and his descendants "for a perpetual holding" (Gen. 17:8), but occupation was always on condition of their faithfulness (Gen. 17:1, 9; Jer. 7:3; Ezek.
33:24-26). Defection from the Lord would cause God to expel Israel
as he had expelled the sinful Canaanites before them. Then the land
would become a barren waste (Deut. 29:22-28; Lev. 26:27-35).

The Charges 4:1c-2

Israel is charged with nine crimes in three different categories. Three
counts of neglect are followed by five specific violations. The accusations end in a single, general charge. The bailiff begins with sins of
omission and then proceeds to sins of commission. They range from
duty and relationship to specific violations. The sins of commission
are extensions of the sins of omission.

Integrity and *faithfulness* ('emet), *covenant fidelity* and *affection*
(ḥesed), and the *knowledge of God* (da'at 'elohim) have been mentioned before (2:19-20). Along with justice, righteousness, and com-

passion, they represent the bride-price with which God will restore the people to himself in the salvation to come. Without these fundamental virtues, Israel's relationship to God and to one another will be little different from that of other nations to their gods. The remainder of the book gathers the prophecies of Hosea around these three themes, but in the reverse order in which they are listed here (see OVERVIEW, above).

4:1c Found Missing: Variations on a Theme

No Integrity: Jezreel. The word *'emet* represents the qualities of reliability, faithfulness, and integrity. God himself is a "God of *'emet*" (Ps. 31:5; 86:15), who calls on his people to practice *'emet* in everyday relationships and in the judicial system (Zech. 8:16, 19; Jer. 4:2). Such integrity is deeply rooted in one's being; it issues from one's heart (Ps. 15:2; Prov. 3:3).

When *'emet* is absent, people are cavalier with the truth in casual conversation, as well as when under oath (Jer. 9:5; Isa. 48:1). Its opposite is deceit, lies, providing false witness, perverting justice, and fickleness. People without *'emet* cannot be trusted; they lack essential integrity. Deep down they are fractured with fissures spreading throughout their being. This absence of *'emet*, signified by the name Jezreel, dominates the prophecies of Hosea 11:12—14:8.

No Family Affection: Lo-ruhamah. There is no ḥesed refers to a failure to maintain community in a wholesome, intimate, caring (*raḥam*) relationship, a theme that will be explored in 6:4—11:11. Ḥesed expresses itself in acts of caring for a weaker person who is in a desperate plight (Sakenfeld). Though ḥesed has no single English equivalent, the word *love* comes closer than most (Jer. 2:2). God's initiative-taking love extends itself to his people. That same love characterizes marriage bonds and the affection one has for one's family. Lack of ḥesed issues in disregard for the welfare of the community. Nearly every dimension of Israel's life is distorted by failure to embrace ḥesed toward one another.

No Knowledge of God: Lo-ammi. The third sin of omission is that Israel no longer possesses the *knowledge of God.* The term itself in its various combinations, "knowledge of God, knowledge of the Most High," is sparingly used in the OT. Yet the concept of knowing God is significant. The way to know God is to reflect on his works in creation (Ps. 100:3; Isa. 40:28-31) and history (Exod. 6:6-8) and to acquire an understanding of his will and his ways through instruction and experience (1 Sam. 3:7; Deut. 34:10; contrast Pharaoh, Exod. 5:2) *[Exodus Tradition, p. 384]*. To know God is to be passionate for the things about which God is passionate (Jer. 9:23-24); this calls for a certain kind of people (*'am*). Those who do not know God go their own ways (Judg. 2:10; 1 Sam. 2:12). That path takes them to destruction. The theme of Hosea 4:4—6:3 centers on the danger of not knowing God and warns Israel against pursuing that course of life.

4:2 A Litany of Evil: Violations of the Law

Five specific sins are listed. The last three of which appear among the Ten Commandments. The Hebrew emphasizes the acts of sinning. This translation results: *Cursing, deceiving, killing, stealing, and committing adultery erupt* (or: *break out everywhere*).

Cursing: Atheism in Action. People commonly invoked the presence of God as Guarantor of their promises. Behind the act of *swearing* (4:2) lies the inclination to deceive others for personal gain or to protect oneself from exposure to the truth or from harm. The third commandment prohibited such misuse of the Lord's name (Exod. 20:7). By swearing cavalierly, one mocked God as weak and useless.

Cursing conveys the impression of integrity. If, however, the oath is made with the intention of deceiving, the basis of good-faith exchanges within the community evaporate in the heat of conflict.

Deception: Destroying Trust. The second sin of commission is that of *deceiving*. Though sometimes translated *lying* (Hos. 4:2), at root this word refers to misrepresentation or deception (Josh. 7:11; Lev. 6:2-3). It does not refer to swearing falsely (cf. Lev. 19:11), though in the Leviticus text it stands as one member in a series of prohibitions which include stealing, deceiving, and swearing falsely.

Deceiving pictures appearance and reality at odds with one another. In the presence of deception, every financial transaction comes under the rubric, *Let the buyer beware!* Unwary or naively trusting persons are fleeced at every turn. Such a society becomes self-protective, suspicious, retaliatory, and vengeful; it breaks down at the level of common, day-to-day relationships.

Murder: Premeditated Violence. Third on the list is *killing* (Hos. 4:2). Capital punishment by the avenger is not at issue, nor is manslaughter, though the underlying Hebrew word applies to both in the Scriptures (Num. 35). Premeditated murder, including assassination, seems to be meant. Such acts pollute the land (Num. 35:33-34). The sixth commandment states categorically, *You shall not kill* (Exod.

20:13). When life becomes cheap, all other values diminish. The meaning of being human is lost; killing reduces human existence to the level of beasts of prey. Blood spilled in violence calls out to God from the ground (Gen. 4:10-12).

Theft: Threat to Livelihood (Hos. 4:2). Some interpreters argue that the eighth commandment, *You shall not steal*, originally referred only to the theft of persons (cf. Exod. 21:16; Deut. 24:7). It is unlikely that this law was ever that narrow. In the Israelite economy, the majority of the population existed only slightly above a subsistence level. In that setting, theft of property took on different proportions than in our Western world. Here most possessions are not essential to life, many people have considerable disposable income, and products are manufactured with designed obsolescence.

Job 24:2-12 is a virtual commentary on the objects prized by thieves. Stealing includes the act of moving boundary stones (stealing land), claiming sheep from the common pasture, confiscating the orphan's means of transportation, taking in pledge the widow's ox (her means of tilling the soil), and seizing the children of the poor to sell them in payment for indebtedness.

Israel's legislation forbade anyone's involuntary enslavement by private persons (Exod. 21:16). Only the courts could assign a person to the role of a slave. Enslavement reduces people to the status of chattel. They become perpetual dependents, and their personhood is violated. In a real sense, that is the result of all theft: it has a dehumanizing effect.

Adultery: Violations of Family Intimacy. Committing adultery is the last of this group of five sins of commission (Hos. 4:2). It reflects the seventh commandment (Exod. 20:14) and specifically addresses the institution of marriage rather than the nature of sexual sins.

Marriage is a covenant (Mal. 2:10-16) *[Covenant, p. 379]*. As such it mirrors the special bonds and history of God with his people, Israel. At one level, then, to commit adultery is to distort the uniqueness of God's election and call of Israel.

Adultery tears at the fabric of society. In the act, the ties that help hold together the families of the larger community are weakened. It creates insecurity in the foundations of social life. Adultery fractures trust, breeds resentment, and results in increased divorce, abuse, degradation, and impoverishment of women and children.

The Snowball Effect. These five sins are described as *erupting* (Hos. 4:2). The verb is used of a child bursting from the womb (Gen. 38:29), of the violent outbreak of a plague (Ps. 106:29), and of the bursting open of wine vats (Prov. 3:10). In its less violent contexts, it refers to a wall broken into pieces (2 Kings 14:13) or to a great increase in family size (Gen. 30:30; 1 Chron. 4:38). This introduction to part 2 of Hosea leaves no doubt as to the scope and severity of the epidemic of sins. No societal restraints exist. All the people are doing what is right in their own eyes.

The ninth charge read by the bailiff is a general statement. The Hebrew is difficult to translate; the NRSV and NIV contain one option: *bloodshed follows bloodshed* (Hos. 4:2). The word twice translated *bloodshed* (lit.: *bloods*) in this sentence connotes violence, which may extend to actual blood being shed. It is probably a more general reference to violence than the word *killing* in the previous sentence. Cogan argues (89-92) that it refers to social wrongdoing, since it is not infrequently included in lists of injustices committed against the weak members of society (Jer. 7:6; 22:3, 17; Ezek. 22:6ff., 25ff.; cf. 2 Kings 21:16; 9:7; 21:6; 24:4).

The verb in this expression ranges in meaning from *touch* to *seize* to *strike*. On the harmful end of the spectrum, it twice speaks of retaliation (Josh. 9:19; 2 Sam. 14:10). Thus read, it means, *One act of violence gives rise to another*, or *violence retaliates with violence*.

The indictments leveled against the people of the land consist of charges representing a rapid escalation of evil. The glue that holds society together is dissolving. Violence of one kind produces violence of another kind until the nation teeters at the brink of anarchy (cf. Amos 3:9-10).

This litany of sins fairly describes what is known about the Northern Kingdom during its closing years. Following the death of Jeroboam II, six kings occupied the throne for a total of 25 years. Four assumed the throne through assassination. With the help of 2 Kings 14:23—17:23, one can sense and imagine the power struggles churning within the nation.

The number and progression of sins covering the Ephraimite landscape creates a dark picture. Only desperate measures can bring about the necessary change. The book of Hosea represents one of those measures.

The Whole World Cries with Them   4:3

Therefore the land mourns. The garden of Eden was to serve as a model for what Adam and Eve could make of the rest of the world. People, animals, and plants functioned harmoniously together. The entry of sin disrupted the created order. The soil yielded its produce grudgingly; animals and plants became competitors for control of the realm.

When God brought Israel to the land of promise, it was to a "land flowing with milk and honey" (Deut. 26:9, 15). As long as Israel destroyed the inhabitants and their idolatrous practices, God would ensure the blessings of Eden (Deut. 7:12-16). The gradual conquest would ensure that God's people controlled the wild animals as well (Deut. 7:22). But if Israel failed to walk in God's ways, they would experience the curses of infertility, drought, disease, and invasion (Deut. 28:15—29:28).

Those judgments are compressed into the three sentences of Hosea 4:3. The process of creation has spun into reverse. In reaction to human violence, nature may go beserk (as with the ten plagues of Exod. 7-12). Unrelenting heat dries up water sources and causes plants to wither and fade. The land's human inhabitants bewail their dead. Creatures inhabiting the sky, earth, and water suffer the effects of Israel's disobedience. They are removed from God's land.

The land and its inhabitants are under the curse. The curse language is made even more emphatic by reversing the Genesis creation sequence (Gen. 1:30) of the wild animals, birds, and fish. The Creator is withdrawing his blessings.

Hosea 4:4—6:3

Defendant, Lo-ammi: You Don't Know God

OVERVIEW

Priests and prophets should know God. We expect them to appear in this category, and they do. Even if these religious persons fail their responsibility of teaching the people to know God, that does not excuse the ignorance of kings or the people at large.

The shift from accusation speeches to judgment speeches can be argued to occur at 5:1 or 5:8. The more comprehensive address in 5:1—priests, people, and rulers—and the specific reference to judgment argue in favor of marking the transition at 5:1.

Indictments Against Lo-ammi

Hosea 4:4-19

PREVIEW

Hosea 4 challenges interpreters. Most of the problems revolve around the question of who is being addressed. Pronouns change rapidly. Verbal subjects are unclear, as in chapter two. There the solution lay in recognizing the multitude of metaphors and images for the same referent (Gomer, Israel, heifer, people, nation, children). The smorgasbord of pronouns and verbal subjects in chapter four may well have a similar origin: God and Hosea speak of or to Israel, Ephraim, Judah, people (Lo-ammi, Not-my-people), priest, prophet, mother, and children.

This exposition will follow the insights and basic lines of interpretation offered by Michael Deroche (185-198). The chapter contains at least three prophetic oracles (4:4-6; 4:7-12a; 4:12b-19). They are linked to one another by the overarching theme of knowing God and recognizing the media through which that knowledge and relationship are experienced and perverted.

OUTLINE

Indictment 1: Rejecting the Source of Knowledge, 4:4-6

4:4-5	I Wasn't Told
4:6a	I Don't Want to Know
4:6b-e	I Don't Remember

Indictment 2: Perverting the Knowledge of God, 4:7-12a

4:7-8	For Personal Gain
4:9	Priest and People Alike
4:10-12a	For Personal Pleasure

Indictment 3: Consorting with Lovers, 4:12b-19

4:12b-13a	Prostitution by Choice
4:13b-14	Double Standards
4:15	Divine Counsel to Judah
4:16-17	Divine Appraisal of Israel
4:18-19	Partners in Shame

EXPLANATORY NOTES

Indictment 1: Rejecting the Source of Knowledge   4:4-6

Five accusing word pairs jolt the reader to attention:

Let no one contend . . .	my contention/contending
You shall stumble . . .	the prophet shall stumble
I will destroy . . .	My people are destroyed
because you have rejected . . .	I reject you from
Since you have forgotten . . .	I will forget

A question and a protest seem to lie behind all three oracles in chapter four: "We are the covenant people, and do you say that we don't know God? That's not possible. We are doing exactly as the priests instruct us."

4:4-5 I Wasn't Told

God, the Judge, refuses to hear the people's case against their priests. To *charge* is to initiate legal suit against someone (cf. 4:1). The word translated *to accuse* is used of the official responsibility of the prophet (Ezek. 3:26) and applies to the truthful denunciation of wrong. Normally, such denunciations are morally right and have God's blessing, but not here.

God prohibits these lawsuits because they represent "the pot calling the kettle black." There is no stratum of Israelite society which can pronounce itself innocent. All share in the responsibility for creating the moral swamp in which Israel is mired.

Accusations meet counter-accusations. Everyone *else* is guilty.

God takes a dim view of such mutual recriminations: *Your people are like those who bring charges against a priest* (Hos. 4:4, NIV; NRSV: *For with you is my contention, O priest*). The law imposed the death penalty on anyone who treated the priest or judge with contempt (Deut. 17:8-13). The people reject the appointed authorities while loudly claiming their rights. Here is evidence that the social order is crumbling. Anarchy will follow. The climate prevailing during the time of Judges (21:25) has returned: Everyone is doing what seems right to themselves.

While the people *stumble* (Hos. 4:5) due to failing strength, the prophets, who should be correcting and redirecting the erring nation, also have lost their bearings. The prophets often received revelation through visions or dreams; if they *stumble* at night, they themselves are no longer hearing the voice of God clearly. All possibility for corrective action has been lost.

Destroy! Reject! The words are harsh; the message, an ultimatum of sorts.

Debate rages around Hosea 4:5c-6a. Many read the *mother* to be the mother of the unnamed (presumed) high priest. More likely the *mother* of 4:5 and the *priest* (singular) and *children* of 4:6 all refer to Israel. The language of mother and children is consistent with the imagery of Hosea 1—3. To *destroy* the *mother* (cf. "daughter Zion," Jer. 6:2) is to silence her, to cut her off from her source of life, the Lord.

4:6a I Don't Want to Know

Israel is the priest on God's behalf to the nations of the world (Exod. 19:6). When God chose his people for himself, he appointed them to represent him. In rejecting God in their national, social, and personal lives, they have distorted the knowledge of God. As a result, God disqualifies Israel from serving as priests.

4:6b-e I Don't Remember

The final recurring word is *forget*. Since Israel has *forgotten* the divine guidance and instruction, God will *forget your children*. Israel's well-being has always depended on their faithfulness to God's commands. Even the promises to Abraham had conditions (Gen. 17:9-14). God assured his people that they would be the vehicle by which he would bless the nations (12:3). But disobedience can disqualify any individual or even a whole generation from that high calling.

Indictment 2: Perverting the Knowledge of God 4:7-12a

The previous oracle ended with orphaned Israel abandoned. This second accusation oracle describes, in a series of disconnected images, the delight of people and priests in the practices of the Baal cult *[Accusation-Judgment-Salvation Oracles, p. 372]*. It continues the theme of many descendants. This oracle is structured chiastically: it consists of two sets of corresponding brackets with a single center *[Literary Patterns, p. 391]*.

Unit	Key words
(A) 4:7	sinned, changed
(B) 4:8	feed, sin
(C) 4:9	punish/repay, ways/deeds
(B') 4:10a	eat, play the whore
(A') 4:10b-12a	whoredom, take away

Here, as in Hosea 4:4-6, the meaning is affected by one's understanding of the addressees. Andersen and Freedman (1980:342-344) account for the changes in person, number, and gender by interpreting the entire chapter as a series of prophetic statements made to the chief priest and his children. The explanatory notes here follow the interpretive direction set by Deroche (see "Hermeneutics and the Hebrew Text," in TBC below).

4:7-8 For Personal Gain

Israel acknowledges her God as the Lord of history but attributes fertility to Baal *[Canaanite Fertility Myth, p. 376]*. As the nation has increased in number, they rejoiced in their strength and gave honor to the pagan gods. Such actions could not be left unpunished by a God who is intensely jealous for the purity of his people.

God declares, *Their glory I will exchange for disgrace*; hence, Israel's *glory* must be the numerous descendants, regarded as gifts from Baal.

The two sentences of verse eight add to the difficulty of this passage. If the larger text refers to priests, then to *feed on the sin of my people* could mean that they eat the offerings made for sin. If Israel at large is being accused, then *to feed/eat* may be translated by *enjoy* (cf. Amos 9:14), *eagerly receive* (cf. Jer. 15:16), or *reap the benefits* (cf. Gen. 31:15). It would then agree with the idiom of the next line, *to lift one's throat*, which elsewhere means "to desire" or "to long for" (cf. Deut. 24:15; Jer. 22:27). Deroche explains the passage as using "a pair of oral metaphors . . . to accuse Israel not only of sinning, but of wanting and enjoying her sinful ways" (197) *[Ba'al, p. 373]*.

4:9 Priest and People Alike

Priests and people have entered the scene as litigants (4:4); they exit sharing a common punishment (4:9-10). The people are the reference point in the proverb (cf. Ezek. 16:44-45). In Israel during the monarchy, priests were royal appointees (cf. 1 Kings 12:31-33) chosen for their loyalty to the crown, not for their devotion to God. The priests, like the people, view their world through the lens of the fertility cult, engaging in the practice of prostitution, and promoting that way of life in their culture. The heart of the judgment will correspond to the sin: The Lord will *visit his ways upon him, and return to him his deeds*. The Judge's verdict, "Guilty as charged!" (4:9), is now spelled out in closer detail by Hosea (4:10-13).

4:10-12a For Personal Pleasure

The gods of fertility provide food and children—or so it is thought. God promises to get Israel's attention by removing fertility from the land. The language is that of covenant curses (Lev. 26:26; Deut. 28:62-63) *[Covenant, p. 379]*. The judgment ensures that no one else may claim God's glory and gifts.

The final word in this oracle details the reasons for the judgment. The book of Hosea consists of one warning after another, of explanation after explanation of the course and consequences of sin. Practicing prostitution and worshiping idols are acts of desertion. They are not minor indiscretions. They represent the adoption of another worldview. They deny the Creator's sovereignty over the processes of nature. They pervert the understanding of who God is.

Apparently Baal worshipers celebrate by eating and drinking in the presence of the Baal (see Hos. 4:18). To *take away the heart of my people* means to deceive or to rob one of good sense (cf. 7:11; the sentence extends across the verse division of 4:11-12). Old *wine and new wine* impair the *understanding*. Instead of bringing one nearer to God, they distort one's perception and experience of God.

Indictment 3: Consorting with Lovers 4:12b-19

Sex and wine have been introduced in the preceding oracles. A third expression of unfaithfulness to the Lord now appears in how they search for guidance.

4:12b-13a Prostitution by Choice

The Israelites seek the will of the gods by *consulting* them! The worshipers lay their question before the god at the shrine, or through the Asherah pole set up beside the altar (Deut. 16:21) *[Asherah, p. 372]*. The cult official or prophet answers on behalf of the god. In the present instance, the god's figurine is of carved wood, possibly mounted on the end of a pole (Hos. 4:12).

Are there no ways open for the people to discover the will of the Lord? Surely! Priests and prophets alike are empowered to receive questions and convey God's answers, even on mundane matters (1 Sam. 9:6-9). But Israel has been captured by a spirit of idolatry. They are taken with the gods of the other nations (Deut. 12:29-31). They follow the seductive walk of those who frequent the hill shrines.

Historically, Baal worship was formally introduced and informally reinforced by Jezebel and other foreigners assimilated into the nation through intermarriage (1 Kings 16:30-33). The appeal of Baal worship had been present from the beginning of Israel's history. Long exposure to Baal had created a pattern of worship and an ethos captured by Hosea in the words *a spirit of whoredom* (Hos. 4:12).

4:13b-14 Double Standards

Their fathers are drawn closer to the gods by the hilltop experiences. Their brothers and husbands honor Baal by worshiping at the hill shrine. Hence, it is natural to expect the daughters and daughters-in-law to duplicate those practices.

Hosea 4:13b does not specify whether the sexual encounters of the Israelite women are a part of their worship of Asherah and Baal. While that may have been the case, Israelite women may simply have been guilty of sexual license. The way of the gods must be good for all! they think.

Israelite (male) society severely judged sexual relations outside of marriage for their women (4:14), acts for which men considered themselves justified or excused. Such double standards are anathema to the Lord. He refuses to judge women and men differently.

Israel seems not to understand the implications of such acts. They think it is impossible to expect purity in marital relationships when sexual acts outside of marriage are a vital part of one's religious life! Yet they must recognize that they are practicing a double standard!

"Evil is evil and needs to be judged," we hear the men say. "The fornicating and adulterous Israelite women should feel God's displeasure!" The words are reminiscent of the story of their forebear Judah, who refused to fulfill his promise of providing a husband for his widowed daughter-in-law, Tamar (Gen. 38). Tamar acted the part of cult prostitute. Given the circumstances, Judah confessed, "She is more in the right than I" (38:26). That insight and that confession are lacking in mid-eighth-century Israel.

Therefore, God refuses to judge the women. That refusal is in itself an act of judgment against the nation. He will allow this evil to take its course. Maybe that will bring the nation to its senses.

4:15 Divine Counsel to Judah

The prophet concludes with messages compressed into one oracle to both Israel and Judah. The oracle comes in its original form, since Israel is addressed in the second person, as you, with a word of concern about Judah. For the Northern nation, the prophetic word pronounces judgment; for the Southern nation, a dire warning.

Judah can still avert the fate facing Ephraim, Hosea's preferred name for Northern Israel [Judah and David, p. 389]. The South has not yet become absorbed with Baal worship and turning away from the Lord. Israel is practicing four sins (Hos. 4:15-18) which Judah should avoid because they lead to destruction (4:19).

First, they shall avoid worship at *Gilgal and Beth-aven*. *Beth-aven*, meaning house of idols, wickedness, or trouble, becomes a by-word for "Bethel," house of God (cf. Amos 5:5). Both places were easily accessible to Southerners. Both were major religious centers and therefore are probably not the hill shrines condemned in Hosea 4:13. Bethel was the royal shrine of the Northern Kingdom (Amos 7:13; 1 Kings 12:30-33). *Gilgal* was an ancient cult center, blessed earlier by the ministry of Samuel (1 Sam. 7:16). The nation took its religious cues from what happened at these two centers. The models of faith and practice presented there were duplicated throughout the hill shrines of the Northern Kingdom (1 Kings 12:31-33). Both these places were within easy reach of Judean worshipers. If the people of Judah frequent Bethel and Gilgal and follow Israel's lead, they will be guilty and subject to the same judgment.

The second sin to avoid is that of swearing falsely. The oath for- mula, *As the Lord lives*, called on him as the sovereign Lord. To do this in the presence of the idolatrous bull calf and other forms of false worship is an insult. If God shall, indeed, guard their promises with his presence, those promises need to be made with integrity. The Is-raelites denied in practice what their oaths affirmed: "The Lord is God indeed."

4:16-17 Divine Appraisal of Israel

The third sin is being *stubborn* and rebellious (4:16a). The famil-iar metaphor of the heifer fits the scene, since the Bethel temple housed one of Jeroboam's bull calves *[Bull Calves, p. 375]*. Attracted by the bull, Israel becomes restless and refuses to heed its owner *[Bo-vine Imagery, p. 374]*.

The judgment of abandonment follows. It is expressed in two par-allel images. The heifer becomes a lamb placed on a wide, open pas-ture *[Bovine Imagery, p. 374]*. It has boundless freedom to go its own way, to search its world. That picture is then recast into human form. Ephraim's worship represents an alliance with idols. The covenant people have become partners with Baal. Let Judah beware! God will abandon the rebels to their own devices. As Hosea with Gomer (Hos. 2), God permits Israel to go her own way. Only then may she be open to the recalling acts of God.

4:18-19 Partners in Shame

The fourth sin consists of endless rounds of *drinking* and prostitution (4:18). The Israelite leaders (Heb.: *shields*) should be the nation's guardians. Instead, they lead the way in sexual idolatry. The Hebrew is difficult; the accusation may be read graphically:

> Having finished with their drink,
>   they indulge themselves in prostitution.
> Their leaders just love female sex organs.

Such attitudes and acts can only end in punishment (4:19). The *spirit (ruah) of whoredom* becomes a *wind (ruah)* which sweeps away the sinners (cf. Ps. 1:4). The sacrifices on which they have depended for success, security, family, and approval will turn out to shower them with shame.

Israel has been abandoned. Let Judah beware!

THE TEXT IN BIBLICAL CONTEXT

Ecology and Salvation: The Land Mourns

Sin not only destroys relationships with God and other people. It also destroys the very soil from which ADAM was taken (Gen. 2:7).

When the prophet says the land *mourns* (Hos. 4:3), he pictures the land as God's agent and presents it as deeply affected by human disobedience. Rarely does the Bible draw specific cause-and-effect connections between human sin and ecological neglect or destruction, but it does affirm that there is a relationship (cf. Jer. 4:22-26).

The Scriptures, as in this example, link morality and salvation to ecology. War, greed, and neglect rape the environment: the land becomes barren, the rains fail, wild animals become a threat to people.

Similarly, Paul describes nature under human sinfulness as groaning in labor pains. Dry rot has set in; creation remains in a state of suffering and decay until the day when it will be set free together with God's people (Rom. 8:18-25).

The link between land and morality is not immediately apparent. A bank robbery does not bring down a nation, but widespread fraud in banks and financial institutions in America affects world interest rates and even threatens the solvency of the world monetary system. Two people fighting over land claims will not ruin the countryside, but armies mine fertile fields and drive farmers from their land, creating famine and leaving a weakened population, susceptible to disease. A man felling a tree will not destroy a forest, but unrestrained slash-and-burn clearing of large forested areas threatens the local ecosystem and over the years even produces changes in the global climate. Nations pump oil at ever-increasing rates to build a modern economy, but they exhaust the oil supplies before they can develop alternative energy sources.

Though unmentioned in the text, the active agent is God. His hand is stretched out against Israel, bringing suffering to every part of the creation distorted by a people's sin.

The Pastoral Calling

The priestly and prophetic calling was to shepherd the flock, not to tear it to shreds. In the OT emphasis is placed on the priestly role in mediating forgiveness through the cult (Leviticus, Numbers) and on the prophetic confrontative, guiding, and intercessory ministry. Many prophets came from the tribe of Levi, so the distinction is not as sharp as some have thought it to be. Since priests were also the guardians of the tradition, their teaching role was significant (cf. 2 Chron. 15:3; Mal. 2:7).

The high priest and his associates were the guardians of the covenant (Deut. 33:8-11). They were also assigned the role of a supreme court (Deut. 17:8-13). According to the law codes of the Pentateuch, the high priest was to wear a special garment, a "a breastpiece of judgment," for making decisions (Exod. 28:15, 29-30). The authorized means of decision-making, the Urim and the Thummim, were placed in pockets of the breastpiece as symbols of the high priest's responsibility to communicate the will of God to the people (cf. Num. 27:21). This was likely a way of casting lots. When one was drawn out, it meant an answer of yes to the question posed; the other meant no if drawn.

Furthermore, priests and prophets were to be models of godliness and sacrificial service to the nation (Hos. 4:5-6; 5:9; cf. James 3:1). Hosea, however, declares that the priests have failed. They have taken on the character of the people at large, so that the moral, social, economic, and political life of the nation has deteriorated. They have turned from Urim and Thummim to consult idols, mere sticks of wood (4:12).

The people lack knowledge, and the priests are held accountable for this state of affairs (4:6). The priests have ignored the law of God (4:6) and thereby opened the door to a multitude of alien influences and distorted views of God. They have exchanged the revealed truth for human constructs, then assumed the right to determine what part of God's truth they wished to follow. Similarly, other prophets in Jeremiah's day were spokespersons for the status quo rather than for God (Jer. 29:9-40; esp. 29:16-17).

The importance of exemplary leadership demonstrated in Hosea is attested to elsewhere in Scripture. Ezekiel (34) uses the image of the caring and the abusive hireling shepherds. Jesus identifies himself as the Good Shepherd, in contrast to the hireling who flees when the wolf comes. Both Samuel the prophet (1 Sam. 12:3-4) and Paul the apostle (2 Corinthians) were deeply conscious of the modeling nature of their lives and ministries. For that reason Paul challenged the flock to test the apostles' motives (cf. Acts 20:25-35) and verify that they as the Lord's messengers had not served out of greed or desire for power.

The church understood the prophetic leadership role to continue into the NT (1 Cor. 12). The hereditary priestly role now embraced the ministry of every member to other members of the body of Christ (1 Pet. 2:5, 9). With apostolic approval, the prophetic teaching ministry continued as the Spirit endued leaders (1 Cor. 12-14).

Hermeneutics and the Hebrew Text

Some scholars emend the Hebrew text rather readily and freely when they encounter what appears to be an uncertain or unintelligible Hebrew reading (as in Hos. 4:7; 5:1c). It is my conviction that one should emend sparingly, and then only as a last resort. Behind this respect for the Hebrew text lie the following assumptions:

1. The Hebrew text tradition has been faithfully preserved. The text underlying the Septuagint (Greek) appears to have come from a different tradition.

2. What appears garbled to us may be due to our distance from the mind-set and/or language of the Hebrew Bible. The scribes and interpreters made sense of the text as it was written. It is cavalier or arrogant for us to judge the writers' ability to understand their native language.

3. When we reconstruct an alternative reading, we inject our sense of the context and its meaning. We do better to persist in trying to decipher the context and meaning from the Hebrew itself.

4. There is nothing inappropriate in admitting our ignorance. My approach is to assume the problem lies with my capacity to under-

stand the syntax, vocabulary, or life setting rather than to assume error in the text.

In this commentary, comments such as "the Hebrew appears garbled" or "challenges interpreters" represent just such points of contention between scholars (cf. notes on 4:7). Unless otherwise indicated, I follow the Hebrew text tradition.

TEXT IN THE LIFE OF THE CHURCH
Covered by Grace: Please Excuse Me!

The history of the church continues that of Israel in many respects. Israel saw herself as elect in that God had committed himself to her very existence; his promises were grants of security, assurances of blessing. That confidence became arrogance. Israel came to believe that God owed her blessings and security, no matter how she treated the land and her own people.

A faulty view of election can lead to a low view of sin and of the call to ethical living. The church has been tempted to claim salvation in its own terms, justifying the status quo and excusing its paganism. In the name of the Scriptures and of religious faithfulness, it has suppressed women and judged men and women by different standards. Those in power tend to rank sins and excuse or even justify sin with religious sanction.

Dietrich Bonhoeffer spoke of cheap grace—the cavalier attitude which assumes forgiveness is free, generous, and unconditional. It expresses itself in such statements: "I know this is wrong, but the alternative is too painful. I also know God will forgive me." That is the sin of presumption.

Worship with the Mind Engaged

Tucked away in Hosea 4:10-12 is the reminder that while worship is intended to be jubilant and emotionally expressive, one does worship with the mind intact. God reveals himself; we "worship what we know." Further, the people of God communicate clearly and intelligibly in normal language and speech acts. Neither wine, which robs one of understanding, nor speaking in uninterpreted tongues in public worship (1 Cor. 14) is appropriate in worship. The fact that God is Spirit does not change public worship into a recitation of the divine names, nor does it validate unintelligible babble, nor mere ecstasy.

An essential element of worship is that we receive and convey the word and will of God.

Worship which pleases God and corresponds to the nature of our God is predicated on awe and obedience; it is intelligible, and it leads to conscious decision and action.

Double Standards: For Men, for Women

Religiously motivated restrictions are the most difficult to recognize as unjust; this is shown by the blessing given to slavery over the centuries. Such restrictions are even more difficult to acknowledge and replace. For much or all of the church's history, it has maintained double standards for men and women. That is true not only of sexual standards; discrimination has also taken place in salary scales, in assuming that hiring the husband obligates the spouse to a joint ministry, in restricting the ministry of women even in areas other than pastoral leadership, and in limiting women's role in decision-making.

It is time men listen to the sisters in the faith and hear their pain. It is time we men listen to God and acknowledge our role in creating and maintaining double standards to this day. Only then will we recognize the true gifting of the body of Christ. Only then will women find release for ministry and experience full participation in the life of the church and in society.

Double standards must go.

The Verdict

Hosea 5:1-15

PREVIEW

The evidence against Israel is now part of the official court record (Hos. 4). The nation is mired in idolatry. While the evidence is being presented, the judge occasionally spells out the consequences of the accusations (4:5b, 6b, 9, 10a, 13b-14, 19). The court, however, has not yet spoken the verdict nor pronounced sentence. That occurs in the two prophetic oracles recorded in chapter five. The first points to the verdict by reviewing the primary evidence (5:1-7); the second announces the nature and the length of the sentence (5:8-15).

The theme of knowing God pervades this section as it has in

Hosea 4. Various forms of the verb *yada'* appear in 5:3-4, 9. In addition, Israel's inability to find God when they seek him in the coming emergency (5:6) shall lead them to seek him in simplicity and honesty (5:15). If that happens, the judgment will have served its restorative purpose.

OUTLINE

Defendant, Israel, 5:1-7
    5:1a   Let the Accused Stand!
    5:1b-4   Guilty as Charged!
    5:5-7   Grounds Found for Leniency? None!

Codefendants, Ephraim and Judah, 5:8-15
    5:8-9   Ephraim: Beyond Any Reasonable Doubt
    5:10   Judah: For Crimes Against a Brother
    5:11-15   The Judge Explains: Circumstances and
                     Conditions

EXPLANATORY NOTES
Defendant, Israel 5:1-7
5:1a Let the Accused Stand!

The accused have their day in court. Three imperatives rivet their attention on the judge: *Hear this! Pay attention! Listen!*

Each command addresses a separate defendant. They have all been charged with unfaithfulness in the preceding accusation oracles. *Priests, people, and royal house*: the categories represent the cross section of Israelite society: the religious establishment, the population as a whole, and the king, army, and political and administrative branches of government.

5:1b-4 Guilty as Charged!

Guilty! All three groups are guilty as charged.

Three segments of the nation are on trial; three accusatory statements are listed. If we read one charge as directed at each group, the Hebrew text does not need to be emended. Merging two triads produces:

Priests! You were a trap at Mizpah.
People! A net is spread out on Mt. Tabor.
Ruling class! Rebels are deep in slaughter.

One may wonder what this means. If the above reading is correct, the *priests* are guilty of entrapment. They have seduced the Israelites to worship at Mizpah. We do not know, however, which Mizpah is meant. It is probably not the Gileadite Mizpah across the Jordan. Is it the Mizpah near Gilgal? The Mizpah in Benjamin? Undoubtedly the listeners would have known what was meant. That is enough.

The people (*house of Israel*) are also guilty. The passive form of the verb in *a net is spread* suggests that they were caught in sin on Mt. Tabor. Does this refer to the shrines which must have been present there? Possibly! Neither Mizpah nor Tabor is treated as a major cult center in the records of the divided monarchy. However, since the earlier accusations spoke of Israel worshiping the idols and practicing prostitution on every high hill, these two centers are sufficiently representative. By avoiding reference to the official shrines, the evidence suggests that Baal worship has become a pervasive, dominating influence in the entire population.

The *royal house* and all those associated with its rule stand next in line for condemnation. Later, when Hosea interprets the national life from the vantage point of covenant love (6:4—11:11) and integrity (11:12—14:7), the royal house will be featured more prominently. Priests and people are given primary attention where the viewpoint is that of the knowledge of God.

No one is sure what *the rebels are deep in slaughter* means. The translation itself is open to question. The NRSV reads, *and a pit dug deep in Shittim.* The noun *slaughter* appears only this once in the OT. The corresponding verb, *to slaughter,* refers mainly to the killing of sacrifices. There are a few occasions, however, in which it describes the assassination of kings and their officials or of rebels (Judg. 12:6; 1 Kings 18:40; 2 Kings 10:7, 14; Jer. 39:6; and parallels). We know that the closing years of the Northern Kingdom witnessed a number of coups and assassinations (2 Kings 15). It is not clear whether the text refers to a particular slaughter of the ruling family, such as the violence of Jehu (2 Kings 9-10), or to the history of such violent actions, which became the object of the judgment embodied in the child named Jezreel (Hos. 1:4-5) *[Historical Summary, p. 384].* Both judgments are addressed to the royal house.

The judge declares that he himself will be the *corrections officer,* the chastising agent. The Lord will take Israel in hand. He will *be a correction to all of them* (5:2b). Their disobedience is a personal thing with God. He is their covenant Lord. It is him they have spurned. He will fulfill his promise of chastising Israel (Lev. 26:28; Deut. 8:5; cf. Hos. 7:12; 10:10). The term *chastising* introduces hope into the very pronouncement of punishment. The word describes parental correction. It is corporal punishment and may even be harsh at times, but its purpose is instruction, growth in maturity, and restoration. It is not the vindictive act of a victim of crime. It is the severe but restorative action of a grieved parent *[Yahweh-Baal Conflict, p. 398]*.

Both God and Hosea comment on the justness of the verdict. God's comment is brief and pointed (5:3); Hosea enters into more detail (5:4-7).

The Lord's verdict comes from his total knowledge of his people. Motives, attitudes, and actions alike have come under his scrutiny. The past and the present are an open book before him. The secret sins of individuals as well as families, social groups, and nation cannot be concealed.

Their central sin, the primary charge for which they are to be punished, is the impurity of prostitution. The parallel clauses are introduced by *Indeed, right now* . . . (5:3c). Implied is the thought that if they had genuinely repented earlier, these judgments need not be spoken. At the very moment the verdict is being pronounced, prostitution continues. What brazenness! What mockery of their Husband and covenant Lord!

This people, called to be a holy nation (Exod. 19:6; Deut. 7:6; 26:19) has become unclean, *defiled,* polluted (cf. 6:10). They are unfit to be the Lord's priests (Lev. 21–22; Hos. 4:6-7). Hence, for a period the Lord is subjecting them to a process of ritual purification, to prepare them once more to serve him acceptably before the nations (cf. 3:3-5).

Hosea's comments (5:4-7) elaborate on God's message. Both the actions and their controlling spirit have become ingrained in Israel's psyche. Habit has rutted the paths to the shrines. The acts of worship and prostitution have become second nature to Israel. They shape the Israelite attitude toward their families, their farming, community life, relationship to the government, and celebrations. Their practices have become part of their worldview. The family and the larger community will suffer judgment if they neglect the high places, they think. Under such circumstances, *to repent* (5:4), *to return to their God* will bring the judgment of Baal upon them, they believe.

Small wonder that Hosea connects the presence of such a spirit of prostitution with inability to *know the Lord,* who has chosen them for himself (5:4b). The pervading mind-set is baalistic. The fertility cult has become the framework within which God is understood *[Yahweh-Baal Conflict, p. 398].* Baalism is no longer merely a temptation. To speak of it as temptation is to stand outside it and be enticed by one feature or the other. Israel has succumbed and is standing within Baalism. Now their true Husband stands on the outside. Baal and the associated fertility rites have become the source and measure of true worship. How can they, indeed, know the only true God from that vantage point?

5:5-7 Grounds Found for Leniency? None!

The testimony on which Hosea bases his conclusions comes from Israel's own lips (5:5). The fertility cult, Israel argues, has made her wealthy, numerous, and strong *[Canaanite Fertility Myth, p. 376].* It is the object of her pride (cf. Amos 6:8; Deut. 8:14, 17-18), even the subject of her boasting. What she regards as evidence showing the pleasure of the gods has become damning testimony against her for being unfaithful to the Lord (5:7). What she relies upon to sustain her has brought her destruction. The word *stumble* (5:5) describes a person tottering or staggering about; the load they carry is too great or they are in a weakened physical condition. For Israel, meaning Ephraim, the Northern Kingdom, the cause of the stumbling is the load of sin which they carry about. It will surely bring them to their knees.

Historical reference points are unclear. The text gives no clue as to whether Judah's stumbling occurs at the same time and will be prompted by the same disaster *[Judah and David, p. 389].* The most likely candidate as God's agent in this judgment is the Assyrian army. Two scenes portray the Israelite response to the judgment. Both confirm the pagan character and the futility of Israel's worship.

Scene 1: Animal Sacrifices 5:6

In desperation the Israelites take their sacrificial animals—sheep, goats, and cattle—to consult the Lord. Surely he will be pleased with the multitude of their gifts. But they are misled in thinking that their God accepts sacrifices in lieu of obedience. They also assume that, having worshiped at the shrine of Baal, one can willy-nilly turn about and bow to the Lord as well. Since Baal worship was polytheistic, adding another god to the list of consultants was perfectly acceptable. But they have for too long been shaped by false worship to understand the total contradiction between Baal and the God of the covenant. The One who met with Israel at Sinai and revealed his will to them there—that Lord will simply not permit himself to be found (cf. Prov. 1:20-32). He refuses to answer their blood-lettings and loud cries and pleading prayers (cf. 1 Kings 18:26-29; Amos 8:11-12).

Scene 2: Child Sacrifice 5:7

If God will not respond to their animal sacrifices, to what will he respond? The nation has reached the point of desperation. Children have been born to them from their prostitution and adultery. They are gifts from God, but the people attribute them to Baal. So they are called *illegitimate, strange,* or *foreign* because they are the offspring of idolatry and the fertility cult. They do not belong to God's family. They are the product of *treachery and covenant breaking* (Heb.: *bagad, dealing faithlessly*; cf. Mal. 2:10-11). Child sacrifices were associated with the worship of other gods, likely at the *new moon* festival (Deut. 12:31; 2 Kings 16:3; 17:17).

Codefendants, Ephraim and Judah 5:8-15

The first judgment oracle (5:1-7) speaks of the judgment in legal, cultic, and agricultural images. God becomes a correctional officer (5:2); he will withdraw himself into silence (5:6); their frantic search for the will of Baal will devour all the resources they attribute to him (5:7) *[Accusation-Judgment-Salvation Oracles, p. 372].*

The scene now shifts to God as the Lord of history. Three historical judgments are identified. The first is set within the covenant community. The second depicts the covenant people and the nation in which they have come to trust for their deliverance. The Lord will expose the futility of all other saviors. The third pictures God carrying his people off into exile *[Covenant, p. 379].*

The specific events alluded to remain in the silence of unrecorded history. The general background is that of the Syro-Ephraimitic wars (735-732 B.C.). The judgment oracle needs to be understood against the background of conflict between the forces of the Syrian-Israelite coalition and the armies of Judah and Benjamin.

5:8-9 Ephraim: Beyond Any Reasonable Doubt

Three Benjamite cities in the South become the staging area for a Judah-Benjamin attack against Israel in the North. These cities are all within ten miles of Jerusalem. While the mustering can be for defensive purposes, two terms suggest offensive action. To *raise the battle cry* or *sound the alarm* is to shout before advancing on the enemy. Elsewhere in the Hebrew Bible, only once does the term describe preparation by a military force about to defend itself, though it is used for the loud cries of defeated warriors (Isa. 15:4). The single mention of the shout in preparation for a defensive stand against foreign forces (Num. 10:9) is to remind Israel where their help comes from. The rallying cry, *after you, O Benjamin!* (Hos. 5:8), confirms that an army is forming for attack. Judah's military might, though unmentioned, stands in reserve.

The attack is directed at Ephraim, Hosea's name for the Northern Kingdom. It is not clear, however, whether this particular battle represents *the day of punishment* for Ephraim (5:9), or whether this is merely a battle in the larger war which results in their devastation. In view of the historical events which brought Samaria to her knees, it is preferable to regard this attack as one in which Benjamin and Judah turn on the Northern Kingdom. They may be taking advantage of the initial Assyrian campaign against the Syro-Ephraimitic coalition to strike back with a vengeance (2 Kings 15-17).

The end result for Ephraim will be devastation. Here is the word of the judge and corrections officer in fulfillment. The word is trustworthy: *I will make sure it is known* (Hos. 5:9). The word also becomes a flaming arrow, shot to alert all the tribes of Israel. The nation has turned against itself. Their unity, created by being formed into a covenant people, is fractured. Their peoplehood stands in jeopardy.

5:10 Judah: For Crimes Against a Brother

The first half of this judgment oracle follows a parallel pattern *[Literary Patterns, p. 391]*.

(A) Judah and Benjamin prepare to invade Israel.
    (B) Ephraim will be devastated.
(A') Judah is judged for invading Israel.
    (B') Ephraim persists in idolatry in spite of judgment.

The attention given to Judah is unexpected. There is no attempt to argue the merits of their case or to condemn Israel for its violence against Judah. Each stands judged for its own crimes. The *princes of Judah* are guilty of action comparable to moving boundary markers (Deut. 19:14). The reference to the *princes of Judah* is to leading officials in the land, such as cabinet members, rather than to the sons of the king. The eighth and seventh centuries saw a dramatic rise in the mention and function of these officials. The action taken against Ephraim grows out of cabinet decision and may hint at internal dissension and policy conflict among Judah's rulers.

A curse falls on those who steal the neighbor's property (Deut. 27:17). Is Judah out to annex Israelite territory? Possibly! But more likely, Judah stands condemned for failing to observe the covenant ties toward a "brother." God has not sent Judah to be his punishing sword. To take the initiative against a brother is to violate community and invite their Lord's wrath.

God's anger will come on this people like *the waters*. Undoubtedly, the Flood account is meant. On that occasion God brought judgment on humanity because dynasties of wicked rulers consolidated their hold against their fellow citizens (Kline). Their deep-seated corruption and far-reaching violence precipitated the Flood (Gen. 6:11-13). So it would be with Judah, responding to violence with violence.

5:11-15 The Judge Explains: Circumstances and Conditions

The result is that Ephraim is *oppressed*. Oppression comes at the hand of the Judeans and Benjamites, but also at the hands of the Assyrians. Yet even this first stage of the experience of *the divine verdict* (5:11, *judgment;* cf. 5:1) produces no change. The translation *determined to go after vanity* reflects the difficulty in understanding the last word in the sentence (5:11). In Hebrew, the word is *statute, law,* or *precept,* and it might refer to continuing on their current course. Most translators regard it as a misspelling. *Idol* would be a euphemism. Andersen and Freedman explain that "the filth of drunkenness is meant. The complete idiom," they argue, "means to join a cult by following a detestable god, called 'Shit' "(1980:410). While the word is uncertain, the message is clear. Even severe judgment is incapable of turning Ephraim from its dependence on idols.

Three metaphors dominate the balance of this judgment oracle. They expand the scope of the judgment on unfaithful Israel. The scene now shifts from the breakdown of tribal relationships within the covenant community to the decay of national life (5:12-13). And finally it moves to the forcible exile of Israel and Judah. They appear in parallel three times within these few verses.

The first scene is that of a severely injured person seeking medical help. God himself consumes his people (5:12). We need not expect total consistency in the imagery. The nations of Ephraim and Judah are described as *sick* and having *sores* (5:13; *wound*). The text describes God's judging action as equivalent to that of a *moth* (5:12; *maggot*), which eats holes into cloth, and *gangrene* (*rottenness*), which devours dying flesh.

The second metaphor takes us in search of a physician. Ephraim and Judah recognize their dilemma. The covenant curses of Deuteronomy (28:59) predict diseases of various kinds as the fruit of the nation's disobedience. "Diseases" is a generic term for illness; *sores* is a more particular description of the curses of the covenant *[Covenant, p. 379]*.

Is Judah deliberately omitted in the remainder of the metaphor? Not if the parallels introduced in 5:13a continue through the verse. The repetition of the Hebrew word for *sores* further confirms this interpretation. The coded text indicates the resultant reading:

> *Ephraim* saw his sickness,
> **Judah** his sores,
> > *Ephraim* turned to Assyria,
> > **He** sent to the great king (for help).
> He is not able to cure *you*,
> Nor will he heal **your** sores.

While there is evidence that Judah appealed to the Assyrians for help, Israel's role is obscure, covered by the dust and ashes of history.

In the context of the Syro-Ephraimitic war, going *to Assyria* for help would suggest some offer of covenant partnership. The nation making such an overture would have to offer the Assyrians something of interest—political and military loyalty, confirmed by paying tribute (2 Kings 16:7-9, 17-18). That implies that both Ephraim and Judah are prostituting themselves to escape God's restorative judgments. But that new covenant lord, Tiglath-pileser of Assyria, will be impotent; he is unable to heal the hurts brought on by the judgments.

The third metaphor of punishment is that of the Lord pursuing Ephraim and Judah *like a lion* which has tasted human flesh. The king of beasts is on the hunt. It seizes its prey, mauls and kills it, and *drags it off* to its lair to be devoured. So it will be with Israel and with Judah.

The emphatic *I, yes, I myself will tear* them to pieces reminds Israel that they are facing their covenant Lord (Lev. 26:22; Deut. 32:24). The lion's attack may take the form of historical judgment by another nation, but actually it is God in disguise. Let Israel be careful to distinguish immediate causes from ultimate ones and recognize that their God is sovereign over the nations of this world. When God acts as a lion, no one can act as rescuer (Hos. 5:14; cf. 2:9-10).

How long, O Lord? How long will this judgment last?

Two conditions must be met before judgment can turn to compassion. First, God's people must confess *their guilt* (Hos. 5:15a). They will need to *acknowledge* wrongdoing. It will not be enough to call out to God for help in times of deep *distress* (5:15b). God answered such pleas during the time of the Egyptian bondage (Exod. 3:7-10), the judges (Judg. 3:9, 15), and even the reign of Jeroboam II (2 Kings 14:26-27). This time God will not respond to distress signals; his ear is now attuned only to confession of sin.

Second, the nation will need to *seek* the Lord (Hos. 5:15a). The altars and sacrifices will not do. When Israel no longer eyes other gods and pursues the Lord only—then the Lord will let himself be found. Neither temporary nor partial measures will serve to restore the nation.

THE TEXT IN BIBLICAL CONTEXT
Knowing God: Three Aspects

Hosea 4:4—6:3 has centered on the theme of "knowing God." We now draw the strands of this theme into a larger whole.

The "knowledge of God" is pictured in Hosea as information and interpretation, experience, and acknowledgment.

Information and Interpretation. The content of the word "know" (in "knowing God") receives little attention in this passage. Hosea assumes that the law sets the framework within which God may be known. That suggests there is "objective" truth which can be understood, described, and experienced. The truth of God and the truth about God are part of the same self-disclosure. People cannot speak about one without the other.

The cultic acts were loaded with the knowledge of God. Worshipers were constantly reminded of the nature and activity of their God. The major festival of the North, the Feast of Tabernacles, commemorated the Lord as the One who redeemed his people out of Egypt *[Tabernacles, p. 396]*. God's providence, his tender care in the wilderness, his acts of covenant-making, and his fulfillment of the promise to give Israel the land—these all were highlighted in worship. The Holy One dwelt among his people (Martens: 81-96).

Israel stands accused of blindness which leads to distortion and eventually to the deliberate suppression of the truth. The end result is that sin so obscures the knowledge of the true God that it renders people incapable of recognizing the acts of God and interpreting them as such. Misinterpretation blinds the mind to God's intentions.

Elsewhere the Scriptures speak of how the Spirit of the Lord prevents the hardened human heart from even recalling the knowledge of God hidden in its subconscious memory (cf. Isa. 6:9-10 et par; Rom. 1:18-32; Heb. 6:1-12; 10:26-31).

Experiencing God. A second aspect of "knowing God" is embedded within these prophecies. Within Israel, to "know" was more than information; it entailed experience. For example, "knowing" one's spouse was to enjoy sexual intercourse (cf. Gen. 4:1, 17). The intimacy of the sex act, the affirmations of love and care which are a natural part of lovemaking, the openness which it promotes—all these are part of the immediacy of knowing God. To know him is not an act of pure reason. It consists of experiencing him in the intimacy of committed love.

To know the Lord intimately is to recognize him in his acts (Isa. 1:3; Jer. 9:24), to experience his saving works (Ps. 9:9-10), to call on his name in petition and praise (Isa. 52:6), and to be shaped by the encounter with the Holy One of Israel (Ps. 36:10; cf. Ezek. 38:23).

When God first spoke with Samuel, the young boy responded to Eli, thinking that the old priest had called him. The historian explains, "Now Samuel did not yet know the Lord, and the word of the Lord had not yet been revealed to him" (1 Sam. 3:7). Samuel had not yet experienced God; he did not recognize the voice of the Lord. The sons of Eli did not know God either (2:12), but their lack of knowledge is rooted and reflected in their misuse of priestly prerogatives and disdain for God.

Knowing God: Response of Love. A third element in knowing God has to do with one's response. The knowledge of God carries with it such conviction of the truth that one *acknowledges* God. Concretely, such acknowledgment may be expressed by admitting to his presence and being open to hear God speak and then to obey his instruction (Gen. 22:12; Jer. 24:7). Sacrifices and worship are ways of acknowledging God (Isa. 19:21), as is the act of developing skill in doing good (Jer. 4:22; 9:3, 6).

The negative counterpart is that some choose *not* to acknowledge the Lord, in spite of ample present demonstrations of power and grace (Hos. 4:6). The negative response may be due to moral obtuseness or to prior decisions and commitment to another way of life; yet it does involve a choice. When people choose to reject God, they discover him gone. They pursue emptiness; all is futile and meaningless when people do not know God (cf. Ecclesiastes).

THE TEXT IN THE LIFE OF THE CHURCH
The Saints

The knowledge of God is understood in the Christian community in our era as spirituality or the spiritual disciplines. The church has variously understood the goal of the spiritual life as sainthood, intimacy with God, or power with God. Over history, most believers have defined the ultimate goal in relation to the person of Jesus Christ. Thus Christ is ultimately the saints' ideal, whether emulated as the Son of God, the Incarnate One, the Suffering Servant, the One who became poor, or the Lamb of God.

The saints of all eras have longed to know God intimately (Ps. 100:3; Jer. 9:23-24; 31:34; John 17:3; Phil. 3:10). That experience has been possible because God revealed himself. He spoke and acted so as to point to himself. God disclosed himself with finality in the person of Jesus Christ (Heb. 1:1-3). The Spirit also bears witness with the human spirit (Rom. 8:16). God's YES! evokes a response, "Yes! You know, Lord, that I love you" (cf. John 21:15-19). Those who love God passionately seek God with every fiber of their being.

Many of the church's institutions have been responses to felt deficiencies in the spiritual disciplines; examples are monasteries, Bible schools, seminaries, and parachurch organizations such as Bible societies or Christian businessmen's associations. Distrusting the efficacy of our own efforts, we try to channel spirituality into defined paths.

But imbalance between information, experience, and life response leads to counteremphases. The catechism can become as sterile as symbolic rituals or confessions of faith, though each may have served the worshiper well in its own time. The same is true of "pure" Bible study or theological studies, of silent retreats, fasting, or direct engagement with the forces of evil. Martin Luther, Menno Simons, and Kierkegaard responded to the current climate and longed for refreshment of spirit. Each found renewal from barren orthodoxy by nourishing their souls through an inner experience of God and by responding to God personally in joyous, responsible living.

Spirituality

In the history of spirituality in the church, one emphasis after another has led to a matching reaction. Correctives lead to aberrations requiring further corrections. We emphasize the one and soon neglect another of the means of grace. One way of reading the story of denominations is to view the church as a pendulum. Each swing of the pendulum represents a corrective to an inadequate or unbalanced spirituality, but each new emphasis is itself limited and in need of correction.

The Roman Catholic Church, for example, contributed the symbols essential for meditation: withdrawal, silence, reflection, prayer, communion with God. These became the rich heritage of the mother church. Within the church, the monastic movement was the source for renewal of these neglected or forgotten spiritual disciplines. Now, the Catholic Church has come to give priority to spiritual directors rather than spiritual disciplines, and it is the Protestant community that is caught up with the disciplines.

Jacques Ellul offers insightful critiques of contemporary society. One such insight concerns the modern and scientific penchant for *technique*, which expresses itself at one level even in our search for spirituality. We look for keys, for shortcuts to spiritual maturity. We promote spiritual disciplines which can be practiced while we are elsewhere doing the important things of life. Too often we resemble Israel in developing spiritual weight-control programs that allow us to keep indulging our love for food.

Balance and vitality can be maintained only as we bear in mind the importance of following mature models of faith and in practicing a broad spectrum of spiritual disciplines. Breadth and depth, joy and endurance in the Christian life come about as a result of consistently opening ourselves to experience God in as many ways as he makes himself known.

Conflict and the Witness of God's People

Members of the same faith family publicly airing their grievances, clogging the courts with their verbal assaults, engaging in thinly disguised war with the advent of each new leader or perceived threat—that scenario fits Hosea's Israel, the Corinthians of Paul's day, and the church in any number of countries today.

· Jesus' high priestly prayer was concerned with the unity of the people of God: "That they may be one as we are one . . ." (John

17:11). The church's strongest witness lies in that unity. Paul preached it as the mystery of God, symbolized by the union of Jew and Gentile (Eph. 2-3).

God bless the witness of the congregation which regularly prays for pastors and congregations of other denominations. God bless those who cross barriers to bring about reconciliation, who bless their brothers and sisters in the faith whom they have not seen. Perhaps someday we may see more peace and reconciliation teams even on our streets, young and old, male and female, black and white, standing between warring factions, brought together in ministry by a common love.

Hope Preserved: The Accused Acknowledges the Conditions

Hosea 6:1-3

PREVIEW

This is the first of three salvation oracles in the second part of the book. Each concludes the section on knowledge of God, covenant love, and integrity. One should not suppose that they represent three chronological time periods. All depict the same salvation event. The author has chosen to repeat the accusation-judgment-salvation pattern in part two, as it was developed in the first three chapters. There words of salvation also occurred three times (cf. 1:10—2:1; 2:14-23; 3:4-5) [Accusation-Judgment-Salvation Oracles, p. 372].

The conditions for restoration in the preceding judgment speeches were: (1) admission of guilt and (2) seeking (returning to) the Lord. Some expositors contend that Israel's words (6:1-3) are insincere or too shallow to warrant divine restoration.

The evidence points to a genuine return signaled by a change of tense. The earlier predictive statement, *I will tear . . . ,* has here become, *He . . . has torn.* Therefore, the salvation oracle is Israel's confession from the lion's den. As God's prey, they have been badly mauled and dragged off to the lair. Punishment is having its desired effect. Yet the nation remains in God's care.

OUTLINE

Genuine Confession and Repentance, 6:1-2
    6:1a   A Common Spirit: Let Us Return . . .
    6:1b-2   A Confident Spirit: God Will . . .

Unreserved Commitment to God, 6:3
    6:3a   All Out for One Purpose
    6:3b   As Sure as the Sunrise—That's a Promise

EXPLANATORY NOTES

Genuine Confession and Repentance 6:1-2

6:1a A Common Spirit: Let Us Return . . .

The language of repentance is sincere. The word translated *return* does double duty. It means "to turn about and go in the opposite direction" as well as "to repent." Indeed, the two meanings are not really distinguishable, since to follow the Lord means to walk in his ways (Deut. 8:6; 13:4; Josh. 22:5). If, after God has visited his judgments upon his disobedient people, they return to him with all their heart, he will restore their fortunes and return them to the land (Deut. 30:2, 8, 10; Ps. 78:34).

Israel's language has been transformed. Instead of mutual recriminations (Hos. 4:4), the people encourage one another to repent and return to their Lord. Earlier they were condemned because their patterns of life were so firmly entrenched that they could not return to their God (5:4). Furthermore, when the nation recognized its sickness, it turned to Assyria for help (5:13). Now, however, they are determined to turn to their Lord. The repentance seems genuine enough.

6:1b-2 A Confident Spirit: God Will . . .

Without a clear recognition of the causes of their downfall, Israel can be accused of superficial apologies to evade the consequences of their actions. Their confession acknowledges two important aspects of life. First, the calamity they are experiencing—being torn and injured—has been God's doing. They understand that their sins have turned his face from them.

Second, their hope for recovery rests in the Lord. They appeal to no one else. Inasmuch as he has punished, in his time he will also restore their fortunes and bind up their wounds. God can be trusted to respond to heartfelt sorrow over sin. God's people have become aware that he is the only Deliverer.

Hosea 6:2 is the source of much debate. Did Israel conceive of resurrection, or was this one way of speaking of recovery from illness (Barre)? Could these words of "repentance" spring from a fertility cult ritual in which the god returns to life on the third day?

Wijngaards offers a more attractive interpretation. He draws on the concept of covenant and its language in international treaties of Hosea's day. Thus he illustrates how the language of killing a vassal may refer to the dethronement of a subordinate king or the act of preventing him from assuming the throne (30-32). Indeed, sometimes it is said that the king was "killed" and then that he "escaped" or was "driven from the land." The act of restoring a vassal king to the throne is described as "raising him from death to life."

The deposition and restoration of the covenant partner is expressed in the language of killing and making alive [Covenant, p. 379]. God will "kill" his people because they have transgressed his covenant (Hos. 2:3; 5:14; 9:15-16; 13:5-6; cf. Deut. 28:45-48, 63). Exile follows "death" (Deut. 28:49-52). If they repent with all their heart (Deut. 30:1-2), the Lord will restore them to the land in order that they may live (Deut. 30:3-6). The choice is theirs (Deut. 30:19-20).

Hosea 6:1-2 also draws on the concept of God and the imagery found in the language of sickness and healing, death and life, as expressed in the Song of Moses (Deut. 32:39). The tradition of curse and blessing as killing/wounding and bringing to life/healing is an ancient one. This is covenant language.

To speak of this "resurrection" as occurring *after two days, . . . on the third day, . . .* is reminiscent of the covenant-making ceremony at Sinai (Exod. 19:10-11, 14-19). God renews his covenant with them. *Not-my-people* will again become *My-people*.

Unreserved Commitments to God   6:3
6:3a All Out for One Purpose

Salvation comes to those who seek to *know the Lord*. Such confidence does not spring from wishful thinking. God covenanted with Noah and his descendants (Gen. 9:1-17) that he would never annihilate the race. Every rainbow signaled that promise. Repentant Israel has seen the promise in a new light and comes expectantly, looking to receive the winter and spring rains from God.

6:3b As Sure as the Sunrise—That's a Promise

Salvation is complete when fertility and hope return to a barren people and land [Yahweh-Baal Conflict, p. 398]. The metaphors of the deeper darkness just before dawn and winter *showers* and *spring rains* depict God's certain return to his people (cf. 2:21-23). Only then will the witnesses hear the covenant renewed:

> "You are my people."
> "You are our God." (2:23)

THE TEXT IN BIBLICAL CONTEXT

Resurrection

The concept of the resurrection as a renewal of this earthly life appears prominently in the miracles of restoration-to-life performed through Elijah and Elisha (1 Kings 17:17-24; 2 Kings 4:18-37; 8:1-6; 13:20-21). All those resurrected in the OT era received an extension of life. Yet they all died again, making these resurrections a form of resuscitation. These miracles of resurrection are extensions of healing. Poison and leprosy (2 Kings 4–5), for example, lead to death unless healing occurs. Resurrection extended healing into the realm of death; it offered a reprieve, though only temporary, from the inevitable and eternal stay in the place of the dead (Sheol).

The NT conception continues the idea of resuscitation (Lazarus, Jairus' daughter). The resurrection of Christ is of a different order: a return to the body characterized and energized by the Spirit, rather than by food and blood.

It appears that Hosea 6:1-3 is the text to which the risen Jesus is referring when teaching the disciples on the road to Emmaus (Luke 24:13-27) and in his later appearance (24:44-49). Jesus identified the theme of resurrection-on-the-third-day as present throughout the OT. That is, he linked the entire body of old covenant literature to show how he himself fulfilled the expectation of Israel's promises and the reality of Israel's death (cf. Hebrews). The covenant made by God with the suffering servant of Isaiah (cf. Isa. 42:6; 49:5-8) is fused with Jeremiah's promise of the new covenant (Jer. 31:31-34). This becomes the basis for Jesus' interpretation of the new covenant in his blood (Luke 22:14-23). All who live in Christ, the Mediator of the new covenant, are invited to live by the explosive power of his resurrection (Phil. 3:10-14; Col. 3:1-17).

In Hosea's time, Israel may not have used the term "raising to life" literally. Yet the concept of the covenant was undoubtedly a major factor in shaping the teaching of the physical resurrection. The faithful will be raised to life from the dead (cf. Dan. 12:1-4; Ezek. 37:1-14; Isa. 26:14, 19) as fully and as dramatically as God brought dead persons to life in the past (2 Kings 13:21).

Thus resurrection becomes the metaphor for a new beginning. In the NT, resurrection is rooted in faith in Christ and symbolized by baptism (John 5:25; Rom. 6:3-11). The dead are hearing the voice of the Son of God and are coming to life. Christ's resurrection becomes the model and guarantee for the hope of all those "in Christ" (1 Cor. 15).

Resurrection begins here and now. For resurrected people, everything is new, great things are possible. The present demonstration of power renders certain the future display of God's glory. Resurrection injects eternity into time.

THE TEXT IN THE LIFE OF THE CHURCH

Repentance: "Let Us Return"

Collective Repentance. Western society is essentially individualistic. This mind-set creates a weak concept of church: it is extremely difficult for us to think of collective accountability, action, or benefits. This mind-set also weakens our understanding and experience of intercession, mutual care, and self-sacrifice for the benefit of the larger whole.

Repentance takes shape when we recognize that all sin affects others, though ultimately every sin is directed against God. Therefore, it is necessary but never enough to confess sin *only* to God. My brothers and sisters need to be released from the constricting effects of my sin, and I from theirs. We confess our sins to one another that we might be healed. And we openly confess our collective sins as we recognize them—sins of denominations, of local congregations, of the faith community. We squirm when the testimony of Christians and the name of Christ are besmirched. But we can be cleansed and the church can be renewed only if we accept that sin through intercession and confession.

Collective sins are attitudes or actions which belong to the group rather than to any single individual. They are part of the atmosphere we live in and which is hard to see. The church sins, for example, in justifying and supporting national wars, in eagerly benefiting from economic oppression at home and abroad, in treating lawbreakers vengefully rather than humanely. We sin in neglecting the poor, the weak, the handicapped, or in promoting politicians who "guarantee" us prosperity and security over the short run.

Repentance and Restoration. Repentance is more than escape from the consequences of sin. It consists of a *return* to God. It restores us to a relationship of equity (justice) and deepest love.

God longs for our wholeness, our health, our restoration. He takes no delight in the death of the sinner. God's concern is for life.

Self-Help and Restoration. Deeply ingrained in each of us is the desire to be mature and self-reliant. "I can do it by myself" comes readily to the lips of children and adults as well. We try to rid ourselves of weaknesses, tame our emotions, and find ways to get what we need so as not to be dependent on others, even on God.

The Israelites tried every conceivable means to stand tall, a few of which appear in Hosea 5. Mountains of sacrifice, even the surrender of newborn children, the use of power through foreign alliances—all were in vain. None addressed the need for human community. None brought lasting security and prosperity, since they violated God's call for obedience to his expressed will—to love God by loving those made in his image.

Each society develops its own ideals and practices that are supposed to lead to maturity and harmony. North Americans are absorbed with the power of the free person to solve problems. We are more likely to try to address life's problems through violence than by conversation. By working at self-improvement, we seek to achieve acceptance and restoration with other people and even with God. Certainly some legitimate gains are made in these ways. But real restoration involves relationships—the other person. The path may be surrender, mutual support, acceptance of help, or confrontation. Broken relationships can be mended only by confession, forgiveness, and reconciliation, those graces and forms of integrity which build community.

Hosea 6:4—11:11

Defendant, Lo-ruhamah: No Family Affection

OVERVIEW

The second child was named Lo-ruhamah, which means *Not Loved.* In part two of Hosea, the corresponding positive theological word for the *Ruhamah* part of the name is *ḥesed.* This word appears as *loyalty* in 4:1 and as *(steadfast) love* in 6:4, 6; 10:12; and beyond this larger block of texts, in 12:7. We were first introduced to the word in 2:19, where it is paired with *raḥam, compassion, restoring love* (Heb.: 2:21). The emphasis of *ḥesed* is on love's genuineness (10:12). The Lord's parental love *('ahabah)* calls out to a wayward son (11:1), who leaves (11:2) and returns *no covenant love (ḥesed*; 6:4, 6; 10:12).

The language and imagery of love pervades these chapters and gathers the message around the larger theme of covenant love. The covenant concept, already present in part one (cf. 2:14-23), unfolds in this section. References to *covenant* occur in 6:7; 8:1; and 10:4 *[Covenant, p. 379].*

The first and last oracles of this section (6:4-6; 11:8-11) begin with similar rhetorical questions, tying the beginning and end together. Each of the three thematic blocks of text in part two contains the progression: accusation oracles, judgment oracles, salvation oracle *[Accusation-Judgment-Salvation Oracles, p. 372]* (see OVERVIEW for 4:1—14:9). Hosea 6:4—11:11 follows the pattern. These themat-ic blocks should not be read as though temporally ordered either within a thematic unit or from one theme to another. They differ only in the share of emphasis given to each type of oracle in the three sec-tions. In 4:4—6:3, the accusations predominate. In 6:4—11:11, the judgment oracles are proportionately dominant. The salvation oracle assumes more weight in 11:12—14:8 than in the previous sections. These changing proportions are presented pictorially below.

Proportions of Accusation, Judgment, and Salvation Oracles

Section	Accusation	Judgment	Salvation
4:4—6:3 verses = %	16 = 47%	15 = 44%	3 = 9%
6:4—11:11 verses = %	24 = 29%	53 = 65%	5 = 6%
11:12—14:8 verses = %	20 = 50%	11 = 28%	9 = 22%

Four Indictments Against Lo-ruhamah
Hosea 6:4—7:16

PREVIEW

Inconstancy is a major preoccupation of this section. A covenant commitment involves a spoken or an enacted oath in which the par-ticipants appeal to God or the gods to guarantee that the covenant will be kept (Gen. 15; 31:48-54; Josh. 9:15, 18-19; Ezek. 16:59). At Sinai, instead of an oath, Israel responded with a solemn promise: *All that the Lord has spoken we will do, and we will be obedient* (Exod. 24:7-8; 19:8). Hesed is covenant love and loyalty. The one who lives by it remains consistently faithful. In contrast to their promise, the Is-raelites are fickle. They flit about from god to god, from one foreign overlord to another. The four accusation oracles review this history of inconstancy *[Accusation-Judgment-Salvation Oracles, p. 372]*.

Each oracle contributes something to the larger whole. That whole consists of Israel's resistance to the acts of God in calling them back to the covenant. We shall be on the lookout for their nature and number. Accusation speeches picture Israel rejecting God's covenant love. God's corrective judgments change nothing (6:4-11a); his kindness proves ineffective (6:11b—7:2). The nation's leaders practice deceit and rely upon policies hatched in intrigue (7:3-13). They try repentance as a last resort, but it is too little, too late (7:14-16).

It is hard to separate the arguments regarding Israel's lack of covenant love from those concerning their lack of integrity (11:12—14:9), since the two themes overlap. Each takes a slightly different perspective. But in both cases, the matter of lying and insincerity are prominent. Each thematic block should be understood to address the same issues. They do not follow a logical or historical progression. Instead, they represent different camera angles on the same scene.

One can distinguish them by viewing covenant love as representing *relationships*, and integrity as descriptive of *character*. Indeed, the accusation oracles represent three expressions of covenant common to the OT: the Lord's covenant with his people (6:4—7:2), the people's covenant with their ruler (7:3-7), and the nation's covenant with other nations (7:8-16) *[Accusation-Judgment-Salvation Oracles, p. 372]*.

OUTLINE

Indictment 1: Breaking Family Ties, 6:4-11a
    6:4-6   Evaporating Loyalty
    6:7-11a   Deliberate Disloyalty

Indictment 2: Corruption at the Core, 6:11b—7:2
    6:11b—7:1a   Pardoned Criminal Returns to Crime
    7:1b-2   Public Exposure of Criminal Record

Indictment 3: Political Chameleons, 7:3-7
    7:3, 7b   Corrupt and Decadent Leadership
    7:4-7a   Revolution: A Burning Oven
    7:7b-d   Might Makes Right

Indictment 4: Foreign Entanglements, 7:8-16
    7:8-11   Senseless Foreign Policy
    7:12-13   Disciplinary Action
    7:14-16a   Rebels Against God
    7:16b-c   Disciplinary Action

EXPLANATORY NOTES
Indictment 1: Breaking Family Ties 6:4-11a

Two originally spoken oracles (6:4-6; 7-11a) may have been shaped
into one text unit to create a design:

> General accusations
> Past judgments
> Specific accusations
> Future judgments

That structure matches the address to Judah in the opening appeal
and in the concluding judgment statement; they identify 6:4-11a as a
single text unit [Judah and David, p. 389].

    Grammatical referents are a problem, but they do not obscure the
meaning. The pronouns shift from you singular in 6:4a, to you plural
in 6:4b, them in 6:5a, you singular in 6:5b, them in 6:7-9, and back to
you (singular) in verse 10. The singular pronouns could refer to the
nation as a collective whole.

6:4-6 Evaporating Loyalty

    The Lord's exasperation shows. There is even a note of frustration
in the double question of 6:4. God's continuous attempts to bring Israel and Judah to their senses have been unsuccessful. What more?
What else is there that might turn them back to their covenant Lord
(cf. Isa. 1:4-6)? The questions convey frustration and compassion.
Adultery drives some spouses to murder. Will God be among them?

    Israel and Judah share a further failing. They are guilty of taking
the Lord for granted. Both fail to recognize God's acts drawing them
toward repentance. By including Judah, Hosea takes us back to the
beginnings of Israel's affairs with other gods.

    The (your, pl.) covenant love and loyalty of Israel and of Judah is
short-lived. All the particular sins God is about to name are expressions of this larger sin.

The Lord's accusation captures the imagination. Heavy *morning fog* and *dew* soon burn off in the heat of the sun's rays (cf. Hos. 13:3a). Confessions of faithfulness made in worship evaporate when Israel's leaders face the day's agenda.

The Lord explains his frustration (6:4a). This is not Israel's first peccadillo, nor is it God's first corrective act (6:4b). Those past punishments were deliberate, consistent with all that Israel (meaning Israel and Judah) knew of God. They came through the mouths of the *prophets* (6:5). The plural suggests a long history of prophetic intervention (cf. Deut. 18:14-22; Jer. 26:4-5). God's appointed agents have spoken corrective words before.

Words have power. Inasmuch as words begin an action by God, the effect of those words is to *chip* or *hack* like a stonemason or carpenter and *slaughter* like a priest or warrior (6:5).

The subject of the concluding clause of 6:5 is *light,* lightning, or illumination. It reads, *Illumination went out in the form of your judgments.* So the judgments throw light on Israel's sin. God first warns of the consequences of disobedience, then he explains the reasons for the judgments. Both types of prophetic messages are common, and both hold up mirrors whereby the nation may recognize its condition and return to the Lord.

The contrast between the prophetic word and how Israel responds to the judgments (6:6) explains Israel's failure to understand their covenant Lord. The prophets have urged Israel toward holy living. The people respond by increasing their sacrifices. The response misses the mark.

Pagan religions in surrounding nations emphasized sacrifices and cultic acts; Yahwism called Israel to be a distinct people in their way of life and relationships *[Israelite Religion, p. 385].* Sacrifices do not necessarily express love and loyalty. The prophets Hosea, Amos, Isaiah, and Micah speak with one voice (Amos 5:4-15, 21-27; Isa. 1:10-20; Mic. 6:6-8), a voice that echoes the prophets of previous centuries (1 Sam. 15:22-23): *Obedience is better than sacrifice.* The psalmist (51:16-17) agrees:

For you have no delight in sacrifice;
   if I were to give a burnt offering, you would not be pleased.
The sacrifice acceptable to God is a broken spirit;
   a broken and contrite heart, O God, you will not despise.

Sacrifices are acceptable, but only after or with genuine confession (Ps. 51:18-19; cf. 40:6-8). Prophets, priests, and faithful worshipers agree: God desires covenant love rather than the blood of bulls and goats *[Bovine Imagery, p. 374]*. The next four verses illustrate the absence of covenant love (sins of omission; Hos. 6:7, 10) and the effect of priestly blood-letting (sins of commission; 6:8-9).

6:7-11a Deliberate Disloyalty

Specific accusations follow to illustrate disloyalty. They draw back the curtain to reveal the larger picture.

Descriptions of covenantal unfaithfulness bracket the sins of the priesthood. Self-evident historical and social references have become an enigma to modern readers. Which covenant is meant? What were the sins of Gilead? Did priests actually assault worshipers on their way to Shechem?

Current interpretation favors the reading, *At Adam they transgressed the covenant; there they acted treacherously against me* (6:7). If we read *Adam* as a place name (cf. Josh. 3:16), the prepositional prefix needs to be changed from *like* to *in* or *at*. The argument in favor of the place name is that the adverb *there* seems to demand it. If we follow this reading, the nature of the covenant-breaking remains unknown.

Traditional theological interpretation reads *Adam* as the name of the first human, the prototype sinner (Gen. 3), or as *people*, referring to all covenant breakers. The objection to this interpretation is that nowhere in Genesis 1–4 is a covenant expressly mentioned, though "Genesis 2–3 suggests covenant without using the word" (Andersen and Freedman, 1980:439).

The adverb *there* appears again in Hosea 6:10b, referring to people, *the house of Israel*. If we follow this line of thought, *there* refers to wherever Israel first violated the covenant.

That takes us back to Sinai. At the very moment God was recording his will on tablets of stone, the people made for themselves a golden calf (Exod. 32). Israel's story from the wilderness to the present has been one long affair with other gods.

That affair had been endorsed by the priests, beginning with Aaron. Details of the priests' crimes are obscured in the Hebrew of 6:7-8. Andersen and Freedman (1980:440) draw attention to the chiastic pattern listing three sins *[Literary Patterns, p. 391]:*

8a	crime	a city of evildoers
8b	murder	deceitful, with blood
9a	robbery	bands of men, lying in wait
	robbery	gangs of priests
9b	murder	on the Shechem road
	crime	enormities perpetrated

This interpretation is appealing.

A more convincing reading focuses on alternate meanings of the words. The term translated *gangs* or *robbers* (6:9a) more often means "sorcery, enchantment, spell" (Deut. 18:11; Isa. 47:9, 12). The word for *monstrous crime* (6:9b) frequently contains the idea of sexual sins and becomes a metaphor for idolatry (Jer. 13:27; Ezek. 22:9, 11). Perhaps the city of Gilead, whose location is unknown, was located on the way to Shechem. If so, then these priests are practicing deceit and violence and murdering people on the way to the place of the Lord's worship at Shechem, particularly through black magic and curses (Hos. 6:8-9).

The case for such an interpretation of 6:8b proceeds along these lines. In pagan worship and religious rites, sexual license, idolatry, and casting of spells go hand in hand (4:12; 2 Kings 9:22; Mic. 5:11-14; Nah. 3:4). Those who practice such black arts are like Balaam, whom the Moabites and Midianites hired to curse Israel, thereby to weaken them, so that they could be destroyed (Num. 22–24). Balaam eventually prompted Moab to weaken Israel by means of idolatry and sexual immorality (Num. 25; 31:16). The linkage of (intended) curse and immorality and idolatry would give a meaning to this accusation oracle consistent with what we know about the Baal cult. A further strength of this interpretation is that it does not require the priests to be robbing the very people whose gifts and sacrifices they are about to receive at the shrine.

Therefore, the priests located at *Gilead* have refined the art of cursing one's enemies, bringing hexes on people, and practicing sorcery for pay (here counted as robbery). They commit *murder* by casting spells on fellow Israelites. Thus the priests at Gilead, experts in sorcery, earned additional income by moonlighting. Their clients' opponents in litigation or spirit included the faithful who went to worship at *Shechem*. This text, then, exposes the enormity of Israel's religious perversions, the effects they have on the community, and the conflicting activities of priests within the cult of the Northern Kingdom.

The closing accusation describes Israel's lack of covenant love

(6:10). It even overwhelms God. The terms *horrible thing, whore-dom,* and *defiled* capture something of the revulsion God feels.

Lest Judah interpret the sins committed at Gilead as unique to the North, God includes the Southern Kingdom in the threat of judgment. *Harvest* may mean what is to be harvested, or the time of the harvest. Both may be intended. Their sins will be harvested by God on the day of judgment when the true nature of Judah's rebellion will be unveiled. *Harvest* occurs when the crop is ripe. That time is in God's hands. When he announces that the nation is ripe for judgment, it will receive its full "reward."

Indictment 2: Corruption at the Core, 6:11b—7:2

6:11b—7:1a Pardoned Criminal Returns to Crime

The previous oracle speaks of the prophetic word as a means to call Israel back to her senses (6:5). That happened throughout history. Judgment was to lead to repentance and restoration. This oracle describes God's acts of mercy and covenant loyalty as another means to bring the people to repentance. Within the recent history, Israel has suffered from foreign domination, but God "saved them by the hand of Jeroboam" (2 Kings 14:26-27). Such acts were pure mercy, since Jeroboam "did what was evil in the sight of the Lord" (14:24). Yet even God's goodness did not turn them back to him.

7:1b-2 Public Exposure of Criminal Record

God took the part of a liberator to *restore the fortunes of my people* and of a physician to *heal Israel,* but neither action brought about new life. Every time God intervened, he exposed more of the nation's (Ephraim's) sin and the leaders' (Samaria's) evil. The physician's diagnostic tests reveal the following moral illnesses:

a chronic case of deceit
burglary
vandalism and looting.

Burglary describes entry into people's homes; *vandalism* and *looting* capture the idea of stripping clothes and valuables off the bodies of war victims. Why this list is so short and narrow in scope is unclear. It may be illustrative. It takes us through a range of sins from the hidden to the most blatant acts of outrage, acts which everyone recognizes as immoral.

Even in the presence of the most obvious and commonly recognized crimes in society (7:2), the people do not acknowledge that God has any investment in what happens among them. In their lack of moral insight, they treat God as though he has amnesia. Sin? Wickedness? Crime? What does God have to do with that? God doesn't remember yesterday's headlines and crime statistics! The nation refuses to recognize God's concern with moral, economic, and social issues of life.

Hosea let Israel know that their wicked deeds are everywhere. That is all God sees when he looks at them. Kindness and loving care have not brought about repentance. What other options are there?

Indictment 3: Political Chameleons 7:3-7

The arena of politics exposes another sphere of covenantal unfaithfulness. Israel's political life is volatile; expediency rules. God's design is that the nation's leaders act as moral guides for the nation. Instead, they themselves wander astray.

The entire passage has a chiastic shape [Literary Patterns, p. 391]:

7:3	the condition of king and princes
7:4a	adulterers = rebels = inflamed persons
7:4b-6	palace intrigue and revolt
7:7a	gluttons = rebels = inflamed persons
7:7b	the condition of kings

7:3, 7b Corrupt and Decadent Leadership

Politicians and government officials survive by brute force, manipulation, or public endorsement. King and princes in Samaria are no different. What works is right! Within that climate, Israel's rulers approve whatever it takes to get the job done. As a result, wickedness becomes a necessity and deceit a virtue. King and princes approve the results and the means used to achieve them.

In coup after coup (7:7b), none of the kings of Israel turns to the Lord. *None even appeals to him.* The Lord does not play a significant role in their lives. Even in the most dire circumstances, their thoughts do not turn to the covenant Lord. How can such leaders guide the people in ways that are true and holy? And those who depose them are cut from the same cloth.

7:4-7a Revolution: A Burning Oven

The politicians are described by a metaphor within a metaphor. The opening and closing lines are parallel:

7:4a	7:7a
all of them	all of them
practicing adultery	devouring their judges
like a burning oven	they become hot like an oven

Adulterers is a metaphor for those practicing covenant infidelity (7:4). Those planning a coup *devour their rulers* (7:7). That is adultery. One day they bind themselves by covenant to support a new leader (cf. 2 Kings 11:4, 17); the next day, they plot to overthrow him.

Heat figures prominently in this extended metaphor. *Heat* is the heat of a fire (Hos. 7:4), the heat of sexual desire (7:4), the heat of anger (7:6), and the heat of intoxication (7:5).

The final ingredient in this metaphor is the baker and the process of baking the bread (7:4). The *tannur* is a specially designed earthenware bake *oven*. Embers are left from the previous baking of bread. The earthenware oven retains heat for a long time, so the baker places well-kneaded dough in the warm oven to let it rise. During that time he does not add any fuel to the remaining embers (7:4b). A hot oven would destroy the yeast in the bread. When the yeast has done its work, the baker stirs up the fire to baking heat (7:6b).

7:7b-d Might Makes Right

The extended metaphor defines the political backstabbing for what it is: lack of covenant faithfulness. The occasion, the festival *day of our king* (7:5), must be some special event. No other record exists of this festival in Israel, unless this is the festival Jeroboam I established to unify the Northern Kingdom (1 Kings 12:32). It may have become the royal anniversary.

Eating and celebrating together confirms friendship and mutual commitment, particularly at covenant-making or covenant-renewal ceremonies (Gen. 31:46, 53-54; Exod. 24:11; 1 Chron. 29:22). Nothing could be more despicable, more deceitful, than to sit at someone's table while plotting evil against them (cf. Dan. 11:27) [Covenant, p. 379].

.The coup leaders are agreed. They will strike down the king in the early morning hours, when everyone is drunk. They bide their time.

In a drunken stupor, the king engages in ribaldry and profane *scoffing*. Like the *mockers*, he derides others and proudly declares himself superior. What a contradiction! While his associates are waiting for the right moment to strike him dead, the king is bragging about his superiority and invincibility.

When morning comes (7:6b), the baker stirs the fire and brings it to baking heat. On that cue the rebels, inflamed by wine and anger, devour their ruler with the sword.

Indictment 4: Foreign Entanglements 7:8-16

Israel is also unfaithful to her international treaty partners. The nations are mentioned in 7:8. They are named in 7:11. Treaty oaths appear in 7:12b. The nation's leaders who guide external affairs are the object of God's judgments in 7:16.

The prophetic message comes through words as well as artistry. There are no fewer than eleven distinct images, analogies, or metaphors in these nine verses. Only a few are connected to one another. Unless we keep the larger theme in mind, our heads may begin to spin like those who try to follow the ball in a rapid exchange by Ping-Pong players. What better way to capture the effect of pragmatic policies? We suggest reading the text unit as alternating accusations and judgments:

7:8-11	Accusation
7:12-13	Judgment
7:14-16a	Accusation
7:16b-c	Judgment

7:8-11 Senseless Foreign Policy

The imagery of baking and eating baked goods continues into this oracle. It suggests that the occasion for the palace revolt previously described (7:3-7) represents a split over foreign policy. The word *mixes* captures some of the character of the underlying Hebrew verb (7:8). It means to mix oil and flour in the preparation of bread. The verb form implies that Ephraim (Israel) is at fault. He has mixed himself with the nations.

A *cake not turned* is burned on one side and not done on the other. It speaks of unprincipled foreign policy. The guiding norm Israel is following in international relations is this: How can we play the two competing foreign powers (Assyria and Egypt) against one another in order to survive? That is dangerous under the best of circumstances.

In carrying out this policy, Israel has to offer inducements to their protecting allies. Menahem, for example, survived by giving the Assyrians a large payoff: 37 tons of silver from the national treasury, raised by taxing 50 shekels of silver from every wealthy man (2 Kings 15:19-20). Details of other payments of tribute are lacking but must be assumed as part of Israel's alliances. *Foreigners devour Israel's resources* (Hos. 7:9), but the nation does not understand the implications. In spite of the wealth of wisdom in the nation (*gray hair*), Israel fails to recognize the impossibility of continuing such a flip-flop foreign policy for any period of time.

The repetition of the clause in 7:9, *but he does not know it*, accents the shortsighted character of the foreign policy as well as the fact that they are not presently consulting God on matters of national survival. Internal conflict has also sapped Israel's capacity to take decisive action for its well-being.

What would possibly create such an impasse in the nation? Hosea answers that question with the simple explanation: Israel's pride. By that he may mean their stubborn resistance to their Lord. He could also be referring to the object of their pride, namely their confidence that God will not permit them to be sent into exile. This mistaken view of election gives them false security.

Pride and genuine *repentance* are mutually exclusive. One cannot strut proudly into God's presence to make a confession of sin. Israel fails to acknowledge the One who invites them back. The implication, reinforced in 7:14, is that the nation no longer recognizes the distinction between Yahweh and the other gods. They appeal to him as they do to idols.

The imagery of the senseless dove sums up Israel's foreign policy (7:11). They flit about, lacking both wisdom and direction. One moment they coo to Assyria, the next they fly off toward Egypt.

7:12-13 Disciplinary Action

The image of birds continues. The Lord acts as a fowler who *will cast* his *net* over doves lured to within the hunter's reach. The birds rise into the air when the net is cast but are brought tumbling down as they wrap themselves in the mesh.

The latter part of 7:12 has given rise to numerous translations. It is difficult to make sense of the Hebrew words as they have come down to us in the synagogue tradition, and that tradition contains alternate readings. (A credible reading would be: *I will punish them according to the report of their treaties.*) Treaties normally contained lists of curses which served as sanctions if the treaty was violated. God was invoked by oath as the Guarantor of the treaty; he would bring those curses on the violator. The Lord, according to this reading, assures Israel that he will act to fulfill the curses on his people because they have violated the terms of their treaties.

Two centuries later, Ezekiel summed up Hosea's metaphor and message and turned it against Judah (Ezek. 17:11-21; cf. 16:59). Israel had violated its treaty with Assyria; Judah stands condemned for violating its treaty with Babylon (2 Kings 24:1, 20).

The imagery shifts abruptly in Hosea 7:14 to the human realm. The first verb, *to flee*, frequently refers to animals, especially birds (Jer. 4:25; Isa. 10:14), though it often serves as a metaphor for people. The parallel *they rebelled* denotes violations of known norms (cf. Hos. 8:1). Their rebellion is against the Lord, even though it takes the form of broken treaties with other nations. The result will be their *destruction.*

Some have argued that Israel's sin referred to here consists of their worship of the victor's (Assyria's) gods. However, there is no evidence that Assyria imposed its own cults on vassal states (Cogan: 112). It is enough that Israel has violated the oath they swore, by the Lord's name, to uphold the treaty (cf. Ezek. 17:11-21). Their foolishness in appealing alternately to Egypt and Assyria for help is compounded by their disregard of God's great name. They have taken the name of the Lord in vain. Such a capital crime subjects them to the death penalty.

Every attempt by the Lord *to redeem* (cf. Deut. 7:8) his people from their oppressive overlord is met with lies. Are these the lies of broken oaths? The lies may also be Israel's continued insistence that they are God's people even though they refuse to walk in his ways. Whatever the historical realities behind this prophecy, Israel is acting out of willful disobedience rather than ignorance.

7:14-16a Rebels Against God

Now the prophetic word quickly transforms the stage set into a banquet room, probably at a royal center of worship. Those gathered together recline at the table (cf. Amos 2:8; 6:4). The occasion? A time of repentance, possibly at a festival, such as Passover-Unleavened Bread. That festival marks God's *redemption* out of Egypt, as well as the firstfruits of the barley harvest. The verb translated *they gash themselves* (Hos. 7:14) might also be read as *they whirl about*, or it may represent another Hebrew verb meaning *they gather together*. Either reading would fit the festival scene. The first verbal root draws attention to the prayer dance before the Lord, and the second verbal root to the element of community. The phrase *they do not call out to me with their hearts* indicates that they mistakenly think they are appealing to the Lord for deliverance. Yet God views their repentance as inappropriate and insincere.

It is inappropriate in that the concerns center in what one brings to God—wailing and offerings. They readily assemble for festivals and proceed with the rituals. To undergo a change of heart is another matter.

The *woe* saying (7:13) suggests that there will be wailing because of the calamity God intends to bring on his people. But he is calling for a deep awareness of sin and a heartfelt repentance rather than preoccupation with how they might escape the consequences. The nation's leaders seem to want God to change the effects of their sins. God longs to have Israel change the unfaithful actions and attitudes which act as lightning rods to attract the judgment.

Their repentance is insincere in that they refuse to put away the idols and their dependence on other gods. They continue *to turn aside* or *rebel* against the Lord. The verb translated *turn aside* frequently specifies from whom or to whom one has or shall turn aside. Common expressions include "turn aside from the evil," "lest your hearts be turned aside," and "do not turn aside to worship other gods." Here they are turning aside *against* God. Hosea 7:15 reinforces this description of their negative attitude toward the Lord. Even though God has been training and correcting them to bring them to maturity, the leaders regard his acts as evil. They label his corrective parental care as vindictive, angry acts; they attribute ulterior motives to the Lord. Israel has come to God as though he were an unpredictable Canaanite deity *[Canaanite Fertility Myth, p. 376]*. They no longer recognize God's acts as a loving call to moral living. What kind of "repentance" can be expected of them? How can restoration take place? They need new knowledge of God; the skewed relationship needs to be healed before God will act with compassion.

The imagery of *turning aside* continues into 7:16a. The leaders are going through the motions and rituals of repentance. But they do not return to the Most High. Their acts of repentance lead them to alternatives other than to their Lord. The nation's leaders are no longer able to recognize that God's corrective acts are meant to draw them back. They view his judgments as displeasure and go to other gods for protection from his anger. As a result, they have become as unreliable as a *defective bow* (cf. Ps. 78:57), which cannot send the arrow to the target.

7:16b-c Disciplinary Action

God's corrective punishments carry within them the evidence of God's persistent grace toward Israel. Then Israel's response becomes an attempt to control God. Israel no longer understands true love.

The end result is punitive judgment. The officials will be killed *by the sword*. War descends on the rulers as they play *Egypt* against Assyria in their negotiations. Their failed international policies will rebound on their heads. Rather than confess her sins, Israel rails against God. The Lord is to blame! He has not proved himself faithful! Covenant breaking leads to God's self-vindication as the guarantor of their oaths. Indignant words against the Almighty bring them to destruction.

Such insolence! Even the nations speak words of censure against his unfaithful people. Covenant breaking is a foolish policy.

THE TEXT IN BIBLICAL CONTEXT

Hesed as Choice, Faithfulness, and Obedience

Hesed (covenant love) is choice rather than feeling, faithfulness rather than intensity of experience, ethical living rather than liturgy. David described Jonathan's act of initiating a covenant as an act of love, an act of sheer grace. In so doing, Jonathan was obligating himself by choice to maintain a commitment freely made. When a covenant partner practices covenant love, that partner keeps the terms of the covenant. Deuteronomy captures the essence of covenant in explaining that the act of loving God is to obey him (6:1-9). The terms of the new covenant are identical: "If you love me, you will keep my commandments" (John 14:15-21).

Covenant love (family affection) is expressed more fully in obedience, in ethical living, than in sacrifice (Hos. 6:6; 8:11-14). That is the purpose of the law. Law is God's *instruction* (8:1, 12). So this love consists of fidelity to another party based on an objectively recognizable and definable norm rather than a subjective experience, private agreement, or casual association. The commandments from Sinai were intended as a means to life, a way to express fidelity to the covenant partner.

The ethical character of covenantal relationships is prominent in each of the saving covenants identified in the Scriptures. The Noachian covenant focuses on the value of human life (Gen. 9:4-6). The patriarchal covenant stresses faithful living symbolized by circumcision (Gen. 17:1, 9-14). The Sinaitic covenant gives requirements of the ten "words" in distilled and expanded form (Exod. 19-24). The Davidic covenant counts on the faithful response of each monarch to the revealed will of God (2 Sam. 7:14; Ps. 89). The new covenant depends on the self-sacrifice and perfection of the covenant Mediator in justice, compassion, and faithfulness (Isa. 42:3-4; 49:10, 13; 53:4-12; Matt. 3:15; Heb. 4:14—5:10).

Covenant unfaithfulness toward God soon translates into deceit toward other covenant partners (marriage partners, family, fellow citizens, nations). The *no-family affection* section of Hosea identifies these violations. Adam is the prototype covenant violator (Hos. 6:7). Israel's subsequent sinning is reminiscent of Cain's murder of Abel. Israel is guilty of breaking one covenant after another (7:3-11; 8:8-10).

The language of covenant breaking connotes willful acts of disobedience. The Israelites practice prostitution (6:10) and relish intrigue (7:6). They stray (7:13), rebel (7:13), and speak lies against their God (7:13). They refuse to act on his clear instructions (8:1, 12). They treat the Lord as an enemy rather than as a covenant partner (9:7). Israel refuses to obey the Lord (9:17). The nation's behavior degenerates into the arrogance of insolence (7:16) and the pride of self-reliance (10:13). They are intent on turning from God (11:7). It seems appropriate, therefore, that faithless Israel—symbolically at least—be returned to slavery in Egypt (7:16; 8:13; 9:3, 6; contrast 11:5). The Assyrians shall serve as God's agents of punishment and, ultimately, of a call back to the Lord. Covenant violation invites the curses (cf. Deut. 27:14-26; 28:15-68; Lev. 26:14ff.). Yet covenant sanctions are never mechanistically applied.

War, famine, captivity, or even death is not the last word. God, the faithful One, will not totally destroy his people. The last word remains: redemption. The lion pounced and carried Israel off to its lair. That same lion will roar, and Aslan (à la C. S. Lewis) will lead a fearful, uncertain people back to their homeland. The Lord has spoken life into the dry bones scattered across the landscape (Ezek. 37).

TEXT IN THE LIFE OF THE CHURCH
Looking for the Large Picture

How does one present the large picture without unduly distorting it by simplification? That constitutes the challenge in this prophetic book. A lifetime of ministry must compress into less than an hour.

Stepping into the book of Hosea is something like viewing wrap-around projection at a planetarium. There is too much for the eye to see and the mind to interpret at once. To take it all in, the viewer may focus momentarily on the northern lights, and then quickly shift to one of the star clusters, the Milky Way, or the streak of light created by an asteroid. The effect is one of depth and breadth. Two camera angles will convey breadth; three are required to capture depth.

The book of Hosea consists of three perspectives from which to view Israel and her relationships to God. *No family affection* provides the second of these dimensions of reality. The series of prophecies condensed and set next to one another creates concreteness, pattern, and depth at the same time. Hosea's concern is to present the large picture: hundreds of years of history lived over large spaces with fluctuating intensity and strange orbits formed by the strong attraction of foreign objects. Hosea pictures the *kinds of things* that concern God about Israel.

To change the metaphor, the book resembles character reference forms which ask for a description of strengths and weaknesses. For each valuative statement, one is to illustrate with an example drawn from personal observation or relationship with the applicant. The example serves to illustrate the behavior pattern as well as the strength of the character trait.

Hosea's method of presenting the large picture offers a model for the pastor or teacher who wishes to affirm growth or encourage change in the larger life of the individual or community. A collage of true-life snapshots or video clips taken from different vantage points conveys the breadth and depth.

When Prophets Succeed (or Fail)

Hosea ministered at the end of two hundred years of prophetic failure (6:5). The failure was not due to incompetence, nor to lack of faithfulness, nor to faulty vision or goals. Israel had not turned to God.

What must it have been like to be told, "I call you to serve this peo-

ple. So far, no one has been successful! Not even Elijah and Elisha."
That places serving God in a distinctive light (cf. Isa. 6:9-13; Ezek.
2:3-7).

It also calls for women and men of character and purpose. Their
critics call such people stubborn; God speaks of them as faithful.
Therapists would label them unbalanced; God sees them as filled
with the Spirit. Society refers to them as out of step with the world;
God delights in their company. Their contemporaries diagnose them
as masochistic; Jesus affirms those willing to suffer for his name's
sake.

Those unusual qualities correlate closely with life lived in awe of
the sovereignty of God, with an intimate friendship with our Lord,
and with the fruit(s) of the Spirit.

The Rule of Pragmatism

Pragmatism and *covenant love* are at odds with one another. This is
true of life choices, response to criticism, national policy decisions, or
international relations. Israel is pictured as a nation whose guiding
rule is pragmatism: Does it work? What is needed to get results? Will
it help us achieve our goals? my goals?

Covenant love embraces worthy goals seen in a long-range perspective. As a guide to life decisions, *covenant love* asks, Does something promote the right, true, and lovely? Will it please God? Do the
weak and poor benefit? Such *ḥesed* is faithful, persistent love. It is
moral, constructive, deliberate, and bubbles with excitement.

Pragmatism creates neither martyrs nor saints—both processes
are too long and demanding. Covenant love creates martyrs and
saints pointing to God's truth and holiness, which will eventually triumph.

God Suffers

The tone and spirit of these accusation oracles spring from a deep
love. We hear the pathos, and we sense the pain Israel's adultery
brings to her Lord.

Throughout the history of the church, suffering saints have asked
themselves, "Does God feel my pain? Does God suffer with his creation?"

Hosea 6-7 assures us that God does feel our pain. But whereas
we are concerned largely with anguish over some loss or with physi-

cal pain due to accident or illness, God's anguish goes much deeper. He sees the destructiveness of sin (Gen. 6:6b). He knows the affront of rejection (Jer. 2:31-32).

At times we rise to challenge God as though he is accountable to us: "Explain yourself! Defend yourself if you can! Why are you allowing this to happen?" And God nowhere silences the cries of his people.

Yet rarely do we see evil in the personal terms or in the breadth or depth spelled out by Hosea. Our view of sin is small and shallow; our view of God is microscopic and distorted. The world takes on a different hue when we recast the earlier question: "Do we feel God's pain? Do I? Are we aware of the depth of his love? Am I?"

Collective Covenant Breaking

Covenants can be personal or collective agreements. Israel treats her international treaties in the same way she treats her covenants with Israelite kings and with the Lord.

This much can be said: an evenhanded approach to covenants is fitting. It implies that the life of God's people, in their relationships to other people, is as important as their faith. Since the Reformation, the Protestant church has largely regarded holiness and ethics of secondary importance, and the profession of love for God as a higher order of confession. They (we?) continue to snub behavior and elevate doctrinal statements, especially regarding the nature of God. Jesus kept the two loves on the same plane; the order "first" and "second" has to do with the fact that love for God forms the basis of love for our neighbor (Mark 12:28-34; et par.). They are equal and necessary expressions of faith. The church does well to reconsider its faith expressions in the light of Jesus' teaching. His words are a corrective to our common bent.

So Israel's evenhandedness is fitting, except that she treated all of her covenants cavalierly!

Sentences for Having No Family Affection

Hosea 8:1—11:7

PREVIEW

The oven full of sins ignites and bursts into a firestorm of judgment. Israel will experience these in two forms: withdrawal of fertility, and the horrors of war culminating in national exile. The accusation oracles establish the theme that Israel seems incapable of discerning the reasons for God's history of judgments. They have lost the covenant perspective from which to view their world. Cult has been severed from morality. Consequently, Israel is no longer able to connect God's corrective and disciplinary acts with the underlying sins. The nation has forgotten how to return to their Lord. As a result they begin to despair of pleasing God.

Hosea addresses that despair by continuing to spell out the principal reasons for the deluge of judgments: they install their own kings, rely on covenants with other nations, reject the corrective prophetic message, pervert worship, and practice the fertility cult.

These accusations are repeatedly cast in historical context. Hosea delights in using Israel's history to highlight their persistence in sin. On occasion he introduces an event from prior to the division of the monarchy to show how Israel has rejected God's gracious earlier action toward them. At other times he reaches as far back as the patriarchs to point to Israel's pattern of sinning. The literary beauty and force of moral argument pack persuasive punch. God has chided Israel for her infidelity for centuries, with no substantive response. The only option left is for God to lash them with his judgments.

A larger pattern emerges as we follow the allusions and references in historical review. The judgments of 8:1-14 come to us in the framework of eighth century (B.C.) events. The judgments of 9:1—10:8 take us further back on a journey into slavery in Egypt (9:1-9). From there the prophet ushers us into the wilderness (9:10-17), to show that disobedient Israel has not changed. Even the entry into the Promised Land is marred. The landscape is littered with Canaanite idols on whom Israel has come to rely (10:1-8).

A distinctive feature of these judgment oracles lies in the interplay between the words of God and the words of Hosea. Sometimes the

146

prophet and his God appear to be in dialogue about Israel's fate. Only occasionally does either speak to Israel directly (8:5a; 9:1, 7, 10; 10:9, 12-15).

A structural element which ties this lengthy judgment section together is the use at the beginning (8:2) and end (11:7) of quotations from Israel. The opening quotation appears in God's statement, presenting Israel's claim to be his people. The closing quotation is cited by Hosea as a confession of faith.

OUTLINE

EXPLANATORY NOTES

Sentences Declared by God: From Palestine Back to Egypt 8:1-14

8:1-3 For Breaking Family Ties

Invasion, Rout 8:1a, 3b

The *trumpet* calling to war sets the tone for the sequence of judgment texts. Though the trumpet is played by the lips, palate and lips occasionally occur in parallel where both refer to speech (Prov. 5:3; 8:7). The word used here is *palate*.

Is this bird the *eagle*, waiting to swoop down and capture Israel in its talons (cf. Deut. 28:49), or is it the *vulture* (Hos. 8:1, NRSV), circling over the battlefield, biding its time until it can devour the flesh of the fallen (cf. Job 39:27-30; Matt. 24:28)? Whether Israel is a silly dove (7:11-13) or those slaughtered in war (7:16), the imagery prepares the reader for what lies ahead. This opening pericope begins with the trumpet announcing the military charge, a charge which quickly reverses itself into a chaotic rout.

The identity of *the enemy* is unimportant (8:3b). Historically, Assyria served that role. But behind the instrument, Hosea sees the hand of God, who stands in judgment over his own people.

Because . . . 8:1b-3a

Israel's destruction is attributed to a single sin: Israel has transgressed the covenant (8:1b). In the terms of the subtheme of Hosea 6:4—11:11, Israel's sin is that they lack covenantal love and faithfulness. Here is abundant use of covenantal categories of judgment.

The term *broken* or *transgressed* commonly refers to someone crossing a border, stream, city limits, or some other clearly definable boundary. Occasionally, as here, it refers to violation of laws or divine commands or God's *covenant* (6:7; Deut. 17:2; Josh. 7:11, 15). The term does not in itself contain the idea of an abrogation or annulment of the covenant. Transgression attracts the covenant curses on those who offend the covenant Lord *[Covenant, p. 379]*.

The central accusation is restated in at least two ways. First, covenant transgression is equivalent to an act of rebellion: *They have . . . transgressed my law*. Rebellion is a word from the political sphere that refers to militant revolt or to passive negative behavior which breaks a relationship. Rebellion produces alienation. The use of this particular verb rules out accidental transgression or sins of ignorance; willful violation has occurred.

Second, in covenant transgression Israel *has spurned the good* (8:2b). *Good* may personify God, "the Good One" (cf. Mark 10:18). More likely, the word *good* carries its normal covenantal meaning of close and formalized treaty friendship (Hillers, 1964:46-47). The treaty document contains instructions to *do what is good and right in the Lord's sight* (Deut. 6:18; 12:28). So Israel is called to decide between life and good on the one hand, and death and calamity on the other (Deut. 30:15; cf. Amos 5:6, 11-12). Hosea's message is unequivocal. Israel has opted for death and destruction and has rejected life and the good.

Sandwiched between these two explanations of what it means to transgress the covenant is Israel's current plea to God: *"My God! We know you! It's Israel here!"* (Hos. 8:2b). As the enemy gathers against Israel, her plea for help rises to God. It contains fascinating features, such as the personal element, *My God*. In the Israelites' minds, the Lord remains their national Deity. Surely he will hear them!

Their insistent *We know you!* speaks of the intimate and longstanding relationship they have enjoyed with their God. From what is

known of the use of images in Israel's worship, we can assume that
their plaintive appeal to God was addressed to one of the idols said to
represent him *[Israelite Religion, p. 385]*. They are appealing to his
memory of their common experience. Such an appeal naturally
paves the way for God to reflect on that common experience in the
judgment speeches which follow.

From the distance of strained relationships, the nation reminds
God who they are. Like the survivor of a capsized boat, shouting and
wildly waving her arms to attract attention, Israel shouts her name to
her supposed Savior. Since judgment is decreed, her frantic activity
succeeds only in alerting the enemy's attention to her position. The
outcome is predictable: *an enemy will pursue him*. That pursuit is described in a series of three extended metaphors in the balance of the
oracle.

8:4-6 For Two Kinds of Rebellion: Slaughter

Political Rebellion 8:4a

Monarchy and cult were closely associated in Israel's world. The
religious personnel frequently played a deciding role in politics. It
was in the king's interest to keep firm control over the priests.

When Jeroboam I led the revolt against the Davidic dynasty
(1 Kings 12), he needed to secure his throne and establish his nation's independence from Judah. Astutely, he created a pair of symbols, the bull calves of Bethel and Dan, to distinguish the religion of
Israel from that of Judah and Jerusalem. The Northern Kingdom
lacked a covenant symbol like the ark in the Jerusalem temple. The
bull calves assumed that function in Bethel and Dan. Shrines multiplied. As a result, *idols* became commonplace aids to worship
throughout Israel (8:4) *[Bull Calves, p. 375]*. Jeroboam also established a priesthood which owed its allegiance to him (1 Kings 12:31).
The result was a religion which legitimated the state and sanctioned
government policies and practices *[Israelite Religion, p. 385]*.

Prophets such as Elijah and Elisha had acted as the nation's conscience and critiqued national and religious policies. They received a
cold reception in the king's palace and in the temples of the Northern
Kingdom. The true prophets were neither endorsed nor sponsored
by the political-religious establishment of Samaria and Bethel, unlike
their counterparts in Jerusalem.

The accusation of Hosea 8:4 identifies two primary national sins
related to the shape of Israel's political and religious structures. First,

with the exception of Jehu (2 Kings 9:1-12), the nation *installed kings* who were not God's appointees. Two distinct but related issues appear to lie behind this accusation. Perhaps the system of succession did not permit God's choice of king to be known. The tradition of selecting the united nation's first three kings established the Lord as the One who chose the king. The "natural" heir, the eldest male child of royal lineage, was not necessarily God's choice. God's pattern in choosing Saul and David set aside primogeniture as the means of selection. Also, Solomon was not a firstborn. At the least, the process of selecting Israel's kings appears to have excluded direct intervention by God. The "system" took care of the political appointments.

The accusation may also be directed at the rapid succession of rulers which was caused by the assassination of kings by competing political groups. The closing years of the Northern Kingdom's existence were chaotic.

The statements *they instate kings* and *they install rulers* are parallels with a common reference. While the word *rulers* does not appear in the second statement in Hebrew, it is embedded within the idea of the verb *śarar* (*rule*). Though Israel claims to *know* their God (Hos. 8:2), they appoint over themselves rulers whom the Lord does not know. It is not that Israel is being ruled by foreigners. Rather, they are governed by kings who do not walk according to God's decrees nor submit to his instruction (cf. Deut. 17:14-20). Israel has substituted rulers of their own choice for rulers God might choose.

Religious Rebellion 8:4b

Second, they *create idols* (8:4). Using the wealth lavished on them by the Lord (cf. 2:8), they have made idols (4:17; 13:2; 14:8; 2 Chron. 24:18; Ps. 135:15). These idols were probably wood overlaid with silver and gold. The idols initially represented God, but in a second stage of idolatry, they have come to be gods themselves. The invisible covenant-making God has been reduced to an image in animal form. How the Northerners justified their idols in the light of the first and second of the Ten Commandments is not known. Possibly they rationalized the idols, as Aaron did at Sinai (Exod. 32:1-25). Or they may have remembered the two names of God, El Shaddai and Yahweh, as the God(s) of the Exodus *[Bull Calves, p. 375; Bovine Imagery, p. 374]*. To this point in the message (cf. Hos. 8:12), there is no indication that Israel depreciates the law or dismisses the Ten Words as irrelevant.

Good Riddance to Those Bull Calves 8:5-6

A result clause links the judgment with the preceding recital of Israel's sins. Since the subject is singular, it is unclear as to whether Israel will be destroyed or whether the bull calf is about to be eliminated. The verb is used elsewhere of cutting down idols, as well as of destroying or exiling people, especially those who have violated the divine instruction.

Hosea 8:5-6 present problems to the translator and interpreter. The NIV reading, *Throw out your calf-idol, O Samaria!* is grammatically unlikely, though it matches the early Greek translations. It is better to read it with God as the unexpressed subject: *He rejects your bull calf, O Samaria.* The Lord's action is an appropriate response to Israel's rejection of what is good (8:3a). The following parallel statement depicts an infuriated God (*my anger burns*) taking action against his rebellious people.

The rhetorical question, *How long will they be incapable of purity?* implies a long history of impurity. *Purity* is associated elsewhere with purity of hands (Gen. 20:5; Ps. 24:4; 26:6; 73:13) and may carry that nuance into this context. If so, the judgment is associated with the act of making or touching idols.

The terse clause, *Indeed, from Israel!* (Hos. 8:6a), takes us back to Israel's earlier appeal to God (8:2). God agrees, *It's Israel alright!* The description matches their claims and their behavior. The judgment has landed precisely where it was aimed.

Prophets as well as psalmists break out in satire against the impotence of idols and the irrational claims that an image made by a person could be a god (Isa. 44:9-20; 46:5-7; Jer. 10:1-16; Ps. 135:15-18; cf. Wisd. Sol. 13-15). Moreover, those who make and worship idols come under the divine curse (Deut. 27:15). The sentence structure is in parallel statements: *As for it—a craftsman made it; and it is no god.* This parallelism contains a verbal derogatory pointing of the finger at "it," the calf-idol (Hos. 8:6). Its destruction is described graphically: *The bull calf of Samaria will become splinters.*

Inherent in the anti-idol argument is an implicit comparison with God's original design. People were made in the divine image. When they rebel against their covenant Lord, they re-create him in the image of the animals they were to rule. At a deeply subconscious level, people attempt to control their gods. They are, like the first humans, intent on becoming and acting like gods.

8:7-10 For Actions Toward Outsiders: Exile

You Reap What You Sow 8:7-8

The dominant image of judgment is that of the harvest, though two other images give shape to Hosea's thought. The structure of these verses accents the judgment.

An opening proverb sets the scene. Some expositors read Hosea 8:7-8 as a sequence of stages from sowing to consumption of the food. More likely, the first two lines are proverbial wisdom: "You get what you sow, and then some." The Hebrew word order emphasizes the results: *Wind they sow; whirlwind they reap.* Grain growers know that a stand which has been severely stressed suffers in yield and quality. Therefore, *when the mature stalk is stunted, one can't make flour.*

The metaphor continues in a futility curse: *If there were flour, strangers would gulp it down.* Curses of this type are common in covenants. They also appear elsewhere in biblical literature (Lev. 26:16; Deut. 28:38-44) *[Covenant, p. 379].*

The reality addressed by the metaphor requires a comment. Instead of pursuing the idea of Israel's crops suffering through the drought of divine judgment, Hosea recasts Israel's remnant as the poor-quality flour (Hos. 8:8a) *swallowed up* by the *nations* who come at God's invitation.

The imagery changes abruptly. Scattered among the nations, Israel will become as useless as a cracked pot (8:8; cf. Jer. 22:28; 48:38). They are destined for the garbage dump. At best, potsherds may be used as scrapers (Job 2:8).

Israel will reap the harvest of her international policies. The nation, reduced in numbers, is headed for exile. Initially given as a source and occasion of blessing for all nations, Israel has become a byword, *a useless vessel* (cf. Jer. 18:1-12).

Failed Policy of Appeasement 8:9-10

Because introduces two causal statements (8:9). The preceding (8:7-8) and following (8:10a; NRSV: *though*) judgments are linked to explanations. Here is what gives rise to this harvest of shame.

Israel's treaty negotiators *went up to Assyria* to negotiate an alliance. The trek comes to life in two metaphors: a wild donkey wanders alone at the desert fringe in search of sustenance (cf. Gen. 16:12; Job 24:5); Israel, the prostitute, hires Assyria as her lover. The *pay for services rendered* consists of treaty obligations, probably including tribute and agreement to support Assyrian military activities in the Palestinian area.

Israel has become isolated in Palestinian politics. Rather than turning to God, her covenant Lord, she wanders off in search of another lord. She finds a lord in Assyria. God intended that his people should be among the nations as *the head and not the tail* (Deut. 28:13). Instead of leading nations in the experience and worship of God, the Northern Kingdom wanders about looking for a lover—some nation to provide her with security and offer her comfort.

God's denunciation of Israel's foreign policy begins and ends with the harvest metaphor (Hos. 8:7-8, 10). While the word *harvest* does not appear in 8:10a, the verb *to gather* can refer to gathering grain or sheaves in harvest (cf. Mic. 4:12). This harvest is for the purpose of punishing offenders.

The balance of Hosea 8:10 yields a number of interpretations. One reading captures the grammar and the vocabulary and fits the context: *But first they shall be profaned* (or: *be made sick*) *a little longer by the burden of king and princes.* Catastrophe is around the corner. Yet God's measure of punishment will not be meted out in full until Israel's quota of kings and abortive foreign policies is complete. There may be a deliberate linkage with the *wild donkey* imagery (8:9) in that the word for *burden* refers to a load carried by donkey, mule, or camel. God will ensure that at the ripe moment, Ephraim will harvest what she has sown by her international policies and practices.

8:11-14 For Attitudes Toward God: War

Using God 8:11-13

Another accusation (8:11-13a) once more issues in an announcement of judgment (8:13b). The pronouns *his* and *they* describe Israel collectively and distributively. The sins spring from the realm of cultic practices (8:11, 13) and religious instruction (8:12, 14).

Sacrifices point out the fatal consequences of offending God. They also symbolize the people's restoration through forgiveness. When made aware of their offense, the nation, if it responds by repenting, may know forgiveness through the animal sacrifices. Only then does the worshiper celebrate restoration by eating a covenant renewal meal in the presence of God (Lev. 7:11-21).

Israel stands condemned. They abuse sacrifices; they reject the ceremonial and moral laws. Since the Northern Kingdom has no central shrine, they worship at many population centers and high places. But instead of experiencing divine forgiveness at their many altars, they pervert the nature of worship through their idolatry, prostitution, and acts of sacrificing according to pagan concepts and practices. Each sacrifice adds to the sin rather than lifting away its weight through forgiveness (Hos. 8:11).

Israel snubs God's commands. He has given careful instructions regarding worship, to protect Israel from sinning. Israel ignores cultic and moral laws alike. Even worse, Israel treats God's *instructions as alien, foreign, strange* (8:12). The Torah is out of step with their practices, which are modeled after the worship of *alien* nations and Canaanite cult centers.

A more literal rendering highlights the tone of the accusation:

Regarding the sacrifices of my gifts:
They sacrifice meat and they eat it,
But the Lord is not their pleasure. (8:13a)

They offer God's gifts (cf. 2:5-8). However, purity is a precondition to eating the fellowship offering (Lev. 7:16-21). The meal is to symbolize a restored relationship; Israel is distorting the most intimate symbol of holiness and fellowship. Small wonder that God so vehemently invokes the sanctions regulating the law of the fellowship offering.

Judgment follows hard on the heels of this perversion of the means of grace (Hos. 8:13b). Sacrifice was instituted to forgive and remove sin. If offered cavalierly, the sacrifices provoke God to wrath. When God remembers sins, he acts (cf. 7:2; 9:9). *They shall return to Egypt* may be a stereotypical way of saying, *I will send them off into exile and slavery.*

Forgetting God 8:14

The oracle ends as it began—with sweeping accusations and pronouncements of military invasion. God *remembers* his people and *their iniquity*; but *Israel, has forgotten his Maker.* Israel was the special, the treasured handiwork of the Creator of all nations (Deut. 26:17-19; 32:6, 15). Yet they reject their Maker by building fortresses and palaces on which they depend for their security.

The traditional judgment follows. Israel's and Judah's sources of security will be razed to the ground. God himself will light the fires which will consume the work of their hands.

The mention of *Judah* is unexpected *[Judah and David, p. 389].*

Is this warning part of the original prophecy to the Southern Kingdom that they are bent on the same course as their Northern counterpart? Is it a word of application introduced by the compiler of the material? Whatever its origin, the fate which will surely befall Israel will
also descend on Judah if they persist in the same sins against their
covenant Lord.

Verdicts and Sentences Supported by Hosea:
Back into Slavery 9:1-9

The previous judgments (8:1-14) have come from God's lips. Those
that follow contain the prophet's Amen! together with advice. In the
mouth of the prophet, advice becomes instruction on how to recognize the destructive consequences of rebellion.

9:1-7a On the First Charge
Infidelity 9:1

    Is Hosea interrupting the national religious celebration with a
warning cry? Is this the "festival of Yahweh (the Lord)" referred to in
Leviticus 23:39 and Judges 21:19? It fits the harvest motif of the passage: threshing floor, wine vat, jubilation.

    That interpretation, however, founders at two points. First, the
great Festival of Booths (Tabernacles), which marked the journey
from Egypt to Palestine, was held in Judah in the seventh month
(Sept.-Oct.; Lev. 23:33-43). In the Northern Kingdom, Jeroboam I
had deliberately changed its date to a month later, to prevent the Israelites from identifying with the Southern Kingdom after his break
with Judah (1 Kings 12:26-33). In other words, the Northern Kingdom festival was not a harvest festival. Grain had been harvested
seven months earlier, and fruit, olives, and grapes more than a month
earlier. That, presumably, is why the festival is associated only with
God's rescue of Israel from Egypt. The words of installation of the
bull calves reflect this historic rescue and are totally silent about an
earlier harvest: *Here are your gods, O Israel, who brought you up out
of Egypt* (1 Kings 12:28).

    Second, the text of Hosea 9:1-9 connects the harvest celebration
with prostitution and with *every threshing floor and wine vat* (9:1-2;
cf. Mic. 1:7). At the same time, it disconnects the harvest from the
worship of the Lord (Hos. 9:4-5) *[Tabernacles, p. 396]*. In particular,
Hosea 9:5 refers to a future *great festival (appointed feast, festival*

day of Yahweh). The explanation of this whole passage as the great eighth-month festival in Bethel does not fit the context.

Yet Hosea does call out his prophetic word during the harvest festivities: *Israel, stop (this) celebrating with ecstasy like the (other) peoples* (9:1).

The majority of translations emend the text to create two parallel verbal clauses:

> *Do not rejoice, O Israel!*
> *Do not exult as other nations do.* (NRSV)

The Hebrew contains only the first verb, reading literally, *rejoicing to (the point of) ecstasy like the peoples*. A parallel Hebrew construction appears in Job 3:22. The emendation is unwarranted. What, then, is Hosea saying?

Israel has come to celebrate their harvest festival like *the peoples* who live among and around them. This is not to suggest that ecstatic celebration was out of place in Israel. In fact, the instructions governing the Feast of Tabernacles (Deut. 16:13-17) uses the same verb for *rejoice* as appears in Hosea 9:1. Exuberance is in place in genuine worship.

What seems to be prohibited is that their pattern of celebration is borrowed from the Canaanite culture. Possibly the form of these celebrations was unique and associated with the Baal and Asherah cults *[Asherah, p. 372]*. The accusation proper spells out the nature of their sin (9:1b).

The specific sin is one of unfaithfulness against their God. The accusation assumes an understanding or at least some formal acknowledgement of Israel's God as the Lord of the harvest (Matt. 9:37). It also assumes an awareness that God is a jealous God who does not delegate fertility to another *[Canaanite Fertility Myth, p. 376]*.

You love the wages of a prostitute on every grain threshing floor; they view their (illicit) relationship with Baal as the true source of agricultural bounty. That is infidelity to the Lord. They regard the grain harvest as the direct result of their fertility rituals. They consort with Baal; the ample results are sufficient proof of their labors *[Canaanite Fertility Myth, p. 376]*.

The Israelites are caught between two worldviews. Each accounts for the harvest, but in different ways. Yahwism draws attention to God as the source of all that the earth produces (cf. Gen. 1:11-13, 20-30). Accepting the Lord as the source of the harvest is to be an act

of faith. No magic, fertility ritual, or sexual acts are needed to stimulate or energize the Deity to produce the crops.

Baal worship invited the worshiper to participate with the god
Baal in generating new life and filling the granaries. It is hard to argue
with vivid experiences. For those preoccupied with the benefits of
worship, Baal more convincingly explained the source of the harvest
than the Lord.

Exile 9:2-7a

Interpreters have long grappled with the imagery of this text unit.
The language of crop failure is prominent (9:2). The judgment of
famine results in such a scarcity of produce that they will not even be
able to worship God in his house at the time of the great festival
(9:4c-5). The language of exile is also strongly present. More accurately said, the imagery of returning to Egypt shapes the passage. The
word "exile" is not mentioned, though the idea underlies the passage.
Instead, Israel is said to *go to destruction* in *Egypt*, rather than to flee
from destruction into Egypt (9:6).

This writer proposes that the background and key to the passage
is the story of the fortunes of Jacob and his family in the land of the
Canaanites (Gen. 34–47). Jacob is the patriarch of choice in the
Northern Kingdom *[Jacob and Isaac, p. 389]*. The majority of his
time in Palestine was spent in the North. Bethel was his spiritual
home. When he returned from Haran (Assyria?), his daughter Dinah
was raped (Gen. 34:2), "defiled" (Hos. 9:4; cf. Gen. 34:5, 13, 27), and
treated like a prostitute (cf. Gen. 34:31; Hos. 9:1) by Shechem, the
Canaanite. His sons avenged the rape of their sister by killing the
males of the city of Shechem. Then Jacob and his family fled to Bethel, where he built an altar to El, who had earlier appeared to him
there (Gen. 35:1-15). This became the family home until the famine
forced them into Egypt (Gen. 45-47).

The themes of prostitution, defilement, famine, Beth-El/El-
bethel/Beth-Yahweh (Hos. 9:4, *house of the Lord*), pouring out
drink offerings to God (cf. 9:4; Gen. 35:7, 14), and the journey to
Egypt to preserve the family—all these are reminders of the precarious existence their forebear, Israel (Jacob), experienced in the land of
the Canaanites *[Yahweh-Baal Conflict, p. 398]*. These themes are interwoven in this judgment text as context to the major events in the
life of their most respected and heralded ancestor.

Specifically, the judgment begins with an announcement of crop failure. The promise of the full vines is deceptive and *shall fail*. The land will refuse to produce for an unfaithful people.

Famine will drive Jacob's descendants out of the promised *land of the Lord* (9:3). Jacob had twice received the promise (Gen. 28:10-15; 35:9-13), yet was forced out. Once he went to Haran to escape his brother's enmity and to marry a relative rather than a Canaanite (27:41—28:9), and finally he went to Egypt to escape death by famine (Gen. 46–49). So the promise is not an unqualified guarantee of continuous possession and prosperity. The condition for Jacob and for his nation's descendants was the same: "Do not intermarry with the Canaanites" (Gen. 24:3; 28:1; Deut. 7:3; Josh. 23:12). The sons of Jacob rejected the Canaanites because Shechem, the Canaanite, had raped their sister and treated her like a whore (Gen. 34). Now the nation has become the whore, flaunting its sins, taking pride in Canaanite practices which had once revolted them. Will not the land reject Jacob's descendants who profane God's gifts of land and harvest?

Only here in the OT does the term *Yahweh's land* appear (Hos. 9:3). The multitude of promises regarding the land, spoken from Abraham to Moses, leave no doubt as to its ownership. Palestine is God's possession, to grant to whom he wishes. The recurring promise, "I will give it to you," is chanted through the pages of patriarchal and national history. Only the undefiled will enjoy the security and prosperity of the promise (Lev. 26). For the unfaithful, the way leads back to slavery in *Egypt* and to further defilement and servitude in *Assyria*.

They will survive by returning to the countries from which they have come, but only at great cost (Hos. 9:3-4b). The mention of *mourners' food,* introduced by *like*, recalls laws which were built on gradations of holiness and defilement (Deut. 26:14; cf. Hag. 2:11-14). Priests could not partake of the sacrificial food if they were in a state of defilement. Similarly, anything in a mourner's tent was impure (Num. 19:11, 14-16). Hosea, doing some sermonizing on these laws, explains that in exile every offering they make will be unacceptable because, to begin with, Israel is defiled through unfaithfulness and ritual aberrations (Fishbane: 199).

Hosea drives home the point by means of the rhetorical question (9:5). If they have all become defiled, how can they celebrate the great festivals of deliverance? The people will need to forgo that celebration because the instructions regarding the Festival of Booths read, "They shall not appear before the Lord empty-handed; all shall give as they are able, according to the blessing of the Lord your God that he has given you" (Deut. 16:16-17; cf. Exod. 23:15).

As in the first descent into Egypt, what begins as a rescue from a famine becomes an indefinite stay (9:6). They will again be enslaved and be buried in the Egyptian city of the dead: *Egypt will gather them, Memphis will bury them.* Meanwhile, the homes they left in Palestine will be inherited by thorns and thistles (9:6b). The country is depopulated from the effect of the famine judgment.

When they left Egypt victoriously under Moses' leadership they took along the wealth of Egypt (Exod. 12:35). When the Israelites asked for a slave's grant on departure, the Egyptians gave them silver, gold, and clothing (cf. Deut. 15:12-15). The judgment spoken by Hosea reverses that gift. Now Israel, on going back to Egypt, will take their liquid assets (silver) with them (Hos. 9:6a) and leave it there.

The background to verse six is also that of the descent of Jacob and his family to Egypt *[Jacob and Isaac, p. 389]*. Of the males in Jacob's family, only Jacob and Joseph were buried in Palestine (Gen. 49:29—50:26; Exod. 13:19). At least four generations of Israelites died and were buried in Egypt. And when the people began to question the wisdom of having followed Moses' leadership, they complained: "Was it because there were no graves in Egypt that you have taken us away to die in the wilderness?" (Exod. 14:11). They preferred captivity with the security of Egypt's year-round harvest to the challenge of trusting in a wilderness God.

Nothing has changed. Israel has not learned from the past. They do not understand the dangers of consorting with Canaanites, nor do they recognize the Lord's claims to their total loyalty. They have not acknowledged the gift of the good land as a grant of love. *The days of recompense have come* (Hos. 9:7a).

9:7b-9 On the Second Charge

Suppressing the Truth 9:7b-9a

Here is a classic response: If you don't like the message, attack the messenger. *What does the prophet know? Fool! Crazy!* Hosea records the people's response and explains it. Their mountains of sins obstruct their vision; the animosities they harbor are dulling their hearing. These are active sins *(iniquity)* and attitudes of the heart: animosities, resentments, *hostility*. Sin of both kinds obscures reality. It deflects accusations and rejects the truth. It ultimately leads to the big lie: God has not said (cf. Gen. 3:1-4; 1 John 1:10).

The first line of Hosea 9:8 is grammatically difficult. It may be continuing the theme of the descent into Egypt. In that case, it could be referring to Joseph, who informed Jacob about the inappropriate behavior of his brothers (Gen. 37:2). But even more to the point, Joseph became the focal point of his brothers' anger because he was Jacob's favorite son and because he dreamed that his brothers and even his parents would one day bow down to him (Gen. 37:3-11). Joseph's seeming foolishness generated only hatred and animosity, even though it anticipated the means for the family's salvation.

The name *Ephraim* connects Joseph to the Northern Kingdom via his younger but more prominent son, Ephraim. Hosea asserts that Ephraim has once acted as a prophet. In the past he (through his father, Joseph) has been aware of God's purposes with the family whom God chose (cf. Gen. 45:4-8). At that time, Joseph was the object of the brothers' opposition. Yet through him the family was delivered by going down to Egypt. Now Hosea occupies the prophetic role, and the nation is attempting to discredit and to silence him. If only the nation will heed his words! Salvation might still be possible.

The text, then, can be read this way:

> *Ephraim is a watchman,*
> *A prophet with my God.*

Or one can read it in a more enigmatic sense:

> *A watchman, O Ephraim!*
> *A prophet with my God.*

Abruptly and without a wasted word, Hosea shouts over the objections of the crowd. He stands before them in the familiar role of a *watchman*, a *sentinel* (cf. Jer. 6:17; Ezek. 3:16-21; 33:1-9; Isa. 56:10). He occupies the high ground, the watchtower from which he glimpses the enemy. While others are still oblivious to danger, the prophet shouts the warning: "Escape! Protect yourselves! Admit to your sins and return to God!"

Instead of trusting the message of the watchman, the Israelites attack God's messenger. This strategy has often been repeated (cf. Jer. 26:8; 36:26). We have no particulars on what *snare* was spread out on *his ways* or how these animosities were connected with *the house of God*. Was Hosea being opposed by counter-prophets (cf. 1 Kings 22; Jer. 28)? Were others trying to defuse or discredit Hosea by accusing him of trumping up charges? The text offers no details. We are simply told that the level of hostility is high. This comment speaks volumes about the reception Hosea received during his ministry to the Northern Kingdom.

Israel's moral decline (Hos. 9:9a) matches the worst example that can be drawn from her past. At the time of the judges, the people of Gibeah had shown their total disregard for social practices and moral values by assaulting a fellow Israelite and his concubine (Judges 19). They brutally gang-raped and killed her; Israel outsinned the Canaanites [Yahweh-Baal Conflict, p. 398]. The Benjamites defended this atrocity. The other tribes attacked, devastating and virtually exterminating the tribe of Benjamin (Judg. 20-21).

Hosea's mention of Gibeah brings to the listeners' minds one of the nation's historic moments of shame. Their moral consciousness has struck bottom. Not only do they openly condone sin, they defend the right of their community to practice it against the helpless. The whole nation justifies immorality. Gross sin prevails. God is about to repeat the judgment which had nearly exterminated Benjamin.

Wait and See! 9:9b

Is Hosea here inviting judgment or announcing it? Either would be in place. If he is declaring the divine decree directly, the people have heard the reasons. They have no basis on which to claim ignorance. If Hosea is inviting God to *remember their iniquities; take action on their sins!* he has the moral right and obligation to do so. That was what the Benjamites should have done to the sinners of Gibeah. Their failure to condemn Gibeah's sin resulted in their own near-extermination. They had become party to Gibeah's sin. If Hosea is publicly inviting God's judgment, he is fulfilling the role of one who is deeply hurt by his people's refusal to hear.

Recess: Judge and Friend of the Court in Conference 9:10-17

This centerpiece of the five judgment sections focuses, appropriately, on Israel's wilderness experience and its sequel, especially the story of the twelve spies (Num. 13-14) [Tabernacles, p. 396]. After a brief accusation, Hosea twice echoes God's announcement of judgment with his own withering announcement. The passage is shot through with curses, using fertility language. The promised blessings are reversed in every possible way [Covenant, p. 379].

9:10 God: The Way It Was

The *fruit* has a double meaning in this passage *[Yahweh-Baal Conflict, p. 398]*. The entire passage draws on the traditions of the wilderness rebellions (Num. 12–25) *[Tabernacles, p. 396]*. In Numbers, those rebellions are set between the two censuses. They mark the destructive effects of disobedience, since in the second census the nation numbered fewer than they did forty years earlier. So the movement in Hosea 9:10-17 takes us from the promise of blessing and increase to the barrenness of wilderness wandering and death.

While the backdrop is the wilderness account, the reader shall understand the contemporary relevance for a disobedient Northern Kingdom. Israel reflects the disobedience of its ancestors in the wilderness.

The forebears whom God rescued out of Egypt represent a pleasant promise, a surprisingly attractive people, *like* finding *grapes in the wilderness*. God enjoyed a time of intimacy with them in the privacy of the desert (cf. Jer. 2:2-3). *Like the first fruit on the fig tree, in its first season*, they were the initial fulfillment of the promises to the patriarchs.

God's hopes for a mature relationship were dashed when they came to *Baal-peor* (Num. 25). At the first peaceful encounter between the Israelites and other peoples, the Israelites bowed down to other gods. They worshiped "the Baal of Peor." They unashamedly indulged in sexual immorality with Moabite women as part of that worship ritual. They quickly turned against the covenant Lord whom they had so recently sworn to love and obey.

The language adds intensity to the accusation. *Baal of Peor* points to the local manifestation of the god to whom they turned. In the very presence of the Creator of heaven and earth, the Lord of history, the One who was giving them the whole land of Palestine, they turned to the god of that town. Could they not understand what God had shown and told them on the mountain?

Furthermore, they *dedicated themselves to Shame*. The word *dedicate* (*nazar*) speaks of bonding, swearing oaths, making a lasting commitment to someone. The noun form is the word for "Nazirite," a person given wholly over to God with special purity, for a designated time (Num. 6). The one they devoted themselves to was *Bosheth* (*Shame*), Baal (cf. Ish-bosheth, man of shame, 2 Sam. 2:8ff. = Ish-baal, 1 Chron. 8:33). As a result, they have become as filthy and detestable as *the thing they loved* (the Baal idol). Their lives imitate the character and actions of their god, Baal, to whom they have given themselves without reserve.

That pattern, begun early in God's care for his people, remains present throughout Israel's history. He can endure the deceit and impurity no longer. Extraordinary measures might break the pattern. God is about to launch the ultimate weapon.

9:11-13 God: The Children Bear the Consequences

The ultimate in judgment is to have Israel defect to Baal, only to experience God as the One who withdraws the gifts she has desired. Israel has pursued Baal, thinking he is the source of prosperity and fertility, the greatest gift of which is children. If there is a failure of the capacity to beget and bear children, or if the life of children already born is removed, they think someone other than Baal must be responsible. The presence of a superior God can be further proved if that God announces the judgment in advance. The prediction here establishes the Lord as God and Baal as incompetent, inferior, or nonexistent.

The first argument (9:11) lists *birth, pregnancy,* and *conception* in the order in which fertility will be withdrawn—a blow to Ephraim, who has gloried in his descendants. The nation stood tall and proud during the time of Jeroboam I (cf. Amos 6:8, 13). When God removes birth, pregnancy, and conception, the future of the nation is in jeopardy. The text thereby declares the impotency of Baal and the sovereignty of the Lord over the processes of nature and the future of the nation.

Judgments are spoken of as sure and shattering, characteristic of covenant curse language. The universals and absolutes describe what the covenant breaker deserves and is about to begin to experience. The first half of Hosea 9:12 makes it clear that fertility is not totally withheld, since children remain. Yet the scope of the judgment includes those already living. The parents of these children shall become childless by God's act through human agents [Covenant, p. 379].

Hosea 9:12b-13 poses a problem to the Bible translator and interpreter. The words do not easily form into intelligible sentences. They seem to say at least two things: (1) God turns blessings into a curse, and (2) Ephraim will see his sons slain. The circumstances are not spelled out. Perhaps they will fall in war. More likely, the nation will resort to child sacrifice in an attempt to coerce the gods to reverse the national calamity (cf. 1 Kings 16:34; 2 Kings 17:16-17).

Since the Northern Kingdom has been depending on Baal to ensure descendants, the Lord attacks the national theology by destroying their children in three ways. He withdraws human fertility, he uses
war and human agents to destroy the children already born, and he
allows the nation to sacrifice its own children in a useless attempt to
empower their weak gods to save them.

9:14 Hosea: Please, Lord!

God predicts families will be in agony and the nation in calamity.
Hosea, like other prophets, is not unmoved by the severe threat he is
called to declare (cf. Jer. 8:21; 9:1). Hosea turns to prayer; he knows
what it means to lose a family.

The ambiguity of this verse springs from the ambivalence in
Hosea's words: *Give them, O Lord—What will you give?* Is this a plea
for mercy or an echo of God's curse? Probably both, with this sense:
"If the barren wombs and dried breasts will bring the people to their
senses, let it happen, Lord! On the other hand, if children are to be
born only to be slaughtered in offering to the gods or by an invading
enemy, then, O God, diminish the pain of this people by withholding
children from them!"

Hosea, the intercessor, stands between a long-suffering, holy, and
just covenant Lord and a persistently sinful people. He lives intimately with the holiness of God; he sees the brazen disobedience of the
chosen people. His heart is torn by love for them.

9:15-16 God: The Children Bear the Consequences

Hosea's thought turns to Israel's leaders. The wilderness tradition
contains a number of accounts of rebellious leaders (Num. 12;
14:36-38; 16). To the backdrop of the Baal of Peor and the wilderness disobedience of Israel, Hosea now adds the name *Gilgal*. Gilgal
has a triple significance in Israel's history. First, it was the base of op-
erations from which Joshua launched the attack against the inhabitants of Palestine (Josh. 9:6; 10:6; 14:6). In preparation Joshua had
the people circumcised (Josh. 5). Circumcision signifies purification
of the means of procreation (fertility); circumcision signals that obedience to God.

Second, Gilgal also marked the end of dependence on manna
and quails. There Israel began to eat the produce of the land. *Gilgal,*

therefore, symbolizes the fulfillment of the promised blessings.

Third, every Israelite would see more in the name *Gilgal.* There Saul was confirmed as king (1 Sam. 11:12-15). There Saul lost the kingdom when he disobeyed Samuel by offering a sacrifice when Samuel did not appear on the seventh day as promised (1 Sam. 13:1-15). So Gilgal also brings to mind the beginning of a disobedient and rebellious monarchy (Hos. 9:15c). God gathers together Israel's failure to acknowledge God's gifts and the failure of leadership in the one word, *Gilgal.*

There also, God's *hatred* emerged against this people (9:15a). They had hardly gained a toehold in the land before he determined to expel them from it (9:15b).

The drought dries up Israel's roots and shrivels the forming fruit. From the first, the Creator has used crop failures as a means to alert Israel to her defection from him, but she has failed to see the natural catastrophes as his acts of judgment (cf. Amos 4:6-8). Even when the Lord slays their darling children (Hos. 9:16c), the nation remains blind and resistant to his recalling grace.

9:17 Hosea: The Way It Will Be

Hosea continues to dialogue with the Lord concerning the fate of Israel. He knows the heart of God. He feels the rejection God has endured over the generations. Israel accepted the land and then profaned God's gift. Such actions cannot continue indefinitely. Since Hosea has stood in the council of the Holy One (cf. Jer. 23:18), he can report its decree: *Because they have not listened to him, my God will reject them.*

One conclusion follows: Israel must be removed from the land (Hos. 9:17b). If they continue untouched by correction, they might become incapable of perceiving God's hand in even the most destructive acts (cf. Gen. 3:22-24). Perhaps in their insecurity as wanderers, as homeless refugees among the nations, their hearts might turn back to the Lord. Here the word of hope, though always implicit, is withheld. Judgment fills the scene.

THE TEXT IN BIBLICAL CONTEXT
A God with Feelings

God appears in the pages of Scripture with emotions unlike the impassive god of some philosophers. The Lord loves and hates, his anger burns, he is filled with compassion and regret, with longing and delight, with pain and sorrow (Hos. 9:7-17; cf. Gen. 6:6; Amos 7:3, 6; Mal. 1:2-3). God, however, cannot be reduced to human categories, even though we relate to God as to a person. God is not a human being (Num. 23:19; 1 Sam. 15:29). Yet we cannot conceive of a personal God in categories other than human. Therefore, all God language consists of accommodation to patterns of human thought and experience. God's self-descriptions of every kind consist of translations across insurmountable barriers. Unless God bridges them, we remain in the dark (Rom. 11:33-36; 1 Cor. 2:6-16).

God's fullest self-disclosure occurs in the incarnate Christ (John 1:1-18; Eph. 1:3-17; Heb. 1:1-3). In that incarnation, God affirms and identifies with our emotional selves as he does with our capacity to choose and to reason. Divine perfection embraces the emotions, suggesting that these are more than mere ways of interpreting the actions and attitudes of God. Those who observed Christ noted the depth of his love for intimate friends (John 11:5, 35-37; 15:9-13; 19:26), the impatience with the disciples when he felt they learned too slowly (Matt. 17:17; Luke 24:25), the anger in his glance and tone of voice when confronting hypocrites (Matt. 23; Mark 3:5), the stress and frustration of decision-making (John 12:27-28), the joy of celebration (Luke 10:21; Matt. 11:19; John 2:1-10), and the agony of facing death (Heb. 5:7). These feelings in Jesus are never represented in Scripture as human frailty or failure. The God who experiences perfect love, also experiences perfect anger and sorrow, joy and peace.

The Word of the Lord

Hosea and God speak with one voice, though not all the prophetic utterances are words spoken by God to Hosea. Indeed, the major portion of the book consists of conversations between the Lord and his prophet concerning Israel. A considerable number of Hosea's comments appear to be addressed to humans concerning Israel.

Prophets and apostles understood themselves to be God's representatives, speaking his thoughts, interpreting his deeds, announcing his purposes to the people. On occasion the word came through dreams or visions as from the throne room of the Almighty (cf. Isa. 6; Ezek. 1; 2 Cor. 12). Like Abraham, these servants of the Lord had become friends of God from whom God did not withhold what he was about to do (2 Chron. 20:17; Gen. 18:17; Amos 3:7; Gal. 1; John 15:12—16:33).

At other times the wisdom of the Spirit came to them as they were meditating on everyday events in the city gate; observing strangers and traders, troop movements, and religious processions; witnessing business transactions; or listening to the fears and hopes of those passing by. As a result, the prophets appropriately came to be known as "those who reprove in the city gate" (cf. Amos 5:10; Isa. 29:21). The word came through them with unique authority because they had become partners with God. Moved by the Spirit, they could not but speak what they have seen and heard (Amos 3; Jer. 20:9; Acts 4:20).

THE TEXT IN THE LIFE OF THE CHURCH
On Choosing Leaders

Hosea scores Israel for choosing leaders whom God has not called (8:4). The church has struggled with how to choose good leaders for nearly two millennia. As with Israel, most segments of the church have adopted the current, national political method of choosing leaders. The method of selection is not as important as the criteria employed and the openness with which the process is carried out. The third-century churchman Cyprian, citing this text (8:4) and the example of the church's selection of deacons (Acts 6:1-7), contends that the key to making good leadership choices is to engage in open and public testing and affirmation of the character and abilities of those being considered (*Epistles* 54, 67).

EXPLANATORY NOTES
Sentences Announced for Crimes in Palestine   10:1-8

Dialogue turns to monologue. Hosea's monologue appears in two more judgment speeches that are identical in pattern *[Literary Patterns, p. 391]*:

Recitation of sins
Announcement of punishment
Israel's despair anticipated

The first speech traces Israel's religious and moral life through past, present, and future. The second lifts the whole to a climax by moving quickly from the present to the future. The forward movement is into exile. In both speeches the people's words are quoted as expressions of despair.

10:1-3 For the First Crime

Misappropriation 10:1-2a

The imagery shifts from fruit to stones to divided heart. The previous judgment message began with the analogy of Israel and the vine and ended with Israel as withered root and perishing infants (9:10).

Israel is a *luxuriant* or *spreading* vine which produces fruit according to its nature. The NRSV reads, *that yields its fruit*. There is another verb spelled exactly like the Hebrew root for *produce* which means *to be like, to resemble*. Since the following lines emphasize the correspondences between God's gifts and their subsequent misuse, that meaning is most likely present here. The grapevine, Israel, *bears fruit which corresponds to its nature*. The harvest matches the nation's character. From the opening line, Hosea launches into a negative account of national religious life.

Three specific indictments follow. First, as the vine has matured and produced more fruit, the Israelites have responded by increasing the number of altars (10:1b). Two sins are represented. The first is the one of providing more centers of worship, an act which bears multiple consequences. The many shrines result in a diminished sense of the larger community. Increasing centers for sacrifice eventually leads to perceiving God as a local deity. A second sin implied in the accusation of multiplying altars has to do with the Israelites' concept of faith and God. Israel places a premium on the activity of the worshiper. Religious ritual has become a means of salvation.

The second indictment is that as the land has prospered, Israel has beautified the symbols of worship at high places (10:1c). Aesthetic pleasure is not the issue; making sin attractive is the problem. Israel was not to use stone pillars (phallic symbols?) known as *masebah*. God repeatedly commanded them to destroy all such pagan aids to worship (Exod. 23:24; cf. Hos. 3:4).

The third indictment touches the heart (Hos. 10:2a). At a deep level Israel has come to pursue the Lord for his gifts and Baal for his benefits. They have come to justify their simultaneous worship of these two gods.

Religion, whether involving one god or many gods, attempts to create a coherent worldview. In polytheism, a common course is to create a hierarchy of gods (high gods, lower gods, household gods) or assign them different spheres of dominance (earth, heaven, history, nature, war, death). Hosea does not accuse the people or priests of deceit in worship, but nevertheless he complains bitterly against them. They have apparently come to integrate the Lord and Baal into a meaningful whole in their religious interpretation of life. The people have come to accept a form of polytheism which honors God as Lord and Baal as his agent in the events of everyday life *[Israelite Religion, p. 385; Yahweh–Baal Conflict, p. 398]*.

Smashed Shrines   10:2b

Israel consummates her guilt at the altars and shrines. God, who will no longer endure them in their sin, will himself *break the neck of their altars.* That graphic language comes from the act of snapping the neck of an animal, rendering it unsuitable for human consumption because it has not been bled. Altars have projections at the corners known as the "horns of the altar" (cf. Exod. 29:12). A person accused of a capital crime could grasp a horn of the altar as the ultimate appeal for justice (1 Kings 1:50-51). Not only will the Lord demolish Israel's court of last appeal and *snap the horns of the altars* (cf. Amos 3:14); he will also destroy the altar itself, what is behind the horn, and erase all possibility of worship at those sites. Together with the altars, the Lord will devastate the *stone pillars*, making them unusable.

Historically, Assyria acted as God's agent in destroying Israel's many shrines. Details of that invasion appear in Hosea's second speech (10:8) *[Historical Summary, p. 384]*.

Defendant's Response: Despair   10:3

A particularly effective rhetorical device is to quote the anticipated response of the adversary or addressee. It undercuts the rebuttal and limits the range of possible responses. Hosea employs this rhetoric of disputation, though not in the technically formal sense of a disputation speech (Murray).

Hosea anticipates Israel's explanation of the enemy invasion: Israel has no king to lead them against the enemy. That state of affairs is due to their social and political disruption. Since God's role is to set up and depose kings, the people wonder if they have shown some *irreverence for the Lord* that led to this lack of a leader.

After soul searching comes disillusionment. Would a king have made any difference? Their experience some ten years earlier (2 Kings 15:19-20) suggests it would not. Perhaps, then, the real problem lies with God's inability to provide for his people. Might that be the real explanation for their calamity?

The historical event which most closely fits this text is Tiglath-Pileser's invasion of Israel in 732/31. The biblical historian lists cities captured by the Assyrian king: Ijon, Abel-beth-maacah, Janoah, Kedesh, Hazor (2 Kings 15:29), as well as the highlands on both sides of the Jordan above the Sea of Galilee. The population of the captured territories has been taken into exile. The area around Samaria became a vassal state under a new pro-Syrian ruler, Hoshea, who had apparently gained some credibility with the Assyrians by staging a coup against Pekah (2 Kings 15:30). Hosea 10:1-3 best fits that historical moment of internal faultfinding and jostling for power. The invasion they have just experienced is merely the foreshock of the more powerful quake to come.

10:4-8 For the Second Crime

The text unit begins and ends with reference to the people's words. The opening words constitute the accusation; the concluding words signal the people's despair.

Perjury 10:4

Here is the fruit which matches Israel's character. It consists of violations of oaths taken to guarantee the fulfillment of covenant. The accusations read:

> *Swearing falsely, cutting covenant,*
> *so litigation sprouts like a bitter and poisonous herb*
> *along the furrows of the field.*

Israel's public affairs are in disarray. When trust deteriorates, alternative means of ensuring responsible community relations become necessary. Israel chooses to replace *covenant love and fidelity* with increasing legalism.

The one who swears oaths invites God as Guarantor. To *swear falsely* is a deliberate act of deceit while using the Lord's name. It shows disdain for God, essentially regarding him impotent and irrelevant. If anything, God has become a means to a greater end—the welfare of the nation state.

Smashed Shrines, Exiled Kings   10:5-8b

The air is thick with irony and satire in Hosea's description of the judgment. The officials of Samaria fear for the welfare of the bull-calf image of that God. People and idolatrous priests alike mourn its departure. The entire nation holds its breath for fear of seeing the golden calf carried off into Assyrian exile, a prize of war (cf. 8:5).

Hosea's satire becomes a taunt directed to the priests and populace through Hosea: *Let them rejoice at his glory* (10:5c). The nation is unaware that the glory of the Lord has already departed from the land because of all its evil and idolatry. The bull symbolizing God will take its place in the caravan of booty carried back to honor the victorious ruler. Sargon reports his subjugation of Samaria: "I counted the gods in whom they trusted as spoil" (Cogan: 104).

What appears to the onlookers to be a victory for Assyria is actually an act of deliverance by the Lord himself (10:6-7). In removing the image of the bull, the Assyrian king will be removing Ephraim's shame. Her so-called "king," the bull calf, is being taken into exile, only to be followed by the people.

The metaphor of the wood chip on the waters reminds the readers that their "god" is a useless wooden idol (10:7). In the previous invasion, the Israelites themselves stripped the image of its golden splendor. Israel now resembles her idol: infertile, broken, to be used as the finder wishes.

Two objects of Israel's false worship dominate Hosea's preaching: the bull calves and the high places with their symbolic pillars [*Bull Calves, p. 375*]. Images of the high gods were important symbols of control over their people. They have already been prophetically dispatched to Assyria. Next come the high places (10:8a-c). They represent worship of a lower level of deity, particularly fertility gods and goddesses [*Israelite Religion, p. 385*]. To destroy them is to destroy the last sources of hope for a conquered people.

High places of Aven (10:8) may refer to all the high places in the country or it may be more specific. House (Heb.: *beth*) of Aven (*wickedness*) refers to Bethel (cf. 4:15; 5:8; 10:5). According to 1 Kings

12:32, Jeroboam built high places in Bethel. These may be intended here. If so, then the Assyrians have connected Israel's worship with high places.

The reference to *thorn and thistle* (Hos. 10:8b) echoes the curse on the first man's disobedience (Gen. 3:18). It signals more than corrective judgment in the form of loss of fertility. The very symbols of fertility (high places) and obedience (altars) become the place where chaos conquers the powers of Baal. That curse comes from the Lord [*Yahweh-Baal Conflict, p. 398*].

Defendant's Response: Despair 10:8c

"We'd rather be dead!" Israel's cries out. In asking for the *mountains* and *hills* to fall on them, the Israelites long for more than death. Their hope, tied to the material symbols of faith, has been whisked away. Despair rules.

Beyond despair, their longing includes the desire to be buried in their own land. Anything, they feel, is preferable to captivity in a foreign land (cf. Ps. 137). To die on home soil would be grace.

Judge Announces Sentences for Earlier Crimes 10:9—11:7

With two oracles (Hos. 10:9-15; 11:1-7), God concludes the judgment prophecies gathered under the theme of *no covenant love* (see OVERVIEW of 6:4—11:16). In them, he presents his case of spurned love. Israel's wickedness has fossilized. They still profess to be the covenant people but no longer live by the terms of the covenant.

Two metaphors describe the nation: a *heifer* and a young *child* [*Bovine Imagery, p. 374*]. Both display stubborn resistance to training. Correction will require firm discipline.

God's patience seems to have exhausted itself. Yet invitations to repentance dot even these final judgment speeches. Intense and severe as the predictions of destruction may be, they contain within them the seeds of hope. Even the starkest condemnations represent what *may* be rather than what *will* be.

10:9-15 For Crimes Since the Conquest: War

Historically, the nations and nature are drawn into service to pronounce judgment. They are represented by Gibeah, war, and sowing and reaping. As with the majority of the prophecies of Hosea, an attempt to date or identify specific contexts for these prophecies is an exercise in futility.

The Crime: Persistent Sinning 10:9-10

Hosea's meditation is brief; his conclusion is pointed. God faults Israel for persisting in the sin of Gibeah: inhospitality, rape, and murder are essentially violations of covenant love (Judg. 19–21). Here is proof that there is *no family affection* in the land. And in this kind of sinning, the nation has remained until the time of Hosea's prophesying.

At Gibeah, Israel came face-to-face with the consequences of her sin. It took a dramatic symbolic act to awaken the moral indignation of the nation. The Levite dismembered and dissected his concubine's corpse, and sent a part to each tribe. The member tribes demanded that the Benjamites deliver the citizens of Gibeah to them for punishment. Benjamin refused. Reluctantly, the nation turned on the Benjamites for harboring the evildoers and condoning their actions. The Benjamites were nearly annihilated in the ensuing war.

The argument of this judgment statement flows as follows: If it was clearly God's will that the Israelites should attack and virtually annihilate an entire tribe of their people, would God do less for similar sins committed by the entire nation? They have persisted for centuries in their sin. God has been long-suffering during these hundreds of years. At the time of his choosing, God will punish the nation by war for its sin. This time God will use foreign nations as his rod. These nations will not act independently, nor by the will of their own gods. They come to act as witnesses in God's lawsuit, casting the first stone against the Lord's covenant-violating people (cf. Amos 3:9-10).

The term *double sin* is ambiguous (Hos. 10:10, Heb.). It may refer to the lack of hospitality and sexual immorality and abuse, as depicted in the story of Judges 19. It may refer to the original sin at Gibeah and the present sins of the nation. It might even refer to the sins of immorality (Judg. 19) and to the disobedience of King Saul, who established his military headquarters at Gibeah (1 Sam. 13:15).

Judge's Appeal Falls on Deaf Ears 10:11-13a

From the stage of history, Hosea transports his readers into the world of agriculture. We observe a young *trained heifer*, threshing, plowing, sowing, reaping, and eating through two harvests. The intermingled images depict judgment intercepted by hope. On the plane of history, they translate into this sequence of events:

God's intention (10:11)
Call to repentance (10:12)
Israel's practices (10:13a)

God's design for Israel was to teach them to serve him. The land was the setting in which they would grow to maturity as his people. The metaphor traces the growth of a heifer to maturity (10:11). The young heifer was frisky and light enough to beat the grain from the stalks without severely damaging the kernels.

Elsewhere, Hosea speaks disparagingly about bovine Israel (2:6; 4:16; cf. Amos 4:1-3). Such satire serves well as an anti-Baal polemic. Here, however, the metaphor describes God's people positively. Or does one sense irony in Hosea's words? Perhaps he means, "So you love to think of yourselves as a heifer and the Lord as a bull. Well, then, consider what he intends for you." One would expect a mating scene, but such is out of character. The absence of sexuality in God's treatment of Israel points to the unique character of his love *[Bovine Imagery, p. 374]*.

Israel is quoted as saying, *I love to thresh* (10:11a). Small wonder. Threshing was a time of relative freedom, light work, and ample access to food. Israel was commanded not to muzzle the mouth of the animal treading out the grain (Deut. 25:4). The nation gained access to the produce of the land of Palestine through conquest. They were spared the difficult task of clearing the land and planting its vineyards and orchards (Deut. 6:10-12). The land came as gift, a promise to the patriarchs.

God intended, however, to lead his people to more mature experiences and expressions of faith. So he himself (Heb. emphasis) placed the yoke on the beautiful neck of this maturing heifer (Hos. 10:11b). To break her in slowly, he planned first to teach her to respond to his commands: *I will drive* (or: *mount and ride) Ephraim*. Only then would the Lord submit his people (Judah, Jacob) to the harder work of plowing and harrowing.

The metaphor dissolves into the drama (10:12). Now the people are tilling the soil. As stewards of the land, they are responsible for the process which produces fruit of character, community, and blessing. It is their job to sow that which will produce righteousness, to harvest that which meets the criterion of unfailing love. But to achieve that, they will need to return to the Lord. Israel's land has remained fallow too long. The untilled land is overgrown with weeds, thistles, and thorns. The garden of God has become a place of wild growth, a place of curse on the human calling (cf. Gen. 3:17-19).

The solution is straightforward and echoes the words spoken earlier through Amos (5:6): *Seek the Lord!* God alone can soften the soil with refreshing rain and cause the land to sprout with right living and relationships. *To seek the Lord* means they are called to devote themselves exclusively to God and pursue his will.

Israel has *plowed (planted) wickedness and harvested (reaped) injustice* (Hos. 10:13a). Both sin words refer to acts of violence or injustice against people. While sin is ultimately a violation of one's relationship with God, it expresses itself when the sinner turns on others. One cannot sow weeds or thistles and expect grapes, olives, or wheat.

What Israel plants, it reaps; what it reaps, it eats (10:13a). All segments of society (*you*, pl.) consume the same moral fare. *The fruit of lies (deception)* has become the staple diet.

At root the word translated *lies* means to fail to produce what is promised or expected. It then comes to mean leanness or weakness. Israel's sin is directed against the members of its society that have weakened the social bonds which hold the nation together. The nation is malnourished; its diet lacks truth, covenant faithfulness, and the knowledge of God. Enemies will find this weakened, discordant people an easy prey.

The King Is Dead! 10:13b-15

Hosea 10:13b-15 depicts the chaos of battle. A massive destruction is descending on weakened Israel. The subject of the verb marks a shift from plural *you* to the collective singular *you*. The national willpower coalesces around its leader, with its armed forces on the ready. Ephraim trusts in its own resources to stave off enemies, relying on trained warriors, garrisoned fortresses, and a military leader.

The language produces graphic war scenes. *Bethel*, the center of national worship, bears the brunt of the attack. *Fortresses* and cities turn to rubble. The enemy fills mass graves with the bodies of mothers and children. The king, chosen by Israel to fight their battles (cf. 1 Sam. 8:19-20), counts for nothing when the enemy strikes at dawn.

Israel's annihilation can be traced back to the people's *great wickedness, excessive evil* (Heb.: *evil of your evil*). If only Israel could see the connection between her disobedience to God in their societal oppression, and the impending judgment!

11:1-7a For Crimes Prior to the Conquest: War

The previous prophecy cast Israel first as a heifer and then as a draft animal, but hardly mature. Now the imagery is that of a stubborn youth. The term *youth* describes males from the age of birth (Judg. 13:5, 7) to adulthood (1 Kings 11:28), but as weak, immature, or lacking in experience.

The Hebrew text of Hosea 11:1-7 challenges scholars. The translation and interpretation offered here are an attempt to discover meaning in its details and cohesion in its parts. A number of factors guide this interpretation. *First,* five action-response sequences contrast Israel and her God. Hosea develops these contrasts in a succession of family and travel scenes and in two scenes of war. The central sequence makes the transition from the family to war (11:4-5b).

God's loving initiative. (11:1)
The nation's faithless response. (11:2)

God's loving initiative. (11:3)
The nation's ignorance. (11:3b)

God's loving initiative. (11:4)
The nation's new bondage. (11:5ab)

The nation's obstinacy. (11:5c)
God sends the judgment. (11:6)

The nation's distress. (11:7ab)
God repudiates a rebellious son. (11:7c)

God's initiative is rebuffed by Israel (11:1-4). Later, Israel's initiatives are rebuffed or negated by God (11:5c-7). *Second,* this reading of the text is supported by its pattern *[Literary Patterns, p. 391].* The passage moves from accusation (11:1-4) to judgment (11:5-7). The transition (11:4-5b) links this text as a unified whole. *Third,* the metaphor traces Israel's response through levels of maturity (cf. 10:7-15). *Finally,* the verb translated *exalt* (11:7) can mean *to rear, train and care for* children (cf. Isa. 1:2; 23:4). It signals that the author is still on the theme with which he began. The results translate as follows:

Sequence 1
When Israel was a child I loved him,
and I designated him my son from (the days of) Egypt. (11:1)
They (also) called them by name
and as a result (of their calling), they went that way:
they sacrificed to the baals
and burned incense to images. (11:2)

Sequence 2
Though I taught Ephraim to walk,
taking them by his arms,
     they did not realize
     that it was I who healed them. (11:3)

Sequence 3
Though I led them with bonds of human kindness,
     with ties of love,
and though I became to them
like those who remove a yoke from their necks,
and though I bent over and fed them, (11:4)
     they shall not return to the land of Egypt;
     instead, Assyria shall be his king. (11:5ab)

Sequence 4
Because they refuse to repent, (11:5c, NRSV: *refused to return to me*)
     the sword will whirl in their cities,
     and its bars will be destroyed,
     and it will eat away at their well-crafted plans. (11:6)

Sequence 5
Though my people live in fearful suspense
because of their apostasy against me,
and though they call him "God Most High,"
     he will not rear them at all. (11:7)

The Crime of Spurning God's Call 11:1-2

God's love and sworn promise motivated him to rescue this slave people *from Egypt.* He freed them for himself and unified them through covenant on the lower slopes of Mt. Sinai. National history began with their release. The *from* marks Israel's point of origin *[Covenant, p. 379].*

Hosea has already introduced Israel as the *children of the living God* (1:10). Here the nation is viewed collectively as God's son. The language recalls God's claim over Israel made through Moses: "Israel is my firstborn son. . . . Let my son go that he may worship me" (Exod. 4:22-23). Though Israel was a son, the newborn nation was a helpless infant.

The Hebrew construction in Hosea 11:1a reads, *From Egypt on I designated you as my son.* No longer were they slaves; they had become the firstborn son, with the attendant privileges and responsibilities. The remainder of this text unit builds the case that judgment is necessary because Israel, God's firstborn, has disobeyed the divine Parent.

If we accept the Hebrew text of verse two as it stands, we are introduced to the following scene. God designates Israel as his son, the legitimate heir. From that point on, he invites this people to follow him to Mt. Sinai and throughout the wilderness years [Tabernacles, p. 396]. But there are other voices calling Israel. They are anonymous and numerous. Israel listens and yields to the seductive accents of these alien voices.

The second half of verse two clarifies the identity of those whose counsel they have been following. The *baals* and the *idols* characterize Israel's way of life. The child has accepted other masters (*ba'al* means lord, master, husband) and the dolls (idols) created by them [Ba'al, p. 373]. Historically, Israel turned to idols before Moses descended Mt. Sinai (Exod. 32-34, esp. 32:8). Even before they arrived at the Land of Promise, they had turned to sacrifice to Baal of Peor and other gods (Num. 25). What a fickle people!

The Crime of Rejecting God's Nurturing Love 11:3-4

A second form of rebellion roots in ignorance and ingratitude (Hos. 11:3). The forty years in the wilderness were special times of God's care [Tabernacles, p. 396]. He graciously provided water, quail, and manna for his dependent child. He taught Israel to walk, to depend on him (Deut. 8). That would confirm their sonship (Deut. 8:5). But God's people seemed not to understand his care. The murmurings and discontent which fill the pages of Exodus and Numbers stand as evidence of this ignorance and forgetfulness.

The word *heal* speaks of salvation (Hos. 5:13; 6:1; 11:3; 14:4). By it Hosea draws attention to pain and pleasure: the pain of God's discipline and the joy of forgiveness so freely granted to repentant people. A child learning to walk takes many falls. Those cuts and bruises were tenderly cared for by the loving Parent and great Physician. Yet Israel never acknowledged the healing touches of God's love.

A third action-response contrast between God's care and Israel's obstinate disobedience is developed by extending the metaphor of the child (11:4-5). God is pictured as the child's mother, who carries the infant Israel strapped to her back or hip in a carrying pouch made of *cords of human kindness, . . . bands of love.* Her touch is warm and affectionate, *like those who lift infants to their cheeks.* The divine Mother holds infant Israel in her lap and bends over to nurse the child (11:4c); the Lord of history suckles Israel. The metaphor breaks our stereotypes of God.

What more can a child ask for? Could any mother give her child more tenderness, more liberating guidance, more ample nourishment?

The image ends abruptly, as though interrupted by a mother's pain at her child's ingratitude. The language turns toward correction (11:5).

Sentence: Assyrian Conquest and Exile 11:5-7a

Many translations and commentators transform the opening clause of verse five into a question on the basis of the statements in 7:16; 8:13; and 9:6, that Israel will go into captivity to Egypt. But Hosea has been using Israel's experience in Egypt as a metaphor for slavery and immaturity, liberation and sonship. Hence, they will not return to Egypt literally, though the nation will return to bondage, symbolized by *Egypt* (11:5). This time the judgment will take them to *Assyria*. In sharp contrast to the loving Parent they knew in the wilderness, Assyria will treat them as harshly as any *king* treats rebels (cf. 2 Kings 17).

Israel's experience of 725-722 B.C. testifies to the fulfillment of this prophecy. Tiglath-Pileser established full control of Israel when Pekah was assassinated by Hoshea (2 Kings 15:29-30), possibly with the Assyrian king's support. Hoshea turned to Egypt and negotiated a military pact to protect him from the Assyrians. He withheld tribute from Assyria. Consequently, the Assyrian king, Shalmaneser attacked Samaria and placed it under siege for three long years (2 Kings 17:3-6). The annals of Sargon II, Shalmaneser's successor, describe the conquest in matter-of-fact terms:

> I besieged and conquered Samaria, led away as booty 27,290 inhabitants of it. I formed from among them a contingent of 50 chariots and made the remaining (inhabitants) assume their (social) positions. I installed over them an officer of mine and imposed upon them the tribute of the former king. Hanno, king of Gaza and also Sib'e [= King So, 2 Kings 17:4], the turtan of Egypt, set out from Rapihu against me to deliver a decisive battle. I defeated them. (*ANET*: 284-285)

The machinations of threatened leaders and nations accomplish nothing. Only vivid imagination can recreate the scenes of war, the death and destruction, and the personal terrors and suffering created by such an event. Fortunately, the author spares us the brutal and agonizing details.

The fourth set of contrasts between God and his son begins with the reason for the judgment. *Because they have refused to return to me* heads the subunit (Hos. 11:5c). Within these deliberate pairs, divine pathos (11:1a, 3-4) gives way to the reason for Israel's severe chastisement. The threats of judgment as well as earlier lesser punishments have not turned Israel to their Lord. This people has *refused* to return—to turn away from its sin and return to God.

Israel has failed to recognize that well-crafted plans are no substitute for repentance. At one level it is clear that repentance does not win battles. But that is precisely the point. Israel no longer sees God as the leader of her armed forces. She fails to own him as Lord. Therefore, the sweep of superior Assyrian forces moving through Ephraim's cities results from her obstinate disobedience; Assyrian military superiority is not the cause of the nation's downfall.

Swords whirl and flash in the streets of her fortified cities. Reinforced city gates hang askew. The rush of enemy warriors tramples carefully drawn battle plans underfoot.

11:7bc Comment by Hosea: Too Little, Too Late

The fifth pair of action-response vignettes pictures Israel's desperate and zealous religious activity as the enemy approaches. Some realize that God may be displeased with them (11:7ab). They appeal to him by the name *El Al* (11:7b, *God Above*). Surely, by acknowledging his supreme power, they should attract his favorable attention.

God refuses to heed their last-minute appeal (11:7c). The nation will receive the judgment specified for a rebellious son: death (cf. Deut. 21:18-21).

Hope in God's Compassion
Hosea 11:8-11

PREVIEW
The recurring pattern of the book of Hosea is accusation-judgment-salvation. Each major block follows this outline. *No covenant love* has been the accusation (6:4—7:16). The Assyrian invasion and conquest dominate the judgment scene. Israelites fill the line of captives.

Hosea has reached back for a reference point to the days of Israel's beginnings. Egypt and the wilderness serve as a reminder of their sin and servitude; they also serve as symbols of hope.

Ephraim, God's grandson, refuses to acknowledge his covenant Lord. The appropriate parental response is discipline. In this case, the corrective acts take the form of expulsion from the land and exile to Assyria. Israel is disinherited. Lo-ruhamah (1:6, Not-loved, Not-pitied).

The framing imagery of parent and child continues from the preceding judgment oracle [*Accusation-Judgment-Salvation Oracles, p. 372*]. It is filled out with historical and geographical reference points, with the roar of lions and the sight of migrating birds. But even more central to Israel's salvation is the tender heart of God. In this oracle God reveals his agony over wayward Israel and the reach of his restoring love.

OUTLINE

The Holy One's Compassion, 11:8-9

The Lord Leads the Way Back, 11:10-11

EXPLANATORY NOTES

The Holy One's Compassion 11:8-9

God, the Parent, is also the covenant Lord. The agony of a mother's compassion and a father's love appears in the *How . . . ?* The exclamation signals deep and intense emotion, usually of grief, occasionally of joy. Here one must picture God, hands extended in love, sobbing at the thought of punishing this rebellious and wayward son. Pain pervades the scene. Those who have known such pain need no description; for others, words cannot serve.

Verse eight expresses two impossibilities: (1) God cannot bear to turn Israel over to the enemy (Assyria) to do with as they please (11:8a). (2) God will not erase the Northern Kingdom as he did Admah and Zeboiim, cities incinerated with Sodom and Gomorrah (11:8b; cf. Gen. 14:2; 19:25-29; Deut. 29:23).

Is God schizophrenic, torn between his love and justice? Does he have multiple personalities, one of whom calls for punishment, the other for mercy? Is the covenant promise of punishment less true than the promise of blessing? No!

Israel has persisted in covenant breaking (Hos. 6:4—7:16). The nation has resisted God's acts of judgment calling her back (8:1— 11:7). Her due is exile and destruction (Lev. 26; Deut. 28:15-68; 29:19-28). Yet, God says, "Yet for all that, when they are in the land of their enemies, I will not spurn them, or abhor them so as to destroy them utterly and break my covenant with them; for I am the Lord their God" (Lev. 26:44). Elsewhere such extraordinary grace is said to flow to them because of his great love and promises to the patriarchs (Deut. 7:7-11) or because of faithful intercession (Exod. 32-33; Deut. 9:25-29).

The text assumes the punishment of exile (Hos. 11:10-11). That punishment is an expression of God's anger (5:10; 8:5). An unrestrained outpouring of covenant curses would bring Ephraim to extinction. In both Leviticus 26 and Deuteronomy 30, God promises to lift the curses when Israel repents. In Hosea, the Lord calls for repentance, but it does not occur. Hosea roots Israel's restoration in divine initiative.

That new initiative with the stubborn, exiled people springs from God's change of *heart* and aroused *compassion*. God's feelings are cast in human terms. There are no other means of conveying the heart of God.

Hosea pursues the same argument found in Leviticus 26. Disobedience in certain circumstances is a capital crime. Yet the compassionate heart of God and his fidelity to the covenant prevent him from applying unrestrained punishment. Unlike humans, who play fast and loose with promises and oaths, the Lord consistently maintains covenant love. Indeed, an essential part of the restated covenant is recorded in Deuteronomy (30:4-10): God will restore his people.

One might expect the following argument: even if the Northern Kingdom rebels and is destroyed, Judah's existence proves that God is faithful. In Hosea, however, God does not treat the Northern Kingdom as apostate and rejected just because it separated from the South. They remain an integral part of the people of God. The covenant promises apply equally to Ephraim and to Judah. Hosea never depicts Judah alone as the faithful remnant.

The motive for God's change of heart lies in his nature. He is God, *the Holy One*. Here, as in Isaiah 12:6, the designation *Holy One* appears in a salvation context. Most frequently it introduces judgment. God takes pleasure in purifying Israel. This time the holy God *will not come in wrath*. Unlike humans, God's emotions do not require time to subside. When sin is removed, God joyfully embraces his restored people.

The Lord Leads the Way Back 11:10-11

While these lines describe Israel's return, it is not a joyful return. Here is Gomer, purchased for fifteen shekels of silver and some barley and wine, instructed to wait until a future time of consummation. Israel is reluctantly returning and not yet gratefully obedient (Hos. 3:2-4).

The Israelites respond to God's demand to return only when he utters it with the voice of *a lion*. The roar brings God's sons *from the sea (the west)*, those parts of the Mediterranean coasts and islands where they have been scattered. They come *trembling* in fear (cf. 3:5).

Some had fled to Egypt as refugees (cf. 2 Kings 25:26; Jer. 42–44). These return from their temporary refuge, though they are wary and easily startled into flight. God draws them back to their homeland, like migratory flocks of birds, directed mysteriously and unerringly by forces deep within. Others had been taken into Assyrian exile. These too return, frightened and insecure, but drawn by the Holy One.

All are settled in the security of their own houses. The absence of any further description of Israel's salvation points to the preliminary character of this act of redemption.

THE TEXT IN BIBLICAL CONTEXT
God, the Mother

God-language frames the Infinite in human concepts and experiences. Describing God as having human form and characteristics is anthropomorphism. God speaks, has hands and feet, and sits on a throne.

With few exceptions, in the Hebrew Scriptures God language is masculine in gender. God is featured as an adult male. This is not accidental, but it is disconcerting in a society in which men and women have equal rights and interchangeable or generic roles. Further, women (and men) who have been abused by men may become alienated from God by male characterizations of Deity. Even the term *Father* can create fear, revulsion, and distancing, rather than conveying the intended solace, security, and affection.

God transcends gender. Unfortunately, however, neither Hebrew nor English has a singular, personal, inclusive pronoun by which to refer to God when the masculine metaphor is not intended.

In Hosea, God is variously pictured as a husband, a lover, the Holy One, the Most High, an offended parent—as well as a mother. Hosea challenges our exclusively male characterization of God. In the likeness of a mother, God carries the child through its infancy in the years of journeying through the wilderness. A mother affectionately and tenderly bonds with her infant by laying it against her cheek and bending forward to offer her breast to the nursing child (Hos. 11:4). The book of Hosea pictures God as a mother.

The feminine characterization of God also surfaces in the book of Isaiah. God, Israel's Creator, embraces the function of both parents: as father, God begot Israel; as mother, God gave him birth (Isa. 45:10). When the child grew to adulthood, he turned against his divine parent in the worship of other gods. God expresses anguish over disobedient Israel in the agonizing cry of a woman in labor (42:14). God could never forget the erring son, Israel. Even if it were possible for a human mother to forget a child to whom she had given birth, it would remain impossible for God to forget the people Israel (49:15). Therefore, let Israel know that God will continue to offer a mother's comfort by restoring the exiles to Jerusalem (66:12). Here the feminine characterization of God communicates depth of bonding, compassion, and nurture of a kind and to a degree which the "father" language and image does not convey.

Hosea 11 and the New Testament

Hosea 11:1 reaches back to the exodus; Matthew has extended Hosea's thought forward to Jesus *[Exodus Tradition, p. 384]*. Moses presented God's demand to Pharaoh: "Israel is my firstborn son. . . . Let my son go" (Exod. 4:22-23). The exodus was God's way of delivering his people. It led to covenant making at Sinai, followed by forty years of wilderness experience, and entry into the Land of Promise *[Tabernacles, p. 396]*.

Matthew portrays Jesus as the One who fulfills the Messianic expectations (1:1, 18; 2:4; 16:16; 26:63). He cites Hosea 11:1 in connection with Joseph and Mary's stay in Egypt as proof of Jesus' messianic role (Matt. 2:13-15). The words in Hosea are historical narrative, not prediction. Matthew may be using rabbinic exegesis to connect fulfillment with prediction. The connection would be in the historical appropriateness of the clause: *Out of Egypt I have called my*

son (Hos. 11:1). The exegetical relevance of the Hosea text is signaled by the code word *Egypt.*

Matthew proceeds to show how Jesus in his life retraced the
course of events by which Israel came to meet with God at Sinai.
From conception (Matt. 1:21-23) to crucifixion (Matt. 27:35), Jesus
fulfilled Scripture.

An illustration will point out the complexity and beauty of Matthew's way of interpreting the life of Jesus. For example, Jesus was
baptized in the Jordan "to fulfill all righteousness" (3:15), as Israel
was baptized in the Sea of Reeds (1 Cor. 10:2). At the baptism, Jesus
is identified by the voice from heaven: "This is my Son, the Beloved
(*ho agapētos*), with whom I am well pleased" (Matt. 3:17). Jewish interpretation connected the word translated "Beloved" to the concept
of the only, the unique child. The Septuagint translates the Hebrew
yaḥid (only child) as *agapētos/ē* (Gen. 22:2, 12, 16; Judg. 11:34;
Amos 8:10; Zech. 12:10; Jer. 6:26). Jesus is the obedient Son, fulfilling what disobedient Israel failed to accomplish (Heb. 5:8).

The writer of Matthew, then, sees the parallel between Israel and
Christ as a deliberate pattern of redemptive history. That shapes Matthew's selection of OT texts in keeping with the Jewish tradition and
in distinct recognition of Jesus of Nazareth as the Messiah.

THE TEXT IN THE LIFE OF THE CHURCH

Trust in Leaders

When the spirit of *ḥesed* (covenant faithfulness and love) disappears,
covenants become exercises in deceit. When trust is gone, agreements are maintained only through brute force or threat of societal
punishment.

Multiplying laws and regulations is a common way to shore up deteriorating bonds within a community, whether of a social, economic,
legal, political, or religious nature. Increased laws call for more law-
enforcement officials and for more prisons. When public officials
themselves treat the laws of the land with disdain or capitalize on every loophole in the law to line their own pockets, the law itself becomes suspect. Trust will grow only where those who lead earn the
public's trust by being open, consistent, and self-sacrificing. The term
servant leadership conveys just such leadership qualities and style.

Uses of Prophetic Judgment Texts

Evidently preachers and teachers addressed Israel differently than they do in our society. It was fitting to warn Israel of the coming catastrophe. Hosea would have been derelict in his duty had he made it more palatable. How does the church use such compilations of verdicts and sentences?

First, we ought not to assume that our society and the church do not need to hear strong words of reproof. The tendency is to underestimate the seriousness of sin and judgment. In the medical diagnosis of cancer, a person who appears to be a healthy specimen is suddenly ordered into surgery. The observer might see this as a heartless act when in reality the operation is a critical step in sparing the person's life. Similarly, clear diagnosis of a society's moral cancer is essentially an act of compassion to spare that society from ruin.

In cases where unrelenting judgment is not the message for the times, one can translate the word into its positive counterpart: "This pleases God; God calls us to deeper love and faithfulness." The audience needs to ask themselves, Are we on God's side on these matters?

Such harsh verdicts against Israel can also serve a protective function for the church. In writing to the Corinthians, Paul explains that these events were recorded for the benefit of future generations, to act as warnings against defecting from God (1 Cor. 10:11). The effectiveness of such warnings depends on the church's capacity to identify with Israel as God's people.

A Consistent Value System

Hosea makes no distinction between the ethical principles and ideals governing Israel's private and public life, between personal and communal practices, between relations to insiders and outsiders. The ethical values and practices of people of faith are consistent in all spheres of life. All are ordered under the lordship of their God.

That reality would seem to translate into our being world citizens and world Christians. Our own nation state and denominational ties then become subordinate to universal values and concerns. The implications of that truth are revolutionary for the church in this global village.

Hosea 11:12—14:8

Defendant, Jezreel: No Integrity

OVERVIEW

Words! Words! Words! While the theme of integrity is broader than that of truth-telling, this last unit of the book strengthens the case against Israel by drawing on the evidence gleaned from speech acts. Consider the following descriptions and instructions: *lies* (11:12; 12:1), *charge* (12:2), *begged* (12:4), *spoke* (12:4), Ephraim's *boast* (12:8), *spoke to the prophets* (12:10), *Ephraim spoke* (13:1), Israel *said* (13:10), *unwise* (10:13), *say* (14:2), *say no more* (14:3), *It is I who answer* (14:8). In addition, this unit contains a number of references to the mouth, jaws, kissing, or eating (12:1; 13:2, 5, 8; 14:2).

Hosea 11:12—14:8 addresses Ephraim from the vantage point of integrity and righteousness. In contrast with the previous perspectives of address, the knowledge of God (4:4—6:3), and covenant love (6:4—11:11), this section does not zero in on the sins of any social institution. It contains general references to merchants (12:7) and the populace as a whole but does not isolate societal groups or institutions for accusation. Even the geographical references (Gilead, Gilgal, Samaria) address the population at large rather than a select group.

The charge against Israel, symbolically named Jezreel (1:4), is not limited to verbal deceit. Their sin also expresses itself in the consequences of such deceit in the form of aggression and injustice. It appears as lies (11:12; 12:1), deceit (11:12), violence (12:1), and treaty breaking (12:1). In the marketplace it shows up as dishonest scales and defrauding (12:7); in their homes, as creating idols from their silver (13:2); in worship, as refusing to acknowledge the source of divine blessings (13:5-6). Some aspect of Israel's lack of integrity lies at the core of every accusation speech in this section. In contrast, the Lord acts as the *faithful* One (11:12), the One who has staked his reputation on fulfilling his promises to the patriarchs (12:5). God's trustworthiness and patience have stood between this people and the appropriate judgment.

Symmetry, balance, and vivid imagery link the accusation (11:12—13:6) and judgment sections (13:7-16) in the artist's hands. The emphasis in this final accusation-judgment-salvation cycle has shifted to salvation as signaled by an oracle which highlights repentance (12:3-4, 6).

Indictment of Jezreel: No Integrity
Hosea 11:12—12:8

PREVIEW

The structure of this oracle resembles a large V, centered and balanced in God (12:5). Each outstretched arm, heavy with accusations, also displays a model of repentance. Unless Israel (Jezreel, 1:4) genuinely repents, the divine embrace will crush this sinful people.

The Hebrew writer links this prophetic word to Assyria in several ways. First, when the names of the two enslaving nations appear elsewhere in parallel lines in Hosea, the order is first Egypt, then Assyria. Here the writer reverses the order, pointing to *Assyria* as the primary reference point. Second, *the east wind* (12:1) refers to Assyria. Third, 12:3-4, 7-8 frames the underlying moral pattern of Jacob's Mesopotamian (Assyrian) experience, now being duplicated (Gen. 28–31).

A thorny problem appears in the double reference to Judah (11:12; 12:2). The problem does not lie in the fact that Judah is mentioned, since that has happened in each of the two preceding subsections. Translators and commentators puzzle over whether to read both as positive statements, both as negative statements, or the first as negative and the second as positive.

OUTLINE

Lies, Deceit, and Violence, 11:12—12:2

Jacob, a Model Repentant? 12:3-4

Remember Me, Your Rescuer? 12:5

True Repentance, 12:6

My Hands Are Clean. Look! 12:7-8

EXPLANATORY NOTES

Lies, Deceit, and Violence 11:12—12:2

The words *no integrity* do not appear in this section, though in contrast, Judah is credited with still being *faithful* (the cognate verb). The concept is carried by the more concrete language of *lies* and *deceit*. The term for *lie* elsewhere serves to depict a gaunt, starved person (Job 16:8; Ps. 109:24). The form or skeleton is present, but the substance has wasted away. Appearance and reality do not correspond. The term for *deceit* denotes spoken misrepresentation. Here it has a twist to it. *False balances* (12:7; cf. Prov. 11:1) may have counterweights too heavy (when buying) or too light (when selling). The claim (to balance) and the reality do not agree. Deceit shades the truth.

God is literally *encircled* by Israel's falsehood. No norm for truth remains in the people's consciousness. They refuse to search out the true God. Every issue—whether in commerce, society, or personal life—is treated according to how it will benefit them. Truth is honored relative to its benefits. As a result, religious activities take on the same tainted commercial flavor. Sacrifices, designed to signal repentance and forgiveness, are not attached to deep sorrow over sin. Even worship, then, becomes a commodity of trade with God.

This interpreter prefers to read Hosea 11:12b as:

> *While Judah continues to have dominion with God* [cf. NRSV note],
> *And is faithful with the holy ones.*

Two arguments favor this translation. First, recognition of some fine points of Hebrew grammar serves to accent the contrast between Ephraim and Judah. Second, the reference to Judah needs to be linked to 12:4, which illustrates it. The nation of Judah is like the patriarch Jacob. Certainly, neither was faultless. But in their wrestling with God, both prevailed in repentance and persistent prayer (Gen. 32). In that respect, both the Southern Kingdom and the patriarch Jacob are models of what is possible when God's people face the truth about themselves and their relationships.

The *holy ones* (11:12b) are probably godly models scattered through Judah's history. These could be people at large (Ps. 16:3), kings (1 Kings 15:5, 14; 22:43), Levites (Num. 3:12-13; 1 Chron. 15:11-15; 2 Chron. 35:3), Nazirites (Amos 2:11-12), or prophets (2 Kings 4:9; cf. "holy ones" as angels, Dan. 7–8). This interpretation fits the use of the model of Jacob, from which Hosea is about to draw meaning for contemporary Israel.

Ephraim's national and international policies are ringed with deceit. Social havoc and lies increase. These further feed distrust, create violence, and disrupt normal life. In desperation, the nation pursues survival as its primary goal. That goal is ephemeral. Like the dry *east wind* from the desert, representing Assyria, it brings only sterility and death.

The ultimate deception occurs when Israel makes a treaty with Assyria. Numerous copies of such treaties are available from that day, though we have no record of this specific treaty. Assyria, the dominant nation, no doubt imposed the terms of the relationship and offered protection. Israel would have agreed to pay tribute, support Assyrian war efforts in the area, perhaps to provide a contingent for the Assyrian armed forces, to offer assistance to Assyria's allies, and to oppose Assyria's enemies (cf. 2 Kings 15:19-20, 29-30; 16:5-18; 17:3-6; 18–19). Israel would also have sworn by all her gods that, should she violate the oath and terms of the treaty, they and the Assyrian gods would speak the death sentence over her.

At the very moment Israel is negotiating with Assyria for her life, she is quietly making overtures to *Egypt* (Hos. 12:1b). The act of sending *olive oil* describes treaty making, not commercial transactions. The occasion for this prophetic attack against Israel may be the treachery described in 2 Kings 17:3-5. Shalmaneser, king of Assyria, reacted like one of his Assyrian predecessors did when he was similarly betrayed:

> When he (Yashub-Addu) became an ally, he swore an oath to me in the temple of Adad. . . . Moreover, I swore an oath to him. . . . (Nevertheless,) having now become my enemy, he has been following the man of Kakmu. He becomes the ally of a king and swears an oath, (then) he be-

comes the ally of a(nother) king and swears an oath, while becoming an enemy of the first king with whom he was allied. . . . When he moves up (for battle), you will he[ar] all that I am doing in his land. (*ANET*: 628)

Shalmaneser's revenge would be sweet to himself but bitter to the Israelites; after three years of siege, Samaria would fall under the Assyrian weapons of destruction and death.

The initial accusation is summed up by God announcing that he *has a court case against Judah*, and *will punish Jacob*. The distinction between God's treatment of Judah and Israel is important. Judah is not yet at the stage where punishment is to be meted out. Yet Judah is called to account for herself. Jacob's deeds have already been named and found wanting. The Northern Kingdom has pressed ahead in moral and spiritual degeneration.

Jacob, a Model Repentant?   12:3-4

Jacob was the patriarch of renown in Israel. The Northern nation was known by the name Jacob (12:2b). In addition, the traditions of Jacob were popular in Bethel and Samaria because the patriarch spent much of his time in that part of the country *[Jacob and Isaac, p. 389]*.

In one quick motion, Hosea sweeps into a single reference the person Jacob and the nation which identified with him. The historical context for the patriarchal events is Genesis 32–33 and 35:1-15. Three events from Jacob's story are here conflated into two verses.

Jacob lived up to his name, Deceiver. The recital of the events of his life reveals of a nearly unbroken series of deceptions. Symbolically, Hosea gathers up the strands of deception in the phrase: *In the womb he deceives his brother* (cf. Hos. 12:3, NIV note; Gen. 25:21-34).

In the prime of life, Jacob wrestled with God until God was prepared to grant him the blessing which he tried to obtain by trickery (Gen. 32:22-32). The blessing has been legitimated through what must be understood as deep remorse and thorough repentance. *He wept and he [God] showed him mercy* (Hos. 12:4b). Jacob's prayer, uttered in great fear and distress (cf. Gen. 32:9-12), captures the spirit of contrition and dependence which pleases God.

Only such life-changing repentance can result in a new self-disclosure of God, as *at Bethel* (cf. Gen. 35:1-7). If Israel is to have any hope for a future in the land, it will require similar repentance and submission. Lies, deception, injustice—these draw the clouds of curse and destruction over the nation. False and foreign gods and their idols must be demolished if God is to speak kindly with them again (cf. Gen. 35:2-5).

Remember Me, Your Rescuer? 12:5

The pillar around which this prophetic oracle moves is the declaration of the divine name. At Bethel, God disclosed himself to Jacob as El-Shaddai (God Almighty, Gen. 28:3). Now God declares his name to be *Yahweh, God of Hosts (Armies)*. The change in God's self-designation recalls God's self-revelation to Moses prior to the exodus event:

> I am the LORD (Yahweh). I appeared to Abraham, Isaac, and Jacob as God Almighty (El Shaddai), but by my name "the Lord (Yahweh)" I did not make myself known to them. (Exod. 6:2-3)

So, two things have changed. First, the name *Yahweh* now represents God in his covenant promise-fulfilling activity. Israel of the exodus as well as Israel of Hosea's day is being addressed by their covenant Lord. His promises as well as his threats are being realized in their experience. This is the One who is inviting Israel to return.

Second, the additional description, *God of Armies*, addresses Israel's national existence in a new situation. The name carries at least two connotations of significance for Israel. One is that in the cosmologies of the ancient Near East, the sun, moon, planets, and stars were the host of heaven (cf. Deut. 4:19; 2 Kings 23:4-5). They were frequently the object of worship. Therefore, when God declares himself *the God of Armies*, he announces his sovereignty over the objects of Israel's false worship. The name *God of Armies* also trumpets his control over every army of this world. If the nation remains unrepentant, God will signal the armies he chooses to overwhelm his people with judgment.

The Lord is the fixed point around which the world turns. Will Israel understand? Will they repent in dust and ashes?

True Repentance 12:6

God is explicit about repentance.

> *Repent* under God's care;
> *Restore* right relationships;
> *Rely* constantly on God.

The Hebrew word order gives emphasis to the clause *But as for you*. Returning to God requires that they rid themselves of the accumulated baggage of foreign gods. It will include a rediscovery of intimacy with their covenant Lord. Frequently such fundamental repentance takes time—time to understand the depths of one's sin and the extent to which it has captured the mind and heart. It is as though Israel is asked to retrace her steps through the wilderness, back to Sinai. There, separated from the paganism to which she has become accustomed, God will again embrace her with his love. And Israel will respond with new affection and praise (cf. Hos. 2:14-23).

Repentance and restitution are closely linked. Genuine repentance presses forward to restore the relationships that have been severed or distorted. Returning to God carries with it concrete responses to people. These are given substance and form in the words *covenant faithfulness* and *justice*. These are faith acts.

The third faith act of a repentant Israel will be to rely on God. The Hebrew word is *wait!* Throughout its history, Israel has proven herself fickle. The flip-flop in alliances between Assyria and Egypt is a case in point. At the national level, social disruption and greed prevail. Power and force speak loudest. The weak have no voice. How different from the design God had for his people (Exod. 21-23)!

Wait continuously on your God! Their faith will develop only over time and with testing. To this point they have not persisted long enough to establish a mature trust in God.

My Hands Are Clean. Look! 12:7-8

The close of this symmetrical accusation oracle focuses on the twin sins of injustice and arrogance. Injustice takes the form of economic deceit and oppression. The *deceit* of the earlier accusation (11:12a) assumes fuller shape in this segment of the literary mirror image (12:7) [*Literary Patterns, p. 391*]. The kind of sins which are tearing at society are *deceitful balances*, dishonest scales. Indeed, defrauding people has become a badge of honor. Overcharging, shortchanging, poor-quality products, exorbitant interest rates, foreclosing on loans—these all fit the category of sin known as *oppression*. And the nation has learned to accept oppressive practices as legitimate. The economic system is justified and validated by the benefits it delivers. Sins of greed are compounded by Israel's arrogance (12:8).

Furthermore, the economic system pays off handsomely for the aggressive entrepreneur. From its own testimony, we learn that Israel attributes its wealth to hard work. The statements are telling commentary on Israel's condition: *I have become rich! I achieved prosperity for myself! Regarding all I worked so hard for, no one will find anything wrong in me which is sinful!* (12:8)

Israel has fallen headlong into the deceitful quagmire of riches. Instead of acknowledging that the bounties of the land come from God, Israel takes credit for good crops and fertile herds and flocks. God anticipated this perversion and warned the people of the temptation (cf. Deut. 8:10-18). Even the warning is not enough. In addition, the people have devised systems of trade and commerce as well as justice which favor the wealthy (cf. Amos 2:6-8; 5:10-15; 8:4-6). Inequity, unfair labor laws, disproportionate taxation of the poor, a justice system run by the powerful—all these discriminate against the average person and vindicate the oppressors.

Probably their boasts are sincere. They believe what they are saying. The structures of society have become so infused with oppression and injustice that only an outsider or one walking in the counsel of God might recognize the nature and extent of the inequities. They confuse what is legal with what is moral. Their eyes are blind to poverty; the claims and policies of the state deafen their ears to the cries of the oppressed.

No integrity! is a penetrating indictment against the nation. Yet God's hands are still outstretched in mercy.

Judgments on Jezreel: No Integrity

Hosea 12:9—13:16

PREVIEW

The preceding accusation speech addressed societal structures, policies, and practices. Now God issues threats of judgment, primarily for cultic deviations. Here there is no plea for repentance, so prominent in the previous oracle. Only one word of hope (12:9) breaks the flow of judgment on Ephraim (Israel, Jezreel, 1:4).

The chiastic structure of the first judgment oracle (12:9—13:8) draws attention to God's extraordinary deliverance of his enslaved people from Egypt [*Literary Patterns, p. 391; Accusation-Judgment-Salvation Oracles, p. 372*]. At the center, Hosea's finger points toward Israel's total misunderstanding and misrepresentation of God's grace. Privilege and position generously given to Ephraim have come to be taken for granted.

The second judgment oracle takes us into the shadowy under-world, where Israel has taken refuge from her Judge. God proves himself superior to all gods, including Sea, Death, and Hades—which in the Ugaritic literature conquer even the Canaanite god of fertility (13:9-16) [Canaanite Fertility Myth, p. 376].

OUTLINE

Once More from Egypt, but in Reverse, 12:9—13:8

12:9-10	God: The Good Old Days
12:11-13	Hosea: Remember Where . . . ?
12:14	Hosea: Payment in Full
13:1-3	Hosea: They Kiss Calves! . . . ?
13:4-8	God: Let Me Refresh Your Memory

Not Even in Hell! 13:9-16

13:9-11	God: I'm Your Nemesis, Israel
13:12-13	Hosea: A Fetus Bloated on Sin
13:14	God: No Place to Hide
13:15-16	Hosea: Stripped and Vivisectioned

EXPLANATORY NOTES:

Once More from Egypt, but in Reverse 12:9—13:8

12:9-10 God: The Good Old Days

The exodus is the supreme act of divine deliverance [Exodus Tradition, p. 384]. However, here it serves as a historical reference point rather than a paradigm of God's redemption. The Hebrew reads: I am Yahweh your God from the land of Egypt. Some translators (such as NIV) supply the additional who brought you, on the assumption that this text abbreviates the common saying. Egypt, however, here serves as the reference point of new beginnings. Such newness should characterize the nation. The annual celebration of the appointed festival (s.), likely the Passover, commemorates that new beginning. Indeed, God's promise for the future—the single word of hope in this oracle—is symbolized by a return to that honeymoon experience. Restoration will occur when they return to the dependence they experienced in the wilderness [Tabernacles, p. 396].

In their dependence, Israel learned to rely on God's guidance through his prophetic messengers (12:10). The messages may not all have been equally clear, coming in speech, *visions,* or parables (comparisons; cf. Num. 12:6-8). Yet they offered the nation direction along the way. The plural, *prophets,* points beyond the exodus and wilderness events themselves. *Prophets* were God's special instruments in providing guidance in matters not part of the law, or in issues that were not answerable by a simple yes or no, as provided by the Urim and Thummim (Num. 27:21; Deut. 18:9-22; 33:8). Since the Northern Kingdom did not possess the high priest's Urim and Thummim, they depended more on the prophetic word.

The Northern prophetic tradition consists more of prophetic accusation and denunciation than of assurances of blessing and hope. Elijah's and Elisha's lives and ministries illustrate the ambivalent and even hostile attitude Northern Israelite kings had toward God's prophets. Ahab summed up the traditional feeling when he addressed Elijah as "you troubler of Israel" (1 Kings 18:17). When Amos the Judean traveled to the North to unburden himself of the divine word, he too was rejected (Amos 7:12-13).

12:11-14 Hosea: Remember Where . . . ?

Two prophetic units (12:11-14; 13:1-3) form the center of this pericope. Both condemn Israel's worship. Both originate with Hosea, since God is referred to in the third person (he). They differ in that the first unit addresses the inadequacy of worship at the holy places where the Lord is worshiped. The second unit turns the listener's attention to the centers of Baal worship.

The first unit (12:11-14; Heb. 12:12-15) is notoriously difficult. Perhaps Hosea's very artistry creates the problems for the modern exegete. He delights in repetition of words and sounds:

gil'ad—bagilgal—kegallim	Gilead—in Gilgal—like piles
zibehu—mizbehotam	they sacrifice—their altars
śaday—śedeh	[furrows of the] field—field [of Aram]
be'iśśah—be'iśśah	for a wife—for a wife
šamar—nišmar	he tended/remained—he was tended/guarded
benabi'—benabi'	by a prophet—by a prophet
he'elah—'alayw	[Yahweh] brought up—upon him

Worship dominates this text unit. In God's economy, the prophetic religious model stands in stark contrast to Israel's preoccupation with the cult, represented by sacrifices and festivals. Focus on the cult fails to direct Israel to the truth regarding God and itself. If the nation is to survive, it must return to the guidance given through Moses.

Two geographical centers represent the totality of Israel located on both sides of the Jordan. The reference to Gilead (12:11) lacks interpretive context. In Hosea, the word *wickedness (iniquity)* takes on the connotation of idolatry (10:8; cf. 1 Sam. 15:23; Isa. 41:29; 66:3). Israel's religious perversions have produced a people who resemble the god they worship. They are *hollow, without substance, ineffective, worthless,* and *come to nothing.*

Gilgal was a major center of Yahweh worship for the Northern Kingdom (cf. notes on Hos. 4:15; 9:15). The imagery merges time, history, and nature's strength. Gilgal will become *like stone heaps.* The action of wind and water over the centuries will so level the city that future farmers will work the land where streets, houses, and altars once stood. The plow jerks as it unearths a pile of stones. Gilgal's altars have become a nuisance even to later generations.

Hosea 12:13-14 contrasts Jacob, the example of human ingenuity and scheming, with the model of Moses, God's spokesman and servant. Jacob pursued security in the *field* (NRSV: *land*), the country of Aram. Genesis 29 records how he indentured himself for fourteen years to obtain his two wives, Leah and Rachel. The storyteller delights in explaining how Jacob's wives brought with them Laban's household gods (Gen. 31:33-34; 35:2-4). Though Jacob deceived his father and escaped, he ended in voluntary enslavement and under the influence of foreign gods.

The reference to Moses as the *prophet* underscores Moses' intimacy with God (Hos. 12:13; cf. Num. 12:6-8) as well as his authoritative teaching (Deut. 18:9-22). The concluding line, *by a prophet he was guarded,* undoubtedly refers to the clear, directive, caring leadership Moses provided through the wilderness years. It may also refer to his intercession by which Israel was spared the full judgment of God for their disobedience in building and worshiping the golden calf (Exod. 32–33). Hosea opens the door for the Northern Kingdom to return, but only on the twin conditions of repentance and obedience.

13:4 Hosea: Payment in Full

Hollow and idolatrous worship vexes God's Spirit and gives *bitter offense* (Hos. 12:14). The verb, capturing God's agitation and anger at Israel for worshiping other gods, appears frequently in Deuteronomy and Kings (cf. Deut. 4:25; Judg. 2:12; 1 Kings 22:53;

2 Kings 17:11). The Lord's concern is not with mere deviations in worship form or style. God has been demoted in Ephraim's heart. For that, judgment will land on them (cf. Amos 3:2; Gal. 6:7).

There is no need to detail the punishment. It is enough to know that payment will be made in full. Israel's perverted worship grows into two cancers. The first is *violence* (*crimes,* lit.: *bloods*) against people and society. The blood of the slain and the cries of the oppressed merge before God. The inhabitants must purge the land of these sins. Israel will receive payment in kind, with violence.

Perverted worship produces a second cancer. Whether through deliberate ridicule, or actions which besmirch his reputation, God's name has been demeaned before the nations (cf. Ezek. 36:20-23). God will vindicate himself. Ephraim must suffer a corresponding punishment of shame and disgrace. God's honor is at stake. In the end the nations will recognize that Israel is receiving her due.

13:1-3 Hosea: They Kiss Calves! . . . ?

Hosea catches his breath and wheels about to attack the pagan centers of worship. These undoubtedly include the high places devoted to Baal and the temple of Baal in Samaria (cf. 1 Kings 16:32). Hosea flashes Israel's past, present, and future before the nation. This prophetic unit begins with acclaim for Ephraim's great beginnings (Hos. 13:1a). Since then, however, their life has all been downhill (13:1b-2). Catastrophe fills the horizon (13:3).

Hosea 13:1-2 traces Israel's decline by reference to the largest Northern tribe, Ephraim. In Genesis, the Joseph story depicts Ephraim as the youngest family member whose descendants later develop into a tribe (Gen. 48). Authority in patriarchal society lodged primarily in birth order. The last should expect to be least. God, however, frequently bypassed the natural right of the firstborn: Abraham, Isaac, Jacob, Judah, Ephraim, Moses, Saul, and David were not firstborn sons. The reference to Ephraim's role in Israel, therefore, reminds the nation that the sovereign Lord chose and has been directing his people.

Following the birth of the nation, the tribe of Ephraim soon established itself in a leadership role. It spoke with acknowledged authority. Joshua, Moses' successor, was its first and greatest military leader (Num. 13:8, 16). Ephraim's next acclaimed leader was Jeroboam I (1 Kings 11:26), who led the revolt against the house of David and reinforced the division of the kingdom by modifying their religion.

Ephraim's downward spiral reads like the inscription on a tombstone: *He incurred guilt through Baal and died* (Hos. 13:1b).

The epitaph-like language highlights two elements. The central factor in the tribe's and the Northern Kingdom's decline was Baal worship. That was the main offense. The *he died* draws attention to Baal worship as the violation of covenant. Wijngaards has shown how the language of dying and killing serves to describe the delivery of judgments resulting from covenant violations. Ephraim's death is marked by the nation's exposure to the curses of the Mosaic covenant. These have been visited upon the Northern Kingdom ever since Jeroboam I violated the conditions imposed on him by God at his accession to the throne (1 Kings 11:37-39; 12:25-33; 13:33-34).

The present shows no change in their behavior. The nation's sins heaped up in their high places have increased to mountainous proportions. The phrase *they added to sinning* implies that they have kept on wandering in search of God but have constantly chosen the wrong way. They are stuck records, mired in deep ruts from which they cannot turn. The specific form of that sinning is spelled out in the following lines.

Israel's turning from God and missing the right way expresses itself in the creation of idols. The nation turns to things they have made. Their skilled artisans use the most advanced technology to shape their silver into images. The gods deserve the best!

A taunt by some worshiper of the Lord captures their sin in vivid color:

> Sacrificers of people;
> They kiss calves.

God intended animals for sacrifice, people to love and care for (cf. notes on Hosea 5:7 about child sacrifice). Idolatry has perverted the nation; they have lost their sense of values. The bull-calf images at Dan and Bethel are the product of human hands. But this people has degenerated so much that they cannot even recognize the absurdity of reverencing the creature *[Bull Calves, p. 375]*. The taunt stands as a commentary on the perversion of the human calling to rule over the animals so powerfully depicted in the creation account.

Therefore (13:3) shifts the reader's attention to the future judgment. In the previous prophetic speech unit (12:10-14), the people were described as without substance. Here their transient and hollow existence occupies four scenes:

morning mist
dew which the sun burns off
chaff chased across the threshing floor
smoke curling out through an open window

Each simile points to something real but fleeting, related to the four seasons of the year. Thus they speak of a continuing condition. The progression is from the valley mist, to the dew deposited on the ground but quickly evaporated by the summer sun, to the dried chaff of autumn, and finally to the indoor winter fire, foreshadowing judgment. God, the unseen Bringer of bountiful harvest, exists without material images; the false gods and their idols of wood, bronze, and silver—these all are without substance, empty. Those who trust in the God beyond nature need no idols. They have evidence of the reality of their God in life experiences. The national deliverance from Egypt vindicates those who trust in him.

13:4-8   God: Let Me Refresh Your Memory

The Lord sets himself in sharp contrast to Israel's shadowy existence. As in Hosea 12:9, God's self-characterization of Deliverer and Caregiver emphasizes that he has been Israel's God from the time they left the land of Egypt. In its long history, Israel has never been rescued by any other deity, as illustrated by the stories during the time of the judges and the monarchy (cf. Judg. 6; 8:33-35; 10:1-16; 2 Sam. 7; 1 Kings 17-19; 2 Kings 18-19).

Moses had warned the people against claiming all the good things as the product of their hands (13:6; cf. Deut. 8:10-20). The pattern leading to forgetting God (cf. Jer. 3:21) is the same in both texts:

satisfaction with good things
pride: my power and my hands have produced this wealth
forgetting the Lord.

That too is part of the big lie: prosperity is not the guarantee for security, health, and leisure. The only available antidote is to remove the prosperity and draw the people back into dependence on their Lord. The LIE will be exposed through further judgment.

Judgments by covenant overlords are frequently compared to attacks by beasts of prey (Hos. 13:7-8; Hillers: 54-56). Israel's foundational covenant documents threaten to treat disobedience that way as well (Lev. 26:22; Deut. 32:24). Ravenous beasts and deadly serpents come to symbolize the land under curse. To annihilate all the inhabitants at one time would leave uninhabited land to the animals (Deut. 7:22). Such exposure to threat would have been a curse and contrary to God's design for his people. God's people were meant to rule rather than to fear the animals. Thus in describing the coming judgment as a ravenous attack by God, Hosea is presenting it as a covenant curse.

Lest Israel interpret the attacking armies as the servants of another God, the Lord explains in advance that it is his doing. The Israelites shall not indulge in yet another form of the LIE. Throughout history they have misinterpreted the gifts of God; he will ensure that they understand the Lord's withdrawal of those gifts and the ravages of judgment that follow.

Not Even in Hell! 13:9-16

13:9-11 God: I'm Your Nemesis, Israel

A statement of divine intent heads this oracle (13:9). Israel is rushing toward national suicide. The Hebrew word for *ruin* (NRSV: *I will destroy you*) describes the act of taking something beautiful, strong, functional, or moral and so distorting it that it becomes ugly, weak, useless, or corrupt. It points to the end of national existence, but it also turns our thoughts to the purposes for which God called his people. He called the nation to be the Lord's "treasured possession out of all the peoples" (Exod. 19:5-6), to walk in his ways. The people, however, wandered from those paths.

Israel rejects the commands which lead to truth, holiness, community, and security. Their inner life as well as their international policies are corrupt. Two examples of that corruption and its effects follow (Hos. 13:10-13).

Israel's king has become the primary symbol of national hope. In a few carefully chosen lines, God unscrolls the sorry history of the monarchy in the Northern Kingdom. The nation resented the insecurity of depending on leaders (judges) whom God chose. So under Samuel, they petitioned for a king "like other nations" (1 Sam. 8; 12). Such a leader would be able to fight their battles and provide security for the people (cf. 1 Sam. 8:20). In that respect, their request was a rejection of God as King.

Still, the monarchy was a gracious gift, a concession to serve a people of little faith. Once established, it would continue if and only if the people and king obeyed God (1 Sam. 12:14-15). Disobedience would set God's hand against his people. The history of the monarchy, particularly in the North, was one long decline. Apparently, at the time this prophecy was spoken, Israel's king had been assassinated or deposed: *Where now is your king?* The removal of the king was God's way of showing the futility of trusting in human resources. That was the act of the One against whom the nation had taken its stand.

13:12-13 Hosea: A Fetus Bloated on Sin

Ephraim's sin, in the matter of the monarchy, was long-standing. The words *wrapped up* and *treasured up* (Hos. 13:12) denote a huge vault filled with packages of carefully wrapped and preserved sin. Israel's national archives contain the record of her failure. Monarch after monarch has added to the sins against God. What Israel has viewed as her glory, God declares to be her shame. This severely deformed fetus will never see the light of God's day of salvation.

When it comes to the time of crisis (*birth*, 13:13), the nation cannot take the appropriate step of repenting and throwing herself in a new dependence on God. The people and their leaders are incapable of changing course. Having come to full term, this child remains in *the womb*. Hope has vanished.

13:14 God: No Place to Hide

The symmetry of the verse is a work of art; its meaning is unclear. A straightforward reading of the Hebrew would take the form of the NIV translation. The ambiguity lies in that the context is one of judgment. So the positive statements,

> *I will ransom them from the power of the grave;*
> *I will redeem them from death,*

seem out of place. This discord with the context is increased by the concluding line of the verse:

> *I will have no compassion.*

Two possible solutions commend themselves to this writer.

The simplest way of resolving the discord is to read the first two lines as questions (NRSV). The Hebrew would permit that reading, though there is no contextual or grammatical cue that signals it. The rhetorical questions imply the answer "Of course not!" The judgment

is assured. Rescue at this late date and under these acute circumstances is out of the question. What follows, then, is a call to *Death*
(*Mot*) and *Sheol* (the *Grave*) to bring on their weapons of destruction
against a faithless Israel. *Death* and *Sheol* are, in this interpretation,
the agents of God in judging his people.

However, the preferred interpretation is to view *Mot* (*Death*) and
Sheol (the *Grave*, the insatiable monster) as representing the
Canaanite god, Mot *[Canaanite Fertility Myth, p. 376]*. Sheol is on
occasion used as a literary parallel to Mot in the OT (cf. 1 Sam. 2:6;
Job 17:13-16; Ps. 49:14; Prov. 1:12; Song of Sol. 8:6; Isa. 28:15,
18). In the Baal myth, Mot and Baal engage in life-and-death combat.
Mot slays Baal and takes him down into the netherworld (the grave).

If the references to *Mot* (Death) and *Sheol* (Grave) in Hosea
13:14 are to the monster who devours people, then the verse asserts
God's power over all the forces of darkness. Nothing, not even the
Canaanite god, Mot-Sheol, can control Israel's future *[Yahweh-Baal
Conflict, p. 398]*. The weapons of Mot-Sheol (plagues and destruction) are ineffective against the power of God. Unlike the psalmists,
whose confidence lay in the Lord's power to redeem them from Sheol (Ps. 16:10; 49:14-15; 86:13), Hosea's word is a dire threat. God
himself will *redeem* or *rescue* those claimed by Death-Sheol—to
bring judgments against them! Even the place of the dead is no refuge for a disobedient Israel (cf. Amos 9:2). In this matter, Amos and
Hosea speak with one voice. The remainder of the judgment oracle
(Hos. 13:14e-16) pictures the nature of that judgment.

13:14e-16 Hosea: Stripped and Vivisectioned

The reason given for God's violent attack on Israel is given: *Because you are against me, against your Helper, your God* (13:16a).
The rebellion is not a one-time act; the verb *marah* denotes a persistent stubbornness, digging in the heels against the advice or instructions of a parent or of God. Israel has had a long history of such rebellion, such obstinate refusal to follow what they know to be God's way.

The severity of the judgment is represented by the opening line.
Translated word for word, it reads:

Sorrow (repentance, compassion) is sheltered from my eyes. (13:14e)

Nothing Israel can do at this point will reverse the certainty of the
judgment nor reduce the severity of the punishment.

Hope Beyond Forgiveness?

Hosea 14:1-8

PREVIEW

These salvation oracles come in two parts [Accusation-Judgment-Salvation Oracles, p. 372]. The first (14:1-3) gives Hosea's advice to Israel as to how to deal with their sins. The second (14:4-8) describes the Lord's restorative love. The text does not detail the connections with the preceding outpouring of judgment. *I will have no compassion* (13:14e) is so definitive that we must assume salvation follows judgment rather than preventing or substituting for it. We proceed with that understanding. The Assyrian whirlwind has brought Israel to her senses.

OUTLINE

Hosea's Counsel, 14:1-3
14:1-2a	Return!
14:2b-3	Start with "I Sinned, Please Forgive"

The Physician-Suitor Says, 14:4-7
14:4-5a	I Will Heal, I Will Love Her
14:5b-7	She's Beautiful Beyond Words

God's Typescript for Israel, 14:8
14:8a	Accept Me for Who I AM
14:8b-d	In Sickness and in Health

EXPLANATORY NOTES

The outline captures some of the intricate development and symmetry of the text. Hosea draws together various strands associated elsewhere with the names and significance of his three children. He also brings salvation full circle in the chiasm of this concluding prophetic word [Literary Patterns, p. 391].

Hosea's Counsel 14:1-3

14:1-2a Return!

Salvation is a sovereign act of God. The presence of sin demands repentance. The restoring work of God meets experientially with human rebellion and failure in repentance, confession, and forgiveness.

The common Hebrew term for repentance is *to turn* or *return* (14:1a, 2a). The concept is rooted in the basic imagery of the life of faith as a way in which one walks. It represents a course of life, a pattern of relationships with God and people. When God's people "walk after other gods" or "turn aside from the way," the required corrective is to *turn/return* to God.

Hosea advises Israel to act without reservation (14:1). They are to *return all the way to the Lord* (cf. Deut. 4:30; 30:2; Amos 4:6, 8-10; Joel 2:12). Partial repentance will not do. Limited return has characterized Israel's history. Whether in the conflict between Elijah and the prophets of Baal, or in the forced reforms of King Jehu, Israel's *repentance* was superficial or selective. Yes, Jehu destroyed Baal worship in Israel, but he failed to remove the golden calves at Bethel and Dan (2 Kings 10:28-29). He did not cut the lure which continuously drew the nation back into idolatry. The sins of deepest significance remained untouched. They were the obstacles over which the people *stumbled* (Hos. 14:1).

14:2b-3 Start with "I Sinned, Please Forgive"

Hosea calls on the nation to confess the truth about its spiritual condition (14:2b-3; cf. Jer. 3:25).

Israel's life has been a lie. Theirs is a history of deceit, false promises, covenant breaking, dishonesty among themselves, and deliberate violation of God's instruction (Hos. 11:12—13:16). Even their way of thinking about the Lord is twisted. If they sacrifice enough bulls, they think, God will be pleased. That may have been true of Baal worship, but it did not capture the way of Israel's God.

Hosea's call is not for the sacrifice of more bulls. Salvation depends on Israel making an about-face and speaking the truth to God. The details of what God desires are spelled out in two positive statements and three negative ones:

> forgive
> accept
>   and we will offer

> not Assyria
> not our military
> not idols
>> you who care for orphans

Israel's downfall has been their sins and their insincere or superficial repentance (14:1). The positive statements of repentance correspond to the analysis of the problem. The Lord must be the object of their return. Their lives need reorientation in him. The quick "Forgive us, Lord, for what sins we may have committed" of the past must become both more comprehensive and more specific.

Their confession of sin has become more comprehensive. It strongly emphasizes, through Hebrew word order, the *totality* of their *iniquity* (NRSV: *all guilt*). Everything that has been a source of stumbling needs forgiveness. Only the *good* can replace it, the active, conscious good. It is not enough to avoid evil. Israel knows the good by reflecting on God's instruction, both as it came to Israel from Mt. Sinai and as it came through the prophetic tradition.

In contrast with large numbers of sacrifices, this confession offers to God promises of faithfulness described as *bulls represented by the lips* (Heb.; NRSV: *the fruit of our lips*) *[Bovine Imagery, p. 374]*. Such vows of new allegiance become access points for a new affection and devotion to the covenant Lord. Words express understanding and commitment. The Israelites have been substituting animals for genuine and deep confession. When they return to their God, that faith will show itself in humbly acknowledging their true condition. Hosea now prompts Israel in choosing words to fit such a genuine confession (14:3). Israel will make new vows, vows they will keep by offering what their lips have promised.

The Israelites are to confess their own inadequacy, their vaunted pride, and their longing for independence from God (14:3a). If they say that the greatest nation of the world, Assyria, cannot *save* them, they admit that God's purposes will not see the light of day through human means. Neither Assyrian treaty assurances nor Israelite *horses* (cavalry) will accomplish God's design for the nation.

This confession also contains the admission that Israel has misunderstood the nature of her dilemma. She thought her most pressing problem lay in her conflict with other nations. The real problem is identified by Hosea: they have been neglecting God, defecting from the covenant, and sinning against the Lord.

Israel is also to promise to reject all idols, *the work of our hands* (14:3b). The phrase *our gods* (14:3b, Heb.) reminds us of the sin of

Aaron and Jeroboam I: both identified the bull calf (calves) as "your gods, O Israel, who brought you up out of the land of Egypt" (Exod. 32:8; 1 Kings 12:28). The people need to make a clean break with the paganism and polytheism around them.

The concluding line of Hosea 14:3 is puzzling. What thread of logic ties God's compassion toward the orphan to the promise to keep the second commandment: having no other gods? The connection may come from awareness that Israel's sin is so great and the punishment due them so severe, that only a God of immense compassion would turn and receive them again. If so, the extent of that compassion is marked by God's sensitivity to the voice of the lone orphan crying out for justice.

There is a reading this writer finds even more attractive. On occasions, a Hebrew relative clause may be separated from its antecedent by another element in the sentence. If we read this grammatical construction here, the text would be translated, *Never again will we say to the work of our hands, "Our God, by whom the fatherless experience compassion."* The Israelites, in turning to idols which represent God, have been addressing the idols as the Lord of the dispossessed and weak. An honest confession acknowledges its absurdity. Hence, Hosea urges the penitents to admit, *How ludicrous, how perverted our sinful ways have been! How could we ever have imagined that a god, created at our workbench, would possess the power and authority to repel oppressors and bring salvation to their victims?*

The Physician-Suitor Says 14:4-7

The language and imagery of this promise of restoration is fittingly drawn from nature. It is fitting because of the fertility cult from which Israel finds release. It is also apt because the language of nature is that of ideals—the garden of Eden and the Land of Promise. Both ideals are present in this picture of restoration [*Yahweh-Baal Conflict, p. 398*].

14:4-5a I Will Heal, I Will Love Her

Israel's repentance cannot in itself bring restoration from exile. Human repentance does not obligate God. The act of healing and restoring a scattered, sinful people roots in the Lord's unfailing love. That act comes to sinful Israel as a promise from their covenant Lord (cf. Deut. 30:1-10). God alone speaks the last word on Israel's future.

In Hosea, *healing* is associated with correction and discipline. The sinful nation has become subject to the Lord's discipline. That corporal correction appears in Hosea in the imagery of corrective punishment of children (cf. Hos. 11:3), and of exposure to beasts of prey which have mauled the nation (cf. 5:13—6:1).

Forgiveness is a gift; it comes to undeserving people. Lest Israel get the impression that God must respond to their repentance by restoring them, he points out that even their repentance is a gift of grace: *I will love them freely.* Healing from the ravages of sin comes from God. It grows out of his *restoring love (raham, mercy,* 14:3).

The Hebrew word used to depict Israel's *disloyalty* and sin is *mešubah,* meaning a *turning* (cf. 11:7) away from their covenant Lord. Despite Israel's repeated defection from their God, his restoring love refuses to be suppressed.

Two words have been used for love in Hosea. Initially, God rejected Israel under the name Lo-ruhamah (cf. 1:6-7). That refers to *compassion, restoring love.* When Hosea received the message to remarry Gomer (3:1), he is instructed to *love* her. This word for love describes the foundations of covenantal relationships (cf. Deut. 4:37; 5:10; 6:5; 7:9, 13). It represents the affection of choice, a willful act. God chooses to *love* (Hos. 14:4) his people so as to restore them to himself. That love knows no boundaries. It replaces the outpouring of divine wrath deserved by those who reject their covenant Lord.

God is the source of Israel's life. *Dew* appears mysteriously from clear skies, unlike rain, which was thought to be brought by the storm god, Baal. God can supply Israel's needs from apparent nothingness.

Here, then, is the source of fertility the nation has so eagerly been seeking. To find it, they have continuously turned to Baal. They have been attributing the Lord's harvests to Baal. Now they will come to recognize the truth about their prosperity as well as of the withheld harvests by which God has so frequently judged them.

14:5b-7 She's Beautiful Beyond Words

Ephraim is God's planting. The changes of subject point the reader to three aspects of new life within the restored people: their vitality, beauty, and bounty.

The *lily* grows in moist soil. God is the *dew* which causes it *to sprout, to break out everywhere through the forest floor* (NRSV: blossom). That is how he will bring exiled Israel back to life. In due time the nation will be revitalized. What has appeared dead, invisible to the naked eye, is really dormant, waiting for the Lord's watering.

In Hosea 9:16, Israel is compared to a grapevine whose roots are dried up. The vine withers, the fruit shrivels. The coming salvation depicts Israel as a *cedar of Lebanon*, striking its roots deep into the subsoil for stability and nourishment. Never again will such judgment be leveled against this people.

Israel's splendor shall be restored when the people return to the land. Three conjoined clauses depict her majesty. Each represents the beauty of a vital and magnificent plan. Israel is frequently depicted as a vineyard or grapevine (cf. Ps. 80:8-18; Isa. 5; Jer. 2:21; 12:10; Ezek. 19:10-14). Like a vine which grows anew from the buds each year, her *new growth shall shoot out*. In the Hebrew plant classification, the vine was regarded as a tree (Judg. 9; Ezek. 15, 17). The reestablished nation may also be compared to the *olive tree*. It provides a staple food (vegetable oil), is highly productive, remains attractively green year-round, and is capable of surviving even in extended periods of drought. The third tree with which Israel may be compared is the *fragrant cedar of Lebanon*. Its pleasing aroma refreshes body and mind. It envelopes the bystander with its beauty.

Why the comparison with trees? First, the imagery of nature moves far beyond the agricultural produce, so frequently associated with Baal worship. All the trees of this passage (cedar of Lebanon, pine/fir, olive), depicting Israel, retain their leaves or needles year-round, as does the *evergreen cypress* (Hos. 14:8). That reinforces the thought of a permanent restoration.

Second, the imagery of trees also draws attention to the inadequacies of Baal. He is a seasonal God, whose power varies with the rainfall and water supply throughout the year. Not so the Lord (14:8), nor his people (14:5-7).

Third, God's concern with Israel's fruitfulness includes the fruitfulness of all creation. Every living thing draws its life from God. Preoccupation with fertility supposedly from Baal detracts from God as the Lord of all creation. Baalism focuses on the limited world of crops, domesticated animals, and humans *[Yahweh-Baal Conflict, p. 398]*. Where is the rest of the created order, which was also blessed (Gen. 1:11-13)? The larger world is God's domain and is also the object of his grace. The promise to Abraham included a word of blessing on the whole world. In Israel's restoration from her captivity, God intends to fulfill that expectation.

The translation and interpretation of Hosea 14:7 (Heb.: 14:8) hinge on five features (bold) of Hebrew grammar and vocabulary:

*The ones who (were/are) **dwell(ing) in its shade will return.***
***They** will come to life (as) grain,*
*and **they** will sprout like the vine.*
***His** reputation will be like the wine of Lebanon.*

Except for the last sentence, the subjects are plural. All refer to this group of people who live in the shade of the tree previously referred to. The opening verb, *they will return*, is frequently regarded as a scribal error because of the difficulty it creates in interpretation. Rather than change the text, we propose this literal translation and an alternative interpretation.

Shade represents comfort; in the blazing heat of the Middle East, it may represent life itself. It is frequently essential to survival (cf. Jon. 4; Ps. 36:7; 121:5). Consequently, God himself is identified as a shade, a source of protection from the burning sun (Ps. 121:5). By extension, he can be described as a shade for the oppressed of Israel (Ps. 17:8; 57:1; 91:1; Isa. 25:4-5). That concept reaches into the political arena.

When a powerful king (or country) makes an alliance with a lesser political power, the less powerful is said to live in the shade of the superior (Isa. 30:1-3). Indeed, Ezekiel, prophesying some 150 years after Hosea, uses the imagery of the cedar of Lebanon (Assyria) giving shade to all the nations of the earth (31:6). Because of Assyria's pride, God sends it to destruction (31:7-16), to be joined by "its allies, those who lived in its shade among the nations" (31:17). By the same token, if a nation does not have an alliance requiring the return of political and economic refugees, these refugees are described as coming under the shade of the protective king or country where they find safety (Ezek. 31:6-7; Isa. 16:1-3).

This extension of the concept of shade into the covenantal sphere fits the text well. The ones who have been living in the shade of Israel prior to the exile of the Northern Kingdom are foreigners. They are the political and religious refugees from other countries. Israel's law protected such persons (Num. 15:13-16; Deut. 1:16). More than that, Israel was to love the resident aliens who had come to them (Deut. 10:18-19) because God loves them. By implication, Israel was not to repatriate refugees to foreign countries because they had come under the protection of God's people and covenant.

These foreigners are the ones intended by Hosea's reference to *those who were dwelling in his shade will return.* They have come under God's protection. They have come to honor Israel's God. When Israel went into exile, their source of protection disappeared.

So the Lord's judgment on his people had profound effects on an even larger group of people—Gentiles who had come to serve and worship God.

Israel's restoration to the land will provide a haven for Gentiles who wish to serve the Lord. This group of people is described as Israel's fertility. *They will be revived/restored as (representing, functioning as) grain* (Hos. 14:7b). It is this body of non-Israelites who *will sprout like the vine*, like Israel itself.

As a result of the gracious inclusion of these converts into the restored people of God, Israel's *reputation* in the world will flourish. It will have a bouquet richer than the superior wine of Lebanon. The bounty includes the spiritual bounty of non-Israelite peoples.

God's Typescript for Israel 14:8

Israel's request had been, "Please forgive our sins. We have acted independently of you. We have worshiped you as the god made by our own hands. Forgive, O Lord" (14:2-3).

The answer corresponds, in reverse order, to the three parts of Israel's confession and plea for forgiveness:

Israel's Plea	God's Response
(A) Restoration	(C') God disassociates himself from idols.
(B) Independence	(B') God promises his care.
(C) Idolatry	(A') God assures Israel of continued provision (security and fertility).

14:8a   Accept Me for Who I AM

The Hebrew of this verse lends itself to more than one interpretation. The alternatives are created by the opening line. How are we to understand the relationship between God's cry to Ephraim and what follows? The NIV has isolated the first statement (spoken as *I . . . you*) from what follows (spoken as *I . . . he*). The alternative here proposed is to read it similarly to the NRSV: *"O Ephraim, I'll never again accept comparison with idols!" I answer.*

The words of God to Ephraim take up an untranslatable Hebrew idiom. The idiom represents an emphatic denial of any correspondence between the Lord and idols. God brooks no rivals. Idolatry needs to be rooted out. Until Israel understands and accepts that reality, she will remain under the corrective effect of the exile. Once and for all, restored Israel will be cured of idol worship (cf. 3:4). Her knowledge of God will be such that idolatry will finally become anathema to her. Israel (Gomer) will be restored to enjoy full marital intimacy (cf. 3:5).

14:8b In Sickness and in Health

I pay careful attention to him (NRSV: *look after you*; NIV: *care for him*). This reminds Israel that they have not been lost from God's sight. The verb translated *pay careful attention* nowhere contains the thought of *watch out for*, but it is still a source of comfort to the exiles. God has not turned his face away. He is looking for signs of repentance. He persists in waiting for his people to turn, fulfilling the words they have spoken (14:2b-3). His restoring love (*ruḥamah*) is patient and sure.

God as a *green cypress/pine/fir tree?* What a strange metaphor! Or, perhaps it is not so strange. The *tree* is green year-round, reminding Israel of the presence of God's life-giving power, even when Baal is dead. All their fruit is found in the Lord. As a source of blessing for others, Israel can draw only on God. All other resources will render Israel's effectiveness in the world null and void. Neither Baal worship nor any form of idolatry will serve the purpose of bringing God's promises to Abraham to fulfillment. Therefore, the identity and purpose of God's people grows from the recognition and acknowledgment that he is their sole Provider.

Surely Israel's focus has been too narrow, their vision too small. When God restores his people, he will open them to new dimensions of his rule and of their calling. The redemptive work of God does more than address Israel's sins; it opens the nation up to a new future in keeping with God's original design.

Restored Ephraim will become the means whereby the blessings of Abraham descend on the nations.

Hosea 14:9

Epilogue: A Word to the Wise

PREVIEW

These words could be read as a concluding comment to this third salvation oracle, inviting Israel to restored integrity. Then the conclusion
would match the opening word (14:1-2a) in mirror image.

This characteristic wisdom saying appears to have a more comprehensive sweep, comparable to the conclusion of Psalm 107:42-
43. It consists of two proverbs. In doubled question-and-answer form,
the first proverb urges the readers to understand their present predic-
ament. The second distinguishes the wise and foolish by whether
they walk or stumble in the ways of the Lord.

OUTLINE

The Way of the Wise, 14:9a-d

The Stumbling of the Foolish, 14:9e

EXPLANATORY NOTES
The Way of the Wise 14:9a-d

The epilogue offers concluding advice on how the readers should respond to the collection of messages first orally addressed to the Northern Kingdom. Those original readers, we have argued, are the Judeans, but the advice applies to readers at other times and places as well.

Earlier Israel was described as a *child without wisdom* (Hos. 13:13). Now Hosea appeals to the readers as adults capable of understanding the implications of God's actions as well as the meaning of his words. Wisdom, understanding, and knowledge are commended to the people as keys to unlock the secrets of God's deliverance. Israel has failed or refused to understand and heed God's warnings. Surely wisdom will guide Judah down a different path!

The questions *Who is wise . . . ? Who is understanding . . . ?* are not answered directly. But any Israelite, hearing these familiar lines, would instinctively respond, *The one who fears the Lord, that is the wise person, and the one who shuns evil has understanding* (cf. Job 28:28; cf. Ps. 34:7-14; Prov. 9:10).

The Stumbling of the Foolish 14:9e

This prophetic collection began with two people entering life together in marriage, a marriage destined for conflict, separation, and only much later, reconciliation and restoration. Foolish Israel walked away from God.

The book ends with a snapshot of two people on a journey. The righteous person walks confidently on the road leading to life; the sinner, the deliberate transgressor, stumbles and trips through a self-charted course.

The epilogue leaves us with the question: Will the reader grasp and appropriate the message of the book or turn from it?

THE TEXT IN BIBLICAL CONTEXT
Integrity

At root, the word *'emunah*, together with its cognates, speaks of *stability, reliability,* and *truth.* It defines the basis on which a relationship proceeds and builds. If trust is broken, suspicion pervades *every* word, act, and relationship. When trust is established and maintained, relationships become open, resistance to change decreases, and justice is practiced. Hosea points toward 'emet as the necessary "prerequisite for justice and righteousness" (*TDOT*, 1:313).

The family of words coming from the same root as 'emet (integrity) is particularly at home in expressions of worship (Psalms) and in the wisdom books (Job, Proverbs, Daniel). In Hosea 11:12—14:9, wisdom language is conspicuously present though not dominant: justice, legal charges, wisdom, the ways of the Lord.

The critique of the nation from the vantage point of integrity is developed largely by pointing to its absence rather than by analyzing its nature. Only the personal story of Jacob, the deceiver, serves to model what God wishes for the nation in this regard. It highlights what can occur to those whose past has been devoted to protecting themselves from the truth.

Israel does not resemble their God. The imagery of the ephemeral and temporary stands in stark contrast to 'emet (integrity). The people *feed on the wind* and *pursue the east wind*. The people have a short memory (13:6) and vacillate constantly (13:9-10). Israel is worthless (12:11), full of foolishness (13:13), turning even against the hand of their Helper (13:9). In their blinded sinfulness, they vaunt themselves with bombast and pride (12:8; 13:6). Israel possesses a fatal character flaw: the people lack integrity.

The consequence is a flood of divine wrath which matches the nation's sin. Appropriately, they *will be like the morning mist, the early dew, the chaff, or smoke* (13:3). All they have relied on for security— their treaties, wealth, sacrifices, many idols, kings, and children— these all will disappear when God withdraws his blessings and brings an *east wind from the desert* (13:15). That scorching east wind is an agent of death, figuratively as well as literally. The baked countryside will be further devastated by a nation blowing in from the east. Assyria will come plundering, destroying, killing.

Is God Obligated by Repentance?

No! Repentance on our part does not obligate God toward us. It does not dissolve or erase sin. It merely expresses the sinner's remorse over sin and the determination to chart a different course in the future. It is a sign of an attitude and intent. People rarely, if ever, plumb the depths of sin and the deceitfulness of the human heart (Jer. 17:9). So repentance cannot address either the full extent or the evil nature of sin.

Yet God forgives our sin. Forgiveness is a divine gift by which God removes from us the consequences of our sin (Ps. 103:7-14). Ultimately, God eradicated our sin by taking on himself our disobedience and wickedness. That is the picture of the Messiah which Israel saw in the prophetic pronouncements (Hos. 14:4-8; cf. 2 Chron. 7:14) and anticipated in the messianic promise (Isa. 53).

Israel is still in a state of disobedience. Yet before the judgment descends, God assures the nation that he accepts and will restore them (Hos. 14:4). God obligates himself to us by his own initiative. He binds himself to the human race through the gift of his Son, in whom he fulfills his promises (John 1:29).

A Blessing on the Nations

The promise to Abraham remained intact even in times of Israel's failure. His name would be used in blessings and his descendants would be a source of blessing to the nations (cf. Gen. 12:1-3). The promise and hope that God's people will incorporate Gentiles of faith runs through the Hebrew Bible. In Hosea, it appears only here (14:7), though it may be regarded as implicit in 1:10—2:1. That theme is found in Amos (9:11-12) as fulfillment of the promise to David, and in Isaiah (45:14; 49:6) in connection with the anticipated new covenant. The NT community of faith recognized it among the followers of Jesus Christ. All who identified with the Messiah as the One with whom God covenants anew, became incorporated as a new community (Isa. 45; 49:6; cf. Matt. 26:26-29; 1 Cor. 11:25).

Ruḥamah: Restoring Love

The case has been made in the notes under Hosea 1:6 that raḥam should be read as restoring love. In the Hebrew Bible, it regularly refers (in the Piel and Pual stems) to a mercy which extends life to one who has come under judgment (cf. Lam. 3:32; Isa. 14:1; Jer. 33:26; Zech. 10:6). The restoring love comes from the very agent who is bringing the judgment, most frequently God. At one point this love is directed even to the dwellings in the city of Jerusalem (Jer. 30:18), resulting in the reconstruction of the city.

The verb raḥam appears in Hosea (in the intensive stems mentioned) in 1:6-7; 2:4 (Heb.: 6), 23 (Heb.: 24, twice); 14:3 (Heb.: 4). Each instance refers to a recovery or restoration of what has been lost or is deficient (cf. 14:3). It never describes the process of initiating a relationship, as does 'ahab, the more common and more far-reaching word for love in Hosea. The verb 'ahab connotes choice and a (continuing) relationship characterized by affection and intimacy (as in 14:4, Heb.: 14:5).

Restorative love characterizes God's relationship to a sinful people; it is motivated by deep affection growing out of a prior relationship. Withholding raḥam is an act of judgment or is motivated by cruelty (Jer. 6:22-23; 50:42).

THE TEXT IN THE LIFE OF THE CHURCH
Integrity in Faith and Practice

The three themes, knowledge of God, covenant love, and integrity, introduce us to a comprehensive way of viewing, understanding, and walking with God. Other similar summary formulations appear elsewhere in the Scriptures. Deuteronomy's essence is summed up as follows: "Love the Lord your God with all your heart, and with all your soul, and with all your might" (6:5). Micah distills the teaching of Israel to "do justice, and to love kindness, and to walk humbly with your God" (6:8). Jesus captured the entire OT in two statements: "Love God" unrestrainedly, and "Love your neighbor as yourself" (Matt. 22:37-40). The three categories of Hosea are distinctive and exceptionally comprehensive. Israel was deficient or lacking in all three.

The knowledge of God is the foundation of faith and godliness. To know God is to understand his ways. It is to recognize ourselves as the reflection of his image. We experience his comforting, guiding, sustaining presence. Meaning, worth, and identity derive from knowing God as our heavenly Parent.

The second theme, covenant love, clarifies the relationships between God and his people, who do not respond with that love. The covenant Lord has spoken and acted. We see his ways, we hear his words, we experience his electing and forgiving grace. The relationships captured by the words ḥesed (covenant faithfulness and love) and ruḥamah (restoring love) embrace all human experience.

What is the distinctive place of integrity in a treatment of fundamental issues of life with God? Where sexual immorality abounds, would not obedience or holiness be more fitting themes? In a society torn by class struggle, crime, and violence, are the moral categories of justice, righteousness, and peace not more appropriate?

Integrity speaks about quality and consistency. As a description of the essential person, one's inner core, integrity underlies actions, attitudes, and motives. Integrity consists of a harmony between one's values, words, and practices. People with integrity face the world with an openness to being challenged and corrected. They are characterized by faithfulness to their commitments. They probe for and eagerly embrace the truth. They are known as people of character. They consistently walk in God's ways. The people of God on both sides of the cross are challenged to walk in God's truth (1 Sam. 12:24; Ps. 43:3; John 3:21; 14:6; Eph. 4:25).

Proclaiming God's word as truth, practicing the truth, living as people who have integrity—these are expressions of Hosea 11:12—14:9. When God grasps people in the depths of their being, they develop a passion for the truth. That transforms them from the inside out.

Unfortunately, Satan, sin, and the self continue to warp the inner person, cloud the mind, and encourage us to ward off danger to ourselves. The human mind is susceptible to the grossest self-deceit, even in the very presence of the truth. The heart is quick to deflect responsibility for its true condition even in the presence of the One who knows its deepest recesses. Integrity exposes what is false and honors the true. It speaks as the restored self.

When people actively experience God's faithfulness and love and reach out to their neighbors with that same compassionate caring, integrity binds up the whole into a consistent and active life of faith. Christians display integrity when they speak up for the cause of justice in Guatemala at the risk of family, possessions, and life. The farmer who is forced into bankruptcy but persists in repaying all his creditors through years of personal sacrifice is motivated by a sense of rightness embedded within his soul. When "in sickness and in health" turns out to be a lifetime of caring for an invalid spouse, the acts and motives of promise-keeping are shown to have deep roots.

Where 'emet (integrity) is present, one's word is one's bond. Swearing oaths becomes superfluous; deception is anathema. Jesus stated it succinctly and comprehensively: "Let your word be 'Yes, Yes' or 'No, No'; anything more than this comes from the evil one" (Matt. 5:37). The simple explanation, "I just don't do that," serves as a profound reason for rejecting evil. To violate 'emet is out of character for the person living close to God.

In the history of the church, such total integrity has frequently led to sainthood and to suffering, to ministry and to martyrdom. One reads the stories of the martyrs of the faith with reverence. (Regrettably, Christians have also been among the informants, judges, and ex ecutioners.) The 86-year-old bishop Polycarp, the 22-year-old mother Perpetua, and the Swiss nobleman Michael Sattler—these had in common a fundamental integrity which led them to welcome death rather than recant their faith in Jesus Christ. Most expressions of faithfulness and reliability are less dramatic, yet nonetheless are representative of the importance of personal integrity.

Such character grows out of sensitivity to the Spirit of God and one's inner spirit. In alert tenderness, it hears the still small voice convicting of evil and feels the gentle nudgings moving one toward maturity. It is more attuned to the voice of God and the needs of people than to the demands of society. It holds conviction tenaciously and hears the brothers and sisters with open grace. It has as its guiding star the One whose will was to do the will of his Father, the One who declares himself to be the way, the truth, and the life (John 4:34; 14:6).

Outline of Hosea

Part 2: TRIAL TRANSCRIPT: GOD VERSUS
    THE HEIRS   4:1—14:9

Preface to the Trial   **4:1-3**
The Case: God Versus North Israel   4:1ab
    Hear Ye! Hear Ye!   4:1a
    The Case Described: Heirs Claim Squatter's Right 4:1b
The Charges   4:1c-2
    Found Missing: Variations on a Theme   4:1c
        No Integrity: Jezreel
        No Family Affection: Lo-ruhamah
        No Knowledge of God: Lo-ammi
    A Litany of Evil: Violations of the Law   4:2
        Cursing: Atheism in Action
        Deception: Destroying Trust
        Murder: Premeditated Violence
        Theft: Threat to Livelihood
        Adultery: Violations of Family Intimacy
        The Snowball Effect
The Whole World Cries with Them   4:3

Defendant, Lo-ammi: You Don't Know God   **4:4—6:3**
Indictments Against Lo-ammi   4:4-19
    Indictment 1 : Rejecting the Source of Knowledge 4:4-6
        I Wasn't Told   4:4-5
        I Don't Want to Know   4:6a
        I Don't Remember   4:6b-e
    Indictment 2: Perverting the Knowledge of God   4:7-12a
        For Personal Gain   4:7-8
        Priest and People Alike   4:9
        For Personal Pleasure   4:10-12a
    Indictment 3: Consorting with Lovers   4:12b-19
        Prostitution by Choice   4:12b-13a
        Double Standards   4:13b-14
        Divine Counsel to Judah   4:15
        Divine Appraisal of Israel   4:16-17
        Partners in Shame   4:18-19
The Verdict   5:1-15
    Defendant, Israel   5:1-7
        Let the Accused Stand!   5:1a
        Guilty as Charged!   5:1b-4

Amos

Introduction to Amos

The Times

Amos comes to us fully formed. Neither the book nor the man appear elsewhere in the pages of the OT. The text even omits the normal family reference, "son of. . . ." Apart from the evidence of this book and that of Hosea, there is little direct biblical data on the nature of Israelite society or of eighth-century Israelite history *[Historical Summary, p. 384]*. The events of the book reflect a moment in the history of Israel since the date *two years before the earthquake* suggests a visit rather than a prolonged stay.

The times were good in Israel (the Northern Kingdom) and Judah (the Southern Kingdom). Jeroboam II (ca. 793-753 B.C., Thiele's chronology) of Judah and Uzziah (ca. 792-739 B.C.) of Israel came to kingship within a few years of one another. Both had stable and long reigns. There is no evidence of conflict between them. Each nation appears to have respected the rights of the other to expand into its traditional spheres of influence. Judah pushed west into Philistia, east into Ammonite territory, and south into Edom, down to the Gulf of Elath (2 Kings 14:22; 2 Chron. 26:1-8). Meanwhile, Israel claimed Syrian territory in the north and east (2 Kings 14:25, 28). Judah and Israel grew prosperous and militarily powerful *[Map of Palestine, p. 403]*.

Outside the country, it is true, dangers to Israel loomed at some distance. Tiglath-pileser III (745-727 B.C.) rallied and organized the might of Assyria to empire proportions. His campaigns in Palestine, exaction of tribute, and policy of mass deportation of conquered peoples (2 Kings 15:19-20; 16) came after the ministry of Amos. Assyrian activities are, however, anticipated in the prophecies of this book. Jeroboam's family line, Amos predicts, will die a violent death (Amos 7:9); Israel will go into exile toward Hermon (4:3), out beyond Damascus (5:27). They will be oppressed throughout the length and breadth of their land (6:14).

Amos ministered before the accession of Tiglath-pileser. Israel was in buoyant spirits. Her armies had been unusually successful (6:2, 13). Her confidence rested in well-fortified cities (3:9, 11). The nation was secure against assault by any conceivable enemy (5:18; 6:1, 13; 9:10). The nation had good reason to be confident (6:8).

The country prospered: ivory was the stuff of status (3:15; 6:4). The citizens—at least the ones who counted—had time to enjoy the summer cottage (3:15), custom-built homes (5:11), the best in dining pleasure (6:4, 6), rich moisturizing skin oils (6:6), and the fine arts (6:5). Vineyards flourished on the large estates (5:11). The grain exchange did a booming business; there were profits to be made (8:5-6).

Religious practice was at an all-time high. Regular services were held at all the main centers of worship (4:4-5; 5:21-22). The music was excellent, the liturgy expressive, and the people were generous with their offerings (4:4; 5:23; 8:3). Meanwhile, the priestly leadership kept close watch to ensure that the preaching built up the people's spirits and promoted the welfare of the nation (7:10-13).

Religion was an important part of national life. The major religious centers, Bethel and Gilgal, focused the official faith (5:5). Religious high places distributed throughout the land catered to local populations with more local concerns (2:8; 7:9). And then there was Beersheba, the city named by their ancestor Isaac (Gen. 26:33; cf. 21:31). It was currently under Judean control, evidenced by the fact that the Northern worshipers are invited to cross over (Amos 5:5). It had become a major retreat center for Israelite pilgrims (5:5; 8:14) [Jacob and Isaac, p. 389].

Yet Israel's fortified cities, conditioned troops, ivory imports, and raised altars could not protect her soft underbelly. Amos's social critique stripped away the objects of national pride and confidence. He laid bare the tattered social fabric in which this people wrapped itself, not realizing that it was really a funeral shroud. Amos placed his finger on one vulnerable and tender spot after the next.

The Message

Amos exposed Israel's success for what it was—a temporary reprieve from certain destruction—unless . . . the nation repented (5:15). The *perhaps* of Amos's prophetic visions and divine pronouncements penetrate the facade of hewn stone and the curtain of wealth to probe the social structures and spiritual condition of this people.

The prophet Amos described the situation. Taxes were a burden to the average landholder (7:1-6). The capital city and the public administration in Samaria were the main beneficiaries (3:9-10) of taxation. Fines (2:8) and exactions (5:11) further handicapped the subsistence farmer and sharecropper. A crop failure would result in mortgage foreclosures and ultimately in the sale of persons to debt-slavery (2:6; 5:11; 8:6). The poor were dismissed as an expendable commodity (8:4). The weight of the national budget and the imposition of surcharges and penalties favored the rich, many of whom probably occupied government posts or contracted for government services.

Added to officially sanctioned financial costs were the manipulation of the judicial system (2:7; 5:5, 12) and deception in the exchange of goods (8:5). The poor person had no real access to justice when the only legal recourse was to appeal to the very rich who also sat as judges in the local courts (2:7; 5:7, 12, 15). Corruption was rampant. Power prevailed. Those at the bottom end of the economic ladder were pawns to be used and discarded at will (8:4-6). Structural injustice (2:7; 5:7, 12), personal unrighteousness (8:5-6), and conspicuous consumption (6:5-6) had become the hallmark of the day.

Is there any question why Amos would characterize Samaria as full of confusion (3:9)? Material prosperity dominated societal values. Class divisions separated people from one another. No society can remain stable and dynamic under such conditions. The seeds of Israel's destruction were already evident to the prophet. Could the nation's leaders be awakened in time to halt its downward slide?

Israel's religion, instead of challenging the moral decline, quietly ignored it. In Amos, the unjust are never denounced as hypocrites, though they are that. The full religious calendar of services was strictly observed (4:4-5; 5:21-23). Sacrifices ensured the offerer of divine blessings, the worshipers thought. Since the rich were capable of the largest and most regular sacrifices, the logical conclusion was that God would favor the rich. But they had gained their wealth unjustly. So they imagined that God was bought off by sacrifices or indifferent to matters of justice and compassion. Hence, ethics and religion became divorced from one another.

Many features in Israel were similar to those in Judah, to the south. This enabled the Judean Amos to communicate effectively in Samaria and Bethel *[Israelite Religion, p. 385]*. The types of sacrifices and the occasions for offering in Israel were identical to those in Judah (4:4-5; 5:21-22). Israelites traveled to Beersheba (5:5), that ancient and traditional patriarchal center of worship. This suggests a close correspondence between the concept of God and the acts of worship of these two nations. An implicit indictment appears in the references to the high places (7:9) and the worship at multiple cult centers (5:5; 8:14). These reflect the biblical historian's standard complaint against the Northern kings' reigns: they "did evil in the eyes of the Lord and did not turn away from any of the sins of Jeroboam [I] son of Nebat" (2 Kings 14:24, NIV). But, then, Judah was also worshiping at Beersheba and at other high places (2 Kings 15:4).

Israel and Judah shared a common conviction that they were the chosen people (3:1-2), freed from enslavement in Egypt (2:10; 9:7), and led by God through the wilderness (2:10; 5:25). They had dispossessed the Amorites and received their territory as Israel's own (2:10). The Lord had given them a succession of faithful witnesses to the way and will of God (2:11; 3:7-8; cf. Deut. 18:14-22; Num. 6). Though there is no reference to Israel's violation of specific decrees (in contrast to the accusation against Judah, 2:4), nor any mention of the covenant at Sinai, the entire book breathes the air of that covenant *[Covenant, p. 379]*.

In Amos, covenant is essential to an understanding of Israel's chosenness and responsibility (3:1-2). It is embedded in the plans he discloses to his prophets (3:7). It underlies the history of restorative judgments by which the Lord has already addressed them, but without success (4:6-11). As covenant-making God, the Lord revealed his name to Israel (Exod. 6:1-8). That name and its significance lies at the heart of three of the major judgment texts of this book (Amos 4:6-13; 5:1-17; 9:1-8). In each instance, a hymn fragment focuses the entire passage on the Lord (Yahweh), the covenant Maker, whose acts of creation and sovereign control over nature remind Israel that they are being addressed by the Creator of heaven and earth. *Yahweh is his name!*

Israel has forgotten that the Lord is the God who calls his people to moral responsibility (3:1-2). The object of their worship at Bethel and Gilgal was surely not the Lord, the God of righteousness and

compassion, justice and judgment (5:5, 14, 16), though they were using his name in the rituals of worship. His moral character and cosmic
sovereignty are reflected in the demands for justice which the nations
have violated (1:3—2:3) and for which they are being held accountable. That same righteousness will burn against the sinful monarch
(7:7-9), the priest of Bethel (7:17), and even the nation whom he
once chose as a special possession (9:1-4).

The Prophet

What is known about the man Amos comes to us as a result of his
strong sense of being called (3:7-8; 7:14-15). God grasped and pro-
pelled him to the Northern Kingdom to fulfill this prophetic mission.
Were the visions of chapters seven and eight part of that call? Possibly. We can only imagine the circumstances and the accompanying
psychological dynamics of the call. Neither serves a purpose in the
book; neither receives attention.

Amos disavows association with any prophetic school. He had no
prophetic credentials, no previous history of prophesying, and no
personal agenda. He was in it solely because God compelled him to
become a messenger to a people rushing headlong to destruction.

Amos participated actively with God in forming the message.
When he had an explicit word from the Lord, he spoke it. He reinforced those words with his own reflections, creating a powerful, focused social critique of Israel (Amos 5-6). As a sheep rancher and
sycamore orchardist, he may have been speaking to people with
whom he was acquainted through his business ventures, or with prospective customers. Therefore, the message becomes even more poi-
gnant. Amos was willing to forgo profit for the welfare of others, a
spirit alien to his listeners (6:6).

It is impossible to read the vision reports (Amos 7-8) and remain
untouched by Amos's compassion. When he sees the calamity about
to descend on the people of Israel, his instinctive response is *O Lord
God, forgive, I beg you* (7:2, 5). There is no vindictiveness, no smug "I
told you so," no casual shrug of the shoulders. Unlike Amaziah, who
was determined to practice political "damage control" by denouncing God's prophet for raising unwelcome issues, Amos burst out in intercession. He stayed, though briefly, the flood of divine judgment.
Eventually God restrained him from further intercession and required him to comply (7:8). Only then did Amos issue the Lord's verdict.

The Book

The book of Amos came into being some time after Amos's prophetic mission (1:1). The actual time or stages of composition are unknown [*Composition of Amos, p. 378*]. It is known, however, that a prophet's messages might be respectfully retained in memory by members of the prophetic guild (cf. Isa. 8:16). The use of the third-person description of Amos's encounter with Amaziah suggests the role of such a "school" in recording the messages of Amos (7:10-17).

The approach in this commentary will be to read Amos as a literary whole without proceeding through the exercise of sorting out what parts may be original, the creation of others, or the work of an editor. The assumption is that the received text is essentially the product of Amos's Israelite ministry in the mid-eighth century and that the editors are faithful to God's intent in their Spirit-guided task.

The book of Amos is stylistically rich and creative. It includes judgment speeches (1:3—2:15), hymn fragments (4:13; 5:8-9; 9:5-6), historical recital (4:6-11), vision reports (7:1-9), a lament (5:2), wisdom sayings (5:13; 6:12), a parable (6:9-11), and disputations (2:9-11; 3:3-8; 5:18-20; 9:7). An artful use of rhetorical devices include irony (4:4-5), understatement (4:12), play on words (8:1-2), quotation of the hearer's words for dramatic effect (4:1), and repetition in the form of chiasmus to center the reader's attention (5:1-17) [*Literary Patterns, p. 391*].

Strength and beauty merge in the sensory imagery of Amos 3-9. The four chapters (3-6) punctuated with the proclamation *Hear this word* capture the imagination with language pertaining to sound, speech, and smell—and the corresponding parts of human anatomy. A subliminal message reinforces the herald's public announcements. Nearly forty such references dot these chapters. Lions *roar*, the trumpet *sounds*, God *reveals his secrets*, witnesses *testify*, and the women of Samaria *speak* to their husbands. The Lord *swears*, the priests *announce* the time for freewill offerings, farmers *lament*, and the populace hates the one who *reproves* in the gate. Their festivals are filled with *songs and harps*, and their houses are built of *hewn* stone. The prudent *keep silent* in such an evil time, and the one who comes to bury the dead is warned, *Hush! We must not mention the name of the Lord.* In related language, the shepherd rescues from the *mouth of the lion* two legs, or a piece of an *ear*; the houses of *ivory (tusks)* will perish, and the women will be led out with *fishhooks implanted (in their lips?).* Famine brings cleanness of *teeth*, they lie on beds of *ivory*, and they turn justice into *poison*.

Amos 7–9 convey God's truth in five visions. While speech is common, visual images dominate. Related language denotes space, dimension, location, motion, and direction; it provides backdrop, foreground, and action. In the visions, grass *sprouts*, fire *burns*, a plumb line *hangs in total silence*. Amos's argument in intercession points out that Israel is *too small*; it cannot *stand*. However, God will not *pass by* his people but will *rise against* the house of Jeroboam and the *high places of Isaac*. Amos is a *seer* whom the Lord *took* from *following the flock*. Amaziah of *Bethel* accuses Amos of fomenting rebellion *in the midst of Israel*. Therefore, he shall *flee* to Judah.

The fourth vision consists of a *basket of summer fruit* and represents *dead bodies*. The judgment consists of an earthquake resembling the *rising and falling* of the *Nile*; the *sun* will *go down* at noon, the earth will *become dark* in *broad daylight*. *Young men and beautiful maidens* will *wander about* from north to east and *run to and fro*. When that earthquake comes, the temple will *fall on the heads of the people*. They will *flee*, *dig*, *climb*, *hide themselves*, and *go down* into *captivity*. Meanwhile, the Lord will *take . . . with his hand*, *bring down*, and *search them out*, and finally *fix his eyes* on them for harm.

Indeed, the *eyes* of the Lord will destroy the sinful kingdom. He will *shake with a sieve* all those who claim, "Evil will not *overtake or meet* us." The salvation to come involves *restoring* the *fallen booth* of David. Fertility is restored; the one *who plows* shall *overtake* the one who *reaps*; and the *treader* of grapes shall *overtake* the *sower* of the seed in near silence. Blessings *drip* and *flow down* the *hills* in the form of wine. The author's artistry comes to life as we read the text aloud and let it stir our imagination.

STRUCTURAL CHART OF THE BOOK OF AMOS

Amos 1—2

Code words: *For three transgressions . . .*

1:1	1:3, 6, 9	1:11, 13; 2:1	2:4	2:6

SYRIA   EDOM
PHILISTIA   AMMON
PHOENICIA   MOAB

(vertical label) NATIONS   JUDAH   ISRAEL

Target Group: aliens | relatives | brother | *us*

Role of Prophet: court herald

Amos 3—6

Hear this word

3:1	4:1	5:1

JUDAH AND ISRAEL

Target Group: whole family | women | virgin Israel

Role of Prophet: reprover in the gate

Amos 7—9

The Lord God showed me . . . .   *I saw . . . .*

7:1	7:4	7:7	8:1	9:1

(vertical) LOCUSTS   FIRE   PLUMBLINE   RIPE FRUIT   EARTHQUAKE

(vertical, right) DESTRUCTION AND REBUILDING

Target Group: poor/weak | rulers | rich worshipers | remnant

Role of Prophet: intercessor, ... | observer of things to come

Amos 1:1-2

Heading

PREVIEW AND OUTLINE

In two tightly compacted verses, the editor of the book lays before his readers the equivalent of the modern title page, foreword, and introduction:

The Prophet, 1:1a

The People, 1:1b

The Time, 1:1c

The Tone, 1:2

We do not know when these verses were written, except that it was after the earthquake. There was a time lag between the prophet's presentation and the writing or editing of the book.

EXPLANATORY NOTES

The Prophet   1:1a

Amos is identified as one of the *shepherds* of Tekoa, a town of Judah some six miles south of Bethlehem [*Map of Palestine, p. 403*]. This

Hebrew word for *shepherd* is unusual. In the OT it appears elsewhere only in 2 Kings 3:4. There Mesha, king of Moab, is called a "shepherd," which qualifies him to supply the king of Israel with a hundred thousand lambs and a hundred thousand rams. The evidence from an earlier culture north of Israel suggests that such a shepherd was a manager of sheep herds being raised for wool and meat (Craigie: 29-33). Later in the book, Amos describes himself as a mixed farmer, earning his living by caring for cattle, sheep, and tree fruit (7:14-15).

Amos is, therefore, superbly qualified to address the administrative, economic, and religious leadership of Israel. Possibly Amos's presence in Bethel and other Northern centers, as well as Beersheba in the farther South, was due to his business activities. In that case, any criticism of the Northern religious practices was bad for his business. His call to ministry took precedence over earning a livelihood.

The prophet's words originated in one or more visions. In contrast to dream messages received while asleep, vision messages were normally received in the conscious state. The precise manner in which this occurred is merely described as *he saw,* suggesting that the manner was the normal prophetic experience (cf. Isa. 2:1; Mic. 1:1).

The People 1:1b

The words of the vision are directed *against Israel* (not just *concerning Israel,* as in NRSV). The preposition carries the weight of a message of judgment for Israel. From the outset, then, the book carries a sense of foreboding. The author refuses to tiptoe around. Let the reader beware!

The first readers were probably the people of Judah. In Amos, the term *Israel* refers to the Northern Kingdom in particular (cf. Amos 2:6; 5:1), or to the united nation before the schism at Solomon's death (cf. 3:1; 9:7), or to the restored Davidic community in the days to come (9:14)—but never to the Southern Kingdom alone.

The Time 1:1c

The time of prophesying is given in typical Near Eastern style, where events were dated with reference to the king's age or rule. Jeroboam II ruled Israel; Uzziah (Azariah) ruled Judah. Though there is considerable debate on the exact years of their reigns, Thiele proposes the years 793-753 B.C. for Jeroboam and 792-739 B.C. for Uzziah

(205). Alternative dating systems vary by only a few years (Hayes and Miller: 678-683). The ministry of Amos probably occurred somewhere around 760 B.C., after Jeroboam's significant military successes (2 Kings 14:25, 28; Amos 6:1-2, 13-14).

The unusual catches the eye. To date the book by referring to Uzziah, king of Judah, before Jeroboam, king of Israel, is unusual and deliberate. Amos delights in drawing our attention to aspects of his message by breaking a literary or spoken pattern. This broken pattern suggests that Judah stands in the path of development of the same prophetic word earlier meant for the Northern Kingdom.

The *earthquake* mentioned here features prominently in the judgment scenes of chapters eight and nine. Amos ministered two years prior to that momentous event. Three centuries later it remained vividly alive in Judah's memory (Zech. 14:5). That event was the break point anticipated by Amos. From the days of the earthquake, the judgments predicted by this seer were launched against Israel and stood as a warning to Judah.

The fact that the book was compiled only after the earthquake occurred suggests that the prophet's words, valid as they were for the Northern Kingdom, came to be recognized as having abiding value beyond their time. The fulfillment of the message was one of God's signs (Deut. 18:22; Jer. 32:8). To be forewarned is to be forearmed.

The Tone 1:2

The words of Amos turn out to be the utterance of the Lord. And the Lord's message comes as a lion's roar. Just as a lion declares its presence and strikes fear into the hearts of all who hear it, so the Lord asserts his sovereignty by this word.

Lions have long since vanished from Palestine, but in the era of the OT they were commonplace, particularly in the thick brush of the Jordan Valley and in the Judean wilderness. The lion appears most often in the Scriptures in association with Judah. Indeed, Judah itself is referred to as a lion's whelp (Gen. 49:9). The throne room of Solomon was decorated with lions (1 Kings 10:19-20), resulting in the proverb: "A king's rage is like the roar of a lion" (Prov. 19:12, NIV). Appropriately, that authority and power is recognized as vested in Israel's God, the One who rules on Mount Zion.

Amos, a Judean, is on a preaching mission to the Northern Kingdom. His opening words are a bad omen. If it is indeed the Lord who roars, then all other gods stand by helpless. Moreover, the priests and prophets of the Northern Kingdom have been assuring the people that God is on their side (Amos 5:18, 21-23). Is God confused? Is Amos mistaken? Are their priests and prophets fakes? Only Amos's message and time will tell.

God's warning comes from *Zion*, the temple hill; from *Jerusalem*, the holy city. Whose voice, then, have the Israelites been listening to in Bethel and in Gilgal? Presumably not that of the living and true God. Yes, God had frequently spoken to the Northerners through his servants, the prophets—through Elijah, Elisha, and the sons of the prophets. None of these genuine prophets, however, is ever associated with the alternative religious centers Jeroboam I had set up when he led the ten Northern tribes away from the Davidic dynasty. So the roar from Jerusalem implies a judgment on all other centers which profess to dispense the oracles of the Lord *[The Yahweh-Baal Conflict, p. 398]*.

It is his shepherd's and fruit grower's heart which guides Amos's mind to select the vocabulary of destruction: *The pastures of the shepherds dry up, and the top of Carmel withers.* When the scorching sun beats down month after cloudless month, even the shepherd's haven (*luxuriant pastures*) becomes parched. And when Carmel's springs cease, this virtual garden of Eden (*karmel: garden, orchard, plantation*) becomes a fruitless waste. The lion's roar brings life in the Northern Kingdom to a standstill. The crucial question arises: Will God's people be able to discern the meaning of that roar?

Part 1

Israel Among the Nations

Amos 1:3—2:16

OVERVIEW

Between two roars of the lion (1:2; 3:8), Amos utters God's judgment on eight nations. Israel and its neighbors were formed from ethnically bonded peoples. These nations had alternately ravaged one another and banded together against common enemies such as the Egyptians, Babylonians, and Assyrians. On occasion they had formed alliances against one or the other of their Palestinian neighbors. At some time each of the first seven nations mentioned had been bitter enemies of Israel. During Amos's ministry, Judah controlled Philistia, Ammon, Moab, and Edom (2 Chron. 26:2, 6-8), while Israel dominated the Arameans (2 Kings 14:25, 28). Only the Phoenicians (Tyre) stood outside the dominance of Judah or Israel.

First the prophet brings charges against peoples with whom Israel shared no recognized blood ties: Arameans, Philistines, Phoenicians. Then he turns to those regarded as distant relatives: Edomites, Ammonites, Moabites. Finally he zeros in on the sister nations, Judah and Israel [Map of Near East, p. 404]. In a culture in which blood ties were a vital part of close relationships, this sequence creates a climax as the tightening spiral of judgment swirls through Judah and settles down on Israel.

The series of judgments takes listeners and readers back to the traditions of Noah, from whom came all families of the earth (Gen. 10:31; cf. Amos 3:1). God covenanted with Noah never again to subject humanity to judgment by water (Gen. 9:8-17). God will mete out judgment against human injustice to prevent such an accumulation of evil which might bring the destruction of the race. God's severity is a measure of grace and of the urgency of the hour.

The message of Amos to these nations is one of unmitigated punishment. Each nation is held accountable for its specific and unique sins. The harshest judgments, however, are reserved for those who claim to be God's special people and who glory in the light of his clear teachings on holy living. The strongest indictments and severest punishments are reserved for the Northern Kingdom, Israel, to whom Amos has been commissioned as a prophet (Amos 1:1).

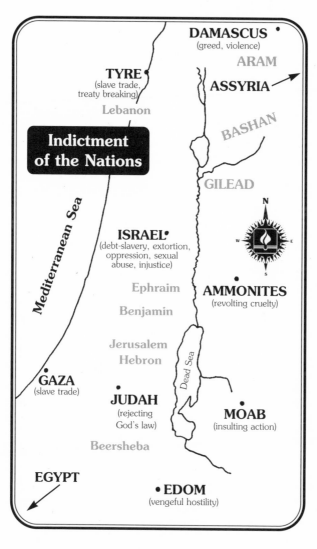

OUTLINE

Alien Nations Indicted, 1:3-10
    1:3-5   Damascus (Syria/Arameans)
    1:6-8   Gaza (Philistia)
    1:9-10   Tyre (Phoenicia)

Related Nations Indicted, 1:11—2:3
    1:11-12 Edom
    1:13-15 Ammon
    2:1-3   Moab

The Lord's People Indicted, 2:4-16
    2:4-5   Judah
    2:6-16   Israel
        A Long List of Crimes   2:6-8
        Worse Than the Amorites 2:9-12
        Punishments to Match   2:13-16

PREVIEW

The editorial comments of Amos 1:1 introduced the message of Amos as directed against Israel. The first prophecies, addressed to surrounding nations, are part of a larger theme directed to God's people.

The series of accusing messages leveled against the nations follows a common pattern. With few exceptions, they each contain:

1. An introductory formula: *Thus says the Lord.*
2. A general charge of sinfulness: *For three transgressions of . . . , and for four.*
3. A general announcement of punishment: *I will not revoke the punishment.*
4. A specific, elaborated charge of sinfulness: *Because they. . . .*
5. A specific, elaborated announcement of punishment: *I will send a fire. . . .*
6. A concluding formula: *says the (Sovereign) Lord.*

The opening line of each prophecy, *Thus says the Lord,* clarifies the source of the message as well as the role of the preacher. These words are not the product of intense nationalism, nightmares, or a creative imagination. They have their origin in the mind of the living

God. The imagery and the shape of the content of the prophecies may well reflect Amos's background, experience, and personality; yet the message is God's. That truth finds its own confirmation in the fact that the opening phrase is a traditional introduction of a messenger speech. The messenger typically quotes or paraphrases his lord's message. In this case, Amos conveys God's words of sure judgment.

In the first three prophecies, the nation is identified by reference to one or more of its prominent cities. Thereafter the references become more personal as each nation is addressed by the name of the ancestor most closely associated with its origin.

Numerical sayings are relatively common in Near Eastern literature, particularly in poetic wisdom literature like that found in Job or Proverbs. Frequently such numbers are followed by an itemization of characteristics or events. Thus, "Three things are too wonderful for me; four I do not understand" is followed by a description of the four enigmas (Prov. 30:18-19). Similarly, Eliphaz's assurance,"He will deliver you from six troubles; in seven no harm shall touch you," is followed by a list of seven adversities from which God will protect the faithful (Job 5:19-23).

In Amos 1-2, however, the specific listing of sins occurs only in the indictment against Israel. There, depending on how one interprets the text, one may discover either four, six, or seven specific sins.

Amos does not need to list all four sins to make his point. The sin mentioned is what puts the measure of transgressions over the top. To this point (*three sins*), God has been gracious, but his patience has limits. Until now God has withheld the hand of punishment; the goal is reconciliation. But persistent rebellion against God, rejection of his recalling and forgiving grace, and the brazen accumulation of transgressions (*even for four*) leads to the inevitable conclusion: *I will not revoke the punishment.*

Literally, the general announcement of judgment declares, *I will not turn him/it back.* The most likely referents for the pronoun *him/it* are the words or wrath of God, as Knierim argues. God is determined not to rein in the word of judgment which expresses his wrath. Once God releases the arrow of his wrath, he will not recall it. The final verdict is in God's hands; he issues it in his time. That time has now come.

The fourth ingredient in these speeches through God's messenger is the recital of specific sins. Since the specific charges represent the distinctive feature of each prophecy, they call for detailed attention. However, some general observations can be made. God offers reasons for his judgment. This seems obvious, but it has profound implications.

Fire is the common element in the specific announcement of punishment in the first six prophecies: *So I will send a fire in . . . , and it will devour its strongholds.* (1:4, 7, 10, 12, 14; 2:2, 5; cf. 4:11; 5:6; 7:4). The scene is that of invasion in which enemy forces have launched an attack against fortified cities. They set fire to wooden gates, platforms around the walls, and the large, carefully constructed palaces and mansions of royalty and nobility. These fortified *mansions* served both as living quarters and protection against violent attack (cf. 2 Kings 15:25; Ps. 48:3, 13).

The lion's roar was heard only as far as Israel (1:2). This suggests that these prophecies, though referring to other nations, are basically addressed to Israel. Amos is prophesying about other nations as a word for those who hear the lion.

Frequently (Amos 1:5, 8, 15; 2:3) God signs off the word of judgment with the formula *says the Lord God,* or *says the Lord.* There shall be no doubt about the source of the message. One may wish for dialogue with Amos, to debate the sinfulness of the transgressions, argue for the innocence of the populace, or question the appropriateness of the timing. But these words, though proclaimed by Amos, belong to God. Whoever wishes to debate, argue, or question will have to address a holy God. Amos makes it clear that this judgment message, though addressed to Israel, is thrust upon the nations with divine authority and urgency.

Alien Nations Indicted
Amos 1:3-10

EXPLANATORY NOTES
Damascus (Syria/Arameans) 1:3-5

God's first word through Amos concerns the Arameans, whose capital is *Damascus [Map of Near East, p. 404].* Damascus was the seat of the monarchy of Hazael. It was a significant center of power west of the Euphrates. The Arameans controlled one of the major trade routes between East and West. The sins for which they are being judged are an extension of their concern for economic dominance. The area known as *Gilead* is the Transjordan Israelite territory originally assigned to the tribes of Reuben, Gad, and Manasseh. It was frequently the prize sought by armies and rulers of Israel and Aram.

Apparently the Arameans had gained control of the territory of Gilead and *threshed it*—probably by extracting tribute. Oxen or heifers pulled threshing sledges over spread-out sheaves of grain on the threshing floor. The bottom of the sledge had sharp stones or pieces of iron fixed to it to break up the sheaves so the grain could be separated from the chaff by winnowing. The good farmer was careful to adjust the type and weight of the sledge to the nature of the grain being threshed (Isa. 28:24-28). Careless threshing could damage the grain and reduce the harvest.

The Arameans' sin lay not in subjugating the Israelites but in their excessive demands for revenue and in the inhumanity with which they extracted their taxes and subjugated the population. They were called to account for demanding "more than the market would bear" from their newly acquired subjects. Before God's tribunal, the Arameans stood adjudged as guilty for the dual sins of greed and violence, sins which are comfortable bedfellows.

God's verdict of "guilty" will be followed by the destruction of the greedy oppressor. God will light a fire in the capital, sending their fortresses up in smoke. The judgment itself does not name or even hint at the identity of God's agent nor does it spell out the time of the invasion. Ultimately, it is not essential to be able to identify the specific Assyrian invasion to which he is referring. It probably occurred around 750-725 B.C., within 25 years after the date of the prophecy. The certainty of the judgment and the source (the Lord) lie much closer to the heart of this text than does the date.

When God summons the Assyrians to do his bidding, he will repay the Arameans for the violence with which they have suppressed Gilead. The *socket-stones* on which the massive gates of Damascus hinge will be smashed, so that the gates can be torn from their moorings (1:5a). The invasion will affect the entire population: rural and urban (1:5a), ruler and commoner (1:5b), the inhabitant of *Sin Valley* and *House of Pleasure* alike. The resulting destruction and deportation to *Kir* (their place of origin, according to Amos 9:7) are God's will, bringing to an end the proud political history of the Arameans. These words were fulfilled, as God predicted through his servant Amos (2 Kings 16:9).

Gaza (Philistia) 1:6-8

As Amos draws another breath, he whirls about to address the Philistine nation under the label of four of their five major cities, Gaza, Ashdod, Ashkelon, and Ekron. Only Gath is omitted, possibly for literary reasons [Map of Palestine, p. 403]. Throughout, the OT pictures the Philistines as functioning as a confederacy of city states.

Their crime? They *took captive an entire community for the purpose of selling them to Edom.* There may well be two sins condemned here. Slavery in itself is not one of them. Slaves captured in war were treated humanely by ancient standards; the alternative normally was death. The nations of the ancient Near East, including Israel, practiced slavery through capture.

The twofold Philistine crime consists first of selling an *entire community* into slavery, and therefore into cultural and ethnic oblivion. Such an act of genocide destroys people's identity. In a world in which one lived on through descendants and culture, the enslavement of an entire people represented a living death. The children they fathered and mothered would belong to their masters. Their virgin daughters would become concubines or wives of the highest bidder, and their sons slave laborers whose children would belong to their masters. Torn from their land and loved ones, even their gods might cease to be worshiped. That was annihilation.

The second crime of Philistia consisted of engaging in wholesale slave trade. It is one thing to enslave an enemy in order to eliminate rebellion. It is another to invade and capture peoples for purely economic gain. Their greed resulted in grossly neglecting compassion; it dehumanized others. People had become goods to buy and sell, to use without regard to their real worth as persons.

Here also God's fire of judgment will sweep through the land (1:7-8). Citizens (*the inhabitants*) and chieftains (*the one who holds the scepter*) will go down together. God smashes all the Philistine centers of violence and avarice. In the end, poetic justice rules when even the *last of the Philistines shall perish*—destroyed with the same destruction they brought on the peoples whom they traded for silver, gold, horses, and perfumes.

Tyre (Phoenicia) 1:9-10

Some two hundred miles north of Philistia lies Tyre [Map of Near East, p. 404]. At the time of Amos, the fortified city of Tyre was located on an island approximately a half mile off the coast. Tyre harbored a large Phoenician merchant and naval fleet. Its location, fortifications, and navy made it virtually impregnable.

Tyre also heaped up crimes against humanity. Her persistent sinning caught God's attention. Like the Philistines, the Tyrians engaged in the slave trade. Unlike the Philistines who sold captives they took in war, the Tyrians merely acted as brokers. They were merchants in human flesh. Their lust for cold hard cash made them deaf to the cries of children torn from their mothers' arms, the groans of the wounded, and the wailing of the bereaved. They, like the Philistines, ignored the longings and hopes of their prisoners as *they sold entire populations* on the auction block (1:9b).

The worst has yet to be told. Those whom they put up for sale were their neighbors and friends. At some point they had bound themselves together in a *treaty of friendship*. Whether or not the captives are Israelites makes no difference for Amos. The sin which caps their list is failure to keep faith. "Treaties are made to be broken," they apparently are saying. One moment the Tyrians are your friends, the next they trade you in the marketplace. Business is business, they glibly say while disregarding a treaty of brotherhood. Nothing—not past relationships, earlier agreements, or even personal friendships—can be allowed to interfere with a good deal.

Such callousness, lack of integrity, and denial of friendship fall under international censure and divine wrath. Fire will sweep along those massive walls and through the gorgeous *mansions* till nothing of worth remains (1:10). The possessions the people of Tyre have grasped and hugged will turn into smoke, dust, and ashes in the day of God's judgment through an unnamed agent.

Related Nations Indicted
Amos 1:11—2:3

EXPLANATORY NOTES
Edom 1:11-12

Edom wraps around the southern end of the Dead Sea. East of the Sea, it shares its northern border with Moab; on the west, it adjoins Judah; south of Edom's habitable land lies the desert. Its two principal cities are *Teman* and *Bosrah* (1:12) [Map of Near East, p. 404].

Amos knows about Edom firsthand; he had lived all his life at the southwest fringe of Judah's agricultural land. He well knows the meaning of the specific indictments he announces on behalf of his God. Edom is guilty and deserves to be punished.

Edom is guilty of blood vengeance, and that against *his brother*. In the absence of international courts or peacekeeping forces, the nations in Amos's day practiced their own form of justice. Edom was not called on the carpet because of attempting to right a wrong done to him. He was called to account for (1) seeking redress only by means of the sword, (2) stifling all compassion, and (3) perpetuating a blood feud with unrestrained fury. Edom has become a wild animal (*his anger tears*) which wantonly slaughters more than it can eat. His initial concern for fairness has been transformed into gross injustice, suppression of brotherly affection, and burning, vengeful hatred.

Can it be that the *brother* against whom Edom's anger was directed is Judah? If so, then the sin may be a continuation of the longstanding hatred first kindled when Jacob stole his twin brother's birthright and blessing (Gen. 25:27-34). True, justice was ill served in those events. But perpetuating and fueling anger from one generation to the next has *distorted* what little *compassion* might arise from time to time *[Jacob and Isaac, p. 389]*.

Neither *Teman* nor *Bosrah* will escape the judgment of the Lord. The enemy whom God will send may not even know that he serves as the agent of the Almighty. But his destroying actions will accomplish the purposes of destruction. Thereby God will declare his hatred of sin and his sovereignty over all nations.

Ammon 1:13-15

The Bible traces the Ammonite ancestry back to Abraham's nephew Lot. The account of Ammon's birth is associated with the death of Lot's wife at the occasion of the destruction of Sodom and Gomorrah (Gen. 19). The Ammonites lived on the fringes of the eastern desert until they gradually settled north of Moab in Transjordan. They were pressed between the Gileadite Israelites on the north, the Moabites to the south, and the constantly intruding desert peoples to the east. The Jordan rift valley hemmed them in on the west *[Map of Near East, p. 404]*. They lacked breathing space.

The concern for national survival has issued in a policy of expansion. That is the occasion for their crime. Specifically, God indicts them for *ripping open the pregnant women of Gilead in order to expand their borders*. The desperate need for land and security led to a simple solution. The Ammonites invaded Gilead, killed all the men, and sold the women into slavery. To prevent the birth of any more Gileadite males who might lay claim to territory when they reached maturity, they ripped open all the pregnant Gileadite women instead of dispatching them quickly; the Ammonites chose to compound their sin of lusting for land with that act of revolting cruelty.

The Lord himself *will kindle the destroying fire in Rabbah of Ammon.* In one climactic day, an enemy will assault the walls of the capital with a chilling battle cry. The unknown assailant will rage like a storm through this "secure" land, laying it waste and taking *their king into exile.* Death and destruction have invited divinely decreed death and destruction. The exiled population will not possess the land they so violently have claimed to create their own security.

Moab 2:1-3

Moab, described in Genesis as Lot's firstborn by his eldest daughter (Gen. 19:30-38), is the next to hear the scathing indictment of criminal acts *[Map of Near East, p. 404].* However, to our ears, *burning the bones of the king of Edom to ashes* seems like much ado about nothing. This accusation speaks neither of greed nor violence. But it does address their attitude of insult toward others.

In a world which reverenced the ancestors and honored the dead, the desecration of bodies constituted an act of ultimate disdain and loathing (cf. 2 Kings 23:16). *Burning the bones* implies that the Moabites robbed the king's grave in order to deliberately desecrate his body and memory. Burning the bones of the enemy's king is directed at the entire nation, since the ruler represents the people and gives them a functional and representative identity.

Moab's brazen act comes under divine scrutiny and judgment. God refuses to restrain the judgment any longer. With devastating fury, the agent of God's wrath will bring Moab to his knees. His fortresses and barricades will go up in flames (Amos 2:2a); his people and leaders (*judge and officials*) will go down to destruction (2:2b-c). Undoubtedly, the reference to *judge* is to the leader of the nation. It is possible that at this time the Moabites have designated their ruler as *judge* rather than "king," though at other times in their history, Moab is described as having a king (1 Sam. 12:9; 2 Kings 3:4; Jer. 27:3).

Amos paints a graphic picture of their impending doom. The invading army launches attacks against major fortified cities. As they breach the walls and batter down the gates, the attacking soldiers set ablaze the timbers of the buildings to which many defenders have retreated to offer their final resistance. The air fills with fire, smoke, noise, and confusion. Trumpets sound, soldiers charge with blood-curdling shouts. Death lies strewn in many shapes and sizes because of Moab's utter disregard for the feelings and dignity of his neighbors.

When that day comes and the survivors recall the prophecy, they will be reminded that behind the devastation lies the hand of Israel's Sovereign: *I will send fire . . . , and I will destroy . . . , and kill . . . , says the Lord.* It is *the Lord's* will that has been ignored.

THE TEXT IN BIBLICAL CONTEXT

God Rules

The Lord's threatening roar receives no challenging response from other gods. Why are the gods of these other nations silent when the Scripture is full of stories about contests of gods?

Here, as on so many other occasions, God shows himself superior to the gods of the nations, whether of Mesopotamia, Egypt, or of Canaan (Deut. 4:15-19; Josh. 24:14-15). Before the fifth century B.C., the predominant polemic in the message of the prophets takes the form of showing how inadequate the other gods are and how God bests them in every power encounter. Israel's Lord is supreme over all that is called God. The exodus, the entry into and possession of the land, and the contest with Baal and Asherah in Elijah's day—these all show that the Lord is incomparable and that his reign is not restricted to the territory the Israelites came to occupy.

When tempting Jesus, Satan claims to rule the kingdoms of the earth (Matt. 4:8-9 et par.). The claim is valid in that he rules in rebel hearts and through human institutions which lend themselves to the oppression of peoples and the distortions of God's presence. Yet when God pronounces judgment, whether through Moses, Joshua, Elijah, or Amos, he asserts his ultimate claim over the world. God reserves the right to judge the nations. When he exercises his right, the gods of this world appear as impotent. They are silenced into submission. The Lord's supremacy displays itself in his international reach and strong grasp. When God shows himself as Judge, the conflict in the realm of history proves to be "no contest."

Ethics and Caring

The rash of judgment oracles with which this book begins informs us that God cares. He cares for saints and sinners. The Father in heaven makes his sun shine on the just and unjust, and sends rain and the bounties of the earth on all alike (Matt. 5:42-48). He censures those whose actions restrict God's gifts of nature to the privileged or powerful few.

A faithful response to God always includes obedience, and obedience is clothed with acts of justice, grace, compassion, and love. Compliance with humanitarian norms is noble and occurs also among peoples who are not guided by God's written revelation (Gen. 14:17-24; Rom. 1:18—2:16). One should not miss the point that the basis for God's judgment of these nations is not his word or his specific revelation or covenant. The evils are evils recognized as such innately, through collective conscience. Even apart from any divine revelation, God has a right to call people to account.

The OT expresses God's ethical character in many different ways. The call for obedience is an essential part of God's covenantal relationships, whether with Noah (Gen. 9:1-17), Abraham (Gen. 17:1-14), Israel at Sinai (Exod. 20-24), or David (2 Sam. 7:1-17). The large body of laws in the OT and also the instructions of Jesus and the apostles in the NT are rooted in the reality of God as an ethical being. On this the Bible is certain. And since God is concerned with ethics, his people should reflect his nature and his concerns. This theme occurs throughout Scripture with amazing frequency.

Be holy, for I the Lord your God am holy. (Lev. 19:2)

Circumcise, then, the foreskin of your heart, and do not be stubborn any longer. For the Lord your God is God of gods and Lord of lords, the great God, mighty and awesome, who is not partial and takes no bribes, who executes justice for the orphan and the widow, and who loves the strangers, providing them food and clothing. You shall also love the stranger, for you were strangers in the land of Egypt. (Deut. 10:16-18)

I give you a new commandment, that you love one another. Just as I have loved you, you also should love one another. By this everyone will know that you are my disciples, if you have love for one another. (John 13:34-35)

If you know that he [God] is righteous, you may be sure that everyone who does right has been born of him. (1 John 2:29)

The fundamental motive force for faithful living rests in God's faithful and caring acts toward his people. Since God is ethical in his very being, those who follow his ways are also ethical in accord with the nature of God. That nature expresses itself in countless acts of love and justice. Suppressing the knowledge of God leads individuals and nations to swerve from the will of God, shutting off the impulses of compassion and justice .

God's self-disclosure always has practical implications. God doesn't specialize in finely woven tapestries of theological thought created for ornamental display. For this reason, the recitation of judgments throughout Scripture is closely tied to explanations (*For three sins of X, even for four. . . . Because. . . .*) and to consequences (*Therefore. . . .*). God is not privately or secretly ethical. He displays his moral and saving acts before humanity so that people may rejoice in them and imitate them.   ·

Addressing the Nations   ·

In both Testaments, God calls nations to account. The OT prophets frequently conveyed words from God to the nations (Jonah; Nahum; Isa. 13–25; Jer. 46–51; Ezek. 25–32). Attention to the nations marks the function of Israel: they are to be a nation of priests (Exod. 19:1-7). John the Baptist stood in this tradition. He rebuked Herod for marrying his own brother's wife. Jesus openly called Herod a "fox," thereby criticizing his political policies and sly practices (Luke 13:32). Paul explained the faith in Jesus Christ to Felix under the topics of "goodness, self-control, and the coming judgment" (Acts 24:24-25). The Hebrew equivalent for "goodness" is "righteousness," a term and concept in Amos *[Justice and Righteousness, p. 390]*. So Paul's message to Felix had to do with his concern for those whom he governed, the manner in which he governed, and his accountability to God for how he ruled. Therefore, when addressing rulers and nations, the good news includes God's interest in their exercise of power and their political and national policies.

Salvation, God's restoring work, extends to the limits of human social structures. Not only are individuals sinners, but every human institution is capable of being used for evil or of serving the forces of evil. In Amos 1–2, the nations' policies and practices are vehicles of evil. The state—not just the king or the armed forces—is responsible. The collective evil has become part of the national ethos. Nations pursue aggression for the sake of national survival, national pride, revenge, or profit. Political and social structures as they exist in this world are not morally neutral. The sin of humanity has infected everything people touch. All those who identify with the affected structures and with the moral ethos they promote must accept responsibility for what they produce. That is why the judgment strikes at the center of power of each nation. And if the center is destroyed, all the dependent parts are affected and included.

THE TEXT IN THE LIFE OF THE CHURCH
Naming the Evils

Over the centuries the church has struggled with the issue of addressing the sins of the nominally "Christian" or the declared non-Christian societies in which it has existed. Most of the prominent sins of society are proportionately represented in the church. Sins cannot be localized or isolated in any given community. But the dominant sins of the surrounding culture tend also to be occasions for struggle in the faith community. The church's response to these issues becomes a touchstone of its faithfulness to the gospel. At the level of concrete example, the high incidence of graft and bribery in Zairean culture, the preoccupation with wealth in American society, the high incidence of Brazilian children born out of wedlock—these are all reflected in the theology and practice of the church in those countries. In that respect, when the church addresses its society, it is usually also addressing sins prominent among the Christians of that society. Israel, during the eighth century B.C., was no exception: witness the correlation of sins between Israelite society and the surrounding peoples. Clearly, the sanctification of God's people is incomplete.

The church has a primary obligation to address the in-house sins of those who claim the name of Christ. Many believers ask, Is the church also under obligation to speak to society (in its own setting or in another nation) regarding the destructive course of that culture? H. Richard Niebuhr has defined the issue in terms of the relationship between Christ and culture; insofar as a culture is destructive, Christ is against that culture. The church has offered a range of viewpoints and taken various positions in practice in the course of its existence.

Most nations addressed by Amos do not identify their national deity as Yahweh (Syria, Philistia, Phoenicia, Edom, Ammon, Moab). However, others do (Judah, Israel). The modern parallel might be between those nations which identify themselves as Christian (Western European countries, the Americas) and those that reject that label and are either consciously secular, identify with another religion, or are atheistic (such as Israel or Marxist or Muslim countries). Could Amos serve as a paradigm of cross-cultural and cross-faith communication?

First, Amos openly traces the message he proclaims to its source, the Lord. It does not grow out of personal opinion but originates in the will of the Creator and Sustainer of the universe (1:2), who is also the Lord of history. Amos leaves no ambiguity in his witness as to whom he serves and to whom the nations are accountable.

Second, every critique of society is accompanied by an implicit or explicit declaration of the grace and patience of God. The phrase *for three transgressions and for four*, while a stock expression, still reminds people that the Lord has been gracious to this point. God did not strike them down on their first offense. Amos himself draws that inference (5:15) when he pleads for Israel to repent. He hopes, *It may be that the Lord, the God of hosts, will be gracious to the remnant of Joseph.*

Third, while it is psychologically preferable to call for repentance and change while holding out some alternative courses of action, Amos proclaims God's disfavor on sin without alternatives to national policy. That is, Amos identifies the shape of evil. He is not an internationally recognized peacemaker. He speaks for God.

The church's witness to society becomes credible when Christian communities immerse themselves in the arena of interpersonal struggle and public life. The prophets call for repentance, but they also comfort the sorrowing, heal the wounded, advise kings and princes, promote specific public policies, and advocate human rights by identifying and suffering with the poor and outcast (cf. Isaiah, Jeremiah, Ezekiel). The prophets immerse themselves in human affairs at every level. When exiled, they (like Daniel) work for the welfare of the nation whose slaves or citizens they have become, even while declaring the will of God for that people.

Fourth, Amos addresses central, crucial issues, rather than attempting to speak to all the sins of the people. That is true for the nations at large as well as Judah and Israel. A universal condemnation is neither true to the circumstances, nor correctable. With the possible exception of Judah, the sin in focus concerns the treatment of persons. This involves their relationships, whether at a personal, social, political, or national level. In every case, the sin is specific: it is something of which people can repent. If they repent in deep sorrow for the sin mentioned, it will transform their attitudes and revolutionize their society. If they treat the helpless and their enemies with integrity and kindness, that inevitably translates at the collective level into a more compassionate and more gentle society.

Fifth, Amos consistently uses language and categories of discourse which those addressed understand. He describes the sins of the nations as violations of international conventions. Thus Amos presents commonly understood norms by which the peoples can evaluate themselves and one another. They had, in effect, violated the UN charter of human rights, which they had signed. No one could hide behind the accusation of prior violation. All deserve judgment.

At the same time, those who declare themselves God's people are called to greater responsibility (Habakkuk; Matt. 11:20-24). The presence of God's people in any nation should be discernible in the private and public life of that society, particularly if that nation professes to hold superior ethical norms. In that respect, the self-declared "Christian" nations of the world, having the greater knowledge, will be judged with greater severity for violations committed according to fuller knowledge.

Blessing the Good

In 1994 business leaders from Europe, Japan, and the United States met in Caux, Switzerland, to develop the first international code of ethics. The statement was eminently practical and rooted in concern for human dignity. Surely the Lord speaks blessing on all who promote the following principles!

Principle 1. The Responsibilities of Businesses: Beyond Shareholders Toward Stakeholders
The value of a business to society is the wealth and employment it creates and the marketable products and services it provides to consumers at a reasonable price commensurate with quality. To create such value, a business must maintain its own economic health and viability, but survival is not a sufficient goal.

Businesses have a role to play in improving the lives of all their customers, employees, and shareholders by sharing with them the wealth they have created. Suppliers and competitors as well should expect businesses to honor their obligations in a spirit of honesty and fairness. As responsible citizens of the local, national, and global communities in which they operate, businesses share a part in shaping the future of their communities.

Principle 2. The Economic and Social Impact of Business: Toward Innovation, Justice, and World Community
Businesses established in foreign countries to develop, produce, or sell should also contribute to the social advancement of those countries by creating productive employment and helping to raise the purchasing power of their citizens. Businesses should also contribute to human

rights, education, welfare, and vitalization of the countries in which they operate.

Businesses should contribute to economic and social development not only in the countries in which they operate but also in the world community at large, through effective and prudent use of resources, free and fair competition, and emphasis upon innovation in technology, production methods, marketing, and communications.

Principle 3. Business Behavior: Beyond the Letter of the Law Toward a Spirit of Trust

While accepting the legitimacy of trade secrets, businesses should recognize that sincerity, candor, truthfulness, the keeping of promises, and transparency contribute not only to their own credibility and stability but also to the smoothness and efficiency of business transactions, particularly on the international level. . . . (*Business Ethics* 10/1 [1996]: 36-37)

The Lord's People Indicted

Amos 2:4-16

EXPLANATORY NOTES
Judah 2:4-5

The crimes heaped up by *Judah* come under the same penetrating examination as those of her pagan neighbors. The final straw, the one which broke the camel's back in Judah's case, is that they deliberately *rejected the law of the Lord*, refused to *keep his decrees*, and pursued *false gods*. The language of this accusation occurs frequently in warning statements in Deuteronomy. There Israel is enjoined to follow God's "instruction" ("torah," 28:58; 29:21; 32:46) and to be sure to observe his specific decrees (4:40; 16:12; 26:17).

Amos explains the most frequent cause of such defection from the law of God as being the pursuit of *false gods* (*their lies have led them astray*). The word *lie* is used elsewhere in Scripture to refer to idols (Isa. 28:15, 17; Ps. 4:2; 40:4). Indeed, in Psalm 4:2 the godless are described as those who seek a divine word from the Lie. No wonder idols lead Judah astray—they constitute the Lie. They promise life but deliver death. They have enticed whole generations of God's people with their deceitful words and have distorted the truth of God. Judah plunged headlong into the way of death instead of walking in God's ways.

The accusation against Judah is given only in general terms. But since these appear so frequently as summaries of the will of God, the message is unmistakably clear. Judah's crime does not consist of any one unlawful act. She denies her covenant Lord. In following other gods (the Lie), her whole way of life has become perverted. The fusion of idol worship with the worship of the true God has resulted in a deeply patterned life, ingrained in successive generations (Amos 2:4c). As a result, Judah has become incapable of recognizing the truth. Such fixed patterns can be broken only by the intervention of God. And intervene he will: *I will send fire . . . and it will consume the fortresses of Jerusalem [Judah and David, p. 389].*

Israel 2:6-16

Israel is caught in Amos's dramatic recital. As he speaks word after word of judgment against the Northern Kingdom's neighbors, one can imagine the delight with which the Israelites nudge one another. Judgment against their traditional enemies translates into success and vindication for them—so they think. Too late do they realize that the circle has become a tightening noose: the last word will wrap them in judgment. There is no place left for them to dodge God's missiles: *For three transgressions of Israel. . . .* Five specific indictments follow.

2:6-8 A Long List of Crimes

Debt-slavery. Israelites were selling fellow Israelites into debt-slavery. Legislation governed the terms of such debt-slavery of Israelites (Exod. 21:7-8; Lev. 25:39-55; Deut. 15:12-18). While the practice was common in Israel and Judah (Isa. 50:1; Jer. 34:8-22; Neh. 5:1-8), it was subject to abuse, as the latter two texts illustrate. God's word through Amos attacks two of the abuses. The first was to sell the *righteous* into slavery. In legal contexts the term "righteous" means innocent (Deut. 25:1; Hos. 14:9), implying that some poor Israelites have been defrauded. Those who hold their mortgages foreclose on the loan and sell the lenders to erase the debt. If the form of the verb in the legislative texts is correctly translated by "sell themselves" rather than "be sold," then debt-slavery is legally carried out only at the initiative of the borrower. The borrower, not the lender, decides how to pay his debts. In the accusation against the Israelites, the text implies that the creditor is taking the initiative in selling the debtor (Amos 2:6). That may represent compounded crimes—forcible seizure and sale.

Extortion. The second abuse (2:6d) consists of *selling the poor for* (or: *because of) a pair of sandals.* The reference to a *pair of sandals* is not to the custom of removing a sandal in the commitment to preserve a brother's family line (Deut. 25:5-10; Ruth 4:7-8), but rather to the sale of people. The Hebrew word for "poor" used here and on four other occasions in Amos (4:1; 5:12; 8:4, 6) refers to a landholding class of Israelites who lost "access to the capital goods of the community—land and money" (Yoder, 1987:129). If the borrowing and lending practices are anything like those that existed in Egypt three centuries later, then the situation is grim indeed. Documents from Egypt indicate that people frequently borrowed grain, whether for seed or food. Interest of 50-100 percent per year was common.

The sabbatical year laws restored the land to its original owners in the fiftieth year (Lev. 25:8-55). Apparently these laws were ignored in Israel because they were poor business practice. An unspoken factor was the pervasive spirit of Baal, which had elevated the role of the independent landholder *[Ba'al, p. 373].* A climate of oppression has settled over the land.

The poor become wage earners or borrow to remain independent (Deut. 24:14). In our Amos text, these poor are already dispossessed of their land. Their last collateral consists of themselves and their families (cf. 2 Kings 4:1-7). In their greed for gain, the Israelite creditors heartlessly sell their own neighbors to erase minor debts, equivalent in value to *a pair of shoes.* Israel's wealthy are preoccupied with accumulating goods; people and community are of little consequence. The conventional wisdom seems to be "Suppress compassion if you want to succeed." No one argues with success. No one except Amos.

Into the trash with compassion goes the sense of community.

Oppression. Israel's third crime consists of oppressing the poor (Amos 2:7a). The poor referred to in this verse consist of the *powerless* (cf. 4:1; 5:11; 8:6) and the *socially or economically oppressed.* These include the permanently poor such as widows and orphans. They drain the economy.

While the translations vary in an attempt to make sense out of what may be terse Hebrew poetry or a copyist's errors, the point of the accusation is clear. Some wealthy take advantage of the poor.

The imagery of trampling on someone's head is drawn from military conquest and implies a class conflict. Society is divided into the conquerors and the conquered. This "defeated" segment of society does not have equal access to the court of law (2:7a). That fact captures the impact of the word *oppressed*. Presumably the wealthy also serve as judges in their communities. That places the subsistence farmer and day laborer at a distinct disadvantage. How much justice does the poor person receive when the judge holds the demand note? Such perversion of justice was clearly contrary to Israel's moral codes (Exod. 23:6-8; Deut. 16:19; 24:17-18).

Not only has compassion evaporated (Amos 2:6b), but Israel violates the basic rights offered to every person under the law of Moses.

Sexual Abuse. The fourth crime lies in the abuse of young women (2:7b), seemingly for social or religious purposes, as with a cult prostitute. The indictment is directed against son and father having sexual relations with the *same girl* (not a slave). In Hebrew the text reads: *a man and his father,* not "a man and his son." The text suggests that *every* man is a womanizer, or that a betrothed man and his father have intercourse with the bride-to-be, or that the young man's father is practicing incest. In any case, they profane the sanctity of monogamous marriage (cf. Deut. 22:13-30). They may even have a religious motive, to ensure fertility and thus to provide security through descendants *[Prostitution, p. 393]*. Whatever the specific motive, this act *profanes God's holy name.* It lays the foundation of marriage in immorality and violates the young woman's personhood. The woman, whether sold, betrothed, or married, serves as the helpless object and victim of men's lust.

Such pagan customs leave Israel's faith and her God indistinguishable from those of other nations; it depreciates women, soon reduces the marriage covenant to a contract, and defiles God's name *[Covenant, p. 379]*.

Injustice and Hypocrisy. Amos hurries on to the fifth crime (2:8), a crime against the poor, justified on religious grounds. Israel's legislation protected the person who borrowed to feed his family. The creditor would take as collateral the man's heavy protective garment, used to shield against the sun by day and the cold by night. The Torah forbade a creditor from keeping the outer cloak after sunset, since it served as the owner's blanket at night (Exod. 22:26-27; Deut. 24:12-13). The wealthy acted in utter disregard for the welfare of their debtors.

Picture the scene. The lender has been "gracious" to the poor by lending him enough food to keep his family alive. He keeps the cloak as collateral when he goes to his favorite shrine to spend the night, to wait for a word from God (cf. Pss. 3-4), or to show his devotion to the

Lord. On other occasions, the wealthy—presumably those in some administrative position—exact fines paid with wine for violations of some law. The word *fines* refers to restitution for damages incurred (Deut. 22:19; Exod. 21:22).

The "other party" in Amos's indictment is the poor person. The prophet does not suggest that the poor are innocent. Indeed, the poor shall not be acquitted because they are poor (cf. Exod. 23:3). The rich and powerful, however, are adjudged guilty of pressing every possible claim against the weak and needy. Against those claims, the poor have limited recourse before the law (Amos 2:7a). Then the rich self-righteously use the collateral and fines of wine to finance their acts of devotion to the Lord. There is an inherent conflict between such attitudes and acts toward the helpless and a declared devotion to God. The presence of sin, whether committed against God or people, renders all such worship null and void.

Israel's institutions, too, fail to embody the divine will. Trade and commerce, the judicial system, marriage and the family, the religious system—all have become perverted. These are representative sins. The description points to customary actions (2:6-8). The societal structures have become weapons of oppression for those in control. If the nation is to be restored to wholeness, the medium of exchange must become compassion, love, and justice.

2:9-12 Worse Than the Amorites

The mind's eye takes in the scene. The backdrop is the city gate, where the majority of significant transactions occur. Beside it stands Amos, delivering himself of the deep compulsion to herald the words of God. One can imagine the city's elite, the rich and the powerful, carrying on business there, but not as usual. They would like to send Amos packing. But if he is a true prophet, they should at least hear what he has to say. You can see their lips move, muttering to themselves: "God wouldn't judge us for such petty faults. Amos is pulling at straws." However, the words belong to God, not to Amos, and God presses home the explanation of why he will refuse to withdraw the judgment.

But as for me, I . . . introduces the sharp contrast between how the Israelites have acted and what God has done. Three of God's gracious acts illustrate his attitude toward the sinful (2:9), the poor and oppressed (2:10), and the ignorant (2:11-12). The message, by implication and blunt application, gives the lie to any thought that Israel's crimes are not worthy of God's scrutiny and judgment.

Amorites is used as a general term for the assortment of peoples whom Israel eventually replaced in Palestine (Num. 13:28-29). The metaphors which characterize the Amorites as *tall as the cedars* and as *strong as the oaks* display people at the height of arrogance and power (Isa. 2:10-18). The divine judgment destroyed their *fruit above* and *roots below* (cf. Hos. 9:16; Job 18:16; Mal. 4:1). The metaphors shift the scene from the hills of Lebanon (cedars) and Bashan (oaks) to the fertile valleys of Palestine, where orchards flourished and were an important part of the economy. Destroying both root and fruit "combines the imagery of both planting and harvesting, imagery which when applied to human beings conjures up images of stability and prosperity" (Wolff: 169). Both are erased in the sweep of God's judgment.

The horticultural imagery contains a double message. In spite of all their security, self-confidence, pride, and strength, the Amorites were felled by their Creator. Yet God delayed their destruction for four generations until the Amorite measure of sins was filled to overflowing (Gen. 15:16). That bushel of sins consisted of idolatry and disgusting practices (Exod. 23:23-24). A second, thinly veiled message is directed against Israel. For many generations, the Lord has patiently endured their smug self-satisfaction, their misuse of power against fellow Israelites, and their worship of foreign deities. Their sins exceed by far the iniquity of the Amorites. So now the ax is about to strike at Israel's roots, scattering her fruit as she comes crashing to the ground (cf. Matt. 3:10).

Perhaps that argument will not impress Israel with the sinfulness of her crimes. So Amos adds another (2:10). Not only did God destroy the Amorites, who lived in opposition to the Almighty, but the Lord also preserved the helpless and oppressed. It was God who brought up a slave people out of Egypt. It was God who nurtured them those *forty years in the desert* until they entered the Promised Land. In their maturity they were given the *land of the Amorites* as an inheritance *[Exodus Tradition, p. 384]*.

That raises the point for Amos's listeners: Who can expect God's mercy? To ask the question is to answer it. The helpless, innocent, disadvantaged, and enslaved shall be rescued by God himself, even in the face of overwhelming power and abundant religiosity. Israel and the Amorites have become a parable of life within the Northern Kingdom. In the exodus event, the Amorites were the oppressors and the Israelites the oppressed, the rich and the poor, the powerful and the weak. In Amos's day, those roles were filled by two classes of Israelites. The Judge will not fail to judge the sinful; the Redeemer will once more rescue those calling out to him for deliverance.

The third historical event which puts Israel's present sin into perspective grows out of God's legislative provision for faithful leaders (2:11-12; cf. Deut. 18:14-22; Num. 6). By appointing *prophets*, God equipped Israel to receive new insights and corrective messages. By making provision for *Nazirites*, God demonstrated for them the special blessings which come on those who devoutly and sacrificially follow his ways. Israel has no excuse for pursuing false gods. The Lord established a continuous line of prophets to be his messengers: Elijah, Elisha, Micaiah ben Imlah (1 Kings 17—2 Kings 13), Amos himself, and others. By following the example of people of faith (Nazirites), the prophetic ideal of devotion to God and service to God's people was possible.

The chiastic structure of these two verses (Amos 2:11-12) beautifies and strengthens their message *[Literary Patterns, p. 391]*.

I raised up	*prophets*
	Nazirites
Question:	*Is this not true?*
You *forced*	*Nazirites*
[You] *commanded*	*prophets*

Israel has consistently distorted the examples of godliness and countermanded God's orders. The people of Israel are not about to honor the self-effacing example of the Nazirites. Self-denial, asceticism, and voluntary poverty do not fit their plans. Nor are the rich and powerful inclined to receive the word of preachers critical of their interpretation of the faith and their way of life.

Early in the Northern Kingdom, prophetism came under the thumb of the monarchy and was nearly squelched by it. Ahab molded Israel's future ruling elite and held the Lord's prophets in fear as well as contempt. He attempted to silence the prophet Micaiah (1 Kings 22). Elijah's Nazirite lifestyle was hardly attractive to King Ahab. With a one-generation interlude of Jehu's revolution (2 Kings 9-10), the pattern remained intact down to Amos's day.

Political, economic, social, and religious structures have become infested with paganism and have sealed themselves against the healing balm offered by God's messengers and saints. Gangrene has set in; the patient cannot survive.

2:13-16 Punishments to Match

Israel's sins have loaded her down like a cart piled high with sheaves of grain. Such a cart, pulled through the soft fields, sinks deeply into the soil. The oxen strain and the axles groan as the wheels rut the ground under their load (Amos 2:13). Israel's harvest of sins is about to be taken to the threshing floor by God, there to be winnowed and disposed of as chaff.

Then the figure of speech changes, in line with Amos's announcement. At God's invitation, an enemy stands poised to harvest Israel by means of the sword (2:14-16). The ultimate blessing for God's people is to enjoy a peace which allows them to "beat their swords into plowshares, and their spears into pruning hooks" (Isa. 2:4; Mic. 4:3). The corresponding curse is to travail under the harvest of war. And what a war it will be!

When the punishing army marches against Israel, the military training, experience, and skills of Israel's armed elite will fail them (Amos 2:14). Every unit in the army—archers, infantry, and chariotry—will be overwhelmed in the rout (2:15). Indeed, the bravest of the professional soldiers (2:16a) will strip themselves of all armor and drop their weapons to speed them on their way from certain death on the battlefield (2:16b).

THE TEXT IN BIBLICAL CONTEXT

God, the Poor, and Violence

A unifying thread is woven into these two chapters. God expresses deep concern for the weak, the downtrodden, the disenfranchised, and the poor. God forcefully demonstrates his interest in this segment of society. Whether addressing Philistia, Edom, or Israel, God leaves no doubt about his concern for the mistreated. God's demand for the exercise of justice affirms human worth and reaffirms the equal worth of each person. Election does not change the value of persons. Here is no special theology for Israel. In all cases, the blatant sins enumerated represent a lust for possessions and power. The consequent oppression is sin, whether in private transactions or in public policy.

Sin frequently expresses itself in violence. Broken relationships of every kind are the product of sin and are themselves sin. The exercise and justification of destructive brute force takes many forms. Within Amos 1–2, it expresses itself in political oppression, slave trade, barbarous cruelty, denial of others' legal or economic rights, lack of compassion, use and misuse of women, and forced conformity to the standards of the privileged. Violence turns people into objects and denies their inherent worth. It negates the creation of human community. Violence perverts truth in its need for self-justification. It drains its practitioners of the capacity for healthy relationships and self-understanding. As Amos points out, it can be directed at anyone: distant nation, neighbor, friend, relative, or wife.

With regard to the expressions of sin in Israel, the text nowhere asks, "Are the poor also to blame for their poverty?" Nor does it point toward a socialist ideal. Differences in the distribution of power are assumed. The problem lies in the exercise of power. God, we are told, consistently exercises his power on behalf of the powerless: the Israelites in Egyptian bondage (Exod. 3:7-10; 6:5-13) as well as the foreigners and Israelites in Israelite bondage (21:1-11; 23:9); the landless poor, orphans, widows, and Levites of Israel (Deut. 14:22–15:17) as well as the aliens (24:17-22).

Amos 1–2 illustrates the larger principle of Scripture: God defends the cause of those who cannot defend themselves (Deut. 10:16-18; Pss. 9:7-9; 35:10; 140:12). That means that God is against the rich and powerful who do not promote the cause of the less fortunate (cf. Amos 6:3-7, esp. 6:6b; Luke 10:25-37; James 5:1-6). God summons the wealthy and powerful as well as every other member of his people to join him in lifting the fallen, caring for the helpless, and relieving the burdens of those bowed by circumstances of life (Lev. 25; Deut. 24:14-22; Luke 4:16-21; Gal. 6:1-10).

THE TEXT IN THE LIFE OF THE CHURCH
Cheap Grace

The Israelites' practices of economic injustice (Amos 2:6-8) reflect a problem in their understanding and exercise of the faith. They forgot when the Lord called them as a covenant people, he was also binding them to one another in the covenant. The very nature of human discourse was at issue. If they would have observed the sanctity of their covenant relationship, they would have mirrored the nature and strength of their ties to the covenant Lord. In violating the welfare of their brothers and sisters in the community of faith, they defamed the name of the God of Israel.

Such a warped concept of covenant faith springs from a weak grasp of the sinfulness of sin and the holiness of God. This perverse thinking does not flourish in the hearts of those moved by the immensity of God's gift of deliverance and forgiveness. The faithfulness of the community of God's people is not nurtured by a shallow, purely individualistic concept of sin and salvation. It rests, instead, in the awareness of the One who stood on Mount Sinai, declaring his will, and the One who hung on Mt. Calvary, demonstrating his love.

Dietrich Bonhoeffer (35) witnessed the harvest of forgetfulness in the church of his day and described its cause with passion and eloquence:

> Cheap grace means grace sold on the market like a cheapjack's wares. The sacraments, the forgiveness of sin, and the consolations of religion are thrown away at cut prices. Grace is represented as the Church's inexhaustible treasury, from which she showers blessings with generous hands, without asking questions or fixing limits. Grace without price; grace without cost! The essence of grace, we suppose, is that the account has been paid in advance; and, because it has been paid, everything can be had for nothing. Since the cost was infinite, the possibilities of using and spending it are infinite. What would grace be if it were not cheap?

On Being a Conscience to the World

Sins against God—whether in forgetfulness, neglect, or rebellion— invariably turn against one's covenant companions. Crimes against humanity are expressions of defiance against the Almighty. Continuous intrusion of sin into the covenant people inevitably frays and eventually snaps the bond of community which holds them together.

Sin seeks the cover of darkness; it resists disclosure. It silences the word calling to accountability, confession, and repentance. It besmirches the garments of those walking with God. A later Prophet (the Messiah) reminded his disciples that society would hate them, as it had hated him, because they were a conscience to the world:

> They will do all these things to you on account of my name, because they do not know him who sent me. If I had not come and spoken to them, they would not have sin; but now they have no excuse for their sin.
> (Jesus, in John 15:21-22; cf. 15:18-27)

Society's opposition to the truth and purity of God is one thing; the church's resistance is another.

The church has both beatified and pilloried its saints. The Oxford scholar William Tyndale invested the years 1520-1536 in translating the Bible into English. Once when a high church official was opposing his translation efforts, he countered with a memorable statement:

"If God spare my life, ere many years I will cause a boy that driveth the plough shall know more of the Scripture than thou doest." The prediction came true. Before he died at the stake in 1536, the NT had been translated and had received general acceptance in England.

Part 2

The Covenant Lawsuit

Amos 3:1—6:14

OVERVIEW

Israel suffers from what some might call attention deficit disorder. Amos shouts for Israel's attention: *Hear this word* (3:1; 4:1; 5:1). The nation is occupied with everything except God. The prophet here fleshes out the earlier sweeping accusations (2:6-16).

The nation has grown moral callouses. It is too set in its ways to recognize its own plight. In an attempt to stop its headlong rush to destruction, the Lord exposes the corruption which threatens to tear this people apart. Israel is unaware that her vital signs are so dangerously weak and deteriorating. Will these warnings startle her into remedial action, or will they fall on deaf ears?

The perspective shifts from Israel as one of the nations (Amos 1–2) to Israel's unique covenant relationship to the Lord [Covenant, p. 379]. Amos begins by describing his reluctant participation (3:3-8). His assigned role is to announce God's legal proceedings against his people (3:1-2, 9-13) and to invite the witnesses to come forward with the evidence they have gathered. The lawsuit follows what in modern legal proceedings amounts to the formal arraignment (2:6-16).

Amos 3–6 contains historical reviews, descriptions of the messenger, witnesses, accused and judge, as well as detailed recitals of the crimes, previous judgments, and penalties about to be imposed. What begins as a lawsuit ends as a funeral.

These four chapters contain sharp warnings uttered more in grief than in anger. The evidence of the present (Amos 3) and past (Amos 4) is overwhelming. Though Israel is guilty, God himself walks among those mourning the death of the virgin (5:1-2).

OUTLINE

Getting Your Day in Court, 3:1-15

Persistent Patterns of Sinning, 4:1-13

Funeral Song: Israel's Last Gasp, 5:1—6:14
  5:1-17   Theme: How (Not) to Meet God
  5:18-27   Stanza 1: The Terrors of That Day
  6:1-14   Stanza 2: Bursting the Bubble of Security and Pleasure

Amos 3:1-15

Getting Your Day In Court

PREVIEW

Israel's court case begins. Judge (3:1-2), prophet (3:3-8), and witnesses (3:9) enter the scene in turn. Samaria and Bethel come under greatest condemnation. They are the nation's political and religious centers (3:10-15).

OUTLINE

First Case: Israel, 3:1-2

Amos's Opening Questions, 3:3-8

Judgment Begins at Home, 3:9-15
    3:9-10   Testimony of Hostile Witnesses
    3:11-15   Verdict and Sentencing

EXPLANATORY NOTES
First Case: Israel 3:1-2

In one long breath, Amos announces the source and the content of his message: *the Lord* addresses *Israel.* Amos refers to the Lord in the third person, and the Lord speaks in the first person, *I.* Israel has enjoyed a long history of intimacy with God. The term *the entire family* reminds Israel of her high calling. The descendants of Abraham were to be the means of God's blessing on "all the families of the earth" (Gen. 12:3; 28:14). The entire history of God's loving care and high hopes for his people compresses into these lines. Israel alone has experienced the special deliverance from Egypt. Surely that act should alert Israel to God's claim on her!

That claim was sealed in God's electing love. As a husband *knows* his wife in the intimacy of marital love, so of all nations, God has known only Israel. He has called her to be a special possession (Exod. 19:4-8; Deut. 10:12-22). Israel was selected as God's sole legitimate covenant partner. *Therefore* he jealously watched over Israel for her purity and welfare.

God, the loving husband, committed himself to his bride, Israel. He expected a corresponding promise of exclusive relationship and faithfulness from Israel. These promises and conditions headed up Israel's founding document: "I am the Lord your God, who brought you out. . . . You shall have no other gods before me" (Exod. 20:2-3). The covenant language prepares us for judgment in place of the blessings God longed to give.

When Israel cried out to God from her bondage beside the Nile, God visited (Exod. 3:16) his oppressed people. Surely, when the poor and needy cry out to God beside the Kishon River, he will hear and rescue them. That future visit will be one of corrective judgment for all the nations to see (Amos 3:2, 14). God will not be treated cavalierly. Nor will he abandon his elective purposes with Israel. His claim as Creator and his invitation to the families of the earth to acknowledge him as Savior—both find fulfillment even in Israel's disobedience ("Election," in TBC below).

Amos's Opening Questions 3:3-8

Amos's seven rhetorical questions build the argument for Israel's responsibility for their failure to hear the prophetic word throughout their occupancy of the Promised Land (3:3-6; cf. 2:9). The pattern of seven-eight here has the same literary function as the prophecies against the seven nations of chapters 1–2, climaxing in the judgment against Israel, the eighth nation.

The series of questions retraces the geography and topography of the conquest of the land. It moves us along from the lonely pathway to the game-filled thickets of the Jordan and other river valleys and fi-

nally draws us into the city where the judgments of God will be executed against Israel. With the exception of the first question, which
provides linkage to the idea of election, intimacy, and wilderness travel (3:1-2), the cause-and-effect imagery is bound up with death and
destruction. The prophet's message is an unpleasant one, to say the
least. In this sequence of destructive metaphors, one moves through
a progression of causal agents: animals, people, God, indicating that
all of life is bound up with the "law" of cause and effect.

The event and message of Genesis 18:16-19 appear to underlie
3:7. Prior to destroying Sodom and Gomorrah, the Lord muses:

> Shall I hide from Abraham what I am about to do, seeing that Abraham
> shall become a great and mighty nation, and all the nations of the earth
> shall be blessed in him? (Gen. 18:18)

God has been voicing warnings to his people through *his servants, the prophets* (Amos 3:7-8). He has not been silent in the past
(cf. 2:11). Let Israel know that none of God's judgments have come at
a whim. In Abraham's day, the sins of Sodom and Gomorrah cried
out to heaven for judgment. In Amos's day, Samaria's sins attract
God's attention and become the object of the Lord's displeasure
(Amos 3:9; cf. Ezek. 16). Israel cannot expect to receive the
Abrahamic blessings when she has failed to do what is right and just.

Those same cues contain a warning for Amos as well as Israel.
Since the message has come to Amos as a lion's roar, refusal to deliv-
er it would surely bring serious consequences: *When the Sovereign
Lord speaks, who can but prophesy?* (3:8).

Judgment Begins at Home 3:9-15

3:9-10 Testimony of Hostile Witnesses

An Israelite court required the matching testimony of two witnesses to convict the accused (Deut. 17:6). Where would one find
two trustworthy and independent witnesses against Israel? Among
the nations—those whom the faith of Israel was to attract so they
could share in the blessings of Abraham (Gen. 18:18) and the promises of Israel (Exod. 19:6).

The court is represented here by heralds or town criers. They
mount the fortresses of the two witnesses, Ashdod (Philistia) and
Egypt, to invite the inhabitants of those countries to observe the sins
of Israel. These past oppressors of Israel can verify that Israel's just
God does judge oppression. Their national representatives are invit-

ed not to the installation of a new king but as witnesses to flagrant crimes. They can observe them from the vantage point of the mountains surrounding the city of Samaria. There is ample evidence against Israel. The catalogue of sins (Amos 3:9b-10) becomes a checklist for the witnesses.

The eyewitnesses will see *great tumults within her.* Israel's way of life has brought social unrest and confusion (cf. Prov. 15:16; 2 Chron. 15:5). Her communal life is no longer ordered by charity, compassion, or concern for fellow Israelites. Distrust, unrest, and anxiety rule a people meant to live in harmony. Trust between God's covenant partners has vanished, leaving uncertainty and social chaos in its wake. Israel has transformed Edenic tranquillity into turmoil.

Within Samaria, the capital, *oppressions* are the order of the day. The context of the same word in Jeremiah points to oppression as the misuse of economic power: "Act with justice and righteousness, and deliver from the hand of the oppressor anyone who has been robbed" (Jer. 22:3; cf. Prov. 28:16; Isa. 33:15). Extortion prevails. In the following lines (Amos 3:10), these money-grubbers and land-grabbers are described as those *who hoard plunder and loot in their fortresses.* Or more aptly put, *They store up the product of murder and robbery in their palaces.*

The administrators of the realm may be the oppressors, since the storerooms served for the collection and distribution of tax revenues (in kind) and other government goods and possessions. If that is the case, then the people of the ruling class are lining their own pockets while collecting scandalously high property and excise taxes.

The witnesses will observe the third sin: the Israelites have lost their sense of integrity (3:10). They live by deceit and lies. Their moral moorings have rotted away.

3:11-15 Verdict and Sentencing

Israel's sins must be punished. Judgment strikes at two points, both representing supposed sources of security. First, a national enemy will move through the entire country, tearing down the fortresses on which Israel relies for security and plundering the mansions in which they have stored their ill-gotten gain (3:11). Second, this unnamed enemy will savage the inhabitants of Samaria who indulged themselves with *four-poster beds* and *silk bedspreads* (3:12).

God is Shepherd as well as Judge. The shepherd simile gains its power from the sarcasm in the word *rescue. Two shin bones and a piece of an ear* is no "rescue" of a sheep from a ravenous lion. Instead, these become evidence of Israel's certain fate. Some expositors, who want to see here a hint of salvation, have thought that the bones rescued suggest a remnant spared. But the tone is one of irony.

Lions appear prominently in the art and artifacts of Egypt and Assyria. The lion had a magical protective (apotropaic) function. As a result, it was often represented in carvings or statues at the entrances to cities, temples, or palaces (Weippert: 15-17). Mittmann has pointed out that the legs of the bed were frequently shaped as lion legs, or decorations were carved in lion motifs (Weippert: 15-17). In the message of Amos, however, the lion destroys rather than protects (3:12; cf. 1:2). Israel falsely depends on beasts of prey. Their sources of confidence will turn and destroy them. Only a few will survive. Instead of being a source of hope, "the remnant motif is here employed as an absolute threat against the national existence of Israel" (Hasel: 181).

The second summons to the witnesses invites them to *hear* the pronouncement of judgment based on the flagrant sinning they have evidenced (3:13). The punishing word comes from the Lord of heaven's armies.

Once more the message strikes at Israel's securities and her comfortable living. The judgment will eliminate the many altars of high places in Bethel, where the Israelites thought that by multiplying offerings, they were assuring themselves forgiveness for their sins and protection by the Almighty (3:14b). In fact, even *the horns of the altar* at Bethel will be cut down as by some giant sword. The significance of destroying these horns lies in their judicial function. The corners of stone altars project upward, serving the fugitive who grasps them as a final sanctuary from which to plead for grace (Exod. 21:13-14; 1 Kings 1:50). A murderer, however, was to be torn away from the altar and executed (Exod. 21:14; 1 Kings 2:28-34).

When the Israelites in desperation flee to the altar to claim sanctuary, they will find the horns missing. Their deeds warrant no more grace. In that judgment day, their well-built *winter homes* and *summer cottages* will become rubble (Amos 3:15). The reference to the *many* (Heb.; NRSV note) *homes* points toward social evils: accumulating properties so wealth is concentrated in the hands of the few. It also implies that a small segment of society lives in opulence. Finally, it may also carry a satirical note regarding the extent of the judgment: many family lines (Heb.: a building or a lineage) will be destroyed in the coming judgment. The ivory decorations found in the excavated ruins of Amos's Samaria confirm the details of this prophetic word.

THE TEXT IN BIBLICAL CONTEXT
Election: Privilege and Responsibility

God's electing grace contained a call to responsibility as well as an invitation to privilege (3:1-2; cf. Deut. 5-11). As Jesus said, "From everyone to whom much has been given, much will be required; and from the one to whom much has been entrusted, even more will be demanded" (Luke 12:48). Israel tended to "hug the promises and play leapfrog with the command." The obedience of faith was to be lived out in gratitude, not compulsion. The memory of God's mighty rescue from Egyptian bondage had been indelibly inscribed in her consciousness. Born in slavery—whether to Pharaoh or to sin—God's people were to delight in the freedom to live for the Lord. Failure to do so was like a slap in the face of the Holy One. Such insults were worthy of severest judgment.

Election does not negate the law of cause and effect by which the world moves to its God-ordained destiny (Amos 3:2-11). That pattern remains impressed on nature, human relationships, human activities, and the work of God. To assume that in election the Almighty locked himself in to the unconditional welfare of this people was to exclude Israel itself from the cycle of cause and effect. Amos stoutly insisted that Israel was not exempt from that cause-and-effect pattern.

However, eighth-century Israel was not uniquely self-deceived about election privileges. Jeremiah echoed this theme in his famed temple sermon to Judah, except that in his day, the magic words were: "This is the temple of the Lord, the temple of the Lord, the temple of the Lord!" (7:4). God assured smug Judah that he would not be inconvenienced by destroying his own dwelling place, since it had been so grossly defiled. And those opposed to the teachings of our Lord and the apostles scoffed, saying, "Where is the promise of his coming? For ever since our ancestors died, all things continue as they were from the beginning of creation" (2 Pet. 3:4). But they forgot that God does not measure time by the movement of the earth or sun. When God's bell tolls, the judgment issues forth against evil and its agents. Even God's people experience judgment against sin (cf. Amos 9:10).

Witness of the Nations

The nations are attracted to the true God through seeing the acts of love among God's people and their devotion to their Lord (cf. Exod.

19:1-6; Deut. 4:5-10; Matt. 5:13-16; 1 Pet. 2:11-12). But if those who have been specially privileged with the good news and the divine favor of salvation turn away from their Lord, God is even able to use that sin in drawing peoples to himself. By summoning the nations to observe Israel's sin, God exposes their shame. The act of judgment vindicates God and preserves the divine integrity. As they witness God's punishment of that sin, his sovereignty and hatred of sin become clear to all (cf. Deut. 29:22-28; Ezek. 36:16-23). God's purposes were not to be thwarted, even by the unbelief and disobedience of his people. In this way the divine judgment becomes a faith invitation to the nations.

THE TEXT IN THE LIFE OF THE CHURCH

Witness to the Nations

Hear this word . . . spoken against . . . the whole family that I brought up out of the land of Egypt. "You only have I known. . . . Therefore. . . ."

Abraham and his descendants were called not merely for their own sake, but because they were to become a blessing to the nations. Amos 3 reminds the nation that they have forgotten their high calling. Egypt and the nations of Palestine were to see and hear of the exodus events and give reverence to the Lord (Exod. 6:5-9; 19:5-6; Ps. 102:18-22; 106; Deut. 4). Israel's disobedience brings on her the curses of the covenant. But even in the act of judgment, God is honored. The church, too, has frequently forgotten or failed to understand her high calling.

The apostles, taking their cue from Jesus, declare the advent of the kingdom of God as present reality in the presence of Jesus, the King. Deliverance and mission are closely tied. The great commissions (Matt. 10; 28:18-20; Luke 10; Acts 1:8) capture the passion of Christ for his people and for their ministry in this world.

Church history records the ebb and flow of the church's grasp and implementation of that vision. The gospel flowered in the first three centuries of the Christian era. Constantine's conversion and patronage of the Christian faith contributed to its domestication, even though he initially involved himself reluctantly in church matters. The fortunes of the Roman empire became, in large measure, the fortunes of the church. The witness of the church was extended in part through force of arms. Yet even in darker years, the monastic movement and individual missioners stood out as beacons showing the visible form of the remnant. Among them stands Patrick of Ireland.

A Briton, Patrick was captured by Irish raiders and sold as a slave. Reared in a Christian home, the sixteen-year-old recalled that his six years as a swineherd were marked by a strong sense of God's sustaining presence. He escaped, went to France, and embraced the monastic life. A Macedonian call came to him in Britain. He responded by returning to Ireland. There he powerfully confronted the Druid religion with the Christian faith. The Christian gospel prevailed; large numbers of Irish converted to the Christian faith. Like Amos before him, Patrick spoke boldly against injustice. In his *Letter to the Subjects of Coroticus*, he indignantly reproved the Christian leader of a band of British raiders who massacred Ulsterites and took captives, some of whom were recent converts. Patrick's death on March 17, 461, remains an important anniversary date even today in the national calendar of Ireland (Bruce: 372-383).

In mainstream Christianity, missionary interest waned considerably until the Protestant Reformation. Yet missioners helped keep the flame alive: Boniface, the Waldenses, Francis of Assisi, Dominic de Guzmán, and Raymond Lull, and others. Mission and witness, however, were not in the forefront of the church's sense of election.

Complacency, inquisitorial and crusading methods, and national identification marked the missional ebb. Its flow was seen in the reform movements, outbursts of spiritual awakening, larger-than-life men and women, and an exploding consciousness of newly discovered worlds. Few incidents capture the conflict within the church on the question of its mission in response to God's gift of deliverance as well as an event in William Carey's life. This former shoemaker, licensed to preach at the age of twenty-five (1786), in that same year,

> attended a Baptist ministers' meeting in Northampton. The group was shocked when the inexperienced young minister stood to declare that they should consider: "Whether the command given by the apostles to teach all nations was not obligatory on all succeeding ministers to the end of the world, seeing that the accompanying premise was of equal extent."
>
> Carey was immediately told to sit down by the moderator, Dr. John Ryland, who said, "When God wants to convert the heathen, he will do it without your help or mine. You are a miserable enthusiast for asking such a question." (Starkes: 155)

Yet the question has not been erased from the lips of many of God's people over the centuries. The faithful are still marked by Amos's concern for a faithful witness as an outgrowth of the confident hope in God who has chosen them.

Amos 4:1-13

Persistent Patterns of Sinning

PREVIEW

Two video clips of Israel's everyday life unmask the evil beneath the surface. Five still shots reveal a pattern of partial repentance: enough to soothe the conscience, but too little to restore the nation to her first love.

The present sins (4:1-5) add to the heap of earlier crimes. Israel is obstinate. She refuses to respond to the covenant Lord's judgments calling her back (4:6-11). That is why she must prepare to meet her God (4:12-13).

OUTLINE

Oracle 1: Conspicuous Consumption, 4:1-3
 4:1-2a The Socialite Sinners
 4:2b-3 Led Out by the Nose

Oracle 2: Invitation to Sin, 4:4-5
 4:4-5a Priestly Invitation
 4:5b   Sarcastic Punch Line

Oracle 3: Incomplete Repentance, 4:6-11
    4:6-11   I Did . . .
    4:6-11   Yet You Did Not . . .

Oracle 4: Watch Out! 4:12-13
    4:12   Get Ready!
    4:13   God's Awesome Identity

EXPLANATORY NOTES

Oracle 1: Conspicuous Consumption 4:1-3

4:1-2a The Socialite Sinners

The prophetic word addresses the *cows of Bashan who are on Mount Samaria*. The women of the leading families of Samaria, the Washington, D.C., of the Northern Kingdom, are intended with this imagery. Bashan, a territory to the east of the Sea of Galilee, was prime grazing land (Jer. 50:19; Mic. 7:14). It was known for its superb breed of cattle (Ps. 22:12; Ezek. 39:18). The designation, *cows of Bashan*, may be an honorable one. It may even be proudly used by the women to describe their religious commitment or social status.

The modified religion of the Northern Kingdom symbolized Yahweh (as well as El and Baal) as a bull (1 Kings 12:28-30; 2 Kings 17:16; Hos. 8:5-6; 13:2) *[Bull Calves, p. 375]*. If that is the life context of the image, the women of Samaria may regard themselves as female partners with their bull god (Jacobs: 109-110). Religion, then, gives sanction to their way of life *[Bovine Imagery, p. 374]*. Or the connotation of this metaphor may be merely economic, pointing to well-being. Another interpretative possibility is that Amos adopts a no-nonsense approach with this indelicate opening sentence in his after-dinner address to that society's jet set.

The ladies of the elite class are guilty of sinning at arm's length. These "aggressive" cattle (cf. Ps. 22:12) are pictured as butting the more docile and smaller cattle about them into submission—they *oppress the poor* and *crush the needy*. The two parallel phrases point up the abuse of the weak and helpless (*dalim*) as well as the landless wage earners (cf. *'ebyon:* Exod. 23:6, "poor"; Deut. 15:1-11, "needy"). By their actions these cultivated ladies have become oppressors of the landless working class. They insist on a higher standard of living. Their demands pressure their husbands into disregarding the rights of others.

There may be another dimension to their sin. The women are demanding more of the best wine. But Israel's festivals were never drinking feasts. Therefore, Amos may be referring to a private religious event in worship of the Lord. The sequence, *Bring* (s.) *that we* (pl.) *may drink!* suggests that a man's wives are in chorus demanding of their common husband that he provide more of the best wine for them. If that inference drawn from the grammar is valid, then the practice of polygamy is exerting pressure on the men.

One function of polygamy is to ensure descendants. As a result of the men's preoccupation with pleasure, reputation, and security (functions of polygamy), the wives and concubines are causing their husbands to demand more of their laborers for less pay. Status requires socially accepted behavior. Here, then, lies one of the motive forces for *selling the righteous for silver, and the needy for a pair of sandals*, and for *trampling on the heads of the poor* (Amos 2:6-7). Sins, indirect as they may be, will not go unpunished.

Another connotation may lie within the bovine imagery. Baal, too, was represented by the bull. His cult was particularly strong in *Samaria* (1 Kings 16:32), the city built by Ahab's father, Omri. Hosea pictures Israel as a heifer in heat, pursuing her lovers (Hos. 2:6). The women of Samaria, then, may be devotees of Baal celebrating his goodness to them in a female family ritual. They may be gathering in something similar to the private club for leading men of the city (cf. Amos 8:4-6).

The oath that follows (4:2-3) secures the judgment on these "noble" women. Oaths are assurances that one will keep one's word. The oath under the formula, *by his holiness*, is the ultimate assurance that God guarantees the promise or threat (cf. Ps. 89:35). That holiness blazes against Israel's sin until the sinners are consumed. Earlier, Amos accused the men of drinking wine taken as fines in the house of their god (2:8). The women of the ruling class are similarly guilty of oppressive behavior.

4:2b-3 Led Out by the Nose

The particular form of the judgment against the *cows of Bashan* fits the imagery of cattle as well as that of capture and exile following a military invasion. On an unspecified day, an unidentified invader will surround Samaria and smash down its walls. After the walls are breached (4:3), many of the inhabitants will die in the onslaught, but *the last* will be taken away (4:2b). According to one reading, the women (*cows*) will be cast out, bloated corpses piled up like so much garbage (Hayes: 140-142). Alternatively, the text may describe them as led out into exile, straight through gaps in the city walls, toward *Harmon* (possibly Mt. Hermon, or *the dung heap*). If their fate is exile, these women, so interested in fashion and feasting, will be kept in line by attaching them to one another with cords run through barbed hooks (attached via nose rings or earrings or impaled in the skin and flesh of the person ahead; cf. 2 Kings 19:28; Isa. 37:29; Ezek. 19:4, 9). They are treated like the cows with which they so proudly identify themselves.

Oracle 2: Invitation to Sin 4:4-5

4:4-5a Priestly Invitation

Sarcasm gets under one's skin. It is most effective when applied to what is sacred or dear to the listener. With power and beauty, Amos parodies the priestly worship instructions. The people of Israel are addressed as faithful religious pilgrims. They have come to worship the Lord. The invitation? *Come, rebel at your favorite holy places. Do it in style!* This rebellion against God resembles the earlier rebellion against the rule of the Davidic dynasty (1 Kings 12:19). It is rebellion against the One with whom they have entered into covenant [*Covenant, p. 379*].

Bethel's fame as a religious center can be traced from Jacob (Gen. 28:10-22) through the ministry of Samuel (1 Sam. 7:16) to Jeroboam (1 Kings 12:25—13:32). Appropriately, the name means "house of God." Lying near the border with Judah, it served the Northern Kingdom as a center of worship, effectively replacing Jerusalem. It also served the royal family of Samaria, functioning somewhat as an Israelite Westminster Abbey. There religion revolved around the worship of God, whose footstool was the golden bull [*Bull Calves, p. 375*]. Gilgal, located east of Jericho (Josh. 4:19), attracted Northern pilgrims from the Transjordan tribes who might otherwise have made their way to the shrine on Mount Zion. The rich traditions and religious vitality of these two centers made them the most popular places for Israel to meet their God.

Does their sin lie in perverted procedure? Is it called rebellion because it takes place at sites unauthorized by God? Or are their sacrifices so despicable because of their attitude and misuse of the religious practices? The text contains clues to the answer.

The scene is that of a worshiper arriving in Bethel or Gilgal in the afternoon or early evening, after one or more days' of travel. The next morning the worshiper brings an *animal sacrifice* (Amos 4:4c), according to prescription, as the first worship act. The following day, day *three* (not NIV: year three), the individual offers *tithes*. Then one is free to return to the temple with *thanksgiving* (4:5a) or *freewill offerings* (4:5b). During the ritual of offering thank offerings and possibly freewill offerings (cf. Ps. 116:12-19), the worshiper testifies publicly to the Lord's gracious acts. The invitation to tell of the Lord's deliverance in personal lives would fulfill the vow made to the Lord (cf. Ps. 40:6-10). The telling is not bragging (as in NIV). The people of Israel are observing the ritual acts with great precision.

Where, then, is the sin of which they are being accused? It lies in the present and in the past.

4:5b Sarcastic Punch Line

Their present sin consists of substituting sacrifices for righteous living (cf. Amos 4:1). This sarcastic parody by Amos anticipates the fuller description of those sins in chapter five. The Israelites are practicing a religion of compensation. They are scrupulous in their ritual observances. They give generously of their goods but fail to consider that those goods have been acquired at the expense of the poor (cf. 2:8). Their moral nerve endings have become numbed, their consciences cauterized. Bulls, rams, tithes, leavened bread—these become a convenient and pleasurable substitute for holy and righteous living: *this is what you love to do* (4:5b). Religious ritual has taken the place of ethical practice.

There may also be an implicit polemic in these words against Israel's worship at these sites rather than Jerusalem. The correspondences between Amos's words and those of Deuteronomy 12:5-7 are more than coincidental:

> You shall seek the place that the Lord your God will choose out of all your tribes as his habitation to put his name there. You shall go there, bringing there your burnt offerings and your sacrifices, your tithes and your donations, your votive gifts, your freewill offerings, and the firstlings of your herds and flocks. And you shall eat there in the presence of the Lord your God, you and your households together, rejoicing in all the undertakings in which the Lord your God has blessed you.

If Amos gives an indictment corresponding with the Deuteronomic tradition, then he is saying that the entire religious system is founded on the wrong premises. The Lord is not even present in the rituals of

Bethel and Gilgal. And even if he were, the social and economic injustices of the worshipers would cancel out any benefit which religious observances might bring.

Oracle 3: Incomplete Repentance   4:6-11
4:6-11 I Did . . .

God chronicles the history of repeated attempts to recall Israel
from her ignorance, disobedience, and pride. These are acts of the
covenant by which God intended to wake up and call back a rebellious people. The Lord threatened his people with punishments if
they rebelled (Lev. 26:14-46; Deut. 28:15-68). Heaven and earth,
acting as the two witnesses, would cast the first stone against this disobedient people (cf. Deut. 4:26; 17:1-7; 30:19; 31:28). Creation acts
as God's agent, though in that action, creation also suffers for the sins
of human alienation. God, the effective Agent, draws on the rest of
the created world to witness against this disobedient people. So while
famine, drought, plant diseases, plagues, and earthquakes serve to
mediate punishments, in the Lord's hand these judgments become
invitations and incentives to repentance. Even the most severe judgments are motivated by the desire to restore rather than to destroy
the nation (Jer. 18:1-11).

Famine (Amos 4:6) may have many causes. None are listed here
because the focus is on God as Agent. Indeed, the opening words
carry over the satire of the previous verses. God explains their past
famines and bare cupboards in Hebrew idiom as *I, however, gave you
cleanness of teeth in all your cities.* The multiplied sacrifices did not
stimulate God to make their cattle more fertile nor to increase the
meager rainfall. Everyone felt the effects of God's past judgments on
nature—city and village dwellers, government officials and farmers.
Yet none turned to God in deep repentance. The Sinaitic covenant
contained the promise that God would bless Israel's obedience in
such abundance that they would not be able to eat all the food grown
in the land (Lev. 26:10). Their experience, however, fit the punishment for disobedience as outlined in the Mosaic covenant (Lev.
26:26-29; cf. Deut. 28:17, 53-58).

In Palestine, where agriculture depends on regular seasonal rainfall, drought symbolizes God's displeasure (Amos 4:7-8; cf. Lev.
26:18-20; Deut. 28:23-24; 1 Kings 8:35-36; 17-18). God withheld
the heavy winter (Nov.-Jan.) rains, causing the sprouted grain to wither. The general rains have been fewer and more spotty than normal

(Amos 4:7c-f), resulting in uneven growth and a lowered water table. Even the wells run dry (4:8). Yet those parched throats did not call out to God in repentance.

At the end of the agricultural year the food ran out and hunger prevailed (4:6). The fields were seeded, but lack of moisture and a burning sun baked the ground (4:8-9). The hand-watered backyard *gardens* and the more drought-resistant *vineyards* and *fig* and *olive trees* survived. These, targeted by the Lord for destruction, were attacked by *plant diseases* and *locusts* (4:9). The "natural" means of livelihood vanished; their hope for survival dimmed. But they did not make the connection between these events and God's earlier warnings (Lev. 26:20; Deut. 28:22, 38-42; 1 Kings 8:37). Still, they did not return to their God.

A weakened populace would be subject to sweeping *plagues* and invading armies (Amos 4:10). The plagues *of Egypt* were events in which Yahweh demonstrated his sovereignty over the pagan deities of that nation. These epidemics are described in putrid detail in the covenant curses (Lev. 26:25; Deut. 28:25-29; cf. 1 Kings 8:37; Isa. 1:4-6). The second form of human destruction is warfare. The elite fighting corps of *your young men*, and *your captured horses* serving as the strength of the chariot corps—these were destroyed in the military camps even before they reached the battlefield (4:10b).

4:6-11 Yet You Did Not . . .

Yes, Israel repented of her sin on occasion. They acknowledged the Lord as their God following Elijah's victory over the priests of Baal (1 Kings 18-19). They identified with Jehu and his militant anti-Baal stance (2 Kings 10-12), though they did not wipe out the worship at the high places (2 Kings 12:1-3).

Šub is the principal word for "repentance" in the OT. The phrase *return to* describes the reorientation in life which marks repentance. Amos 4 describes Israel's failure to *return all the way back to me*, to the Lord, from whom they strayed (Deut. 30:2). Genuine repentance of this kind involves rejecting all other gods in favor of the Lord of the covenant (1 Sam. 7:3; 2 Kings 23:2-5). Israel's persistent rejection of the divine invitation carried life-and-death consequences (cf. Amos 6). She had consistently chosen foolishness and death. Partial repentance will not do, nor will the multiplication of objects of worship.

Since Israel refused to *return* to Yahweh, the Lord *overturned* his people (4:11). The analogy of Sodom and Gomorrah accents the catastrophes and points toward final and ultimate destruction (cf. Deut. 29:23; Isa. 13:19; Jer. 49:18; 50:40). *A brand snatched from the fire* is normally a source of national hope in promising the preservation of a remnant of the people, but here it becomes a symbol of annihilating judgment. It destroys Israel's false hopes. Amos "confronts Israel in such a radical way in order to shake her out of a false sense of security, to bring to her attention her desperate situation before Yahweh, to warn her of the real danger of complete destruction, and to provoke reformation" (Hasel, 1972:190).

Oracle 4: Watch Out! 4:12-13

4:12 Get Ready!

Prepare to meet your God, O Israel joins a final appeal for repentance with a threat of punishment in the face of continued obstinacy.

4:13 God's Awesome Identity

The hymn fragment which follows seems out of place at first glance. That it is a hymn is established formally. A hymn focuses on the name of God (Yahweh), and uses participles (at least initially) to denote the characteristics of this God who is addressing Israel (4:13; cf. Ps. 103:3-9; 104:2ff.). The God who confronts Israel is no petty deity. All domains of human existence are under his control. He is not at Israel's beck and call, nor can anyone manipulate him into serving Israel. No, God addresses his people as Lord and comes to them in his own time and way. The best Israel can do is to *prepare* (Amos 4:12; cf. Exod. 19:11) *to meet* their *God.*

The hymn (Amos 4:13) extols the majesty of God in the language of creation and of the Sinaitic covenant. The presence of God is the ultimate hope for a trusting people. When they reject the God of Sinai, they need to remember that he is the One who forms the mountains, brings the breath of nature (wind) and of humankind (spirit) into existence, and discloses his most intimate thoughts to those who love him (cf. Gen. 18:17; Amos 3:7).

In addition to being Creator and to revealing himself, God acts as Judge within the world. *He makes the morning darkness* and superintends the affairs of individuals and nations from his vantage point on the *heights of the earth.* When God steps onto the mountaintops, the earth trembles (Exod. 19:18; Ps. 68:7-8). This word from Amos irresistibly leads us to God's self-disclosure at Sinai. Now, however, God addresses his people with what appears as a final appeal.

Though the precise nature of the judgment remains hidden in the threat, the metaphor of an earthquake dominates the scene.

THE TEXT IN BIBLICAL CONTEXT
The Role of Corrective Judgments

How is one to recognize God's corrective judgments? Not every stressful event nor every trying experience is to be interpreted as a judgment brought because of a particular sin (cf. Job; John 9:1-12). The Deuteronomist points out that God sometimes withheld blessings to test Israel's obedience and dependence on their God (Deut. 8:2-5). But if a similar event can be attributed to different causes, how is one to identify the intended cause? How was Israel to determine that their thirst and hunger in the wilderness years (Deut. 8) was a test of their dependence on God, but understand the drought and famine in their settled Palestinian existence as an act of judgment for their sins?

At the level of purpose, it does not matter. God's intention in either case was to draw Israel to himself. In one case, it is called "discipline"; in the other, we call it judgment. The experience itself could be identical, though the causes may vary.

At the level of cause, the misfortunes of life need interpreting to be properly understood. Historically, this function was performed by the prophets whom God sent:

> From the day that your ancestors came out of the land of Egypt until this day, I have persistently sent all my servants the prophets to them, day after day; yet they did not listen to me, or pay attention. (Jer. 7:25-26)

The Northern Kingdom (Israel) of the eighth century is guilty of the same sin: suppressing the truth of God (cf. Amos 2:10-12). Therefore they are called to account for the distinctly judgmental character of the acts by which God intended to lead them to repentance.

At times the Northern Kingdom did have rulers or prophets who led the people back toward God. Jehu was one of the few Northern kings zealous for Yahweh (2 Kings 9-10). Others are described as *doing evil in the eyes of the Lord.* Even the spectacular prophetic ministries of Elijah and Elisha did not produce large-scale repentance. At most, the return was toward God rather than fully to him. The nation was set in its way. It seemed that nothing could swing the ship of state and the mass of the populace all the way back to God.

The string of corrective judgments also implies the patience and long-suffering character of God. Repeatedly, generation after generation, the Lord had brought his judgments on Israel. Repeatedly, each generation repudiated God's call to repent. There are a number of occasions in the Scriptures where the first sin of a particular kind was judged immediately and drastically. The execution of the first Sabbath-breaker (Num. 15:32-36), the deposition of the first king because of disobedience (1 Sam. 15), the death of Ananias and Sapphira when they lied to the apostles (Acts 5:1-11)—all fit this pattern.

If similar judgment had fallen on all others who sinned like them, none would have survived in their calling. Yet in severely judging the first transgression, God pointed out how sinful sin really was and how he abhorred it. Therefore, every interim or corrective judgment expressed God's patience and grace. When God's people refuse to heed his warnings and corrective acts, the living Lord himself will confront them. If God's people, or any people for that matter, will not discern the presence of the Lord in his acts of calling them to repentance, eventually he will present himself with unmistakable displays of majesty and power in retributive judgment. "It is a fearful thing to fall into the hands of the living God" (Heb. 10:31).

The Relation of Ethics, Theology, and Doxology

The climax of Amos 4 (in 4:12-13) raises for us the question of the relationship of theology, doxology, and ethics. The preceding calls to repentance were invitations to return to Yahweh. Israel had gone through all the motions of worship (4:4-6). They had enjoyed God's bounties when they had received them (4:1-3). But they had failed to recognize and acknowledge the One with whom they publicly identified. Their way of life denied the reality of God.

One's faith in God (expressed in doxology and awe) expresses itself in eager response to the will of that God. Repentance is returning to the God whose will we have violated. Obedience is walking in the ways of God (Deut. 4:5-7, 32-40; John 14). Therefore, the nature of one's ethical life will reflect the extent and the nature of one's knowledge and experience of God (Rom. 1:18-32). Since "God" represents our understanding of the Ultimate, a person's actions, will, decisions, values, and relationships will accurately reflect the nature of that Ultimate Being. Therefore, the beginning, the reference point, and the culmination of the walk of faith is the ethical life lived out of gratitude (doxology) to a lovingly faithful God (theology; Job 28:20-28; Rom. 11:33—12:2; Eph. 4-5).

Repentance

Partial or halfhearted devotion is not devotion. God invites people to pursue his presence with abandonment. All else is secondary and inconsequential. God has harsh words for those who only move their lips in pursuit of God. That is the way to death. Life exists in the hope that genuine repentance will turn the people back to God.

Amos has moved beyond encouragement, beyond reminder, beyond chiding. Israel is confronted with stark reality: decide between life and death. The call to repent is a call to consider the truth and severity of the situation. It is a call to acknowledge responsibility for the state of affairs, and to reorient one's life so that the motivating forces giving rise to the sinful behavior are transformed. God's and Amos's call to repentance is generated by a loathing of sin and a longing for the restoration of Israel.

The biblical accounts of repentance, whether individual or collective, usually occur in crisis. Unless people recognize the true nature of their defection or deviation from God and accept the situation as critical, there is little likelihood of change. Occasionally dramatic confrontations open the sinner's eyes. Nathan's parable of the poor man's sheep forced David to open his eyes to his own sin against Uriah (2 Sam. 12). Sadly, calamities or the threat of dire consequences are often necessary to bring about repentance. The cycles of sin, servitude, sorrow, and salvation which characterized the period of Judges illustrate the human resistance to self-examination.

The primary task of the prophets was to awaken God's people to the dissonance between their professed allegiance to Yahweh and their disregard of the divine will. Ezekiel's appeal shows this:

> Therefore I will judge you, O house of Israel, all of you according to your ways, says the Lord God. Repent and turn from all your transgressions; otherwise iniquity will be your ruin. Cast away from you all the transgressions that you have committed against me, and get yourselves a new heart and a new spirit! Why will you die, O house of Israel? For I have no pleasure in the death of anyone, says the Lord God. Turn, then, and live.
> (Ezek. 18:30-32)

Genuine repentance requires integrity with openness. If Israel recognizes her sin, will she be ready to acknowledge it? Theologically, admission of sin is known as confession. Sin needs to be named for what it is as well as what it has done. The sin rampant in Israel is societal and personal injustice. It has destroyed the neighbor, caused truth to be depreciated, shredded the community, and led God to avert his face from them in all their religious acts.

Specific sins have been committed. They need to be confessed. Confession, when genuine, is accompanied by restitution. Such restitution was ordered by Israelite legislation (Exod. 22:1-7; Lev. 6:5; Num. 5:7). God would not accept the deceitful restitution practiced later by the Judean slaveholders as a bargaining chip in negotiations with the Almighty (Jer. 34:8-22). Genuine repentance involves renouncing—decisively renouncing—one's former ways in favor of a new course. Models of such litanies of repentance appear in Hosea (6:1-3; 14:1-3) and Jeremiah (3:22—4:2). Jesus recognized in Zacchaeus's restitution (Luke 19:8-9) and in the prostitute's act of humble anointing (7:36-50) the marks of true repentance.

Since all sin destroys relationship with God, it is necessary to restore that relationship for repentance to be completed. So Amos calls Yahweh's invitation to Israel: *Seek me and live; but do not seek Bethel* (Amos 5:4-5). God stands at the center of life. Repentance means returning to the covenant Lord. Nehemiah led his fellow citizens in such repentance, binding themselves by solemn oath to maintain the specific elements of the law (Neh. 10:28-39; cf. Jer. 34:10-11, 15-16). Repentance which leads one back to God will always restore one to holy living as well. Then God's people will also be willing to confess their sins in litanies of repentance (cf. Jer. 3:22—4:2; Hos. 14:2-3).

THE TEXT IN THE LIFE OF THE CHURCH
Between Feasting and Famine

The moral distance between feasting and famine is bridged by fasting and generosity. The feasts of Israel commemorated the Creator's providential care in providing fertile soil, regular and sufficient rainfall, freedom from diseases and destroying insects, and an abundance of sunshine. Yet God never guaranteed equality of opportunity or giftedness. Diversity is inherent in God's design for the exercise of community. Indeed, variety is the basis and measure of community; it stands as the antithesis of individualism and self-indulgence.

At this time of writing, Rwandan refugees are pouring into neighboring countries, desperate for food, shelter, clothing, and security. Continuous exposure to the plight of such refugees can induce compassion fatigue, though fatigue may set in early because of lack of exercise. Yet even our Lord accepted and enjoyed religious festivals, wedding celebrations, and invitations to banquets, while some people begged in the streets.

How do the people of God live with gratitude and compassion, and resist the temptations of cynicism and despair? The moral antonym of self-indulgence is self-discipline, not self-abnegation. Likewise, the answer to gluttony is to eat healthy, balanced food in moderation rather than to starve oneself. That is not to discount fasting, abstaining from food with specific objectives for limited periods of time. The selfishness displayed by the elite women of Samaria confirms that when turned inward, appetites become insatiable. These women have not understood the electing grace of God (Amos 3). Chosenness points out the significance which life acquires when divine acceptance, personal worth, and witness to the covenant Lord's presence and saving grace receive due attention within the faith life.

The teaching of the later Testament describes self-denial as an essential of discipleship: "If any want to become my followers, let them deny themselves and take up their cross daily and follow me" (Luke 9:23). Self-indulgence, an unbridled concern for self-gratification, is alien to the Christian way of life. As with the women of Samaria, occasionally self-indulgence is even falsely sanctified by religious teaching or by placing it in a religious context.

Injustice at Arm's Length

On Tuesday, November 8, 1994, the voters of California voted YES on Proposition 178, a measure restricting the right of undocumented aliens from the full range of essential public services. Only a few days later, delegates of a church convention responded with applause to the testimony of a young man who escaped abject poverty and possible death in Central America and was in the country illegally. The convention delegates celebrated his newfound faith and love for Jesus Christ and affirmed the priority of compassion over legal niceties. Christians struggle with their consciences in sorting out the claims and counterclaims of Christ and the state. Part of the struggle derives from a deep-down awareness that we contribute to evil in this world through arm's length injustice.

Suppose we vote for representatives who promise to promote policies that increase our market share and disregard the plight of human beings because they happen to be citizens of other countries. Are we not practicing injustice? We may be silently grateful that our government is placing restrictions on cigarette and chemical production because of the toxic effect of their products. But are we not participating in the injustice of selling those products to citizens of countries that do not have similar laws in force?

The further the sin and its consequences are removed from one another, the less likely we are to establish causal connections. This makes it more difficult to recognize the sinfulness of a lifestyle of conspicuous consumption. We might summarily reject the suggestion that the developed nations' insatiable appetite for oil contributes to flooding in the river plains of India. Nevertheless, it is a fact that inhabitants of mountainous drainage areas use oil as a heating fuel, and that the jump in fuel prices at the time of the Gulf War put oil out of reach. When the Indian population turned to wood as an alternate source of energy, rapid deforestation caused erosion, silting up the large and effective flood-control dam system. Flooding resulted.

Amos 4:1-3 focuses our attention on the indirect injustice of an extravagant lifestyle. People are responsible for the unintended effects of their way of life as well as for the intended effects of their conscious choices. Such sins are included in the psalmist's prayer: "Who can detect their errors? Clear me from hidden faults" (Ps. 19:12).

The fact that one's actions only indirectly hurt another does not exonerate the offender. In God's eyes, the person remains responsible. Two reasons can be adduced. There are actual, multiple consequences which flow from every human action and reaction. We live in a complex, dynamic world. We are under moral obligation to think through the implications of our actions. Inasmuch as it is possible for us to foresee some consequences of our actions, we can choose to pursue ends which are constructive and benefit others. Fortunately, God has also spoken to what is good and just and loving. If we violate those ethical instructions, the results will be destructive for us and others. Responding to the divine will, on the other hand, brings vitality and life to the person of faith and those affected by her deeds, even though the response may be accompanied by pain and deprivation.

Another reason people are responsible for indirect consequences of their actions is that we exist as a community of persons. God calls people to accountability to and for one another. When we focus on self-gratification, we suppress or ignore the welfare of the community. Such a community cannot long survive. It tears apart at the seams—the seams of ethnicity, politics, or economics. The Scriptures remind us elsewhere that it was God's pleasure to bless the nations through Abraham's seed, not to disperse or destroy them (Gen. 12:2-3; Exod. 19:6). And the NT adds to that insight: it is God's purpose to take the hostile polarities (male-female, slave-free, Jew-Gentile) and bring them together in Christ (Eph. 2:15-16; Gal. 3:28). God's intention is to reconcile rather than to alienate or separate humankind.

Amos 5:1—6:14

Funeral Song:
Israel's Last Gasp

OVERVIEW

The sights, sounds, and smell of death permeate these chapters in the form of war, exile, earthquake, and plague; funeral processions, mourners, burying the dead, and a decimated and scattered remnant. The reader, like Israel's contemporaries, would rather not hear the gory details unless . . . unless that might lead to repentance.

The imagery of killing and restoring to life is the language of existence under the covenant (cf. Hos. 6:1-3; Deut. 32:39; Wijngaards). To kill a covenant partner is to subject the covenant violator to the consequences of disobedience. To raise such a partner to life is to restore that exiled person to the blessings of the covenant. Israel is a fallen virgin who cannot *arise* (*qum*) because there is no *restorer* (*qum*, Hiph. participle; Amos 5:2). The theme of death saturates Amos 5-6.

Amos 5 and 6 contain three sermons on related subjects (5:1-17; 5:18-27; 6:1-14). Israel's religious veneer, her pride, and her blindness to the reality of her condition invite divine punishment. The prophet has argued that Israel has made no fundamental or permanent change in response to God's corrective acts (4:6-13). They have exhausted the Lord's patience by their superficial repentance and obstinacy. Therefore God decrees the ultimate consequence: death and destruction.

The funeral song (5:1-17) is followed by two prophecies of woe (5:18-27; 6:1-14). Together they form a death chant against a disobedient nation. Janzen has shown that "woe" oracles were originally associated with funeral processions. The "woe" oracles reinforce the stress on death in this rush toward Israel's meeting with God.

The sermons of these chapters fuse the words of the Lord and of Amos. Frequently one can distinguish them on the basis of whether God is referred to in the first person (I) or the third person (he). Using that criterion, God is the direct Speaker in 5:3-5, 12-13, 16-17, 21-27; and 6:8, 14. The prophet's words are none the less authentic and authoritative than those attributed directly to God. The prophet illustrates, expands, supplements, and affirms what he has received by divine act. Amos's practice anticipates the apostle Paul's statements regarding the validity of the message of an authorized spokesperson, even when not quoting the Lord (1 Cor. 7:6, 8, 10, 25, 40). By the work of the Spirit, God and the prophet's words are formed into one Word.

How (Not) to Meet God
Amos 5:1-17

PREVIEW

The code words denoting Israel's sin and God's judgment fill this poetic unit. The reference to women, for example, shifts from the abused Israelite wife in 2:7 to the abusive wives of 4:1-3 and appears in this section as the virgin Israel ravaged by an invader. God appeals for repentance with growing intensity. The rhythm of the funeral song leaves no doubt about the consequences of delay in responding to God.

OUTLINE

This sermon is marked by balanced symmetry (De Waard: 170-177) [Literary Patterns, p. 391]. Its chiastic pattern catches the eye and the ear:

It's Your Funeral, 5:1-3
  There's One Way Out, Maybe, 5:4-6
    Cause of Death, 5:7
      God's in Charge: I AM! 5:8-9
    Cause of Death, 5:10-13
  There's One Way Out, Maybe, 5:14-15
It's Your Funeral, 5:16-17

Since the parallel pairs explain and reinforce one another, we will treat them together. That way today's reader may recapture what the original hearers and readers understood.

EXPLANATORY NOTES
It's Your Funeral 5:1-3, 16-17

Let the mind's eye take in the scene. Amos's place of preaching is at the entrance to the temple at Bethel (7:13). A lively atmosphere prevails: the hustle and bustle of commerce, the dancing and singing processionals of religious festivals, and the streams of worshipers carrying or leading their offerings destined for sacrifice on the altar. Abruptly and dramatically the prophet shatters the peace with the piercing notes of a wail in the form of a funeral song.

> *Fallen no more to rise*
>   *is virgin Israel,*
> *forsaken on her land,*
>   *with no one to raise her up.* (Amos 5:2)

Why *virgin* Israel? Not because of her purity (5:7, 10-13; cf. Jer. 18:13; 31:21). Nor is she described as a virgin because of her special relationship with the Lord, since God uses the same language of other peoples (Isa. 23:12; 47:1; Jer. 46:11). Probably the term *virgin* appears because in that culture, the death of an unmarried girl suggests the absence of a protector, shattered dreams, unfulfilled promise. Ravaged, Israel lies exposed to the world while her life ebbs away.

The catastrophe will be of such proportions that all the city dwellers (Amos 5:16b) and farmers (5:16b) join in the lamentation. Normal activities cease. Everyone will be mourning a loved one. Town squares and broad streets will be filled with professional mourners. Yet the death toll will be so high that even nonprofessionals—*the farmers*—will be commandeered as mourners. Death and mourning will spill over into the *vineyards* (5:17). These very vineyards, which normally symbolize joy and celebration (Judg. 21:21), have become witnesses to the pain brought on by God's judgment.

Concretely, this judgment takes the form of an invading army which will decimate Israel's military strength (Amos 5:3). The city which sends out a battalion will be left with only enough to form a company; the town which conscripts a company will conclude the battle with a platoon. The identity of the military opponent is inconsequential. The foe is not even named. It is enough to know that this is the Lord's doing. The Lord of armies is passing through his people with judgment (5:16-17).

There's One Way Out, Maybe 5:4-6, 14-15

Is there any way to forestall this calamity? Only one. Both God and Amos shout it out:

> Seek me (the Lord) and live. . . .
> Seek good, not evil, that you may live!

To seek (daraš, finite verb or infinitive) God or gods means that a worshiper enters God's presence to ask for guidance or instruction (1 Sam. 9:9; 2 Kings 22:13, 18). One who seeks God goes into his presence and walks in his ways, doing his will (Ps. 24:3-6; Isa. 55:6-9). This encounter normally occurs at a holy place, though the focus is on the submission to God. One who seeks God from the heart can expect God to disclose himself and respond with salvation (1 Chron. 28:8-9).

Here Amos's instruction contrasts seeking the Lord with seeking Bethel. On this act of Israel hangs the fate of the nation. The people have become so accustomed to the stench of sin that they are not aware of their festering wounds. The Israelites claim to be worshiping the Lord at Bethel (cf. Amos 5:14, 18); Amos rejects that claim. They are using the name of the Lord in worship but ignoring his guidance for daily living. Under such conditions, religious rituals become self-deception. Instruction offered by the priests and prophets of those centers is not of divine origin.

Bethel, Gilgal, and Beersheba were three prominent historic religious centers frequented by the Israelites [Map of Palestine, p. 403]. Israel's religion was bankrupt, her appeals to the Lord were a sham, and her claim to divine favor was mistaken. Only in returning to Yahweh was there hope.

Relying on these cult centers is useless, the Lord declares: Gilgal is destined to go into captivity (note the wordplay: *haggilgal galoh yigleh*, 5:5c). *Bethel* (the religious capital) will be so thoroughly devastated and depopulated that it will *come to nothing* and be known as "catastrophe" or "nonexistent."

Injustice and evil have replaced goodness and truth. The perversion has become so deeply rooted for such a long period of time that, while repentance is called for, even it might not turn the tide of God's judgment (5:14-15).

Seek me/good and then/so that you will live! The only alternative to repentance is to face the certain and unquenchable firestorm of the Lord's fury (5:6). But even the option of repentance may be lost, since the best word of hope is only this: *It may be that the Lord, the God of hosts, will be gracious to the remnant of Joseph* (5:15b). There is no guarantee of reprieve; God does not count or measure out delay or deferral of judgment. The final hope lies purely in the grace of God and in the extension of his pardon.

Cause of Death 5:7, 10-13

The reasons for this destruction lie in Israel's character. They are guilty of fundamental failings rather than occasional transgressions. They have transformed the judicial system into a tool for personal benefit. It has been turned into *wormwood* (5:7), a bitter aromatic plant (King: 124). *Wormwood*'s promising odor is offset by its unpalatable taste. Israel is a nation of law, but the laws have been interpreted to favor the rich at the expense of the poor. Justice is supposed to be a deliberate empowering of the weak and helpless, not a neutral evenhandedness. But Israelite justice has become the tool of the powerful. Those who object to the state of affairs on moral and humanitarian grounds are despised in the places of power (5:13) *[Justice and Righteousness, p. 390]*.

The specific nature of the accusations is not intended as a comprehensive listing of all the sins. The list is incomplete when considering the indictments in the remainder of the book. Why not give the entire catalog of sins and then deliver the knockout punch? Why this piecemeal approach? A number of reasons come to mind.

First, the text units probably were originally delivered as street-corner sermons. They are brief and pointed. That format permits the prophet to catch the passerby with an entire message while within earshot. Second, these prophetic mini-sermons were probably delivered at different places in the cities of Samaria and Bethel. Amos 5:1-

17 would fit the setting of the city gate. It is the location from which one sees off the army and welcomes its return (5:3). The *city gate* is mentioned three times in this text (5:10, 12, 15) as the place where justice is to be practiced. Indeed, the city gate was the place where justice was normally dispensed in Israel (Deut. 17:5; Ruth 4:1, 10-11; Isa. 29:21).

The prophet acts as the conscience of the nation in the most public arena of Israelite life. In that role the prophet observes negotiations regarding matters as varied as the purchase of property or the bride price. Proceedings at the city gate reflect the community's concern with justice. When judges succumb to bribery or self-interest, the weak cannot obtain redress for their complaints.

This text unit turns on the call to justice and the accusation of justice perverted. The injustices identified here match those listed elsewhere in Amos, but are focused on the judicial system (Amos 5:10, 12, 15), not on occasional practices. The judiciary as well as the judicial procedures have become corrupted. No hope remains for the one who seeks redress for crimes. The plaintiff approaches the bench, knowing that the judges to whom he has come to appeal for help are the very oppressors from whom he seeks relief. Justice has been transformed into bitterness, and fairness is ground into the dust.

The God of justice looks in vain among his people for fairness, equity, right relationships, and consideration for the weak, poor, and helpless. Justice in these terms is the highest priority (Ps. 89:14; Isa. 61:8). If they were truly "seeking the Lord," they would hear his concern for the protection of the powerless and for the promotion of justice and ethical living. In the end, goods acquired by unjust means will be a hollow benefit because the rich and the powerful have the most to lose through the ravages of war.

The meaning of Amos 5:13 is unclear. Is this a righteous victim or an advocate for justice whom the prophet advises to "let sleeping dogs lie"? Or is God through the prophet calling the silent majority just as responsible for oppression as those actually practicing the injustice? The indirect injustice of the *cows of Bashan* (4:1-3) is paralleled by the social critic who privately bemoans the fact that "the world is going to the dogs" but refuses to confront the oppressors.

God's in Charge: I AM 5:8-9

Here stands the centerpiece of the sermon. Amos's listeners would have caught it by the change in his voice. The wail of the lament (5:1-

7) gives way momentarily to a hymn of praise (5:8-9), only to be followed again by the second verse of the funeral song (5:10-17). The translators of the NIV, together with many commentators, interpret this hymn as an intrusion. It appears misplaced until one recognizes the chiastic structure of the sermon. Then it becomes the hinge point.

The description of the Judge reminds hearers of this word that it is God, not law, which takes center stage in the life of his people. This is the One they are to seek. He is not some petty chieftain, some hungry pagan idol to be appeased by rituals, incantations, or offerings of cereal and steak. The Creator of the cosmos (5:8a-c) and Lord of history (5:9) stands before his people. This Sovereign of the stars, sun, and rain is unimpressed by the height of mountain citadels and the strength of hewed-stone walls. Israel has ignored the divine perspective; she is caught up with life on the horizontal plane.

5:8d I AM

At the very heart of the sermon, as pivot point for the whole, is the testimony, *the Lord is his name.* The mention of the name immediately brings to mind God's self-disclosure to Israel at the time of the exodus from Egypt:

> I am the Lord. I appeared to Abraham, Isaac, and Jacob as God Almighty, but by my name "the Lord" I did not make myself known to them. . . . I am the Lord, and I will free you from the burdens of the Egyptians and deliver you from slavery to them. I will redeem you with an outstretched arm and with mighty acts of judgment. I will take you as my people, and I will be your God. (Exod. 6:2-7)

The personal name of God, Yahweh (= the Lord), was first explained to Moses at the burning bush (Exod. 3:14-15; cf. 6:1-3) as "I AM." In context, the significance of the name appears to identify the Lord as the One who can be trusted to fulfill the covenant promise made to his people. God is present to act, usually and preferably for a people's salvation, but at times such as these, for judgment.

Within the Amos 5:1-17 text, the mention of the name *Yahweh* draws attention to the two themes surrounding it. First, since God promised to ensure an orderly world after the Flood (Gen. 8:21-22; 9:11-17), he remains faithful to his covenant oath. The One who set the stars in their heavenly patterns, who regulates the sequences of day and night, who majestically loads the clouds with moisture from the sea and pours it out on the land (Amos 5:8a-c)—this One will keep covenant forever.

Yahweh is his name!

The other side of the meaning of the divine name is that the Lord will visit with judgment those who claim the name but refuse to observe his decrees of justice and compassion (Amos 5:9; cf. 5:10-13). Those who desecrate the name of the Lord will experience the faithfulness of God, the Judge. The Lord has promised blessings on obedience and judgments for disobedience (Deut. 27–30). If Yahweh is to live up to his name, fulfillment demands judgment.

Yahweh is his name!

The judgment is imminent unless Israel repents and returns to her covenant Lord. The people have not yet acknowledged that the funeral procession is for them. They continue to hold out the hope that God will still intervene on their behalf. God dashes that hope to the ground in the wailing crescendos of two woe oracles (Amos 5:18-27; 6:12-14).

THE TEXT IN BIBLICAL CONTEXT

Seeking God: Refocus on Justice

Seek God! The words are simple enough; the practice is all-consuming. The call is not to find something lost, but to pursue someone or something unrelentingly, to commit one's whole life to finding God so as to remain close to him. This is a summons to pursue God with passion.

Justice seeks well-being by providing everyone equal access to livelihood and opportunity, regardless of status, power, or role in society. Justice is blind to color, clothing, and creed, since it concerns itself with society as a whole, and the powerless or repressed in particular. When God's people promote justice, they align themselves with God's intentions for society and for the world at large. Such justice even accepts escaped slaves and resident aliens, and pursues the welfare of the widow and orphan (Deut. 23:15-17; 24:10-22; cf. Job 29:11-17; Luke 20:45-47; Acts 6:1-7; 9:32-43; James 1:27).

God's concern for justice and righteousness in the human community pervades the Scriptures. It transcends the limits of covenantal relations inasmuch as justice and righteousness express respect for persons as persons. These virtues are to prevail in the human community without regard to the existence of prior ties of affection or historic commitments based on preferred relationships. They are foundational expectations, core values. Paul presents them as the message of the gospel (faith in Jesus Christ) in addressing Felix, the governor (Acts 24:24-25). They are the substance of the Spirit's conviction of divine expectations in all people: "He will prove the world wrong about sin and righteousness" (John 16:8-10). Jesus himself reminded his disciples that greater privilege and enlightenment should translate into a righteousness greater than that of the Pharisees (Matt. 5:17-20).

THE TEXT IN THE LIFE OF THE CHURCH
Renewal

Not all renewal is the product of the preaching of judgment on sin and the need for repentance. God's goodness can also lead one to repentance (Rom. 2:4). However, all renewal results from a deeper consciousness of sin. Whether that sin appears in the public domain or is harbored in the inner recesses of the heart, repentance is a deep sorrow over what displeases God and an about-face regarding the course of life. When Christians individually or collectively as the church are not continuously being renewed, God sends messengers of the prophetic order to recall his people to new faith and holy living. Jonathan Edwards was one such prophet. His Amos-like message in the sermon "Sinners in the Hands of an Angry God" symbolizes the dramatic preaching that led to the Great Awakening in New England in the second quarter of the eighteenth century.

The biblical record and church history contain abundant evidence of renewal among God's people. Of some of the kings it is said, "He walked in the ways of his father, . . . doing what was right in the sight of the Lord. Yet the high places were not removed; the people had not yet set their hearts upon the God of their ancestors" (2 Chron. 20:32-33; cf. 24:2, 17-19; 26:3-5, 16ff.). Selective repentance is a sign of shallowness. Thoroughgoing repentance searches for and uproots the causes of sin as well as its manifestations. Confessional statements such as "If I have sinned against someone, please forgive me" are frequently evasions of truth, a refusal to confront reality. Repentance and confession need to lay bare the specific acts of rebellion, neglect, disloyalty, or selfishness, as well as the motive which gave it expression in the first place. Such repentance has re-creative potential. Perhaps the deepest reach of repentance is found in the psalmist's words:

Indeed, I was born guilty
a sinner when my mother conceived me.
You desire truth in the inward being;
therefore teach me wisdom in my secret heart. . . .
Create in me a clean heart, O God,
and put a new and right spirit within me. (Ps. 51:5-12)

When repentance transforms the spirit, one is turned back to God.

Modern Western society has a penchant for reducing or eliminating the sinfulness of sin. In *Whatever Became of Sin*, Karl Menninger analyzes the moral decline in the postwar era, observing that the language of sin has disappeared in this society. Sins, he observes, have become crimes (against impersonal society). Personal crimes have become illnesses. Collective sins, distributed across the population, are diluted to an acceptable pollution level of parts per million.

Genuine repentance moves one back toward the center, toward God. Anthropologist Paul Hiebert poses two alternative ways of describing conversion and the life of faith. Traditionally, Christian conversion is viewed as an outsider becoming an insider. Many texts can be harnessed in this way of thinking about becoming and being a Christian. Hiebert proposes an alternative way of conceptualizing the faith. One is either moving toward the center (Christ) or away from it (Hiebert: 95). The mere suggestion opens up a whole range of possibilities in the way we think of evangelism, renewal, maturity in the faith, the danger of being "so close," yet not knowing Christ, and the possibility of delighting God every day. We wonder what the church would look like if it considered its relationships as contributing or hindering people in a movement toward the center, Christ.

Stanza 1: The Terrors of That Day

Amos 5:18-27

PREVIEW

This first woe oracle counters Israel's claim to practice superior worship. God, they assert, will vindicate them on the day of his approval because they engage in the ritual in the appropriate manner and numbers. God declares their hope to be unfounded; anything short of justice is unacceptable.

OUTLINE

EXPLANATORY NOTES
This Is What It Will Be Like 5:18-20

The cry *Woe* or *Alas* is rooted in mourning (1 Kings 13:30; Jer. 22:18b; Janzen). It marks the presence of death. The nature of that death has been anticipated in verse 17: *I will pass through the midst of you, says the Lord.* The phrase echoes the description of the final plague brought against Egypt (Exod. 12:12, 23). God will now be to Israel as he once was to Egypt. He will engage in a holy war against his own people. Consequently, the wailing of the Egyptians for their firstborn shall become the mourning cry of God's firstborn, Israel.

The *day of the Lord*, declares Amos, will be contrary to the people's expectations. By implication, Israel's concept of that day is one of salvation [*Day of the Lord, p. 383*]. They expect it to be a time of victory, celebration, and *light* (5:18, 20; cf. Isa. 13:10; Esther 8:16). Amos, however, reverses the meaning of the day of the Lord. It will be a time of *darkness* and *gloom*—language typical of God's decisive judgments against Israel's foes (Zeph. 1:15; Joel 2:2, 31). In the time of Moses, the ninth plague brought darkness to the Egyptians and light to the Israelites (Exod. 10:22-23). However, the coming day will cast Israel in the role of the disobedient and judged. They expect vindication in their identification with the Lord; yet the Lord, in turn, announces that day as a vindication of his name. God is turning on his people [*Day of the Lord, p. 383*].

Amos describes that day in vivid countryside imagery (5:19). The traveler escapes a chance encounter with a lion, only to be met by a bear. By good fortune, he reaches the safety of his home. Trembling with fear and relief, he supports himself with his hand against the stone wall, only to be bitten by a poisonous snake. Surely the message should strike home to Amos's listeners. The acts of judgment Israel has experienced are not chance events; they have occurred through divine appointment. The source of ultimate security and

confidence, one's own home, symbolizes the *day of the Lord* and becomes the guarantor of death.

Here's Why 5:21-25

The prophet's word concerning the true character of the day of the
Lord gives way to the message from the Lord himself: *I hate, I
despise. . . .* In this passionate outburst, God startles the worshiping
crowd into deathly silence. The setting? Probably Bethel, the center
of fervent religious worship. The time? Maybe some major festival. Indeed, the concept of the day of the Lord may be associated with
God's historical inbreaking. Could it be that we have here the Northern Kingdom's version of the Passover? Or does it represent the special festival begun by Jeroboam I to draw his citizens away from their
former allegiance to Jerusalem (1 Kings 12:25-33)? *[Tabernacles,
p. 396.]*

The ingredient missing from Israel's religion is *justice* and
righteousness (Amos 5:24) *[Justice and Righteousness, p. 390]*. The
demand for its recovery is braced from above and below by arguments from the present (5:21-23) and past (5:25-26).

The text uses plurals for *religious feasts, assemblies, burnt offerings,* and *grain offerings* (5:22-23)—what *I hate, I despise.* This suggests the Lord's wholesale condemnation of their religious activities.
These statements are particularly jarring because they run counter to
other commands to attend the feasts and celebrate the assemblies, to
offer burnt and grain offerings (Lev. 1-2; 4:1—7:10; Deut. 16:1-17).
Clearly, the current practices as well as the specific instructions of the
priestly laws point to the normative nature of these religious rituals.

In addition, since the *fellowship* (NRSV: *well-being*) *offering* was
not required, its voluntary nature gave it a special status as a symbol
of devotion to God and identification with fellow Israelites (Amos
5:22; cf. Lev. 3; 7:11-36). The details governing the fellowship offering mark this sacrifice (aside from the Passover lamb) as the only one
of which the offerer may eat. The grateful offerer probably gathered
relatives and friends together to confirm the fulfillment of a vow or to
commemorate the saving deeds of God in a concrete life situation
(Exod. 32:6; Deut. 27:7; 1 Sam. 11:15; cf. Ps. 116). In lists of offerings, the *fellowship offering* regularly follows the *burnt offerings.* The
symbolism is vivid and rich with meaning: fellowship with God and
with one's neighbors is grounded in repentance, confession, and the
forgiveness of sin.

There is no suggestion in this text or elsewhere in Amos that God's renunciation of Israel's worship is due to anything other than their attitude of heart and unethical practices. Even the call to repentance (Amos 5:4-6) contrasts seeking Yahweh with seeking Bethel, Gilgal, or Beersheba. The chosenness of Mt. Zion is not at issue. Nor is there any reference to the bull calves at Bethel or Dan as the reason for this somber appraisal. Amos does not even breathe a word about the fact that non-Levites are serving as priests (1 Kings 12:31-32; 13:33). The writer of Kings attributes the exile of the Northern tribes to ritual deviations (2 Kings 17). But in Amos, none of them serves as the stated reason for God's judgment upon Israel. The text's silence on those issues highlights the crucial character of justice and righteousness. Worship is inconsequential when justice and righteousness are lacking [Justice and Righteousness, p. 390].

No wonder God bursts upon the scene with such vehement words. The trappings of worship are all present: the best animals and vegetables, the instruments, the singing. But they revolt the Lord. Where are the just and righteous relationships? Where is the care for the needy? Whose eye catches the plight of the weak? Which ear is attuned to the cries of the forgotten and neglected of society? Justice has dried up, righteousness has evaporated. The stream bed of mutual care is empty of compassion and covenant fidelity. It is littered with smug piety, celebrative worship experiences, and generous offerings. Yet they are offensive to God.

One thing is needed: *Let justice roll down like waters, and righteousness like an everflowing stream* (Amos 5:24). One student paraphrased and modernized the text this way:

Let justice burst forth like a rocket,
    And righteousness like an ever-circling satellite.

Justice and *righteousness* are not seasonal streams. If they truly tumble down ravines and valleys in seasons of prosperity or peace, they do not evaporate in the adversity of summer heat. Their absence symbolizes drought and death; their presence is a sign of the work of the living God [Justice and Righteousness, p. 390].

The rhetorical question of Amos 5:25 invites Israel to recognize the secondary role of worship rituals. The question implies that during the years of wilderness wandering, the laws requiring sacrifice by individuals and the general population were not yet in force or were temporarily suspended (Num. 15:1-3, 17-19). Even the Passover was celebrated only twice before entering Canaan (Exod. 12:21-28; 13:5;

Num. 9:1-5; Josh. 5:10). The festivals marking the harvest year would not have had meaning for Israel in the desert because they would not have harvested grains or vegetables. Amos utilizes the Northern Israelite tradition to argue against Israel's overemphasis on the place of sacrifice and cultic ritual (cf. 2:10) [Israelite Religion, p. 385]. His argument: At the time of Israel's greatest intimacy with God, during the wilderness years, the people were not sacrificing. Yet God accepted them. Therefore, ritual sacrifice is not essential to maintaining a dependent and faithful relationship with God.

Off You Go! 5:26-27

The grammatical relationships in Amos 5:25-27 are unclear. Verse 26 may be read either as a continuation of the rhetorical question begun in 5:25 (Wolff: 265) or as introducing the therefore of 5:27. The NIV leaves this verse suspended without context. The most natural reading: Therefore you will lift up. . . . On this interpretation, followed here, 5:25 clinches the preceding argument concerning the relationship of sacrifice and justice, while 5:26-27 contain the announcement of the judgment.

Translations vary on Amos 5:26. The NIV takes the text as describing the royal chaise and the home-crafted deities, resulting in the picture of king and gods going into exile. It is doubtful, however, that a captive king was ever carried into exile in royal style. The text may be referring to Assyrian astral deities worshiped in Israel: Sakkuth = Moloch/Molech, the Canaanite god, and Kaiwan = the planet Saturn (cf. 2 Kings 17:16; Acts 7:42-43 in TBC below). Sakkuth and Kaiwan may be a name and an epithet of the planet Saturn, taken as a star-god (ABD, 5:904). On this interpretation, Israel is still probably on favorable terms with Assyria, and the text is heavy with irony: Israel will carry into exile the very gods of those people (the Assyrians) who are ravaging and deporting them.

Another possibility commends itself to this interpreter. Some 170 years earlier, Jeroboam I had led the ten Northern tribes in secession from Judah and the leadership of the Davidic monarchical family line. He astutely identified with the wilderness tradition and with the symbols of the kingship of El Shaddai and Yahweh, the two manifestations of Israel's God, by the images of the bull calf. The text would translate as: And you will take along Sikkuth (Heb.) your king, and Kiyyun, the star (heavenly representation) of your gods, which you have crafted for yourselves. That is, when the time of judgment overtakes the nation, they will carry with them these symbols of their god. How useless, since he was unable to rescue the nation from the invading Assyrians! *[Bull Calves, p. 375.]*

The words *I will send you* . . . indicate that Israel is not going into captivity because the Lord is incapable of defending his people. No, the Lord, *the God of hosts* (NIV: *God Almighty*), is personally in charge of this devastating experience. He is the Writer and Director of the unfolding drama; the conquering nation (Assyria) merely marches onto stage on cue.

In a few bold strokes, Amos paints the judgment scene. One sees in the mind's eye a long line of Israelite captives trudging northward, beyond Damascus. Some are bowed under the weight of the very idols and other religious paraphernalia which they themselves fashioned. The gods have become an unshakable burden imposed on them by the enemy. The text is rich with irony.

One can visualize the shocked expressions which greet the words of their God: *I hate, I despise your festivals*. . . . How could Israel have deluded itself so severely? What could have given rise to this separation of judicial integrity and religious ritual?

Three reasons may be proposed, with some tentativeness. First, they have separated moral responsibility from election privilege. Their defective concept of what it means to be the covenant people has far-reaching social consequences (cf. Amos 3:1-2).

Second, it appears that the monarchy has introduced some separation of the royal and religious courts. Presumably that would reflect a difference in the type of issues addressed by each. The Chronicler records that David assigned the role of judges to the Levites "for everything pertaining to God and for the affairs of the king" (1 Chron. 26:29-32). The existence of these (and only these) two categories suggests that the interests of the two spheres were best served by specialization. Administrative efficiency was a controlling concern. The effect would be eventually to dissociate the morality of royal decrees (regarding matters of defense, taxation, trade, and commerce) from the ethics of one's religious life.

The story of king Ahab and Naboth's vineyard illustrates well the conflict between royal decree and morality. The elders and nobles who served Ahab's administration kept silent about the immoral character of Jezebel's demands (1 Kings 21:8-14). Political loyalty prevailed over morality. Inevitably that silence on morals associated with issues in the civil domain infiltrated society, particularly in the case of royal appointees and officials of the realm who functioned as the king's representatives.

Third, if the circumstances of eighth-century Judah resembled those of the Northern Kingdom, then taxation and property laws were being passed which favored the rich and disadvantaged the poor and the peasant landholders. Isaiah pronounces judgment on the legislators who established discriminatory laws and on the justices who favored the causes of the rich (Isa. 10:1-2). Dearman notes that these administrators were not accused of being derelict in their duty. Instead, they took "advantage of their positions to plunder the helpless for their own personal gain" (80). He argues, further, that the pattern of oppression condemned in Amos and Hosea mirrors Isaiah's pronouncements.

Realists know that archaic laws and religious fervor are no match for pragmatism and decisive action. Furthermore, the priesthood of the Northern Kingdom had, from its first appointments by Jeroboam I, served the interests of the state. Only meddlers like Elijah dared oppose national policies. They had been silenced by royal decree.

Years of prosperity under Jeroboam II had confirmed the benefit of strong, decisive government and the appropriateness of existing administrative and social policies. God's blessings on the realm were seen as an endorsement of royal policies and the nation's piety.

In 5:18-27, Amos addresses the issues of national priorities and moral posture. He announces the primacy of fairness, compassion, and virtue over worship. Sacrifices, prayers, celebrations—all these mean little unless they are expressions of one's love and obedience. That love and obedience can be felt, seen, and heard in maintaining integrity and community, in compassion and justice for the weak and the poor among the governed. God's people can exist without the elaborate trappings and rituals of worship. They cannot survive the drought of justice and righteousness. The Lord refuses to receive the prayers and sacrifices of uplifted hands when those very hands are stained by the mixed blood of cattle and covenant partners.

THE TEXT IN BIBLICAL CONTEXT
The Use of Amos 5:25-27 in the New Testament

Stephen draws on the words from Amos 5:25-27 as prophetic confirmation of Israel's repeated defection from the Lord (Acts 7:42-43). While the Hebrew stresses the absence of offerings in the wilderness years, Stephen draws on this text because it serves his purpose in a threefold way. First, it permits him to reflect on the wilderness years as a time of defection from the true faith (cf. Exod. 32). The emphasis in Stephen's quotation of the text is on "to me." Second, the Amos quotation adds weight to Stephen's argument that Israel was inclined to search for guidance from sources other than God, such as star deities of Mesopotamia: "Rephan," the planet Saturn, and images thereof (cf. Acts 7:40, 42). Third, by interpreting "beyond Damascus" as "beyond Babylon," Stephen is able to bring to mind the imagery of Israel's pagan origins as well as her later exile (cf. 7:45).

Stephen's argument assumes the historical meaning of Amos 5:25-27 but then modifies the text and its emphasis so as to have it serve the flow of his argument.

Cult, Creeds, or Conduct?

True prophets discern the hour and focus the issues. The twelfth hour is no time to entertain theological niceties or endless qualifiers. Those open to the Spirit recognize the prophets as the voice of God.

The prophetic word in both Testaments confirms the priority of ethical living and discipleship over creeds or cultic acts; obedience to God is the litmus test of faith. Even worship was never intended to stand on its own as a mark of the covenant people. The sacrifice of animals or grains, the offering of prayers, the recitation of the Shema (Deut. 6:4-5), the celebration of God's historic or material provision in festal song and dance—these had three primary functions: to symbolize and mediate forgiveness for sin, to express gratitude and praise, and to reaffirm their covenant commitment to the Lord. Sins violated God's covenant (cf. Lev. 4-7).

Cultic acts symbolized the worshiper's repentance. The accompanying priestly word concretely and specifically conveyed God's forgiveness. Those whose sins were forgiven would bring additional offerings and tithes as expressions of gratitude and praise. These were reminders of God's goodness, of his abundant provision according to promise, and of the binding oath of allegiance once made at Sinai and periodically renewed (Exod. 19-24; 32-34; Lev. 26; Deut. 6:1-25; Josh. 24:1-28). Early in the history of the monarchy, Samuel had addressed the dilemma pointedly:

> To obey is better than sacrifice,
>   and to heed (is better) than the fat of rams. (1 Sam. 15:22)

The same attitude is reflected by the very psalmist who encourages sacrifices (Ps. 51:16-19). The obedience which transcends sacrifice and worship is neither mechanical nor onerous. It flows from the relationship with the living God. God is a moral God who calls for the evidence of moral transformation before accepting gifts of praise or sacrifice from his people.

The prophets Isaiah and Jeremiah condemn the hypocrisy and moral blindness of Judah. The Southern nation, like her Northern neighbor, developed this perversion: they took the gift, the temple, and its provision of symbols of repentance and counted them as a guarantee of forgiveness and acceptance. God declares:

> Even though you make many prayers,
>   I will not listen;
>   your hands are full of blood. (Isa. 1:15)

> Will you steal, murder, commit adultery, swear falsely, make offerings to Baal, and go after other gods that you have not known, and then come and stand before me in this house? (Jer. 7:9-10)

The incongruity is overwhelming; Israel's inability to recognize the contradiction is incomprehensible. How can a people be so utterly devoid of moral capacity?

That same attitude toward cult alongside ethical living occasioned Jesus' instructions to his disciples: If, in the act of worshiping God in the holy place, you are reminded of a discordant note in the relationship between two of you, "First be reconciled to your brother or sister, and then come and offer your gift" (Matt. 5:24). Similarly, even when accompanied by religious acts, creedal confession fails to please God, who invites obedience prompted by love (Matt. 7:21-23; James 1:26-27; 1 John 2:3-8). Paul's vaulted theology and ecstatic doxology (Rom. 1–11) translate into a service of God consisting of nonconformity to this world, a renewed mind, and sacrificial living (12:1-2). Amos (5:18-27) points in the same direction.

THE TEXT IN THE LIFE OF THE CHURCH
"I Have a Dream"

Nobel peace prize winner Martin Luther King Jr. caught the core of Amos's passion for justice and righteousness in his life and thought (Amos 5:24). In a "Christmas Sermon on Peace," in the face of escalating violence in America and in Vietnam, he reaffirmed his dream that "one day 'justice will roll down like water and righteousness like a mighty stream' " (M. L. King: 77). If God's people would be captured by a similar vision, the world would yet see how glorious is his design for the human race. Righteousness exalts every practitioner and brings honor to all who live by it.

The Priestly Vocation

The priestly vocation is made difficult by the priests' constant exposure to sin and its attendant pain and destruction. Compassionate people long to reduce pain and release sinners from bondage. Those are priestly functions. They are appropriate and necessary. Unrelieved pain, misplaced guilt, a cold shoulder in times of failure—these can drive people to despair. The priestly role also involves exposing sin as a destructive reality. Harsh and peremptory treatment of those who sin is cruel. It alienates sinners from a loving and forgiving God. Yet church leaders have an awesome prophetic mandate as sentinels to warn sinners from their wicked way (Amos 1:1; Hos. 9:8; Ezek. 3:16-21; 33:1-7; Lind).

The history of caregiving in the church has tended to be one of reaction to excesses of past or present. It moves between the bipolar concern for a pure church and the desire for peace within the community of faith, between ignoring the sin and acting with severity toward the sinner (White and Blue: 15-75). The extreme consequence of concern for God's honor has resulted in the Inquisition, Zwingli's persecution of the Anabaptists, and the Salem witch trials.

On the other hand, believers want to be compassionate with those struggling over painful decisions or circumstances. This has contributed to the church's ambivalence toward the slaughter of unborn millions, its muted voice on marital breakup, its justification of taking part in war or "peacekeeping" violence, and an inability to recognize and reluctance to address the sinfulness of homosexual practice.

Those who engage in the therapeutic arts draw heavily on tradition as a stabilizing factor for those in spiritual distress. The prophets decry such religious tradition (*the day of the Lord!*) when it serves as a placebo replacing genuine repentance and forgiveness. The church's pastors and other caregivers are called to discern when to bind and when to loose, and how to lead the church in mutual accountability before God (Matt. 16:13-19; 18:15-20; Gardner).

Imaging God: Icons or Idols?

We perceive God through our imagination. Ezekiel, Daniel, and John of the Apocalypse depict biblical visions of God which stimulate us in

creating pictures of God in our own minds. Paintings, sculptures, poetry, and other art forms further help reflection on the nature and
person of God. They expand the ways we have traditionally been encouraged to think of God. They introduce or highlight aspects of God
we may not personally have experienced. And they allow us to perceive God through the senses and spirits of others who have meditat-
ed long and deeply on the One who is the way, the truth, and the life
(John 14:6). When images themselves become objects of trust and
worship, they are idols. Amos 5:18-27 warns against three forms of
icons which have become idolatrous images: an inflexible self-serving
theology, ritualistic worship, and material symbols of God.

Protestants were not the first to object to the misuse of certain
icons. Commonplace from before the sixth century were paintings,
frescoes, mosaics, amulets in the form of the cross, and carvings of
Jesus, Mary, and the saints. The issue of the place of icons raged in
the church for over a century (A.D. 726-843). The iconoclasts were
sensitive to the accusations of Muslims and Jews that Christians were
idolaters. Those who favored the use of icons saw them as valuable
for instructing illiterate Christians in the faith (Latourette, 1:293). The
temptation to venerate the aids to faith is real. Whenever the church
loses the ability to stimulate new ways of perceiving God, its material
icons become wooden, jaded, and limiting.

Even the Bible, biblical study, and theology can become idols. The
experience of God is limited when the church declares that the Vul-
gate or the King James Version is the only acceptable translation, or
when the church stifles genuine questions of faith or restrains those
who pursue creative explorations into biblical truth. When the church
claims its doctrine, confession of faith, creedal statement, or catechism is the ultimate test of true faith, these have become idols.

A third type of icon which can become idolatrous is that of worship. Knowing and experiencing God can be facilitated by the rituals
of worship, but these can also obstruct the faith. There is, of course,
no form of worship which in and of itself is life-giving. The high-
church liturgy formed through centuries of use and recorded in flowing language and classical music cannot guarantee us access to God.
Nor necessarily can the unrecorded liturgy and weekly re-creation of
"extemporaneous" ritual and choruses. Even the image of God as
loving Father can be defective when one has known only an absent
or abusive earthly parent.

Our mental images of God need constant renewal lest icons become idols.

Stanza 2: Bursting the Bubble of Security and Pleasure

Amos 6:1-14

PREVIEW

The first woe addressed religious values and judicial practices; the second strikes at the nation's false security. These oracles take the literary form of diatribes containing rhetorical questions, quotation of the opponents' words, verbal outbursts, irony, and graphic judgment vignettes. This second woe prophecy divides into two halves: the first is largely accusation (6:1-7), and the second is judgment (6:8-14).

OUTLINE:

Just Look at Yourselves! 6:1-7
      6:1-3   Smug, Secure, and . . . Sick
      6:4-6   Lifestyles of the Rich and Famous
      6:7   The Day of Reckoning

Watch Me! 6:8-14
      6:8   I Swear . . .
      6:9-10   Don't Get God's Attention
      6:11-14   Devastation

EXPLANATORY NOTES
Just Look at Yourselves! 6:1-7

While Amos is lamenting the death of the nation, the elite of Israel are banqueting, oblivious to the condition of their people.

6:1-3 Smug, Secure, and . . . Sick

In one sweeping stroke, Amos paints the party scenes in the capitals of Judah and Israel. Some scholars suggest that the reference to Zion was added by a disciple of Amos to make the message apply to Judah after the exile of the Northerners. Others suggest that it may be the result of a copyist's error. Yet others contend that Amos would have us think of Samaria as the *Zion* of the Northern Kingdom.

Perhaps, however, the reference to Zion is a pointed way of indicting all the leaders of God's people, North and South. In both kingdoms, the monarchy has created a ruling elite. Samuel warned the people of these consequences of choosing a king after the model of other nations (1 Sam. 8). But Israel insisted on having its way. The monarchical administration concentrated power and the powerful in the royal cities. Israel was reaping the harvest of an earlier disobedience that had run its course. Judah strained toward similar national goals, even though the historian's evaluation of Uzziah and Jotham was positive (2 Kings 15:1-7, 32-38).

In the time of Amos, the court personnel in both Zion and Samaria are smugly self-confident and secure. They are *notables*, living in defensible cities, there by special appointment or because of their outstanding qualities. They speak proudly of their nation as a superior people, a *foremost nation* (cf. Num. 24:20). These elite relish the attention and pride of place that come with their leadership roles. It is gratifying to be wanted and needed by the common people.

The precise function of Amos 6:2 in this oracle is unclear. Was the verse added after 734 B.C., when the Assyrian king, Tiglath-Pileser III, had already drastically reduced the size and power of the states of Calneh (northern Syria), Hamath (north of the Lebanese mountains), and Philistia? *[Map of Near East, p. 404.]* If so, the message is a warning that a similar fate might befall the myopic leaders of Judah and Israel. If, however, the saying is earlier than 734 B.C. and from Amos, it may be connected with the phrase *foremost nation* in verse one. In that case, it would be saying, satirically: Close investigation of each of these nations proves that none of them matches the quality nor the territorial size of Judah or Israel. You truly are superior!

The specific indictments leveled against Israel in this oracle occupy 6:3-6. The sins are highlighted in 6:3, 6b; the spirit and attitude in which they are embodied are portrayed under "the lifestyles of the rich and famous" (6:4-6a). The first sin consists of an absence of moral discernment (Amos 6:3). These civil leaders should recognize the inevitable consequences of moral decay. The day of reckoning, the *evil day*, cannot be postponed indefinitely. The nation's leaders seem blind to the obvious: someone, some time, must pay the piper.

In addition to blithely dismissing signs of internal rot and external threat, Israel's leaders occupy themselves with short-term gains. Their policies, decisions, and practices are devoted to ensuring continuing benefits for the ruling class. Their exercise of power can more properly be termed a *reign of violence* (6:3b). Position, power, security, pleasure: these dominate their way of life.

6:4-6 Lifestyles of the Rich and Famous

Amos hits hard at extravagant furniture, elegant dining, elaborate entertainment, excessive drinking, and exotic perfumes. The nations' leaders live in idle opulence. They have the latest in design and the most expensive modern furniture (6:4a). *Ivory* is "in" in Samaria. One envisions ivory-inlaid furniture. Furthermore, in a society where the average person rarely eats meat (except for festive occasions), Israel's elite dine on *lambs* and *fattened veal* (6:4b; Beach, 1992:130-139). They twitter away their time composing songs extemporaneously, in what they regard as the great lyrical tradition of their foremost ruler, David (6:5). Wine is served them in widemouthed bowls, probably to permit the wine to be mixed with spices (6:6a). The aroma of the best anointing oils wafts through their spacious houses (6:6b).

Details of this account can be illustrated from archaeological findings. Ivory figurines and furniture inlays have been discovered in Samaria (King: 142-149). Megiddo, a city of major importance, has yielded an ivory carving, depicting "a prince drinking from a bowl, while in front of him stand a servant and a lute player" (Wolff: 276). The later Assyrian king Esarhaddon described the dedicatory banquet of his palace in language that also captures the opulence of Israel's rich: "The nobles and the people of my land, all of them, I made to sit down therein, at feasts and banquets of choice dishes, and gratify their appetites. With grape wine and sesame-seed wine I 'sprinkled their hearts,' with choicest oils I drenched their foreheads" (Wolff: 277).

Amos's indictments are not due to his rural mentality, to disgust with officialdom, to jealousy, or to sourness about wealth as such. Instead, these are God's appraisals of a decadent society. But they are more than that. The language of these verses points to three specific sins.

First, the references to the lambs, calves, music like David's, the widemouthed bowls (like those used in the temple), and anointing (*mašah*, generally used for the cultic act) suggest that private feasting has taken on a religious character (6:4-5). What better way to sanction extravagance, self-indulgence, and intemperance than to wrap it in a halo?

Second, the word for *lounge* (6:4) is used of spreading vines (Ezek. 17:6) or the overhang of the temple curtains (Exod. 26:12-13). The rich were idle rich, draping themselves over their costly imports. They were preoccupied with personal gratification. Indeed, the problem may be even more acute than that. The last two Hebrew words of

6:7, *revelry of the loungers* (NIV: *feasting and lounging*) may actually refer to an exclusive, elitist club (*marzeah*) dedicated to distinct social and religious values.

The main feature of the *marzeah* was the banquet. This sacred meal, sometimes associated with funerals (Amos 6:7; Jer. 16:5), was a time of eating and drinking to excess (Barstad: 127-142). The larger lyre (Amos 6:5; NRSV: *harp*) used at this feast was "customarily reserved for a religious function" (King: 154). The wine-bowl, usually referring to a sacred vessel (King: 158), may be another mark of the religious character of this funerary feast. This miniature covenant community exerted a stranglehold on the economic and social life of the nation. Consequently, the *notable* men who recline together in their private clubhouse will one day lead the way into exile (6:6b).

Third, and most serious, is the sin of omission: *They are not sickened* (6:6, lit.) by the shattering of their people. They cannot see the destruction of society around them. They seem incapable of feeling the pain of others. Their thoughts are for themselves alone. Here is the crux of Amos's critique. The wealthy are called to account for serving self alone. Gone is compassion for broken people. Absent is any concern for the well-being of God's people (*Joseph* = Israel).

6:7 The Day of Reckoning

Therefore the symbols of wealth and ease will disappear when God sends these leaders, these select people, to the head of the line of survivors into foreign exile (6:7). With this common announcement of judgment, the accusation oracle now gives way to the final description of Israel's death.

Watch Me! 6:8-14

This oracle consists of five literary snippets. The end has come for Israel. What true prophet could announce the death of his people in clear, calm speech? The thought leaps from image to image, like the semicoherent account of an accident victim or the reminiscences of the recently bereaved. A common thread unites these short outbursts: Yahweh has turned against his people.

6:8 I Swear . . .

The most memorable oath uttered by God in the story of his people is this:

By myself I have sworn, says the Lord: Because you have done this, and have not withheld your son, your only son, I will indeed bless you, and I will make your offspring as numerous as the stars of heaven and as the sand that is on the seashore. And your offspring shall possess the gate of their enemies, and by your offspring shall all the nations of the earth gain blessing for themselves, because you have obeyed my voice.

(Gen. 22:16-18)

This promise made under oath is referred to by God or his people more than forty times in the OT. That oath was fulfilled in Israel; the current oath cited by Amos replaces those earlier blessings with curses (cf. Deut. 32:15-42).

Instead of relying on her Lord, Israel has come to trust in her military prowess and the defensible position of her capital city, Samaria (Amos 6:8). Stone walls, well-equipped armies, and esprit de corps have replaced God in their political and international policies. These are abhorrent to the Almighty.

6:9-10 Don't Get God's Attention

The parable of Amos 6:9-10 picks up the last part of the previous verse: *I will deliver up the city and everything in it.* If the marzeaḥ or banqueting described in 6:3-6 is part of a funerary cult, the following parable of Israel's death is particularly fitting.

The parable's life setting is that of a ravaging epidemic. Even if a family has ten males in it, that will be no guarantee of survival. If the next of kin discharges his responsibility of removing and burning the bodies (lit.: *bones*), that relative may find someone still alive and inquire of the fate of the others; he will be told to be quiet. Presumably the name of their God is be a common part of everyday speech, as in "If it please the Lord," or "Lord forbid." But mentioning the Lord's name will be thought to draw the Lord's attention to the speaker and his situation. The inhabitant of the house is eager to forgo this when God is not favorably inclined toward his people—the condition shown by the current decimating judgment (1 Kings 17:18).

6:11-14 Devastation

Verse eleven explains the extent of the destruction of the *city* (Amos 6:8). When the Lord is done judging the city, it will appear as though an earthquake has struck. The stone mansions will be smashed to bits, and the dangerously large cracks in the commoners' homes will make them uninhabitable. Why? Because God has given his word of command in fulfillment of his oath.

Amos assigns the cause of the divine judgment to two sins: injustice (6:12) and pride (6:13). The fundamental character of the people of God has been violated by the nation's leaders. The judicial system, which should empower the poor and create equity between covenant members, has been poisoned. It has become the tool of the powerful in suppressing the helpless and in promoting their own welfare. What should show itself as the results of righteousness—wholesome, creative relationships—has been transformed into bitterness and enmity. Such perversions on Israel's part should be as improbable and contrary to nature as having *horses gallop on rocks* or *oxen plow the sea*.

The second sin—pride—expresses itself in self-congratulation over their military achievements. Lo-debar (cf. Josh. 13:26) was probably a strategic Ammonite city; Karnaim was the capital city of an Aramean kingdom [Map of Near East, p. 404]. Both fell during an Israelite invasion. But the historical record indicates that this eastward and northward expansion of Israelite power was prophesied by Jonah. It occurred because of the Lord's compassion on his oppressed people (2 Kings 14:25-27). Instead of acknowledging the divine compassion, the nation prides itself in these military accomplishments.

Israel has been sentenced to the death of exile for crimes against humanity and God. Only the means need to be disclosed (Amos 6:14). The national agent of execution remains nameless; the Judge who orders the execution is the One with whom disobedient Israel has to do. He is the Lord of armies. And the death sentence will be protracted, taking the form of oppression (as in Egypt) from the Lebanese—anti-Lebanese (*Lebo-hamath*) passes to the reaches of the Dead Sea (*Arabah*). The length of the land from north to south will be affected.

The wail of lament, begun in Amos 5:1, has reached every segment of society and every nook and cranny of the country. Only the prophet, peering into the future with eyes of faith, can make out the funeral procession and hear the mourners. The rest of the nation bustles about the marketplace, crowds into the sanctuary with offerings in hand, administers the officially sanctioned forms of justice in the city gates, and lines the public squares to cheer the victorious armies. Why should this people give attention to such a doomsday preacher?

THE TEXT IN BIBLICAL CONTEXT

Spotlight on Leaders

Leaders shape the destiny of those for whom they are responsible. Precisely for this reason, the Lord holds accountable not only those who are called to lead the people of God but also all leaders.

Throughout the Scriptures, leadership is portrayed as an appointment under divine accountability. Kings are the stewards of their nation's human and natural resources. In describing the land conquered by Joshua, the list of 31 slain kings becomes representative of the whole of the population (Josh. 12). When a king is killed, his nation is said to have been killed: "there was no one left who breathed" (Josh. 11:11, 14). Yet the book of Judges describes the Israelite tribes as clinging precariously to a few areas of Palestine. Such extravagant claims of extermination are due to what has been called "representative universalism" (Mattill: 8-11). The nation was identified so fully with the king that his death could be said to be the death of the entire nation, and his life stands for their life.

The divine pronouncement against the nation is frequently centered in the failed responsibilities of its leaders: kings and princes, priests and prophets, government officials and judges. Rarely do the people escape unscathed when judgment strikes. But the primary charge and punishment is leveled against the leaders (cf. Kings, Chronicles).

Leaders are accountable to God for those in their charge. This implies that God treats leaders as essential to human institutions which possess the power to build or destroy. Elsewhere in the Scriptures, these human agencies are called principalities and powers (as in Rom. 8:38; Eph. 3:10; 6:12). They consist of the human leaders, the power structures, and the domains ruled by the ethos and spirit of the age. Societies develop a collective character which leaves their imprint on those living within them. God holds leaders responsible for the ethos they encourage or produce as well as the specific acts and direction they give to the institutions over and with which they exercise their power.

All who follow the leadership of a civil, religious, judicial, or other leader, are subject to the effects of the divine evaluation of that leader. That is why, for example, judgment falls on all the generations (three or four) living under the authority of a parent who rebelled against the Lord.

On the role of leaders, a second implication concerns the level of responsibility. Leaders will have to give an account for those entrusted to them (Heb. 13:17). Those who teach falsely and lead their charges astray are subject to greater scrutiny and more severe judgment (James 3:1; Matt. 18:6-9). On the positive side, "whoever welcomes one such child in my name welcomes me [Christ]" (Matt. 18:5).

Third, this concept of leadership is extended to society in general in that governing authorities (Rom. 13:1-8) are charged by God with the faithful fulfillment of their societal obligations. They have been assigned their place in the divine economy, regardless of their political or economic philosophies. When their methods or the principles by which they govern ignore justice and distort human relationships, they are accountable to God for their deeds.

Fourth, nowhere in Scripture are those who are oppressed ever encouraged to rebel against authority. The oppressors will be judged by God; he will vindicate his name. The NT picks up this theme explicitly in calling citizens to submit to authorities (Rom. 13:5; cf. 1 Pet. 2:13). At times, that may involve suffering (2:18-25), but God promises to stand by his people. If we serve those in authority, even if they are demanding overlords, that is an act of reverence to God, who has charged leaders with performing the duties assigned them by society (1 Tim. 2:1-2; Rom. 13:1-7). Consistently, in Amos and the other prophets, the word of judgment from Yahweh begins: "Therefore I will. . . ." This implies that God honors the leadership choices of communities.

Fifth, the prophetic example informs us that submitting to authority does not mean silence or passivity in the face of injustice. Amos's presence and message are dramatic illustrations of the role of God's people in calling the leaders of their society to justice and compassion. Perhaps, also, the example of the prophets guides us in promoting the welfare of others rather than concentrating energies in objecting to injustice. That means that all of God's people need to be alert to what is happening in their society, to understand the issues, identify with the downtrodden, and promote justice and righteousness.

THE TEXT IN THE LIFE OF THE CHURCH
Materialism

Materialism is much, much more than greed, money, wealth, or prosperity. It is an attitude of the heart fed to bloating by the inability of things to satisfy the person or provide security for the future. The church has not always been helpful in its teachings in the area of wealth, money, and economics. The church has frequently given attention to secondary matters—to the things themselves rather than to what they represent. It has condemned the wealthy for possessing wealth and in turn salved their consciences by blessing their contributions to the church's building and missionary projects. These responses miss the point. Furthermore, such teaching and actions create confusion and guilt. They also separate many of the wealthy from the kingdom.

The Scriptures, especially those of the OT, promise well-being and prosperity as a reward to those who walk faithfully (Schneider). Many interpret this at the personal level to mean the following: If I am faithful, I will receive a promotion, my salary will increase, or my business will prosper. If I have committed this area of life to God in prayer and been honest in my dealings, I am justified in using more of the disposable income for myself. Were we not meant to enjoy God's world? So, travel, enjoy good cuisine, relax in the summer cottage.

This mind-set translates at the national and international level into an economic philosophy which undergirds the achievements of the majority of the wealthy countries. Its principal adversary has collapsed: communism, which many equate with atheism. The free market system (an essential element of capitalism) appears to be validated by the superior effectiveness with which it creates and distributes wealth, by the benefits of mass consumption and production across the globe (Nash). Supporters of this view of economics argue, for example, that without the massive influx of capital, fundamental research, biological and medical discoveries, and technological advances would be impossible. The entire world benefits in innumerable ways from this economic system. Today even environmental concerns are receiving a hearing. God made this world good for all to enjoy.

A contrary stream of thought links wealth and its accumulation with ungodliness, and pairs poverty with divine endorsement. It reminds us that God loves the poor and stands as their Defender. The kingdom of God belongs to the poor. True Christians identify with the marginalized of this world. The church has struggled with the matter of wealth over the centuries. Vows of poverty are one response, and generosity is another.

We do well to reflect on distinctions: between accepting a challenge to develop a business and being consumed by greed, between hoarding wealth and expanding a business, between preoccupation with things and the development of quality products, between self-sufficiency and preparation for the future, and between enjoying the amenities of life and living selfishly. Since riches can readily become a substitute for dependence on God, the love of money is called idolatry. Yet covetousness is not limited to those who possess more than they need of this world's goods.

Neither Amos nor any other prophet of OT or NT blesses the poor for being involuntarily poor. The prophets, however, do remind their hearers and readers (including the church) that strong divine censure falls upon conspicuous consumption, disregard of the poor, and injustice. Conversely, a commendable spirit of stewardship is reflected in good vocational choices, devotion of one's energies and resources made possible because of early-retirement plans, encouragement of governments to promote effective international aid programs, and the personal generosity of many Christians. Is it possible, however, to hide behind generosity?

As many as one-quarter of the American population professes to be "born again." However, even with self-declared Christians composing such a large proportion of the population, we make a relatively small impact on the crime rate and the criminal system, on poverty in rich America, on attitudes toward even legal immigrants, on the entertainment media, and on the divorce rate. Hence, the character of that Christian faith stands open to doubt. It feels more like self-indulgence and self-justification. Godly materialism may exist, but it hardly seems the right message for this time and place.

Let us consider the wars being fought over pieces of land or what lies under its surface. Arable soil stands fallow while whole populations starve. Greed for power controls even national policies by bartering votes in legislative sessions. And there is our own consumptive lifestyle. Is not the basket of summer fruit (Amos 8:2) a more appropriate word than "godly materialism"?

Part 3

Visions of the End

Amos 7:1—9:15

OVERVIEW

The sounds of death give way to silence. The earlier summons to "pay attention" is replaced by visions of the future. Has the nation gone stone deaf (Amos 5–6)? Doesn't anyone care? Have their hearts turned to stone as well? Are leaders and commoners in denial? Or are these pantomimes, shadows on the screen of history?

The ears of the nation are shut to God's word calling them back and threatening them. Only Amos seems to grasp the nature and extent of the crisis. If they will not hear, perhaps they can be made to see what the sights of the future hold for them. Five visions follow in rapid succession. The first four take us from early spring to fall; the fifth will come without warning in God's good timing. The first two concern the common people; the third, the royal house; the fourth, the rich and powerful; the fifth, all those who gather to worship in Beth-el, the house of God, the national shrine. Amos announces these visions in the temple at Bethel, probably in the middle of the eighth month, during the Festival of Tabernacles (Oct.-Nov.) [Tabernacles, p. 396]. The judgment could arrive within the year.

These are visions of dying rather than death. Locusts, fire, the sword, famine: these consume the nation silently. Even the earthquake is a silent destroyer. Watch and see what God is about to do!

If only there were someone to intervene, one to mourn! The visions come in rapid succession. Twice Amos is able to respond before the sight vanishes from his mental screen. Following the third vision, he is declared persona non grata by the nation's highest religious authority, the priest who claims to represent God's interests as well as those of the king.

326

The artistic beauty of these visions appears in their imagery. Locusts and fire are indiscriminate and affect the whole nation. The plumb line has to do with construction, appropriately preparing the way for the judgment on the *house* of Jeroboam. The basket of fruit leads to commentary on the fate of the merchant. In the end, after the judgment on the populace as a whole, only the sovereign Lord remains (vision 5).

Symmetry occurs in other ways as well. The first and fourth visions involve the farmer and the produce of the soil; the second and third visions may reflect God's action in regard to the work of people's hands. The first two visions contain Amos's intercessory response; the next two visions contain a sequel to the explanation of the vision. The fifth vision breaks the pattern, pointing to the dramatic conclusion.

OUTLINE

A Vision of Locusts, 7:1-3

A Vision of Fire, 7:4-6

A Vision of a Plumb Line, 7:7-17

A Vision of a Basket of Summer Fruit, 8:1-14

A Vision of the Lord: Judge and Restorer, 9:1-15

A Vision of Locusts

Amos 7:1-3

PREVIEW

To this point, Amos's word has been directed against those who live lavishly and frivolously in Samaria at the expense of the poor. The prophet sees God's coming judgment adding to the oppression they have already received from their fellow citizens (Amos 6:12, 14). This transforms Amos's compassion into an outburst of prayer.

OUTLINE

The Judge at Work, 7:1

A Catastrophe in the Making, 7:2a

The Prophetic Appeal, 7:2b

A Change of Mind? 7:3

EXPLANATORY NOTES
The Judge at Work 7:1

Locusts were commonly understood to convey the divine judgment. They represent one of the futility curses threatened against a covenant-breaking Israel (Deut. 28:38, 42) *[Covenant, p. 379]*. Joel depicts them as a marauding army, leaving death and destruction in their wake (Joel 1-2). Here they are expressly said to be *prepared* or shaped (cf. Gen. 2:19) for the divine purpose.

A Catastrophe in the Making 7:2a

The timing is crucial. The *latter rains* have come and gone. The first and fullest crop of hay, *belonging to the king*, had already been harvested (April). Destruction of the initial stages of growth of the second crop would so devastate the grass that little if any growth would develop as the temperatures climbed through the spring. The effect of this locust plague would strike hardest at the sharecropper, local landholder, shepherd, and the poor who lived off the gleanings. Instinctively Amos calls out, *O Lord God, forgive, I beg you! How can Jacob stand? He is so small!*

The Prophetic Appeal 7:2b

Amos, the Southerner, transcends nationalism. In an apparently instinctive response to the image of destruction, Amos bursts out in intercession. Prophets, official and occasional, were known as intercessors (Gen. 20:7; 1 Sam. 12:19-23; Jer. 7:16; 11:14; 42:1-6; "Intercession," in TBC below). The prophetic voice may at times sound harsh and even vindictive, but the reflex action of the prophet to words of impending doom is *Lord God, forgive. . . .* These messengers are not vindictive. Their response reflects a spirit of compassion, an identification with God's people which transcends expectations of office or social obligation.

Forgive! How can Jacob stand? He is so small! Amos appeals to God, using the argument that Israel is insignificant. Without special divine care, the Northern nation faces a certain and destructive future. The description *small* is more frequently a reference to significance than to size. It appears as a deliberate literary linkage of this final part of the book with what preceded. As such, it represents Amos's confession of the sin previously mentioned: Israel is a proud people, claiming God's victories as their own doing (6:13).

A Change of Mind? 7:3

God cancels the vision with the words *It shall not be.* Amos's appeal to God is rooted not in his promise or covenant but in God's concern for the weak and poor. In contrast with the inflating pride and arrogance of the leaders of the nation (6:6), Amos recognizes Israel's hazardous condition and relative frailty. Indeed, that has been his message throughout: in spite of seeming prosperity and security, the nation teeters on the brink of disaster.

The plea to *forgive* and *stop* represents intercession on behalf of a morally blind and unrepentant people. The verb *forgive* (*salaḥ*) is reserved in the Bible for God's treatment of sin. Such forgiveness does not require an offering (except when the verb is used in the passive). God, by sovereign act, frequently at the request of repentant or righteous persons (cf. Jer. 5:1; Dan. 9:19), cancels the sin with which they or others are charged. It is an act of pure grace. This ultimate appeal for forgiveness is rooted in the nature of the Lord (Ps. 103:3).

The word for *repent* (NRSV: *relent*) used here of God denotes an intensely emotional response, charged with compassion or sorrow. God does not act with detached coldness, nor does he erratically change his mind or course of action. The nation is standing at the brink of a precipice. For that reason, these final words of warning are sounded with the urgency and intensity of tough love ("When God Repents," in TBC below).

A Vision of Fire

Amos 7:4-6

PREVIEW

These first two visions are reported in identical literary form. Their parallel messages reinforce one another. Each of the seven nations whose judgment was declared in Hosea 1-2 saw its elaborate forti- fied dwellings disappear in fire. Israel's turn has come. The nation as a whole has become fuel for the fire.

OUTLINE

The Judge at Work, 7:4

A Catastrophe in the Making, 7:5a

The Prophetic Appeal, 7:5b

A Change of Mind? 7:6

EXPLANATORY NOTES

Locusts and fire appear together in judgment texts here and in Joel 2:3-25 (cf. Joel 1:4) and Nahum 3:15-17. Chronologically, the locust normally arrives in spring and is followed by the searing heat of sum- mer, which sucks up moisture reserves and bakes the denuded coun- try as would a spreading fire. One can imagine the heat waves com- ing off the scorched land, appearing as a flame. Fruit withers on the vine, the immature spring grain crop shrivels. Day laborers and others lose hope because they depend on the annual crop cycle.

It is unimportant whether Amos's plea is part of the vision or whether it represents his conscious response to the threatened hor- ror. In either case, it bares the soul of the prophet. Amos again breaks the stillness with a deep-throated cry: *O Lord God, cease, I beg you! How can Jacob survive? He is so small!* Again God cancels the vision.

Indeed, the multiplied warnings and threats of this book are a re- minder of the reluctance with which God acts against his chosen peo- ple, Israel. The sentence is executed only when all means to create re- pentance as well as all other avenues of appeal have been exhausted. Twice God responds to the intercession of his prophet.

THE TEXT IN BIBLICAL CONTEXT

Intercession

Intercession is typically prophetic but not uniquely so. The writer of the story of Abraham and Abimelech connects Abraham's prophetic "office" and intercessory acts (Gen. 20:7). Abraham's intercession for Sodom and Gomorrah (Gen. 18), about to be torched, finds an echo in Amos's intercession. Similarly, Moses (Exod. 32), Samuel (1 Sam. 12:23), Jeremiah (11:14; 14:11), and Daniel (9:4-19) all obtained reprieve for others' sins through intercession (cf. Neh. 1, 9).

The prophet typically stood as an intermediary between God and people, taking God's word to humankind and bearing people in their frailty and sin before the Almighty. He was both messenger and advocate (Limburg: 115). This picture of the dual prophetic role appears in the description of Moses' relation to God and Pharaoh. Moses was given words to be conveyed to Pharaoh. But he also took back Pharaoh's words to the Lord and interceded for the Egyptian king and his people (e.g., Exod. 8:8-12). This twofold messenger role may be displayed in graphic form:

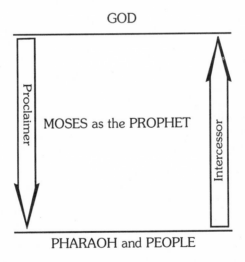

GOD

MOSES as the PROPHET

Proclaimer

Intercessor

PHARAOH and PEOPLE

The deeply compassionate character of the true prophet is shown in the transmission of the concerns of those being addressed by the prophetic word. Frequently these requests for intercessory prayer sprang more from fear of the consequences than from genuine repentance (Num. 21:7; 1 Sam. 12:19; 1 Kings 13:6; Jer. 37:3; 42:1-4,

19-22). However, God honored the prayers of his prophets for a sinful people. Our Lord Jesus and his disciples also taught and modeled such intercession (Matt. 5:43-48; John 17; Rom. 10:1; Heb. 7:25; James 5; 2 Thess. 1:11).

There are, however, limits to the divine forbearance, as shown in Amos 7:8; 8:2. Indeed, three times Jeremiah is told to stop praying for the people (7:16; cf. 11:14; 14:11). The repetition of this instruction implies that Jeremiah persisted in intercession and that God's hand was stayed by the prophet's appeal. This illustrates both the limits of the divine forbearance and the power of intercession. Elsewhere those limits are stated yet more dramatically: God announced that even the prayers of intercessors such as Noah, Daniel, and Job will be impotent (Ezek. 14:20).

When God Repents

What does it mean that God *repents* (*naḥam*)? The phrase appears frequently in the OT (cf. Gen. 6:6-7; Exod. 32:14; 2 Sam. 24:16; Jon. 3:10; 4:2). On the other hand, Balaam's God-given oracle for Balak seems to contradict this statement: "God is not a human being, that he should lie, nor a mortal, that he should change his mind (*naḥam*)" (Num. 23:19). The parallel between "does not lie" and "does not repent" reinforces the fact that a fundamental aspect of the person of God is at stake. God will not and cannot act contrary to his nature.

An even more puzzling text is 1 Samuel 15. Twice it is said that God repented (*naḥam*) that he had made Saul king (15:11, 35). And twice the word *naḥam* is used to describe the impossibility that God might reverse his decision to replace Saul on the throne (15:29).

Perhaps the clue is to be found in Jeremiah's experience at the potter's house (Jer. 18). There God enunciates a fundamental principle governing the relationship between human repentance and the sovereign acts of God: God's promises of wealth or threats of woe to the nation are conditional. Repentance from sin or defection from the covenant Lord may cancel an earlier threat or promise (18:6-10; cf. Ezek. 18).

The principle suggests that God has included human choice and responsibility as a factor in ordering the affairs of individuals and nations, in shaping our destinies. Good and evil will always bear their fruit in the form of curses or blessings. If, however, defection or repentance (or intercession) occur, the conditions have changed so that other consequences take effect. God's *purposes* are never altered by human choices. He is not a human that he would change his objectives or act contrary to his nature. Saul's rejection of God resulted in God removing him from the throne. This eliminated the possibility of his family creating a ruling dynasty. The timing of the consequences, while incorporating human participation or lack thereof, rests in God's hands. With Israel as with Saul, the verdict *I will spare them no longer* (Amos 7:8; 8:2) is divinely ordered. The end has come. Even intercession will no longer delay the judgment.

The biblical report that *God repented of the evil he had intended* is in anthropopathic terms, the language of human emotions. It is an accommodation to our finitude. That is, if we were to act toward others as God dealt with Israel (or Saul), we would speak of that as changing our behavior because of the intense compassion (or disappointment) we felt. That is what it means that God repented (*naḥam*). When God's repentance is directed toward those who harden and assert themselves against God, it leads to judgment. His repentance toward those who humble themselves, personally or representatively, roots in his deep compassion (Ps. 106:45).

THE TEXT IN THE LIFE OF THE CHURCH

Polar Viewpoints on Prayer

Intercession is a vital part of the ministry of those who proclaim the Word of God (1 Sam. 12:23; Acts 6:2-4). A pastor embodied this prophetic intercessory ministry creatively as he offered regular prayer for the members of his congregation. He knew where each member normally sat for worship. During the week he would move through the sanctuary, kneeling in intercession at each pew. A singular blessing attended his presence among the people and his preaching ministry.

Twentieth-century Western Christians congregate around two polar positions regarding the character of intercession. One pole stresses the sovereignty of God and views prayer primarily as an acknowledgment of what God is doing. Thus Edward Willis says,

> Prayer does not change things. Prayer changes people who change things. On the psychological level, prayer is an instrument of change because it continually reinforces the changed self-understanding of the persons praying. Prayer effects a change of heart in the Christian community. . . . Ethical responsibility derives from the freedom which comes of knowing that we are part of God's movement in history, that our actions have weight in his sovereign purposes. (120-121)

Intercession, then, becomes a way of immersing our spirits in the work of God and of empathizing with the plight of the suffering and the lost. The emphasis here is on engaging God in intercessory prayer because we are instructed to do so. The one praying benefits in exercising faith in the living Lord.

Those near the other pole stress intercession as a way of doing the work of God. The intense, persistent prayers of the saints effect God's purposes and actually change the course of individual lives and of history.

> Intercession is the climax of prayer. . . . Just now in certain circles it seems quite the thing to lay great stress upon the subjective value of prayer and to whittle down small, or deny entirely its value in influencing others. . . . The scriptural *standpoint* always is this: that things quite outside of one's self, that in the natural order of prevailing circumstances would not occur, are made to occur through prayer. . . . For prayer in its simplest conception supposes something changed that is not otherwise reachable. (Gordon: 40-42)

The emphasis here is that we pray because God (for one reason or another) has bound himself in the accomplishment of his redemptive purposes, with individuals and the church, to the faithful intercession of the saints. For example, many Christians firmly believe that the disintegration of the Iron Curtain and the destruction of the Berlin Wall were answers to prayers of millions of suffering and peace-loving Christians.

Scripture points to the effect of intercession as well as its limitations (the divine restriction, e.g., Amos 7:1-17; Ezek. 14:12-23). Perhaps we do well to retain both perspectives, held together in tension. The mystery of intercession parallels the mystery of proclamation. If God's people will be silent, the very stones will call out the word of salvation (Luke 19:40). If God's people neglect intercession, the redemptive plan will not be thwarted. But those who fail to pray, do so to their harm, and they affect the way God does his work. "As long as Moses held up his hands, the Israelites were winning, but whenever he lowered his hands, the Amalekites were winning" (Exod. 17:11, NIV). The victory depended on the grace of God invoked by Moses.

Surely God sustains the universe by intervening in a fallen world. He changes people, things, processes, and events directly and indirectly. He further invites those who know and love him to engage with him by interceding for a fallen and disjointed world.

Still, intercession has boundaries. Some deny the existence of limits to prayers of faith. They invoke the promise of Christ as absolute:

"I will do whatever you ask in my name, so that the Father may be glorified in the Son. If in my name you ask me for anything, I will do it" (John 14:13-14). It is dangerous to forget that many of God's answers reflect a different perception of how the divine purposes are to be accomplished than we might imagine. Even Jesus' prayer for release from the impending suffering was answered unexpectedly by the supporting presence of a strengthening angel (Luke 22:42-43). God has answered the faithful prayers of many saints by fortifying them to face the struggles, burdens, and trials of life rather than by removing them from trials.

Intercessory prayers may receive similar answers. God may choose not to heal, open prison doors, or restore the erring brother or sister. On the other hand, God delights in doing the impossible, frequently acting on the vital and persistent faith of those who love and serve him, though he also graciously sends rain and sun on all the earth for all people. The mystery of intercession remains a mystery of grace. It yields more readily to the test of practice than reason.

A Vision of a Plumb Line

Amos 7:7-17

PREVIEW

This vision (and the next) contrasts with the earlier ones in four respects. First, whereas the visions of the locusts and fire speak of imminent action on Yahweh's part, the vision of the plumb line denotes a condition. The symbol is a static one, describing the very nature of the people. Second, a swarm of locusts might be stopped, a fire might be quenched. But who can recondition a leaning stone wall? Who can prevent soft ripe fruit from spoiling? Third, God prevents intercession, implying that judgment is inevitable. Fourth, judgment oracles replace the prophetic appeal for mercy.

OUTLINE

The Plumb Line, 7:7-8a

Down with the Wall! 7:8b-9

The Official Report: Sedition, 7:10-11

Priest and Prophet in Deadly Dialogue, 7:12-17
   7:12-13   Prophet, Go Home!
   7:14-17   Don't Blame Me!

EXPLANATORY NOTES

In this passage the literary craftsman has spliced together a vision report and its narrative sequel. The references in each section to both the religious and political establishments bind the parts together. The *plumb line* is a builder's tool. The *wall* (*ḥomah*) is a city wall, not a house wall.

The Plumb Line 7:7-8a

Modern interpreters disagree on the meaning of the word translated *plumb line*. The corresponding Akkadian (and Assyrian) word means "tin." On the assumption that plumb bobs were made of lead, some interpreters have ruled out the idea of the plumb line (Holladay: 492-494; Stuart: 372-374). The Hebrew phrase "stone of tin," appears in Zechariah 4:10 as a plumb bob or plummet. The tin, then, stands for the plumb bob. The phrase *wall of tin* (Amos 7:7, Heb.) means a wall built by use of the plumb line to make it truly vertical. Perhaps Amos, in using the Assyrian word for tin, is hinting at the identification of the enemy who will destroy the city.

Down with the Wall! 7:8b-9

The king's palace and the temple frequently adjoined the city wall and were located at the most defensible part of the city. The construction engineer in the vision is *standing on* (7:7, Heb.; not *by* or *beside*, as in NIV/NRSV) *the wall*, holding the plumb line that all may see how seriously the wall is out of plumb. The danger is evident; their most formidable point of defense is tottering. Enemy sappers might easily undermine the wall at its weakened point and permit their assault troops access to the city through the breach. Or an earthquake could bring the wall crashing down.

   Israel is that leaning wall. The religious centers, whether local cult *high places* or sanctuaries in major fortified cities, as well as the heavily defended royal administrative cities—all will fall to the enemy. The royal family will go down in defeat. The prophecy does not spell out the reasons nor the time; the fact is sufficient. In preventing intercession (7:8b), the Lord ensures the fulfillment of this prediction. Historically, the prophecy against the dynasty of Jeroboam was fulfilled in the assassination of his son Zechariah, after a six-month reign (2 Kings 15:10). The destruction of the walled cities occurred some 25 years later, in 722 B.C. (2 Kings 17; cf. 15:29).

The Official Report: Sedition 7:10-11

Amos may be delivering his prophecy within earshot of the religious shrine at Bethel. Or the priest Amaziah may have heard of his words secondhand. An archive of documents uncovered in Mari (northern Mesopotamia), inscribed a millennium earlier, holds a local official responsible for keeping the king informed of any prophecies affecting affairs of state [ANET: 623-626, 629-632]. Similarly, the priest in Judah was appointed to ensure that only "genuine" prophecies, those approved by the ruler, be proclaimed at the religious centers (Jer. 29:24-28). The king of Judah was also apprised of words directed against him or his policies (Jer. 36). Amaziah, then, appears to be fulfilling a double obligation: informing Jeroboam of the content and source of prophecies directed at him, and expelling prophets who have spoken as madmen or without authorization (cf. Jer. 29:26).

The charge of *conspiracy* raised against Amos is a serious one (7:10). Earlier prophets were involved in creating new rulers or overthrowing the existing dynasties of Jeroboam I, Baasha, Ahab, and Jehu. Amos's prophecy was another such prediction (7:9). Since he was a Judean, his words could be seen as part of a conspiracy, joined possibly by Jeroboam's opponents in Israel. Here, then, was the religious propagandist inciting and abetting the king's enemies to rebel. And he was doing it brazenly, not in the occupied territories, but *in the very center of the house of Israel.*

The fact that Amaziah's report does not quote Amos's words precisely as they are given in 7:9 has raised some questions. It may be that Amaziah is deliberately misquoting Amos (*Jeroboam will die* rather than *I will rise against the house of Jeroboam*). Yet the remainder of the message corresponds with what Amos has said elsewhere about punishment by exile (cf. 4:2-3; 5:27; 6:7). On the other hand, the report may represent poetic license, or may be an acceptable paraphrase. It may even reflect the liberty and creativity of the writer and editor in shaping the contents of the book. The report to the king repeats the gist of Amos's prophetic word.

Priest and Prophet in Deadly Dialogue   7:12-17

7:12-13   Prophet, Go Home!

Amaziah addresses Amos as *seer* (see-er), possibly because Amos has been recounting his visions. The term was a perfectly normal one (cf. Isa. 29:10; 30:10) used most frequently in Israel's early history to designate a prophet (1 Sam. 9:9). Amos's answer (7:14) shows that *seer* and "prophet" are synonyms, and so does Amaziah's command for him to *prophesy* elsewhere.

Amaziah's words carry a threatening tone. A modern colloquial English equivalent might be, *Get out of the country if you know what's good for you. Go do your thing in Judah. Bethel is off limits to you* [Map of Palestine, p. 403]. The advice *Earn your bread there* (in Judah), *and do your prophesying there* implies that professional prophets earned their livelihood by giving prophetic counsel (cf. 1 Sam. 9:7-8; contrast Mic. 3:11). From Amaziah's perspective, Amos's prophesying in Israel means that some enemy of Jeroboam's is financing a revolt, or perhaps the prophet is being paid to invoke evil on the kingdom, in the manner of Balaam (Num. 22–24).

Amaziah, Jeroboam's high priest, is responsible to see that only messages acceptable to the king are pronounced in his domain (cf. Jer. 29:24-28). He does not deny the integrity of Amos or the source of his message. He merely frees himself from deciding between the word of the Lord and the wrath of the king.

Amaziah represents civil religion, domesticated by Jeroboam I and his successors. Unlike the religion of Judah, Israel's priests existed by royal appointment (1 Kings 12:31; 13:33). Her kings resisted the intrusion of true prophets in national life and political matters and made life unbearably difficult for persons like Elijah and Elisha. Note the story of the old prophet of Bethel who deliberately deceives the prophet from Judah, resulting in his death (1 Kings 13). This illustrates how quickly and thoroughly the Northern Kingdom created a powerful synthesis of religion and politics, and how devastating its effects were on the nation.

Amos has already established Israel's guilt in her acts of silencing the prophets and tarnishing the Nazirites' reputation (Amos 2:11-12). Amaziah's present action follows true to form.

How might Amos' hearers have recognized his message as genuine? ("Testing the Prophets," in TBC, below). True, he did point out Israel's failures and predict ruin. Furthermore, he was an Israelite and did speak in the name of Yahweh. Yet, since the test of fulfillment is the display of coming fiery judgment, that fulfillment is not yet available to bring about the repentance Amos is calling for, so the people might avert that very judgment. What remains is the test of consistency between Amos's pronouncements and prior revelation. That becomes the crucial norm (cf. Jer. 28:8-9). If the Israelites are to recognize the truth of Amos's prophecy, they need to reflect on their past and act with integrity.

7:14-17 Don't Blame Me!

Amos's answer to Amaziah's demands is twofold. First, he denies the charge of professionalism (7:14-15), thereby repudiating the accusation of conspiracy. Second, he confronts the demand to hold his tongue in Bethel with a judgment speech aimed directly at Amaziah himself (7:16-17).

The words of 7:14 (lit.: *Not a prophet, I, and not a son-of-a-prophet, I*) have been the occasion of much scholarly debate. The discussion revolves around the question of tense: should these verbless clauses be translated, *I was not . . .* or *I am not . . .*? Wolff observes that "this is a heated discussion because it includes the question of the self-understanding of Amos, and thereby also the problem of distinguishing between independent and officially sanctioned prophetism" (Wolff: 312).

The point of the contrast in 7:14-15 is not between Amos's past and present occupations, but between those prophets who prophesy at some other person's request or initiative and those who, like himself, are grasped by the Lord and empowered to prophesy without regard to vocation. Amos is not a card-carrying member of the institutional guild. Amaziah has accused Amos of preaching for pay. Amos rejects that accusation by pointing out that he has earned his living as a livestock breeder (cattle *herdsman*) and *slitter of sycamore* figs (to produce a sweeter and softer fruit). By occupation, Amos is in agribusiness.

The term *sons of a prophet* applies to apprentices (2 Kings 9:1). Amos contends that he is neither a vocational prophet nor a prophetic disciple. God's call to prophesy is irresistible (cf. Amos 3:8). In this he stands in the tradition of Moses (Exod. 3-4) and Samuel (1 Sam. 3). The call to prophesy has aimed him at Israel, and that validated his ministry in Bethel. So much for his self-defense.

Amaziah's order for him to leave Bethel and desist from prophesying there will have severe consequences (Amos 7:16-17). This priest of the Lord is more concerned with pleasing King Jeroboam, and thereby maintaining the security of his own position, than in doing the will of God. The fitting punishment? All that he holds dear will be lost; he will come to feel the weight of the curses of the covenant [Covenant, p. 379]. His wife will be deserted in a ravaged land, reduced to prostitution for survival (cf. Deut. 28:30). His children will die by the hand of an enemy (cf. 32:25). His land will be parceled out as a permanent possession to others (cf. Lev. 26:32). He himself will die in exile on unclean soil (cf. Deut. 28:36-37, 64).

The fate of the nation will enclose his own fate. The national sin of consistently silencing God's spokespersons (Amos 2:12) is mirrored in Amaziah's rejection of Amos for personal and political reasons. For Amaziah, exile is certain. The story of the interchange between Amos and Amaziah may be inserted between these visions as a way of pointing to overall unresponsiveness. This prepares the reader for the subsequent vision of judgment. Nothing can any longer avert the judgment.

THE TEXT IN BIBLICAL CONTEXT

Testing the Prophets

The writer of Deuteronomy had warned that Israel would be tempted to follow the ways of the nations in determining the will and ways of God (Deut. 18:14-16). Rather than consulting the dead, the entrails of animals, witches, or the stars, Israel was to heed the divine word as it came through authorized prophets (18:17-22). The message could be tested for authenticity by the fact of fulfillment.

Some gray areas remained. An authorized prophet might deceive (1 Kings 13:11-32; 22; Jer. 23:25a). An unauthorized or false prophet might produce credentials such as signs and wonders ("miracles"), and thereby convince the people of genuineness (Deut. 13:1-5).

There were no infallible proofs of a genuine word, though a number of tests were offered. The first test evaluated the prophet: Was he an Israelite in the pattern of Moses (one who communed with God)? A second test evaluated the message after the fact: Did the prophecy (of warning or weal) come to pass (Deut. 18:21-22)? Fulfillment presumably authenticated the prophet. But it was precarious as a test, since the message of false prophets might also be fulfilled or be supported by a sign or wonder (Deut. 13:2). A third test lay in determining whether the prophet's word was consistent with Yahweh's previous self-revelation (Deut. 13:1-5; Jer. 23:21-22, 25-32). A fourth test turned on the morality of the prophet (Jer. 23:14; 1 Kings 22:8-17).

Apparently the Judeans used additional (or alternative) tests of genuineness for the prophetic message. They evaluated the message as authentic if it promoted the permanence of the temple in Jerusalem (Jer. 7:4), if it reinforced God's reign over his people as one of peace (6:14; 8:11), if it came to the prophet in the form of a dream (23:25), or if it was announced as an "oracle of Yahweh" (Jer. 23:34, NIV). The only criterion of historical record applied to Northern Kingdom prophets is the one implicit in King Ahab's exchanges with Elijah (1 Kings 18:16ff.) and Micaiah ben Imlah (1 Kings 22): if the message was one of woe, it was most likely true (22:8).

THE TEXT IN THE LIFE OF THE CHURCH
On Recognizing the Prophet of the Lord

How does the church recognize true prophets today and distinguish them from the false? The question remains as critical in this century as during the days of Amos. What criteria may guide the church in distinguishing the true from the false? Is there a standard which can be applied to the prophets of the Charismatic Movement, the Vineyard Movement, The Church of Jesus Christ of Latter-day Saints (Mormons), and the African Independent Churches, or to persons like Thomas Müntzer, John Wesley, Jimmy Jones, David Koresh, or Billy Graham? Or is time the only infallible winnowing agent?

Sometimes a prophet may promote the ways of God, but imperfectly. Is such a prophet a false prophet? If so, is that prophet to be followed with reservations? What does a qualified commitment to the church's leadership do to the ability to lead?

In 1988 a self-proclaimed "prophet" announced the return of Jesus Christ under the slogan "88 reasons why Jesus will return in 1988." Should Christians take such prophecies seriously? Some pastors accepted the arguments of the apparently qualified writer (a former NASA engineer) and preached the message, leading Christians to repent and renewed commitment. Does that result make it right? Or must we wait, in such cases, until the designated time passes?

Questions accumulate more quickly than answers. Yet some relevant clues can be drawn from the text we have explored. The church draws on the Scriptures to identify ways of testing the spirits.

First, any messenger who purports to be a prophet must clearly be oriented in the truth of the Scriptures. It must be the final authority for faith, life, and godliness. That constitutes the reference point of "the previous revelation of Yahweh." Just as the prophets repeatedly drew Israel back to the Lord of the covenant, so contemporary prophets must be tested for their faithfulness to the Word of God. Therefore, every Christian is obligated to know and search the Scriptures so that they might determine the truth of the message (cf. Acts 17:11). Testing, probing, and evaluating the prophet's (or preacher's) message, when done with the intention of obeying the truth, is a mark of faith, not rebellion.

Second, the moral character and ethical practices of the prophet should be exemplary and embody true godliness. Amaziah was right in raising the issue of motivation and character. Prophets who prophesy for pay or personal advantage are definitely suspect in the public mind. The prophetic message springs from inner compulsion of the Spirit, compassion for people, identification with the poor and the needy, and an intense longing to see the kingdom of God established. For the true prophet, compassion is reflected in faithful intercession. Intercession is the (often) silent and unheralded ministry of those who know the heart and holiness of God, the sinfulness of sin, and the eternal destiny of both the ungodly and the saints.

Third, the experience of Amos warns us that prophets who promote an identification with the political and social structures of society—any society—are often false. True prophets like Amos, with few exceptions, confront society and its institutions with calls to repentance. By their very nature, the structures of the world are coercive; in their values they are essentially materialistic; in their practices they utilize almost any method which assures them of self-preservation. Those who invite uncritical and unqualified obedience to national or civil leaders and institutions are probably false prophets. The true prophet penetrates society with the call to repent, to turn to God, and to cast off reliance upon this world's power structures, its methods, and its weapons.

On Silencing the Prophets

Israel is not alone in silencing the prophets among them. Church historian Albert Newman reflects on the first 19 centuries of the church:

> The church has persecuted Christians far more cruelly, and has destroyed many more Christians than pagans have done. (1:316)

The institutionalized church, like other societal structures, tends toward self-preservation. Prophets threaten the status quo. They threaten the stability of church and society. Their ministry creates ferment, dissonance, and frustration. Yes, it may well do that.

Like society at large, the church has frequently rejected the prophetic word and silenced the prophets. Examples may be drawn from nearly every era of its history and every theological branch.

Florence, Italy, of 1490-98, was a city in political and religious turmoil. Its most prominent preacher of righteousness was the friar Savonarola. He preached the coming of a new age and the need for repentance by the city's leaders and people alike.

> There followed a startling transformation of the life of the city. Women threw aside their finery and dressed plainly, bankers and tradesmen restored ill-gotten gains, there was much reading of the Bible and the works of Savonarola, churches were crowded, alms to the poor increased, and some scions of leading families and several mature men of outstanding ability entered San Marcos as monks. (Latourette, 1:673)

Savonarola made political and religious enemies. The pope ordered him to stop preaching; he defied the order and was excommunicated. The city government was hostile to Savonarola; they arrested and tried him. The trial was a farce, the verdict predetermined. The rack and the noose ended his life. Fire reduced Savonarola to ashes. Following his death, "The majority of Florentines returned to their old ways" (Latourette, 1:674). A prophet had been silenced.

Oscar A. Romero was archbishop of San Salvador for three years (1977-80). Death squads roamed the city streets, kidnapping and murdering critics of the oppressive regime, killing priests and commoners. In that setting, Archbishop Romero's sermons sound like those of a modern-day Amos as he addresses the sins of the nation:

> When we preach the Lord's Word, we denounce not only the injustices of the social order. We denounce every sin that is night, that is darkness: drunkenness, gluttony, lust, adultery, abortion, all that is the reign of iniquity and sin. Let them all disappear from our society. (Romero: 5)

While the message was addressed to all segments of society, he saw his special calling as that of speaking for the poor.

> The world does not say, Blessed are the poor. The world says, Blessed are the rich. You are worth as much as you have. But Christ says, Wrong. Blessed are the poor, for theirs is the kingdom of heaven, because they do not put their trust in what is transitory. (Romero: 33).

Romero's fellow bishops and the political rulers opposed him and complained to Rome about his "communist" activities. He rejected the accusation, explaining,

> When we speak of the church of the poor, we are not using Marxist dialectic, as though there were another church of the rich. What we are saying is that Christ, inspired by the Spirit of God, declared, "The Lord has sent me to preach good news to the poor" (Luke 4:18). (Romero: 40)

Like the OT prophets, the archbishop kept calling his parishioners and the rulers of the country to repentance and faith in Christ: "I cannot change except to follow the gospel more closely. And I can quite simply call to everyone: Let us be converted so that Christ may look upon our faith and have mercy upon us" (Romero: 62).

The end came when this pacifist priest made a pointed appeal to soldiers, national guardsmen, and policemen:

> Brothers, each of you is one of us. We are the same people. The *campesinos* you kill are your own brothers and sisters. . . . No soldier is obliged to obey an order contrary to the law of God ("Thou shalt not kill"). It is time that you came to your senses and obey your conscience rather than follow out a sinful command. The church, defender of the rights of God, the law of God, and the dignity of each human being, cannot remain silent in the presence of such abominations. (Buckley: 98)

He had gone too far. Archbishop Romero had called the military to choose between national policy and God's ways, between oppression and justice. Two days later, while saying mass for cancer patients, he was shot to death by a rifleman. A modern prophet had been physically silenced, but his faith still speaks (Heb. 11:4; Gen. 4:10).

There are other ways of silencing the prophets. Various subversive tactics are employed today in the North American church: slander and unfounded accusations, endless criticism, complaining and murmuring (Exod. 15-17), creation of opposition power blocs, boycotting services, and sometimes cutting pastors' salaries. Silencing the prophets eventually results in a famine of the Word of God.

From Civil Religion to World Christian

Civil religion results from a national sense of divine calling or a fusion of religious and political goals. By their very nature, both church and state address issues of great importance. Therefore they claim the right to order the life of their citizens or adherents, even to the extent of expressing or defending their values at the risk of life itself.

The doctrine of "Manifest Destiny," advanced in the USA in earlier decades, tends toward civil religion. Signs of civil religion exist everywhere. Politicians identify with a church to gain adherents, they call on the nation's religious leaders for counsel, they authorize national prayer days, they quote the Bible in their election campaign speeches. But at a deeper level, civil religion is seen in that the major religious denominations have blessed virtually every "Christian" country's war efforts. The Korean War, the Vietnam War, the Gulf War, and the invasions of smaller countries in the Caribbean—these all were blessed by religious leaders. Is this fundamentally different from Hitler's gaining support of the state church in Germany? Or is the difference one of degree rather than kind?

As long as the church is in this world, national and racial identity will shape its life to some extent. The more the church enjoys the benefits of stable government and the opportunity to present the claims of Christ to our society, the greater will be the tug to equate the kingdom of God with our national, racial, or tribal privilege. Persecution or antagonism toward the followers of Christ loosens the world's grip on the Christian's national or racial allegiances. Such opposition may even pry the church loose from its ethnicity and release it to function as a counterculture. When that happens, world Christians are born.

The gospel invites us to become world Christians who hold as secondary all other identities, all other allegiances. World Christians engage their own society in constructive critique and appropriate approval while acknowledging the contribution and worth of other societies. Their strongest allegiances, however, are to the people of God across cultural, social, and political boundaries.

The church seems to have made little progress toward achieving its worldwide identity. The NT gives prominence to God's purpose of uniting all people into one new humanity in Christ. Yet world Christians are truly rare, even after centuries of cross-cultural mission activity. Nationalism, racism, and prejudice have deep taproots reaching down into the reservoir of our unacknowledged fears and unconquered pride. World Christians, however, are nurtured by the vision of the one body brought into wholeness by the Spirit of Christ.

A Vision of a Basket
of Summer Fruit
Amos 8:1-14

PREVIEW

One does not ordinarily associate a basket of peaches or plums, berries or tomatoes, with a spiritual message. Yet God has pictured the Amorites as trees and described their destruction in the words, *I destroyed his fruit above, and his roots beneath* (2:9). In the first three visions, Israel is pictured as grass being eaten down to the ground, consumed by the sun's fire, and withering away down to the roots. Israel is a city wall out of plumb due to faulty foundations. In this fourth vision, the nation becomes the summer fruit carried in a basket. The threat of destruction is very real and is comparable to God's expulsion of the Amorites.

OUTLINE

A Vision of Soft Summer Fruit, 8:1-2a

Play on Words in Dead Earnest, 8:2b-3

Catastrophe in Real Life, 8:4-14
8:4-6	The Responsible Parties: Merchants and Bankers
8:7-14	God's Monologue on the Nation's Destiny

EXPLANATORY NOTES

This vision and its explanation are characterized by play on words and metaphors of contrast and reversal. The writer gathers together strands of thought from chapters 5–7. The air of death and sounds of mourning carry over from the funeral scene. Here is the last appeal to those still able to hear the word of the Lord. The temple songs of praise have become wailings for the dead.

A chiasm binds the disparate parts of Amos 8 into one larger whole. The subtle artistry prepares us for an even greater and more intricate design in the last chapter. Here are the correspondences.

(A) Blessings withdrawn (8:1)
   • disclosure of vision by Yahweh
   • basket of moisture-filled summer fruit

   (B) Explanation of judgment (8:2-3)
      • the end has come
      • my people, Israel

   (B') Blessings withheld (8:11-19)
      • word withheld by Yahweh
      • young virgins and men in prime

(A') Description of judgment (8:9-10)
   • the end like a bitter day
   • an only son (Isaac)

A Vision of Soft Summer Fruit 8:1-2a

Like a basket of summer fruit (*qayiṣ*), the nation appears to be at its prime. The word *qaiṣ* occurs in an early document (the Gezer calendar) as the month of harvest of summer fruit (Paul: 253). While it probably refers to the fig harvest, other summer fruits may well be included in the term. Most fruit which ripens in the heat of summer deteriorates quickly after it is picked. Is that the mental image which now occupies Amos? The Israelite corpses, like so much decaying fruit, are flung outside. The month of moral harvest has arrived.

Play on Words in Dead Earnest 8:2b-3

The end has come. Note the wordplay in Hebrew, with similar sounds for summer fruit (*qayiṣ*) and for end (*qeṣ*). The summer fruit is a metaphor for the conclusion of the harvest. The end in view is God's bountiful care for his people in the Land of Promise. They can expect no further delay in the judgment.

I will never again pass them by. This reminds readers of the first Passover and the escape from Egypt. The angel of death did "pass over" the homes of those who applied the blood of the Passover lamb to the doorjambs of their houses (Exod. 12). God has again come to visit his people, but this time the oppressors are the Israelites themselves. Will the sovereign Lord distinguish between those who are the oppressors and the oppressed as he did in Egypt? Or will all suffer alike? The answer rushes forward on the heels of the question: *The end has come for my people, Israel.* The nation has passed the point of no return. The prophecy carries a strong note of finality.

What appears in translation as a straightforward statement contains the power of the literary artist. God was earlier said to despise
the songs of the temple because they replaced justice and righteousness (Amos 5:23-24). The location is Bethel; the *songs* are accompanied by instruments. Hallelujahs (Heb. verb: *halal* or *hallelu*) will be
transformed into *howls* or *wailings* (Heb. verb: *yalal*, in this form:
helilu). Howls are not accompanied by instruments, nor are they sung
in the temple. The *wailings* (*howls*) locate the howler in desert areas,
indicating that Israel is on the march into exile. Instruments of worship will be unnecessary baggage, even if they have been rescued
from the fires and destruction.

Dead bodies shall be many, cast out in every place. This is a sign
of the scope of the enemy attack and of the continued existence of a
remnant, inasmuch as the bodies are being *thrown out.* The demand
for silence reminds the readers to connect this word with two themes
from earlier prophetic utterances: Israel's attempt to silence the prophetic voice (2:11-12; 3:7-8) and fear of drawing the Lord's attention
to Israel, which might mean more judgment (6:10).

Catastrophe in Real Life 8:4-14

8:4-6 The Responsible Parties: Merchants and Bankers

The vision of judgment grows into a wail of four or five stanzas.
The mourners are addressed as though they were the subject of a
praise song. The wail will come from these merchants. They are the
propertied and monied people. They may be the husbands of the
cows of Bashan, who earlier felt the lashes of the word of judgment
(4:1-3) *[Bovine Imagery, p. 374].* Without using the word, Amos describes this powerful group of people as Canaanite traders (cf. Hos.
12:7). Some of their many sins are enumerated here. At root, all the
sins mentioned grow out of greed and materialism. Instead of addressing the outrage of poverty, the well-to-do focus on ridding themselves of *the poor* (Amos 8:4), probably by enslaving them or forcing
them into exile and out of their sight. Out of sight, out of mind, they
reason.

They are so totally preoccupied with commerce and trade, that
communal times of rest and celebration are endured with regret:
good opportunities for making a living are going to waste (8:5a).
Their times of worship are taken up with calculating how they can increase their earnings and what measures they need to employ to im-
prove their profits. They cheat at every turn (8:5b-6). They *sell grain*

(or *food*, generally) with an undersized measuring basket. They buy goods using overweight counterweights. They rig the scales in their favor. They buy people as readily as goods (see notes on 2:6). In the assembly, while others worship, they worry about selling the *wheat screenings*. They have desecrated the land.

The land of Israel, as distributed to the tribes, clans, and families at the time of the conquest, was unevenly productive. It almost seemed that God permitted inequalities to exist so as to give occasion for the development of community. Some families reaped bountiful harvests, others eked out a living. But God's ideal was that all should receive ample blessings as demonstrations of God's gracious care (Deut. 15:4-5).

The ideal and the reality did not fully match. Not all people are equally gifted. Sloth, neglect, poor management, illness, inferior soil, and the weather contribute to the creation and plight of the poor. So how is poverty to be addressed in a nation which practices justice? In large measure through the generosity of those more amply blessed. The unevenness is an occasion for community building. The presence of the poor constitutes a test of love (Deut. 15:7-11).

The wealthy addressed in Amos 8 are far removed from the Deuteronomic ideal and practices. Indeed, they appear to be acting in measured contradiction to the divine instruction. Injustice prevails. Charity does not cross their minds, let alone the palms of their hands. Community means nothing to them, except for the community of those who belong to the same dining club (*marzeah*, 6:3-7). The community of covenant partners as envisioned in the revelation at Sinai has become an alien concept.

Underlying this rejection of covenant community, which cuts across the variety in giftedness, opportunity, character, and resources, is the lust for money and a distrust in the providence of God.

8:7-14 God's Monologue on the Nation's Destiny

Here is a metaphor of judgment. Its fulfillment is doubly ensured by the oath of the Lord taken, not on a holy book, but *by the pride of Jacob*. Is this the false pride of the nation, boasting of being invincible (6:8, 13)? If so, the phrase tastes of bitter sarcasm. Or does the nation pride itself in the Lord, their covenant-keeping God? This too bites with sarcasm. Even in the display of anger, God preserves a sense of humor.

The central feature in the coming judgment is a massive earth-

quake (8:7-8; cf. notes on 1:1). God has come to fulfill his word of
threat; this earthquake authenticates the prophecy of judgment conveyed by Amos to the Northern Kingdom. Indeed, it is a confirmation
of the message to Judah as well, since the Lord will shake the entire
land (8:8). Those who experience its roller-coaster effect will later
compare it to the annual rising and falling of the Nile (8:8b). The aftershocks and effects will add to the devastation (8:9-10). Even the
heavens are said to share in this act of judgment when night comes at
high noon.

The description of the judgment of darkness is probably intended
to recall the plague of Egypt (Exod. 10:21-23; cf. Deut. 28:29). Since
heaven and earth are affected, the prophecy also points to this event
as one of the promised consequences of persistent disobedience.
The Sinaitic covenant, as contained in Deuteronomy, called heaven
and earth as witnesses to the covenant commitments (4:26; 30:19).
But a witness does not remain a neutral observer of events. When
willful violations of the covenant occur and judgment is decreed, the
witness casts the first stone (13:9). In the case of the judgment described in Amos 8, both heaven and earth convulse in revulsion at
the sin of Israel (cf. Deut. 28:20-29, 38-42) [Covenant, p. 379].

One can imagine the consequences of such an earthquake. The
city walls in which they trust, the mansions in which they loll, the altars at which they worship—all will be reduced to rubble. When they
dig themselves out from beneath the debris, the whole country will
mourn its dead (Amos 8:10). The Egyptians mourned the death of
their firstborn (Exod. 12:30); the people of Israel will mourn as for an
only son (Amos 8:10).

The inevitable deluge of questions will follow: Why? Why? Why,
O Lord? In desperation the nation will search its world for answers
and hope (8:11-12). They will find none. God will be silent. Israel refused to heed the Lord's words when he spoke in warning (cf.
Amos 4). Now even the warnings have ended, and God will not listen
to their prayers, no matter how shrill the pleading. Israel has been depending on her own resources, reveling in luxury and gluttony. The
people's sumptuous fare, elegant robes, and vaulted hairdos are replaced by fasting, sackcloth, and shaven heads. The land will mourn
its dead.

Aftershocks follow the quake. One result of God's shaking the
land is that the sources of water have been disturbed. What is stored
in cisterns has seeped through the cracks. The land and its people die
of thirst.

Even the most vigorous and promising young men and women will suffer. These too have compromised their faith and promises, swearing by the names of the gods of their major cult centers. Out of a distaste for even pronouncing the names of other gods, those names are probably omitted by Amos (though some would argue that *Ashimah of Samaria* and *the Way of Beersheba* are the names of patron deities). In the time of calamity, the youth will run about looking for answers from the gods in whom they have trusted. The gods are silent. As a last resort, they search for the Lord's word, but it is nowhere to be found. Previously their elders have silenced the prophets; in their supreme distress, Yahweh answers with silence.

All the sources of pride are brought to ruin in one sweeping act of destruction. The image of earthquake already introduced in 8:8 is sharpened in what follows. The final vision (9:1-10) overlaps with this fourth vision in that it begins with the earthquake and progresses through the military conquest of the weakened nation.

In this climactic act of withholding his word, God reminds Israel "that one does not live by bread alone, but by every word that comes from the mouth of the Lord" (Deut. 8:3).

THE TEXT IN BIBLICAL CONTEXT

The Silence of God

Prophets are called to announce the message from God. Even threatening messages indicate that God is still concerned. But what happens when the prophets no longer speak? We presume the silence is intended by God.

The perception that God is silent could be the result of someone's disobedience. Jonah, for example, initially withheld the message from the Ninevites for personal reasons. Jeremiah found the message so dreadful that he attempted to hold it in (20:8-9). But it became like a fire in his heart, a fire which could not be quenched.

On other occasions God's silence constitutes a test. There may be a reason for this silence, but that explanation is unknown to the one who feels abandoned. For example, God left Hezekiah to his own resources "in order to test him and to know all that was in his heart" (2 Chron. 32:31). God has chosen to withdraw himself. The agonizing cry from the cross reminds us that the silence of God is terrifyingly real: "My God, my God, why have you forsaken me?" (Mark 15:34). The request in the Lord's Prayer that the Father would "lead us not into testing" refutes the assumption that the life of faith is one continuous intimacy with God (Matt. 6:13).

God's silence may also be due to sin. Persistent rejection of the word of God can lead to the inability to hear or see it even though it is present. Pharaoh hardened his heart ten times, each act confirmed in that God matched it with a corresponding act of hardening (also ten times). God's commission to Isaiah addressed the issue of divine silence, a silence due to Israel's callousness:

> Go and say to this people: "Keep listening, but do not comprehend;
>   keep looking, but do not understand."
> Make the mind of this people dull, and stop their ears, and shut their eyes,
> so that they may not look with their eyes, and listen with their ears,
> and comprehend with their minds, and turn and be healed. (Isa. 6:9-10)

At other times God chooses to withhold the word altogether. Saul, living in the downward spiral of disobedience, in desperation appealed to Yahweh for guidance, but "the Lord did not answer him by dreams, or by Urim, or by prophets" (1 Sam. 28:6). He experienced the silence of the word of God. Similarly, Yahweh placed a restraining order on Ezekiel to prevent him from rebuking the recalcitrant nation until the news of Jerusalem's capture arrived (3:26; cf. 33:22). It was never the prophet's calling to determine when and where the word of God was suitably proclaimed. That remained the divine prerogative.

THE TEXT IN THE LIFE OF THE CHURCH
Greed

Greed is a lusting after things which represent power to us. These may be in the form of money, resources, people, or circumstances (opportunities). One need not be rich to be greedy, since we all have a need for personal power, a need to feel we have some say in our own well-being or in the choice and direction of our lives. Most often greed consists of an insatiable desire to have more things. As such it is an expression of materialism as well as a hunger for security.

Greed sets its practitioners against other people, destroying community, and isolating those who grasp for it. Greed for power acts like an addictive drug, offering a false security while destroying the addict and separating those whom it touches. Israel's economic injustices represent an agreement between the ruling and the merchant classes in the legal exercise of greed. The unjust laws and practices of Israel's political leaders and economic class have shattered the unity of the nation. The subsequent judgment will shred the economic structures, exposing the vulnerable foundations on which they have been built. Neither economic nor legal institutions can ever substitute for the strength which comes from people living in community.

Avarice also represents distrust in divine providence. It places in doubt the willingness or the ability of God to provide for the material needs of his creatures. Is it not characteristic of deeper realities, that idols are made out of silver and gold (Ps. 135:15; Hos. 8:4), and that the Scriptures refer to the love of money (covetousness) as idolatry (Col. 3:5; Eph. 5:5)? Inevitably, those who worship this idol succumb to immoral methods to feed their greed.

Preoccupation with security and material welfare starves the spirit. For such a person, God becomes a supporter of the status quo, One who responds to my needs at my bidding. But the Lord will not be bound by the timetable of those who name the Name. Continued resistance to the call for repentance induces spiritual hardening of the arteries. God treats the disease by withholding his word. Preoccupation with the blessings of God gnaws away at community.

The antidote to greed is generosity. It recognizes God as the Giver of all good gifts. It acknowledges the other persons with whom we occupy limited human and natural resources. It frees people from selfish addictions. It releases the work of the Spirit of God in binding people to one another. This results in a sense of security, acceptance, and worth.

A Vision of the Lord: Judge and Destroyer

Amos 9:1-15

PREVIEW

This fifth vision is different from the others. Here is neither grasshopper, fire, plumb line, nor summer fruit (7:1—8:3). The Lord himself is the centerpiece of this experience.

Hosea 9 consists of as many as four prophecies merged into one coherent whole. Verses 1b-4 and 7-10 appear to have been a single original unit, delivered from the mouth of God. The hymn of 9:5-6 comes to us in the third person. It accents the theme of the vision, though its source is unknown. Verses 11-12 constitute the third unit.

The time signature, *in that day* (9:11), marks its beginning and appears elsewhere in Amos (8:3, 9). In 8:3 it is clearly not a signal of a new prophetic unit. This raises the distinct possibility that 9:11-12 (and 9:13-15?) were part of the original vision. A second, more general, time marker, *the days are coming* (9:13; cf. 8:11), introduces the concluding prophetic speech. More will be said about the integrity of 9:11-15 in the notes below.

OUTLINE

[A] [I'm Taking It All Away, 8:11-14]

    (B) You Can't Escape, Even in Hell, 9:1-4

       (C) I Am the Lord; Remember Me? 9:5-6

    (B') You're Not That Special, 9:7-10

(A') I'm Giving It All Back, and More! 9:11-15
    9:11-12   Restoration of the Booth of David
    9:13-15   Restoration of God's People

This chiastic literary structure brackets two pair of matching bookends: A, B, C, B', A'. The cues marking the outer bookends (A, A') of this structure consist of identical words or phrases in the corresponding sections (Limburg: 123-125).

8:11-14	Removed	BLESSINGS	Restored	9:11-15
8:11		the days are coming		9:13
8:14		fall . . . rise/raise		9:11
8:13		in that day		9:11

EXPLANATORY NOTES

Amos 9:1 signals a new vision, but the vision introduction does not follow the earlier pattern. This encourages the reader to look for a variation in structure. That variation occurs in that 8:11-14 serves as the conclusion to the fourth vision as well as the opening element of the fifth (9:1-15). The effect of this literary device is to speed the action toward the consummation. Amos 8:11-14 has already received our attention.

You Can't Escape, Even in Hell   9:1-4

The symbolic objects of locusts, fire, plumb line, and fruit basket in the first four visions are replaced by the presence of the Lord himself. The veil has been removed. God stands at center stage. His stance is not casual; it has a definite purpose.

The location is significant. He is positioned *on* (NIV: *by*) the altar, on the platform surrounding the raised part of the altar. The particular altar is not specified, but it is at a major center, probably at Bethel (cf. 3:14). This is shown by the description of the major pillars located there (9:1b), implying that its destruction affects the entire nation.

God is acting with malice aforethought. While one would expect to see God in connection with the place where he is worshiped, his stance is one which conveys foreboding. It speaks of judgment, not forgiveness. And if God's first destructive act strikes at the court of last appeal (the altar and the priests who serve there), the future is indeed menacing. The Lord has turned on his own people.

The acts of God will take two forms. The earthquake will destroy Israel's religious center(s) (9:1b-c). An enemy force will mop up the survivors (9:1d-4).

Only an earthquake can do the type of structural damage envisioned: *Strike the tops of the pillars so that the thresholds shake* (9:1a). These pillars (literally: *capitals*) may support a roof over a shrine or several rooms reserved for priests. On the other hand, they may be free-standing pillars (male sex symbols?) like those placed before Solomon's temple by his Phoenician craftsman, Hiram (1 Kings 7:15-22). In both cases, each pillar is topped by an elaborately carved or cast *capital*. These pagan symbols are to be brought down on the assembled worshipers with such a crash that the thresholds will tremble. The temple is destroyed from top to bottom (cf. Judg. 16:23-30). False gods will be unveiled for what they are: impotent. The people who worship them must bear the consequences of their perversion.

Earthquakes, including severe earthquakes, are common in Palestine. A major fault line runs beneath the Jordan and extends southward to form the Great Rift Valley in Africa. But the event of which this prophecy speaks should not be interpreted as merely a phenomenon of nature. It occurs at God's express command. It is to be understood as an act of divine judgment on the Northern Kingdom.

The second stage in the coming destruction will be military invasion and wanton killing. God is on the side of the invader. He stands as the warrior against his people (cf. Isa. 63:10).These are his acts: *those who are left [after the earthquake] I will kill with the sword.*

The similarities between Amos 9:2-4 and Psalm 139:7-12 raises the question of literary dependence. While the question is academically interesting, the outcome does not alter the meaning of the text. Both Amos and the psalmist affirm that the Lord is present and powerful everywhere. For the psalmist, that fact is a source of comfort; in Amos, it serves as a threat to the ungodly.

The hypothetical hiding places (Amos 9:2-4) are transparent to the piercing eye of the Lord. His long arm reaches them wherever they may conceal themselves. Neither the underworld nor the heavens, not the lush vegetation of Mt. Carmel nor the murky depths of the ocean, nor even the scattered lands of the nations—nothing can prevent God from fulfilling his judgment on this people.

Gods were thought to have their special domain where they were strongest. Thus the Arameans understood Israel's God to control the mountains (1 Kings 20:23). In Canaanite thought, Baal together with his daughters Dew, Rain, and Irrigation, controlled the fruitfulness of the soil and animals; Yam dominated the briny deep; Mot ruled the underworld, the realm of the dead [Ba'al, p. 373].

Israel receives prophetic assurance that God is unlike other gods. He rules in every domain and will ferret out sinners no matter where they flee, whether by his own hand (Amos 9:2), by means of one of his creatures, such as the dragon of the ocean deep (NRSV: *sea-serpent*, 9:3), or by people (9:4). God's actions are designed for their misfortune (evil) rather than their welfare (good). Here is retributive justice.

I Am the Lord; Remember Me? 9:5-6

The extended description of the severity of judgment (9:1-4, 7-10) revolves around a crucial center (9:5-6). The vision has as much to do with God as with the destruction of the people's security. The prophetic messenger sees what is hidden from this myopic people. If only they knew God, their hearts would melt in fear at the words of judgment they now dismiss with haughty confidence.

The description of the Lord comes in hymnic form. Its opening and closing lines proclaim his exalted name: *the Lord, the Lord of Armies, . . . the Lord is his name.* Israel's self-confidence is badly misplaced.

The one confronting them merely *touches the earth,* and it shakes in a convulsive fit. A single light move will generate the earthquake which will send the nation into wailing for its dead. The whole land undulates in waves as high as the annual rising and falling of *the Nile* (9:5; cf. 8:8). Fortunately for the human race, the Lord makes his home in the heavens. Not all are destroyed when he tiptoes across the land (9:6).

The scene is one of graphic majesty. Up above the dome of the sky, in the midst of the upper waters (cf. Gen. 1:6-8), is the Lord's *upper palace.* Its noble supporting arch rests on the earth at the horizon, where earth and sky meet. At his pleasure he summons *the waters of the sea, and pours them out* through the windows of heaven to water *the earth,* as in the Flood (Gen. 7:11; 8:2). This is the God whom the sinners in Israel have outraged and whose will they have persistently ignored. He will now begin to demonstrate to Israel his power and anger as the sovereign Lord.

The hymn fragments in Amos have all centered in the divine name, the Lord (4:13; 5:8-9; 9:5-6). In each instance they constitute the climax of the message, whether as the concluding element in a linear development of thought or the central element of a chiastic literary structure. The effect is to press home to Israel that it is God with whom they have to do. In form and function, hymns focus attention on the nature and acts of God. This God is awesome. Escape from him is impossible, a point made initially with the lion's roar (1:2), and again in conjunction with the day of the Lord (5:19), and now in the finale.

The hymn fragments also draw attention to Israel's preoccupation and perversion of worship. The defective worship consists of things—animals, offerings, gifts. God intends to be the center of their worship.

Finally, these hymn fragments present God's alternatives to the lamentations of a nation in mourning (5:1, 16-17), the shallow worship of a pleasure-oriented people (5:21-23), and the entertaining compositions of the idle rich (6:5). God commends worship which acknowledges the Lord of nature and history from the core of one's being.

You're Not That Special 9:7-10

Two themes flow from the previous description of the searching pursuit of God. The first theme is election. One can almost hear the plaintive cry of the doomed Israelites: "How can you do this to your chosen people, Lord? We are the seed of Abraham. You rescued us from Egypt and gave us this land." The divine word anticipates their claims and reminds them: "I have created all nations, the *Lybians* as well as you. Furthermore, just as I brought you *out of Egypt*, I also brought *the Philistines, your enemies, from Caphtor and the Arameans*, another foe, *from Kir [Map of Near East, p. 404].* You are not alone the objects of my care and kindness."

The land of *Cush* (NRSV: *Ethiopians, Nubians;* Heb.: *Cushites;* present-day Lybia) is probably meant to highlight God's concern for people at the fringes of civilization and the outer limits of communication with Israel. *Caphtor* is the island of Crete. This connection with Crete is upheld by the fact that part of the Philistine coast was called the "Cretan" South (1 Sam. 30:14), and Cretans are sometimes described with Philistines in the Bible (Ezek. 25:16; Zeph. 2:5) *[Map of Near East, p. 404].*

At the beginning of the twelfth century B.C., the Philistines swept down through Palestine by land and sea, looting, burning, pillaging. They finally settled on the fertile south Palestinian coastlands, where they established themselves as a formidable foe, opposed to Israelite settlement and contending for control of the highlands.

The location of *Kir* is unknown. Scholars suggest that the original Arameans were nomads who began settling down on the fringes of the Syrian Desert between 1500-1250 B.C. Shortly thereafter they invaded Syria and the Euphrates basin to settle in the fertile valleys (*CAH*, 1991:532). Surely the lessons of history should not be lost on Israel, particularly when both the Arameans and Philistines frequently contested Israel's land claims and control of major trade routes.

Israel has presumed on her election. She has assumed that God locked himself into her existence. She has assumed that election contains privilege without responsibility. Both election texts in Amos denounce Israel's presumption (3:1-2; 9:7). In forgetting their priesthood and witness function in the world, the nation is to share the fate of all others who ignored the Most High God, despised his gifts, desecrated his land, or violated his call for justice and righteousness. Amos has earlier conveyed God's word of judgment on the Philistines (1:6-8) and Arameans (1:3-5). Israel, *the sinful kingdom*, can not suppose herself to be exempt from a similar fate. That fate consists of the curses which covenant-breaking entails (cf. Lev. 26:23-39; Deut. 28:49-68).

The second theme is that the "total" destruction will not be total (Amos 9:8-10). In this respect, Israel's election remains intact as a blessing, but only for the qualified few. On first glance, the closing statement concerning the preservation of a remnant appears to conflict with the earlier announcement of annihilation (9:1d). The text reflects the literary practice of placing the universal or general statement before the exception or the more specific one. Universal or otherwise extravagant language may be employed in the Scriptures to denote a great intensity, extent, or degree. Thus, Joshua is said to have taken "the whole" land (Josh. 11:23) when there was still much land to be conquered at the close of his life (Josh. 13). The perception of a contradiction occurs when one separates the two corresponding sections (B from B': Amos 9:1-4 from 9:7-10) of this single prophecy. When we recognize the chiastic character of this text, these two sections must be read as one comprehensive statement.

The threshing metaphor is familiar to Amos's contemporaries (9:9-10). Threshing involves removing the grain from the stalk on the threshing floor. Cattle may serve this purpose by trampling on the grain or by dragging a threshing sledge on the threshing floor (1:3; Hos. 10:11). Winnowing removes the straw and chaff. It is then scooped off the pebbled ground and sent through a large sieve to remove the heavy debris and stones. Then it is sent through a fine sieve to remove the dust and sand and separate out the grain (Weippert: 22). This last stage is represented as the function of the exile.

The earthquake and invasion have threshed and winnowed Israel. Hope lies in what is left. The remainder, then, will be sifted in exile until all the foreign matter has been removed. The sinners—the foreign matter—are those who in Amos's day boastfully claim immunity from attack by any enemy. Their view of God's purposes with the people of Israel exclude his ever turning against them in this way. Nothing can shake their security. Yet God declares that their future lies, not in the Israel which remains (the stones and heavy debris), but in the grain which is to be spread among the nations. In so describing the judgment, Amos already prepares the way for the message of restoration to which he is about to proceed.

I'm Giving It All Back, and More! 9:11-15

9:11-12 Restoration of the Booth of David

The idealized past is frequently used by the prophets to present and interpret the events and hopes of the future. The primary reference points which serve this purpose are the garden of Eden, the exodus-wilderness-conquest complex of events, and the Davidic era. The text before us draws upon the Davidic motif; the following text builds on the entry-into-Canaan motif.

The time of fulfillment is *in that day*, the day of the Lord (cf. 5:18-

27) *[Day of the Lord, p. 383]*. It is the day of God's decisive inbreaking for judgment. This is Amos's first assertion that the day of the
Lord will be anything other than full-scale judgment. Earlier, the divine word hinted that the judgment would not be total. Now we are
told, however, that this event will constitute salvation. How do these
two perspectives mesh?

They can be understood when placed in a continuum with the
previous messages. The first two chapters outlined the context of
Amos's severe reprimand and threat of judgment against Israel, an island among the heathen nations. The Northern Kingdom's failure to
respond to God is much more worthy of punishment than that of the
other nations (Amos 2-3). Warnings of the storm of God's judgment
go unheeded (Amos 4). By the time the thunderclouds appear on the
horizon (735-722 B.C.), Israel is beyond saving (Amos 5-6). The
flood of judgment sweeps over the nation like a tidal wave generated
by an earthquake, only momentarily stayed by Amos's intercession
(7:1-6). But nothing can restrain the towering wall of destruction that
demolishes the countryside (7:7—9:8a).

As the winds of judgment die down and the waters recede, a few
chastened survivors appear (9:8b-9). The prophetic voice comes to
those few survivors with the word that help is on its way (9:11-12).
The hope for reconstruction lies not in the survivors' strength, in
number, nor in history, but in God alone. This restored people will experience the full complement of blessings promised within the covenant but previously experienced only in limited measure (9:13-15)
[Covenant, p. 379].

In all this, it is important to remember that these concluding sections are visions of what will be. The vision traces Israel's future to its
end. That end, in spite of the frightening destruction which precedes
it, will be glorious. The Lord's purpose with his people remains intact;
hope is not totally extinguished by the divine wrath against the covenant people (cf. Deut. 30:1-10). The specific nature of that restoration first appears in Amos 9:11-12. The majority of translations and
commentators interpret all the pronouns of 9:11 as referring to
David's fallen tent (cf. NIV; NRSV notes). The Hebrew text says:

> I will restore David's fallen booth,
> and I will repair their broken places,
>   and restore his ruins,
>   and build it as it used to be.

Walter Kaiser (101-102) argues that *their* refers to the two kingdoms of the divided monarchy (cf. Ezek. 37:15-28). This points forward to the reunification of the ten Northern and two Southern tribes. The *broken places* (lit.: *breaches*) refers to the many sources and occasions of conflict between the two kingdoms. These are to become compounded by the exile of the Northern Kingdom (722 B.C.) and the subsequent religious, social, and cultural breaches between Jews and Samaritans. Such an interpretation of future events is valid if one remembers that this is divine revelation rather than human foresight or wishful thinking.

The Davidic kingdom is designated as a *booth*. The word originally referred to the temporary shelters erected during the Feast of Booths, commemorating God's gracious care during their precarious existence in the years of wilderness wanderings (Lev. 23:42-43; cf. Neh. 8:14-17). The term could also refer to overnight shelter (possibly a light tent) on the battlefield (1 Kings 20:12, 16). Here it would probably point to the dynasty of David, as promised by the Lord (2 Sam. 7:11-16, 27), existing as a fragile reality in its current disobedience *[Tabernacles, p. 396]*.

The person representing the restored line of David is intended by the singular pronoun: *his ruins*. A specific person is referred to, as later prophesied in closer detail by Isaiah (11:1-16, esp. 1-2, 10):

A shoot shall come out from the stump of Jesse,
    and a branch shall grow out of his roots.
The spirit of the Lord shall rest on him. . . .
On that day the root of Jesse shall stand as a signal to the peoples.

Ezekiel also prophesies in connection with the reunification of the twelve tribes: "My servant David shall be king over them; and they shall all have one shepherd" (37:24-28). The *ruins* to be restored are the descendants of David, not the empire or the palace. They represent the exiled and disgraced family of David.

The final phrase, *and build/rebuild it as it used to be*, refers to the Davidic *dynasty*, the succession of kings who ruled Israel. The Davidic family ceased to rule over the North after the death of Solomon. In the South, the Davidic royal family remained on the throne until 586 B.C. This text refers to restoration which anticipates a united kingdom under a descendant of David. "The resurrecting of the dilapidated Davidic fortunes would involve a *kingdom*, a *seed*, and a *dynasty*" (Kaiser: 102).

The purpose of this restoration is spelled out in Amos 9:12: *in order that they may possess the remnant of Edom and all the nations*

who are called by my name. The plural *they may possess* points to
the people of God in the restored Davidic kingdom. The thought of
possessing these other nations is drawn from the language of the rule
of David himself; he conquered Edom, Moab, Syria, Ammon, Philistia, and Amalek (1 Chron. 18-20) *[Map of Near East, p. 404].* They
were either annexed to Israel or became vassals (subjects) of David's.

Those called by the Lord's *name,* in the language of the OT, are
God's special possession (Deut. 28:10). When he places his name on
a people, God is present among them (Jer. 14:9). When they stray
from the Lord, he judges them "like those not called by [the Lord's]
name" (Isa. 63:19; cf. Hos. 1:9-10; 2:23). The prospect outlined for
the future Davidic kingdom is modeled after the military expansion of
David's reign. He conquered and gathered tribute from six nations,
including Edom (2 Sam. 8:11-12).

The language of *possessing the remnant of Edom* implies conquest with the focus on people rather than territory. Only here in the
OT are Gentiles designated as a *remnant.* This remnant of the future
consists of those peoples who shall identify themselves as worshipers
of the Lord. Israel will yet become a light to the nations (cf. Isa. 19:18-
25; 49:5-7). Israel's restoration will be even more glorious than the
Davidic kingdom because it enfolds that remnant of the Gentiles
which are called by the Lord's name.

9:13-15 Restoration of God's People

Amos has predicted the exile of the Northern Kingdom (Amos
4:2; 5:25-27; 7:10-17). Restoration must include the reinstatement
of God's people in the land and its return to fertility (9:13). The vision
of future days is lush with vegetation, filled with produce yielded by
the rich soil. It is a land flowing with milk and honey, a land in which
the thorns and thistles of the curse are no longer present. All that is
needed is to plant and reap. The soil will produce continuously in
abundance (cf. Ezek. 47:12). The hills shimmer as new wine flows in
ripples down the terraces. Famine has been transformed into abundance (cf. Amos 8:11). Paradise at last!

God's restored people will reconstruct the world they once knew
(9:14). Cities, vineyards, gardens—all the sign of God's blessing will
mark their return to covenant fidelity (cf. Deut. 30:1-10). Unlike their
first entry into the land, this occupation of it will be permanent (Amos
9:15). That implies a new relationship with their God and a new kind
of people. Such a prospect agrees with the visions of restoration sung

by other prophetic bards (cf. Isa. 60:21; Jer. 31:35-37; Ezek. 37:25; Mic. 4:7). In concert, across the centuries, these prophets announce the presence of the long-awaited kingdom.

THE TEXT IN BIBLICAL CONTEXT
Israel's Misinterpretations

How could a people come to believe themselves immune from judgment? Earlier, Amos provided two dimensions of the answer to this question. The first has to do with their misunderstanding of election (3:1-2). Since the promises (confirmed by oath) are irrevocable, the land and blessings are regarded as permanent possessions, so they think. Sending Israel into exile would violate the assurances of their continued statehood and special relationship with Yahweh.

Second, Israel's military successes and economic prosperity under Jeroboam II have blinded her people to the true condition of the country (6:1-8). They are committed to a straight-line interpretation of history. If the nation is strong at the moment, the future can provide only more of the same.

A third reason for the nation's self-deception is that their God—or at least their perception of Yahweh—is too small. Israel has failed to appreciate that they exist by the grace of the Lord of heaven's armies. They have neglected the implications of the majestic sovereignty of the Creator (9:5-6). The "one who inhabits eternity" (Isa. 57:15; cf. Amos 9:6) will surely exercise his dominion in the world of his creating. God's shaking of the earth (9:5; cf. 1:1) will signal the purifying act of the One who harvests the nations (9:9). Only a remnant will remain. It is a sufficient seed for the accomplishment of the divine objective in keeping with the promise.

The fourth reason for the Israelites' failure to perceive fully their role in God's economy is that they missed the compassion of God for all humankind. In this text, that compassion is represented by both the remnant of Israel united with Judah under the rubric of the restored Davidic monarchy, and the remnants of Edom and of the nations who identify with Yahweh. In the context, this latter category (nations) must be interpreted as a *remnant* composed of believing Philistines, Lybians, and Arameans (9:7), or as representatives of the nations of the world.

Our reading of the book of Hosea sees Gentile representatives as participants of the eschatological salvation of a reunited Israel (cf. Hos. 1:9-11; 14:6-7). That hope is present in Israel's perception of its origins and call (Gen. 12:1-3; Exod. 19:1-7). The concept appears even more frequently in Judean texts. Isaiah 19, for example, pictures a chastened and repentant Egypt being saved from their oppressors by Yahweh (19:18-22). Indeed, the redeemed of the world, represented by Egypt, Assyria, and Israel, will worship together (19:23) and know the Lord's blessing:

> Blessed be Egypt my people,
>   and Assyria the work of my hands,
>   and Israel my heritage. (Isa. 19:25)

Similarly, Isaiah 56:1-8 and 66:19-21 depict the remnant of the Gentiles (though the term *remnant* is not used in these passages) as enjoying the full benefits of the redemption experienced by the remnant of Judah. Finally, Ezekiel 16:53-63 appears to draw on the same salvation tradition found in Amos 9:11-12 in identifying the recipients of the coming restoration. In Ezekiel 16, a triad is said to be reunited to form the new community of faith: Israel (Samaria and daughters), Judah (Jerusalem and daughters), and Edom (Sodom and daughters). Meanwhile, the Arameans and Philistines mock the wicked and lewd descendants of Isaac (cf. Amos 9:7; Isa. 9:11-12).

The restoration is the product of God's concern for his besmirched reputation among the nations; it cannot be attributed to the honor or integrity of his people (cf. Ezek. 16:61-63; 36:21-23; Lind). *I will restore, says the Lord your God* (cf. Amos 9:8-9, 11, 14-15). Here is a regathering of Israel and Judah, and the inclusion of a segment of their traditional enemies. In Judean tradition, this occurs under the guidance of the royal line of David (Isa. 11:10ff.).

Israel has failed to perceive God's larger purposes with the human race, and that has contributed to their claims of invincibility.

New Testament Interpretations

The writer of Luke-Acts takes up Amos 9:11-12 as part of James's argument during the debate of the Jerusalem council (Acts 15:16-17). The quotation does not accurately reproduce the Greek equivalent of the Hebrew (Massoretic Text) of Amos 9:11-12. It is not clear as to whether James is quoting freely from the Septuagint (Greek version of OT; Richard: 44-52) or whether he is quoting from a better Hebrew text (Braun: 116-117). While the decision we reach is important for the larger understanding of the NT use of the OT, we can address the crucial concerns without resolving the matter of the reason for these variations.

The tension in the Jerusalem council is resolved by an appeal to Amos 9:11-12. James rephrases the line referring to Edom: *so that all other peoples may seek the Lord—even all the Gentiles over whom my name has been called* (Acts 15:17). No one at the council debates the fact that Amos referred to Gentiles being incorporated into the faith community. Nor is there any debate about the accuracy of the quotation.

At the center of the debate is the question: Must the Gentiles become Jews, subject to the law of Moses, before they are eligible for redemption in Christ (Acts 15:1, 5)? Implicit in this statement of the problem is the assumption that observance of the law is essential for all Jews who are being saved. How can the Gentiles experience God in a manner different from Jews?

Peter addresses the stated question as well as the assumption. Gentiles, he says, have been coming to faith in responding to the same message received by the Jews (Acts 15:7, 9). God confirmed that salvation in both groups by the evident empowerment of the same Spirit (15:8). So why impose on the Gentiles the Torah as law, in which role it is not presently the means to salvation, nor has it ever been (15:10)? In this new era, Jews are being saved through the grace of the Lord Jesus, just as the Gentiles are. That makes the law unnecessary for Jews, just as it is unnecessary for the salvation of Gentiles (15:11).

Following Paul and Barnabas's testimonials of the great work God has been doing among the Gentiles, James draws on the Amos text to summarize and seal the argument. First, his use of Amos assumes that the participants share the view that Jesus Christ is the new David. Therefore, the restoration of the Davidic line, the establishment of the hope of the Jews, has already taken place. It is historically being fulfilled right now. It has existed in the church, initially consisting only of Jews, until the apostles began proclaiming Christ to the Gentiles as well.

Second, God's purpose in rebuilding David's booth, as Amos announced, is to incorporate into his people the remnant from outside Israel (Acts 15:17). That too has been taking place (15:14). Since, then, Jews and Gentiles are both entering the kingdom through the person of Jesus Christ, it is inappropriate to add to the requirements for Gentile entry into the Davidic kingdom. In fact, the raising up of the Davidic booth via the Messiah is *so that* (15:17) other peoples (interpreting Edom as humankind) might be incorporated as God's people. The Gentiles should, however, be considerate of Jewish sensibilities so as not to alienate Jewish Christians or potential converts from the Jewish community (15:20-21).

Amos 9:11-12 admirably captures the emphasis on this new work as God's initiative, the reality of the remnant of Israel as well as of Gentiles entering the kingdom, and the central character of the Davidic figure.

THE TEXT IN THE LIFE OF THE CHURCH
The Church's Use and Neglect of Amos

Apart from the closing verses of Amos 9, the book of Amos is conspicuous by its absence in the church through the centuries. The church fathers and the Reformers make occasional references to words of Amos. But in general, they overlook the social dimension of the message of this prophet. References to Amos 9:11-12 are more common, because the Acts 15 passage in which they are cited entered the debates about the means of salvation and the nature of the Messiah.

Prior to the twentieth century, the church virtually ignored the moral dimensions of the teaching of Amos. That is not to say that it disregarded issues of social justice. It simply did not ground its social conscience in the words of this "minor prophet." William Wilberforce, the prime mover of the abolition of the slave trade in England, for example, rooted his religious and moral argument against slavery primarily in the life and teachings of Jesus (Wilberforce). Since his appeal was specifically addressed to the middle and upper class, the arguments from Amos would have been appropriate, especially if his audience had held the social message of the prophets in high esteem.

A second theme in this text addresses the church. Throughout church history, segments of the Christian community have interpreted themselves to be the "faithful remnant," suffering because of the sinfulness of the larger church. The Puritan settlement of Massachusetts Bay (1630) under John Winthrop was one such restorationist movement. Miller describes this maneuver as a deliberate act of a people who saw themselves as "an organized task force of Christians, executing a flank attack on the corruptions of Christendom."

These Puritans, Miller points out,

did not flee to America; they went in order to work out that complete reformation which was not yet accomplished in England and Europe, but which would quickly be accomplished if only the saints back there had a working model to guide them. (Miller: 11)

Regrettably, the effect of creating a relatively closed community was comparable to what happened to many other similar groups of saints: the world flooded into their community, leaving it less rather than more like their ideal.

The remnant described in the Bible consisted of a people purified through sufferings, cast about by the winds of political and religious persecution to emerge as a powerful witness. God preserved them as a holy community through their suffering rather than their withdrawal from the world.

The third point of relevance of this pericope is that it contains a much-needed message of hope for God's people in trying circumstances and in the face of their own sinfulness. Not everyone in Israel was equally guilty, yet all would experience the horrors of war, and the survivors would enter the degradation of exile. One may acknowledge the appropriateness of the coming devastation on the sinful leaders of the nation, on Jeroboam, Amaziah, the "Cows of Bashan," and the members of the (*marzeaḥ*) dining club. But how about the faithful? How do they face such realities?

In hope. In the deep confidence that the Lord who is shaking the heavens and the earth, who is summoning a nation against his people, will also preserve a remnant through whom his work will come to fruition. The truly faithful are more concerned to see God's glory than to ensure their own welfare. For them the continuity of the promise provides the assurance of God's sovereign and gracious fulfillment of his purposes with humankind. Yet in that surrender to God's design, there is also a word of assurance: a remnant will be saved. Indeed, hope lies in what God will achieve through only a remnant. In hope for that fulfillment, their spirits are encouraged in the time of testing, and their faith will be vindicated.

Finally, for many in the church, these closing verses of Amos have been a reminder that the advent of the descendant of David has introduced the concluding chapter of world history. We live in the messianic era. The kingdom of God has come and is coming. It will be fully effected at the time when the Davidic king appears once more at the end of this age.

Outline of Amos

Essays

CONTENTS

ACCUSATION-JUDGMENT-SALVATION ORACLES Some readers may object to calling these speech units "oracles." The term is a technical one and implies literary structures recognizable by their standard form and content. In this commentary the term "oracle" refers to a literary text unit; the written form takes priority over their original structure. Some text units appear to consist of summaries of two or more sermons. Amos 3:1-15 may summarize up to eight sermons; Hosea 9:10-17, five original units. This essay sets forth the basis of this classification: accusation, judgment, and salvation (AJS) oracles.

The main problem lies in differentiating between accusation and judgment oracles or speeches. Both contain accusations; both threaten or predict judgment. Accusation oracles in both books begin with a litany of Israel's sins; judgment oracles with death, war, or destruction. Though both oracle types define the reasons for the punishment and outline something of the nature of that punishment, the proportions differ, allowing us to distinguish them as accusation or judgment. Classification of oracle types in part 1 of Hosea (1:2—3:5) is complicated by the fact that the accusation section contains a complete AJS cycle in its subunits (1:2-3; 1:4-9; 1:10—2:1).

Amos 1:3—2:16 consists of prophecies beginning with accusation and containing a proportionately larger text unit describing the nature of the nation's sins. The judgments which follow appear in more stereotypical form. Amos 3:1—9:10 (except for 5:1-17) consist of judgment oracles in a variety of forms, including woe oracles (5:18—6:14) and vision reports (7:1—9:10).

Salvation oracles, too, vary in form in both books. They contain promises of God's work (Hos. 1:10—2:1; 11:8-11; Amos 9:11-14), historical recital and prediction (Hos. 3:1-5), invitation to repentance (Hos. 10:12; 14:1-3; Amos 5:1-17), and words of confession and repentance (Hos. 6:1-3). The coming salvation is described in both books as the act of the Lord in reestablishing the Davidic kingdom (Hos. 3:5; Amos 9:11-12) and restoring his people to their land and its blessings (Hos. 11:10-11; Amos 9:13-15).

ASHERAH: SYMBOL AND GODDESS Asherah refers to both the wooden symbol of the goddess Astarte (Ashtoreth, Ashtaroth) and the goddess herself.

In the Gideon and Jephthah stories, the worship of this goddess is associated with Baalism (Judg. 6–8, 10; cf. 1 Sam. 12:10). Under Samuel, Israel renewed her covenant ties with the Lord and committed herself to the exclusive worship of her covenant Lord (1 Sam. 7:3-4). Renewal consisted of serving this God only.

The literature of the OT makes no mention of Baal or Baal worship between Samuel's reforms and the accession of Ahab. The goddess Ashtaroth is reintroduced by Solomon (1 Kings 11:5, 33; 2 Kings 23:13), yet she does not reappear with the Baal figure. Probably she had become an independent object of worship. Thereafter the historical texts repeatedly refer to asherahs as part of non-Yahwistic worship of Canaanite origin and influence in Judah as well as Israel. The asherahs were not necessary in Baal worship (cf. 2 Kings 21:7).

The term Asherah may have come to replace Ashtaroth as a reference to the Canaanite goddess Astarte. In any case, it referred at one and the same time to cult objects and to the goddess it represented (cf. 1 Kings 16:33 with 18:19; 2 Kings 23:4 with 23:6; *TDOT*, 1:438-444). The frequent and specific references to "removing the high places and the asherah poles" suggest that the worship of the asherah was a particularly popular and serious defection from the Lord.

In the Baal myth, Asherah is the consort of El, the bull, and the mother of the great gods. She is also known as the mistress of the sea (Heb.: *yam*). Asherah's favorite son, whom she set forward as the heir apparent, was Yam, god of the sea. Baal was a contender for the throne who successfully displaced Yam through the use of superior weapons. El settled the dispute by assigning the land masses to Baal and the oceans to Yam.

There is some extrabiblical evidence that in practice, the Israelites associated their God with the cult object known as asherah. Kuntillet 'Ajrud is an archaeological site in the Sinai desert which has yielded valuable data regarding Israelite religion in the earlier part of the eighth century B.C. The site appears to have been controlled at the time (790 B.C.) by the Northern Kingdom. The inscriptions of names "Yahweh of Teman" and "Yahweh of Samaria" resemble Absalom's reference to "Yahweh in Hebron" (2 Sam. 15:7-8). These designations suggest that the Lord was worshiped in his different local manifestations at many cult centers throughout the land (McCarter: 137-142).

BA'AL: FROM COMMON NOUN TO DIVINE NAME

The Common Noun The name "Baal" grew out of everyday use in early Hebrew. That early usage is reflected especially in proverbial literature. There it refers to one who is responsible for, and is able to, master a personal dimension of life, an area of life frequently difficult to control. The tongue, one's temper, one's desire for food, or the possession of riches are good examples (Prov. 22:24; 23:2; 29:22; Eccl. 5:11, 13). Similarly, "wisdom," we are told, "preserves the life of its *ba'al*" (owner, possessor, the one who masters it).

The word *ba'al* is also used of the owner of domesticated animals, particularly draft animals such as the ox (Exod. 21:28-29, 34, 36) or the males of donkeys or sheep used for breeding purposes (Exod. 22:11-12, 14-15).

Further, *ba'al* serves to describe a citizen of a city, one who is a "voting member" of the city council (Judg. 9:2-3, etc.; 20:5; 1 Sam. 23:11-12; 2 Sam. 21:12).

Within the family, the male head of an independent household is a *ba'al*, and the female in charge of the household, a *ba'alah*. The ideal woman (Prov. 31) has the full confidence of her husband (*ba'al*, 31:11, 13, 23, 28), to whom she gives due honor so that even the community acknowledges his qualities. He in turn shows her nothing but love and respect.

The word *ba'al* originally resounded in Hebrew with a positive ring. When applied to one's god, it described nobility of character, harmonious marital relationships, and responsibly exercised authority. It conveyed an image of virginity and an initial (ideal) marriage. Is it any wonder that the Lord was once called "my *ba'al*" (Hos. 2:16, *my master*, NRSV note)?

The God Ba'al   The name was most appropriate for the Lord. But the overlays of meaning which came from associating it with the Canaanite god, the son of Dagan, led to a misunderstanding of Yahweh, the God of the Exodus. The Canaanite Baal was present in many local manifestations, called (lowercase) *baals*. God had directed Israel toward monotheism by centralizing worship and guiding the interpretation of God's self-disclosure through the prophets. Baal worship, inherently polytheistic, tended to create a variegated and multiple rather than a multifaceted and synthetic concept and experience of God.

Baal's subjects and worshipers occupied the land when Israel appeared on the scene. Baal exercised control of the fertility of the soil. Baalist concepts and constructs of morality and family values, land ownership, political structures, and authority conflicted with those of the God of the patriarchs and the Sinaitic covenant, as well as with the meaning of the term *ba'al* in Hebrew. Hence, when the prophets speak of Israel "prostituting herself to foreign gods," they bring all the significant values of their religious society under that umbrella. But the Israelites did not understand. They did not differentiate their *ba'al* (husband), Yahweh, from *Baal*, the Canaanite god of fertility.

Some of the gods of the Canaanite pantheon were apparently more easily distinguished from Yahweh than was Baal. The history of Israel's faith is a story of conflict between the Lord and the gods of Canaan. Those which were readily distinguished from Yahwism receded; others, like Baal, contested the Lord's claim inch by inch. The soil of Palestine was strewn with the bones of the contenders.

BOVINE IMAGERY   Cattle, whether bull calves, heifers, cows, or oxen, carry symbolic weight in Hosea and Amos. They represent the gold-overlaid thrones of El and Yahweh, and they serve as religious and literary images of Israel in Hosea (2:6-7 [see notes]; 4:16; 8:5-6; 10:5-6; 10:11; 13:2) and Amos (4:1-3).

Bovine symbolism is rich because cattle were such a highly valued possession (cf. Amos 4:1-3). They served as the draft animals. Heifers were used in threshing, and mature cows in pulling heavier carts and in the more-difficult work of plowing and harrowing (Hos. 10:11). Normally the heavy work was done with teams of cows or with oxen. Cattle also provided food in the forms of milk, cheese, curds, and meat.

Bulls in the neutered state (oxen) were used as heavy draft animals. Their commercial value also gave them religious value. In both Canaanite and Israelite religions, they served as primary sacrifices for individual and collective cultic atonement. In Canaanite religion, the bull represented El, the supreme god, as well as Baal, the storm god. Most powerful of all domesticated animals, bull Baal came to rule over his brothers. His consort was Anat, symbolized by the heifer. She conceived a new bull calf by Baal. According to the myth, when Baal annually succumbed to Death (the god Mot) in the drought of summer, Baal descended and remained in Death's clutches until Anat, the goddess of war, defeated Death and gave birth to the young bull calf, in whom Baal is reborn. As the placenta broke, life flowed back to the earth in the form of rain and dew.

The texts of Hosea and Amos are filled with bovine fertility language and concepts. The notes draw attention to many of these as God, Hosea, and Amos point to Israel's God, Yahweh, as the true source and Creator of all life.

BULL CALVES, THE TWO The prophetic historians of the Northern Kingdom make much of the bull calves. They were the creation of Jeroboam I when he separated from Judah after the death of Solomon (1 Kings 12:25-33). Making them was an astute political move. He created two visible symbols, probably in the shape of bulls, to serve as thrones or footstools for the invisible God. In all likelihood, they did not directly represent Israel's God but signified the presence of their God under two different names. One and the same symbol served for both Yahweh and El. In so doing, Jeroboam connected the patriarchal and national histories (Exod. 6:1-9). Jeroboam identified these bull calves with that complex of great historic events, the exodus, law giving, and wilderness journey, by connecting them to the Festival of Booths, which he held in the eighth month instead of the seventh, as practiced in Judah.

How did Jeroboam avoid the association of these images with the sin which God judged so severely at Sinai (Exod. 32-35)? We do not know. He must have avoided this association enough to satisfy the majority of the nation. Surely he would not have taken alien symbols to promote the worship of his God at a critical moment in national history. Furthermore, we do know that the people of Judah also had relics from the wilderness years which they revered and then began to worship (2 Kings 18:4). One reconstruction which seems reasonable is that the the bull calf (representing a virile young animal) was probably the pedestal, throne, or footstool of God. This was comparable to the ark of the covenant in Jerusalem.

Why two, we wonder? If our reconstruction of the historic connection of the bull symbol is correct, then the two represented Elohim in both manifestations, El and Yahweh. Jeroboam placed the one permanently (Heb.: śim) in Beth-El, the historic Canaanite and patriarchal center of El worship (Gen. 28:19; 31:13; 35:3-16). The other, representing Yahweh, God of the Exodus and the wilderness Guide, was placed (Heb.: natan) "as far as (Heb.: 'ad) Dan" (1 Kings 12:29-30). That is, the bull calf serving as Yahweh's throne was a movable one. It may have traveled through the country, remaining at different locations for a fixed period of time, been used in processionals connected with the Festival of Booths, or represented the image associated with the "house of high places" at Bethel (13:31-32, NRSV note). Perhaps it served as a visible expression of the monarchy at coronation ceremonies, or it may have functioned in more than one of these purposes.

THE CANAANITE FERTILITY MYTH Canaanite religion is most fully depicted in the documents unearthed at Ras Shamra (Ugarit), on the coast of northern Syria. The gods El, Baal, Anath, and Asherah figure prominently in these mythological accounts (Mullen; L'Heureux; Fleming; Walls).

Bull El is the father of the gods, the head of the pantheon; Athtarte/Ashtarte/Astarte *[Asherah, p. 372]* birthed the seventy gods. It is natural to hear Bull El referred to as the creator, but that creative role is limited to the heavens (including the gods), the earth, and humans. It does not include the annual cycle of fertility in the animal and plant worlds (Mullen: 12-22).

El rules the other gods as undisputed king, though compassionate and merciful. He is pictured as an old, wise, gray-bearded divine patriarch. As ruler, he determines the disposition of authority in the created world. He also determines the boundaries of each nation's territories (cf. Deut. 32:8). Each of his divine children is assigned a particular sphere of influence or country of the earth: Yam is the god of the sea; Mot rules the realm of death; Anath wages war; Ba'al is the god of storm and fertility (Mullen: 36-41; L'Heureux: 10-11). If disputes between the lesser gods persist or become too intense, El eventually resolves them by divine decree.

If need be, El also engages in war. In the Canaanite mythological literature, however, he does not actively fight; his role is limited to sanctioning and directing warfare and to dividing the spoils of war (Mullen: 30-35).

Just as El dispenses power and kingship to the gods, he also dispenses power and kingship to human rulers. Consequently he sets up kings and dethrones them (Mullen: 24-25; cf. Dan. 4:17, 25, 32). Associated with this divine regulation of human affairs is his function of ensuring that justice is done among humans.

Ba'al appears to have been a latecomer to the Canaanite religion. There are indications in the mythology that his father was Dagan (grain), but that as time progressed he was incorporated into the family of El. L'Heureux describes the process of merger as "incomplete assimilation between the circle of Ba'al and the family of El" (14). Whatever the process of assimilation, within the Baal myths Baal's authority is subordinate to El. He is called the son of El ("Bull El his father") and El grants him kingship ("Prince, Lord of the earth") as the storm god who defeats the chaos god, Yam (Sea).

Much of the available Baal literature features his right to build a house as a sign of his victory over Yam (Sea) and as a mark of his kingship. Its significance for our purposes may be summed up in a few lines. The implication is that unless a god has a dwelling, he cannot be king. This is true in the earthly realm as in the heavens. The construction of a temple, then, is a sign that the god has come to reign in the realm given to him. It symbolizes his kingship (Mullen: 46-74).

Following the construction of Ba'al's house, his rule as storm god faces another challenge. The god Mot (Death) rules in the underworld. Fertility, provided by rain, is constantly being challenged by the forces of death. Mot desires to rule the earth.

> Ba'al had already extended his power over the force of Chaos-Sea. Now it was necessary for him to constrain the dominion of Sterility-Death. Only in this way could the cosmos be made secure and fertile. (Mullen: 76)

In this cosmic battle, Ba'al can rely only on his sister-consort (Anath) for support. In anticipation of the battle and of defeat, Ba'al, in the form of the bull, mates with the goddess (heifer) Anath, to ensure progeny. Mot and Ba'al enter into conflict, seen on earth as the gradual drying up of the water sources in the heat of summer drought. Ba'al is defeated and taken to Sheol, the abode of Mot.

El and Anath, heaven and earth, mourn the defeat of Ba'al. These mourning rites are appropriately mirrored by Ba'al's human subjects, and so they become part of the ritual of Ba'al worship.

Anath, Ba'al's consort, refuses to accept the outcome of the battle. As goddess of war,

> She seized 'El's son, Mot,
> She cleaved him with a sword,
> She scattered him with a sieve,
> She parched him in flames,
> She ground him in a hand-mill,
> She sowed him in the field. (Mullen: 80)

The description of Mot's (Death's) destruction takes us from the harvest (sword, scythe), through the care and use of the harvested grain in winter, to the spring seeding. This life and death battle pictures Anat victorious at the moment of the birth of the new bull calf. The destructive forces of nature have been overcome. Anat, the goddess of fertility, has survived the gestation period. She stands triumphant, the blood of the birth process covering her hocks. Baal is revived, fertility returns. His restoration fulfills El's vision:

> The heavens rain with oil,
> The wadis run with honey.
> Indeed 'Al'iyan Ba'al lives,
> Surely the Prince, Lord of the earth exists! (Mullen: 81)

Though Mot has been ritually slain by Anath, Ba'al must still personally win the day. Mot and Ba'al engage in battle to the death. Both fall, exhausted and beaten. At that point, El intervenes and stops the conflict. He assigns them their domains. Ba'al rules the earth and life; Mot rules the underworld of death.

Ba'al's sovereignty over the earth is marked each spring by the coming of the rain in the storm, which ensures fertility. Yet in all the battles in which he engaged, Ba'al was incapable of defeating the opposing forces alone. His hold on fertility is fragile and must be regained each year. Thus is introduced the annual cycle of the fertility ritual to ensure the survival of plants, animals, and humans.

Unfortunately, the Canaanite mythology gives no evidence of how these battles between the competing gods translated into cultic worship. For that we will need to examine the polemics of the books of Amos and Hosea [Yahweh-Baal Conflict, p. 398].

COMPOSITION OF AMOS Some scholars claim to be able to identify the stages of literary growth of the text of Amos. Most of these claims rest on two assumptions: first, that the prophetic message does not contain genuine predictions of future events (as, for example, the restoration text of 9:11-15). In their opinion, texts always and only reflect the circumstances present at the time of their oral delivery or composition. Second, Amos would not have addressed Judah in a work aimed so pointedly at the Northern Kingdom [Judah and David, p. 389].

The first assumption is connected with the perception that prophetic utterances are generated in the sensitive consciousness of the prophet, not received or occasioned by divine revelation. But prophecy came through both media. Amos declares, *This is what the Lord says.* Then he proceeds to quote Yahweh's words in the first person, *I* (5:3b-d, 4b-5, 12a, 16b-c, 21-27). At other times, he appears to introduce or develop a theme in his own words and way (5:1-2, 6-11, 12b-16a). The very fact that this distinction is made draws attention to the unique oracular character of the divine speeches. The admixture of the two suggests the active interpretive role of the prophet as he molds his speeches for delivery. Or it may reflect the work of a prophetic tradition in fusing announcement of the divine word and prophetic analysis and commentary on the contemporary situation.

This first assumption also raises questions about the prophetic self-understanding. Central to Amos's defense against Amaziah is the assertion that he was divinely compelled to prophesy (7:14-17). The descriptions of the messenger call of Moses, Isaiah, and Jeremiah suggest that the people called to prophesy were generally reluctant to do so (Exod. 3-4; Isa. 6; Jer. 1). The same is true of Amos (7:10-17). Unless those call narratives are fictionalized, it is more likely that a reluctant messenger would withhold some of the message (particularly a message of judgment) than enlarge upon it (cf. Amos 3:7-8; Jer. 20:7-18). Since that is the case, would the prophetic disciples not be similarly inclined out of respect for the message and its source? If there are genuine, discernible signs of editorial work, could they be pointing to the "editing down" of a much more extensive body of messenger speeches and prophetic sermons rather than the incorporation of later expansions into the text (cf. John 21:25)?

The second assumption and the corresponding criteria for separating the later from the earlier materials has to do with the references to Judah in a book said to be the outgrowth of a preaching mission to Israel. Surely, it is argued, Amos would not have addressed Judah in the same work! What relevance would it have had for Judah at that time?

Yet if he could address Syria, Philistia, Phoenicia, Edom, Ammon, and

Moab (Amos 1:3—2:3), why not speak to Judah as well (2:4-5)? By the middle of the eighth century, their social and religious conditions were roughly comparable. Literarily, the Judah prophecy creates a powerful argument through the progression to Israel itself (2:4-5). Furthermore, while Uzziah initially followed the ways of God (2 Kings 15:3), later in life he vaunted himself against Yahweh (2 Chron. 26:16-23). Meanwhile, the high places continued to be used by the people of Judah (2 Kings 15:4), in defiance of the divine will. This syncretism is reflected in Amos's oracle against Judah (2:4).

Equally problematic is the act of assigning 3:1 to a later period because it incorporates Judah into the accusation under the phrase *Israel, the whole family I brought out of Egypt*. If a school of disciples is responsible for the final shape of the book, they may have deliberately included the Judah prophecies (including 9:11-15) because the earthquake (1:1) had confirmed the veracity of Amos's words. Therefore, Judah needed to heed the words of Amos which were particularly addressed to her. Wolff's comments alert us to the caution with which we should approach the process of distinguishing literary strands in the text, and the conclusions we draw from this process: "In any given instance it is often difficult to distinguish between the *ipsissima verba* of the prophet and the new formulations and supplementations of the disciples" (Wolff: 109).

A final argument may be offered for an early (eighth-century) date of composition of the book. The precise dating formula of the prophecy (*two years before the earthquake*, Amos 1:1) suggests a time of composition nearer rather than further from the event. Here it is simply *the earthquake*. Later it needed to be distinguished more clearly from other earthquakes: "as you fled from the earthquake in the days of Uzziah king of Judah" (Zech. 14:5).

COVENANT Covenants punctuate the biblical story. They provide the primary formal and conceptual framework by which God communicated his will and within which Israel understood her relationship to God. The church carried forward this concept of covenant in identifying herself with the new covenant people of Israel as well as in describing the Hebrew and Christian Scriptures as the Old and New Testaments (covenants).

The concept and practice of covenant making was common in the sphere of international and interpersonal relations in Israel's world. In the OT, individuals, clans, and nation participate in covenant making. Thus covenants were sufficiently morally neutral conventions to serve God's self-revelation without undue distortion.

Formally, a covenant (*berit*) is a solemnized interpersonal agreement defining the mutually beneficial future relationship of the covenanting parties. The biblical record does not differentiate between types of covenants; most distinctions are modern attempts to classify and understand the many aspects of covenant. Whether the variants have any bearing upon the basic concept of covenant is not clear. Covenant language has become freighted with theological significance through the history of the church, and much of it depends on fine distinctions. So we remind ourselves that the Scriptures make few distinctions regarding the many covenants. For example, the OT does not distinguish formally between covenants involving equals and those between people of different social status. For *renewing* covenants, the OT does not use language different from that used for originally *making* them.

When humans make a covenant *(berit)* they "cut" *(karat)* it. The language comes from the rite of cutting up an animal and swearing an oath of self-imprecation, such as: "May I be cut up as these animals are cut up if I do not keep this covenant" (cf. Gen. 15). Its common form consists of words and symbolic action: "May the Lord do so [possibly illustrated by a slashing movement of the hand across the throat] to me and even more if I don't observe. . . ."

God, however, both cuts *(karat)* covenants and establishes *(qum)* them. The initial act of covenant making is to "cut" the covenant. But God makes covenants which extend beyond a single lifetime. The confirmation of the covenant with multiple generations is spoken of as "establishing" *(qum)* the covenant, as with Noah (Gen. 6:18; 9:9, 11, 17), Abraham and Isaac (17:7, 19, 21), plus Jacob/Israel and later generations (Exod. 6:4; Lev. 26:9; Deut. 8:18), David, Solomon, and kings (2 Sam. 7:25; 1 Kings 9:5), and restored Israel (Ezek. 16:60, 62; cf. Jer. 31:31-37). These transgenerational covenants are designated in the OT as "eternal" or perpetual *('olam)*. With the exception of the covenant with Noah and the promised new covenant, the God-initiated covenants are conditional. The promise remains intact, but individuals who refuse to comply with the conditions will not become beneficiaries of the blessings (Gen. 17:9-14; Exod. 12:1-27 and 19:5-6; 2 Sam. 7:12-17).

Covenants enacted within the social sphere include marriage (Mal. 2:14; Prov. 2:17), friendship (David and Jonathan, 1 Sam. 18:1-5; 20:12-17; 23:15-18), intergroup relationships (Abraham and Abimelech, Gen. 21:25-34; Isaac and Abimelech, 26:26-33; Jacob and Laban; Gen. 31; David and Abner, 2 Sam. 3), a king (or leader) and his subjects (Joshua and Israel, Josh. 24; David, 2 Sam. 5:1-5; Asa, 2 Chron. 15:8-15; Jehoiada, 2 Kings 11:17-20; Josiah, 2 Kings 23:1-3), and international relations (Israel and the Gibeonites, Josh. 9; Solomon and Hiram = Israel and Phoenicia, 1 Kings 5:12; Asa and Ben-Hadad, kings of Judah and Syria, 1 Kings 15:19).

These covenants have a number of features in common in addition to the oath. They include a gift or an exchange of symbols of the covenant, such as Jonathan's robe of office, his armor, sword, bow, and belt (1 Sam. 18:4). Abraham gave sheep and cattle to Abimelech, as well as seven ewe lambs, to confirm the covenant (Gen. 21:25-30). Apparently the gift symbols serve as a form of witness (Josh. 24:26-28; cf. Gen. 21:25-30), comparable to the stones and pillar set up by Jacob and Laban (Gen. 31:43-50), or the altar built by the Transjordan tribes after the conquest of Palestine (Josh. 22). If the treaty is violated, the stones cry out against the violators. Witnesses cast the first stones against the willfully disobedient judged worthy of the death penalty (cf. Deut. 17:2-7).

Covenants of peace or friendship are frequently sealed by a meal. Jacob and Laban eat together as part of the covenant-making ceremony (Gen. 31:54), Abimelech and Isaac eat a covenant meal signaling their harmony and celebrating amicable future relationships (Gen. 26:30-31), and the elders of Israel eat and drink in the presence of the Lord (Exod. 24:11), just as

Israel did at the first Passover (Exod. 12).

All covenants except for the Noachian and the new covenant contain conditions of fulfillment. Compliance with the conditions permits the benefits to flow to all concerned. The gods and other witnesses judge violators until they die or repent. This judgment is referred to as "bringing the curses on the disobedient" (Gen. 17:9-14; Exod. 19:5; 23:20-33; Lev. 26; Deut. 26–30). If the violators repent, the aggrieved party may accept the repentance and graciously restore them. Covenants remain in effect until one of the parties dies (1 Kings 5:1-12; cf. Gal. 3; Rom. 7:1-3). Even covenants obtained through misrepresentation remain binding on both parties (Josh. 9).

In international political treaties of this type the curses include famine, drought, pestilence, infestations of locusts, death by lions, leopards, snakes, and other animals, barrenness, hunger to the point of eating one's own children, exposure to the avenger, sleeplessness, bitter family relationships, weakness in the face of the enemy, torture, no burial, destruction of houses and cities, exile, no forgiveness from the gods and many more dread consequences.

The curses were symbolically represented during the covenant-making ceremony by killing an animal and by action and/or word identifying with the death and destruction of that animal. In the treaty between Ashurnirari V of Assyria and Mati'ilu of Arpad, the enacted curse is accompanied by the words:

> If Mati'ilu sins against (this) treaty made under oaths by the gods, then, just as this spring lamb, brought from its fold, will not return to its fold, will not behold its fold again, alas, Mati'ilu, together with his sons, daughters, officials, and the people of his land [will be ousted] from his country, and not behold his country again. This head is not the head of a lamb, it is the head of Mati'ilu, it is the head of his sons, his officials, and the people of his land.

The lamb is then killed, beheaded, and torn apart, limb by limb, with the accompanying curse, "Thus shall the head . . . shoulder . . . of Mati'ilu, of his sons, his officials, and the people of his land be torn out . . . (*ANET*: 532-533).

A similar ritual is described in Yahweh's oath with Abram (Genesis 15) in which God himself takes the oath by passing between the two rows of matched pieces of the animals which God commanded Abram to slaughter. In this way God confirmed his promise with an oath.

The curses spoken against a disobedient Israel are symbolically enacted in Exodus 24:5-8 and are recorded in Leviticus 26:14-46 and Deuteronomy 28:15-68. The explanatory notes of this commentary make frequent reference to these texts, inasmuch as the prophetic books use these categories of curses to remind Israel that God's covenant has been violated and after fair warning, the consequences of covenant breaking are finally being implemented.

When God makes covenant he begins his relationship with people by inviting them to an act of trust and obedience. God acts on behalf of his people and fulfills his promise. Finally, God offers a continued relationship of blessing on the condition that the people will remain faithful.

In case of failure, covenants can be renewed. Following the worship of the golden calf at Mt. Sinai, Moses smashed the tablets, in the pattern of use of the Egyptian denouncing texts, signifying the breaking of the covenant and Israel's exposure to the curses (Exod. 32:19). At Moses' intercession, God stayed his hand of judgment and graciously received them again in a covenant renewal ceremony (Exod. 34). Similar renewals occurred in connection with national repentance under Samuel (1 Sam. 7:2-13), Jehoiada (2 Kings 11:17), Josiah (2 Kings 23:1-30), and Nehemiah (Neh. 9:5-38).

Provisions were made for the regular reading of the covenant document (and, presumably, its reaffirmation) at the Feast of Tabernacles every seventh year (Deut. 31:9-13). The covenant may also have been reaffirmed at transitions of leadership, so that the new generation would receive their leaders with a renewed commitment to Israel's constitution (cf. Josh. 24:1-27).

The covenant concept incorporates the language of family and nature into itself. Father-son language is common in Near Eastern suzerainty-vassal treaties (cf. Exod. 4:22-23; 2 Sam. 7:14; Ps. 2:7). The language of brothers appears frequently in descriptions of equals who exist in treaty relationships (cf. Lev. 25:25-43; Deut. 15:1-12; 1 Kings 20:33-34). The relationship within this family metaphor is described as that of love (cf. Deut. 4:37; 5:10; 6:4-5; 10:12-19; 11:1, 13, 22; 30:6, 16, 20). Love transfers readily to the description of the bond between Yahweh and his people as that of husband and wife.

The overt husband-wife language, however, is absent outside Israel in describing treaty partners. It appears prominently in the description of the Sinaitic covenant partners, particularly when describing Israel's pursuit of other gods (Hos. 1-3; Jer. 3; Ezek. 16, 23). Presumably the marriage metaphor was used because the concept of marriage itself became elevated in Israel to that of a covenant relationship (cf. Mal. 2:14; Rom. 7:1-3).

The language of nature is associated with the original intent of the exodus—the giving of the land. But nature is also related to the formal features of covenant in two other respects. First, many of the continued blessings associated with the covenant exist in the domain of nature. Fertility, good harvests, descendants, prosperity—these are much of the substance of divine favor; their removal shows divine disfavor. Second, heaven and earth are called upon to witness the terms of the covenant and to act as witnesses (Deut. 4:26; 30:19; 31:28). The witnesses to covenant-making are not detached observers; they are active participants who ensure that the blessings and curses are carried out (Deut. 17:7). Near Eastern international treaties invoke the gods of the heavens and the earth. From the perspective of Israel's faith, these are not gods. They serve the interests of Yahweh, the Creator.

The nature of the covenant is important for the understanding of Amos and essential for the grasp of the textual particulars and larger conceptual structure of Hosea. Both books appear to reflect the specific content of the book of Deuteronomy, which itself follows the literary pattern of the second-millennium (B.C.) international treaties. The implication is that the deuteronomistic tradition was present in essentially its present form during the eighth pre-Christian century. The literary and theological discussions of

Amos and Hosea rest in part on this perspective of the nature of covenant and its relationship to the traditions embedded in the book of Deuteronomy.

THE DAY OF THE LORD The "day of the Lord" becomes a technical term in the prophetic literature, standing for a time of the Lord's incisive inbreaking for purposes of judgment and salvation: judgment of those opposed to God, and salvation for those whom he wishes to vindicate. The origins of the term have most prominently been located in the wars of the Lord (Gressman), the cultic enthronement of Yahweh (Mowinckel), the holy war (von Rad), or some combination or variation of these occasions or themes (Barstadt: 89-93). The concept also appears in many places where the term itself is not present, but a decisive moment of Yahweh's majestic appearance in history is indicated (Isa. 34:8; Jer. 31:1, 31, 38; Zeph. 2:2-3; cf. Amos 9:11, 13; King, G.: 16-17).

This examination of the theme includes passages which refer to the coming day of Yahweh's incisive judgment and decisive saving acts without using the technical term itself. The great majority of the references connect this great day to judgments against the foreign nations (Isa. 13:6, 9; 34:8; 63:4; Ezek. 30:3). The references to the day of the Lord seem to have initially been understood by Israel as directed against her enemies. Salvation would come to Israel, it was supposed, when God judged the foreign nations. But in Amos as in Joel, Isaiah, and Zephaniah, the judgment against Israel's enemies did not automatically translate into mercy and blessings for the remnant of Israel (Amos 5:18, 20; Isa. 13:9; Joel 2:1; Zeph. 1:7-9).

The earliest recorded reference to the day of the Lord appears in Amos 5:18 (twice) and 5:20. Amos uses the term to correct Israel's misconception of its character. They have been anticipating that day and even longing for it as a time of success, probably of military victory or deliverance from their enemies. That represents a faulty understanding of God's relation to his people.

The reference to "those who long for the day of the Lord" (Amos 5:18) points to a specific or limited group within Israel. If it is a specific group, it may refer to the false prophets and priests who predict peace and victory for the Northern Kingdom at a time and under circumstances when they should be warning the people about the impending judgment (cf. 1 Kings 22:12-13; Jer. 6:14; 8:11; Smelik: 246-248). If it is a limited group, they probably consist of those segments of society (administrators, judges, and the wealthy) being addressed elsewhere in Amos's prophecies. Their greedy longing has come to translate every event of history to their economic and political advantage.

Underlying all the references to that day, the day of Yahweh, is the covenantal character of Israel's relations with her God. The conditional character of covenant curses and blessings fuse the themes of judgment and salvation for Israel and the nations (Deut. 30, 32). The prophets repeatedly declare God's judgment on his people as the reversal of the holy war; God will wage war against his own people if they act with injustice toward one another and in disobedience toward him (Deut. 28:45-68; Zeph. 1:7, 14; Isa. 13:6, 9). The last word, however, is to be one of salvation rather than judgment, restoration to the Land of Promise rather than dispersion and death (Zeph. 3:16-18; Jer. 31; Amos 9:11-15).

THE EXODUS TRADITION A major religious reference point in Northern prophetic texts is the exodus from Egypt. Essential to Israel's self-understanding is the Israelites' keen awareness that the Lord took them up from Egypt. With only a few exceptions, the verb "go up" is characteristic of the language of the rebels in the wilderness (Exod. 17:3; Num. 20:5; 21:5), the account of the worship of the golden calf (Exod. 32:1, 4, 7-8, 23; 33:1), the concluding words of the Ephraimite Joshua (24:17, 32), the Northern book of Judges (2:1; 6:8, 13; 11:13, 16; 19:30; but 2:12, "go out") the book of 1 Samuel (five times, one exception), and Jeroboam I's installation of the calves in Dan and Bethel (1 Kings 12:28). "Go up" is used exclusively in Hosea (2:15; 12:13) and Amos (2:10; 3:1; 9:7). Neither of these prophetic books mentions Israel's slave status. Elsewhere, the description of the exodus is conveyed by the word meaning "to exit."

The exodus set Israel apart from surrounding nations. God led them forty years in the wilderness and then ushered them into the land which he gave to them. Emphasis on the wilderness journey of forty years marks both books (Hos. 2:3, 14-15; 11:1-4; 12:9; 13:5; Amos 2:10; 5:25).

The exodus was equally important in Judah's self-understanding. In Judah, however, the focal point of the exodus tradition lay in the demonstration of power the Lord exercised in redeeming his people through the plagues, climaxing in the angel of death's destruction of the firstborn of Egypt and the miraculous annihilation of Egyptian military might at the Sea of Reeds. With the Passover, Judah commemorated the exodus. In the North, however, there is virtual silence regarding the mighty miracles by which God wrested them out of Pharaoh's hand (Amos 4:10; 8:9-10). The Northern Kingdom's metaphor of deliverance becomes the festival of Booths/Tabernacles. It focuses much more on the wilderness years and the Lord's preservation in the barren wastelands (Mettinger: 72-79).

HISTORICAL SUMMARY Under Tiglath-pileser III (745-727 B.C.), Assyria moved aggressively westward. By 738 he was receiving tribute from Hamath, Tyre, Byblos, Damascus, and Israel (Bright: 270-271). Israel's military and political leaders disagreed on the nation's foreign policies.

Between 746 and 736 B.C., five kings ascended the throne in Samaria, three through violence. When Pekah seized the throne in 736, he became leader of an anti-Assyrian coalition. His major confederates were Rezin of Damascus (Syria) and the Edomites and possibly the Philistines. Judah refused to join the coalition and so was invaded by them (cf. Isa. 7:6; 2 Kings 15:37; 16:5). In desperation Ahaz, king of Judah, appealed to Assyria for help (16:7-18). In response, Tiglath-pileser destroyed the coalition by moving against Philistia in 734. The next year he struck Israel, Galilee, and Transjordan (15:29-30). In 732 he waged a third campaign (16:9) in which he ravaged Damascus and deported the Syrian population (Bright: 274-275).

In 725 or shortly thereafter, Hoshea of Israel rebelled against the Assyrians and allied himself with "King So of Egypt" (2 Kings 17:4). The alliance was doomed. After a three-year siege, Samaria fell to the Assyrian king,

Shalmaneser V, in 722. Two years later, Sargon II retook Damascus, deported 27,290 of its residents, and recolonized the Israelite territory with new refugees. Samaria then became an Assyrian province (Cogan: 98-101).

Meanwhile, Judah remained an Assyrian vassal until 712, when Hezekiah became involved in a rebellion against Sargon. A second rebellion in 701 resulted in severe punishment by the new Assyrian king Sennacharib. Hezekiah surrendered when "46 walled cities and countless small towns in their environs" (cf. 2 Kings 18:7-8, 13-16) were captured by the invaders. The war indemnity was oppressive; it was added to the annual tribute imposed on a greatly diminished Judah (Cogan: 66-67).

ISRAELITE RELIGION, DISTINCTIVE FEATURES OF The thesis underlying the following reconstruction of the religion of the Northern Kingdom is that the process of integration of El and Yahweh was not completed when Israel seceded from Judah under Jeroboam I. This incompleteness would give significance to the designation of the bull calves as "the gods who brought you up out of Egypt" (1 Kings 12:28). Those gods were understood to be El and Yahweh, both represented by the bull (like El and Ba'al in the Canaanite myth). At the beginning of the divided kingdom, the functions of El and Yahweh had not yet been totally assimilated or integrated, particularly in the North. Within the two succeeding centuries, their identities and names fully merged, the El traditions absorbed by Yahweh. The major moments contributing to this state of affairs occurred during the reigns of Jeroboam I and of Jehu.

Jeroboam I's Restructured Yahwism When the Northern Kingdom seceded from the union of the twelve tribes, its religious development took a turn which set it apart from official Judean Yahwism. Jeroboam astutely recognized that the ultimate unifying force in the nation was Yahwism, as centralized by Solomon (1 Kings 12:25—14:20). Jeroboam's hold on the Northern Kingdom remained tenuous as long as his citizens worshiped at the temple in Jerusalem. His response was to initiate changes in five crucial areas.

New Locations of Worship First, he created official centers of Yahweh worship at Bethel and Dan. The heralds must have announced far and wide: "Come, worship the Lord at conveniently restored holy places." Bethel intercepted pilgrims traveling south to Jerusalem to worship Yahweh. Dan attracted worshipers from the northern part of the country, particularly when the mobile image of Yahweh was located there *[Bull Calves, p. 375]*.

New Symbols of Yahweh Second, Jeroboam created two bull calves, installing one in Bethel and the other in various locations and as far north as Dan. The words of installation linked the Northern Kingdom's worship to the God of Sinai: "Here are your gods, O Israel, who brought you up from the land of Egypt" (1 Kings 12:28; cf. Exod. 32:8). The choice of words distinguished the symbols from idols. These symbols represented Yahweh and possibly El, the supreme God. The symbols captured the imagination of the nation, concerned with fertility, not unlike the bronze serpent (Num. 21:9), which served Judean worshipers as a symbol of faith and salvation for centuries (2 Kings 18:4). Even in Solomon's temple, bulls served a prominent and symbolic role (1 Kings 7:25-33). Jeroboam's words did not identify the bulls as God; they merely associated the two. Presumably the bulls represented thrones on which the deities were imagined to be sitting, not unlike the ark of the covenant.

As a next step, it would have been relatively simple to transfer such symbols from one level of meaning (creation, virility, power) to another (the god's throne), lending the bull calves authenticity and validity.

Similarly, the same measure of respectability could readily be transferred from the Solomonic temple's two free-standing bronze pillars (1 Kings 7:15-22) to comparable stone pillars representing Baal and the wooden pillar representing Asherah at the high places.

Inasmuch as Solomon's major designer of bronze work was Hiram of Tyre, the Phoenician/Canaanite influence was undoubtedly incorporated into the construction of the temple. The Lord continued to be worshiped at the official Yahwistic shrines in Bethel and Gilgal until Israel's demise. Baalism was practiced elsewhere, even while the kings gave lip service to the Lord. A certain compatibility had been created between Yahweh and Baal.

New Centers of Worship   Third, Jeroboam created a new category of worship centers, called "houses of high places" throughout his kingdom. These "houses" (pl., 1 Kings 13:32) were officially sanctioned, enclosed places of worship. In addition, the "house [s. in Heb. and NRSV note] of high places" established in Bethel was a chief sanctuary (12:31-33). The temple at Bethel contained the newly built altar and one of the golden bull calves made by Jeroboam, who worshiped there (1 Kings 13).

There is no evidence that this temple and the shrines of high places which it represented were originally anything other than centers of Yahweh worship. Indeed, apart from the valuative comments and criticism by the *Judean* compiler of Israel's history (2 Kings 17; esp. 17:9), the writers of *Israel's* history do not blame that nation for worshiping at high places. The writers of *Judean* history condemn pagan worship at high places (2 Kings 16:2-4; 21:2-9). They hold their own kings responsible for not destroying the high places even when non-Yahwistic worship had been eradicated there (cf. 1 Kings 15:14; 22:43-47; 2 Kings 12:2-3; 14:3-4; 15:3-4, 34-35).

The Northern Kingdom historians do not condemn worship at high places (1 Kings 13:33-34; cf. 15:33-34; 2 Kings 10:28-31; 14:24). Instead, they accuse their kings of sinning in the pattern of Jeroboam I, who worshiped the golden calves (2 Kings 10:28-29) and installed non-Levitical priests at the shrines of the high places (1 Kings 13:33-34). The difference between prophetic evaluation of South and North seems to reflect centralized worship of God in Judah versus decentralized worship in the North. In Israel (the North) it was not possible to worship except at some center already compromised by asherah pole, bull calf, or location (at high places). Jeroboam I introduced or sanctioned the asherah poles before these altars (1 Kings 14:15) as aids to worship. It appears that the official, national Yahwistic centers of worship were located at Bethel and Gilgal, while the high places attracted people in a more popular and life-related expression of religion *[Bull Calves, p. 375]* Hosea 8:5-6 may tell us that by the time of Hosea, the itinerant bull calf came to be lodged in the capital city, Samaria.

In short order, however, the Lord's prophets confronted the prophets of Baal and of the goddess [Asherah, p. 372]. That conflict is described in the stories of Ahab, Elijah, and Elisha.

New National Festival Fourth, Jeroboam modified an existing festival (Feast of Booths/Tabernacles) by changing the date to a month later (the eighth month) so as to disassociate it from the fall harvest festival (1 Kings 12:32-33; Lev. 23:34-36; Deut. 16:13-17; notes on Hos. 9:1-9). That linked the major Northern national festival only to the exodus from Egypt, the covenant, and the years of wilderness wandering. The linkage is confirmed by the dedication of the altar and the identification of the bull images as "your gods, O Israel, who brought you up from the land of Egypt." The harvest festival component of the Feast of Booths was still practiced at the fall harvesttime (the seventh month) but by local initiative. Harvests were connected to celebrations at threshing floors (Hos. 9:1) and worship at high places. However, the national festival celebrated Yahweh as the God of history but no longer associated him with the realm of nature and fertility.

New Priesthood Fifth, the temple in Jerusalem was served by the Levitical priests of the house of Aaron. The Aaronic Levites were officially designated as the priests in the Jerusalem cult. According to the description of their allotted inheritances (Josh. 21:9-19), these priestly families all lived within the territories of Simeon, Judah, and Benjamin. The schism placed the non-Aaronic priests living in the North in a dilemma. It forced them to decide on their political affiliation as well as their religious service. Many identified with the Davidic monarchy and the Jerusalemite cult. Some even left their assigned properties and migrated to Judah. Religious and political loyalties became increasingly fixed as border skirmishes followed, driving a wedge between Aaronic and non-Aaronic priests. Abijah and Asa, kings of Judah, are said to have invaded the territory of Benjamin and Ephraim, establishing control over this southern part of the Northern Kingdom (2 Chron. 13:2-20; 15:8). Jehoshaphat, Asa's successor, fortified the cities which had been captured (17:2) and reestablished Yahwistic worship in those territories.

This development is important. The cities of the Northern Kingdom associated with genuine Yahweh worship (Bethel, Gilgal, Jericho) are all located near the territory of Judah and all come within the area controlled by the Judean kings, Abijah, Asa, and Jehoshaphat (ca. 910-870 B.C.). While it is explicitly said that Asa did not remove the high places from Israel (2 Chron. 15:17), he did remove the idols from Ephraimite territory (15:8). His son Jehoshaphat, also a zealous Yahwist, carried his reforms further into the Ephraimite territory he had inherited (19:4).

The Chronicler details the intermarriage between Jehoshaphat and the house of Ahab (18:1), and the covenant he made with Ahab's successor, Ahaziah (20:35-37), but gives no indication when the southern territory of Israel was restored to Northern control. Possibly the covenant itself ceded captured territory back to the Northern Kingdom. At the very latest, the weak reign of Judah's king Jehoram, Jehoshaphat's son and successor, would have been an occasion for the reassimilation of these border cities into the Northern Kingdom (21:4-20). The proximity of these cities to Judah, the reforms of Jehoshaphat, and the anti-Baal pogrom of Jehu were likely the prime factors in preserving these southern Ephraimite cities as Yahwistic centers of worship.

The books of Chronicles offer an additional dimension to the interpretation of the development of the Northern Kingdom's religion. The Chronicler explains that Jeroboam's religious actions met with severe resistance from the priests and Levites throughout his realm (2 Chron. 11:13-17). At the same time, the role of the priests and Levites extended beyond the religious sphere. From the time of David, Levites served in significant political and administrative roles (1 Chron. 26:30-32; 1 Kings 4:5; Toews: 132-146). In 2 Chronicles 11:16-17, the Levites and their followers who came to Judah after the schism are said to have supported Rehoboam and the kingdom of Judah *for three years*. Presumably, they turned against Rehoboam when his policies changed and his devotion to the Lord waned. Thus, Jeroboam was not alone in having to contend with the political power of the priesthood.

The descriptions of Jeroboam's institution of a new priesthood explicitly associate these priests with the high places which he built throughout the kingdom (1 Kings 12:32; 13:33). The high places were Yahwistic centers of worship (cf. 3:1-4; 18:30; 19:10). Therefore, we must assume that the Levites who remained at those centers pledged their allegiance to Jeroboam. Levites seem not to have been automatically excluded from serving in the additional religious centers so conveniently established by Jeroboam (cf. 12:31).

It is precisely this appointment of non-Levitical functionaries as priests which is described as the "sin of Jeroboam" (1 Kings 13:33-34; cf. 15:26, 34; 16:25, 31). It may also be that the story in Judges (17–18) of the Levite who served as clan priest to Micah, and later to the Danites, represents a pattern of priesthood present throughout other parts of the Northern Kingdom. He is described as a non-Aaronic Levite (a descendant of Moses, 18:30) whose "sons were priests . . . until the time the land went into captivity."

The effect of this reformed priesthood was soon felt in the religion of the Northern Kingdom. By appointing priests from the laity, Jeroboam strengthened his hold on the religious system. The religious leaders were indebted to the king. The historian provides a snapshot of the extent of the politicization of religion in the North in the account of the Judean prophet who delivered the prophecy against the altar of Bethel (1 Kings 13). The deception of the old prophet of Bethel can be understood as rooted in his submission to political power. The national faith had become a civil religion. Disloyalty to the crown was also disloyalty to God. Furthermore, the priests would be less likely to retain a strong tradition of practice and teaching, so the nation became increasingly susceptible to foreign and alien influences. Worship, especially in the high places, developed quite independently of what was normative at the official, royal shrines.

Jehu's Violent Reformation Thirty-six years after the death of Jeroboam, Ahab became king of Israel, the Northern Kingdom (1 Kings 15:25; 16:29-33). He married the Sidonian princess, Jezebel, a devout worshiper of Asherah *[Asherah, p. 372]*. Ahab turned to Baal worship and built a temple to Baal in the capital city of Samaria, sanctioning the official worship of this Canaanite deity. His son and successor, Ahaziah, went as far as to consult the god Baal-Zebub, the god of Ekron (2 Kings 1). Yet within thirty years (by 841 B.C.), Baal had been deposed. This reversal of Baal's fortunes was brought about by Jehu.

Jehu set in motion a military coup against the ruling family, Ahab's descendants (2 Kings 9–10). By concealing his loyalty to the Lord and pretending to be a Baalist devotee, he lured all the prophets, worshipers, and priests of Baal into the temple of Baal in Samaria. Then he ordered them all to be slaughtered. He demolished the sacred stone of Baal, tore down the temple, and made it into a public latrine (10:18-36). The concluding comment offers a clue as to the subsequent place of the Baal cult: "Thus Jehu wiped out Baal from Israel" (10:28). The Northern Kingdom never again officially sanctioned the Baal religion. The Lord ruled as the high God.

The "sins of Jeroboam, son of Nebat," however, remained the primary obstacle to religious reform. Inasmuch as these sins were never addressed, the nation continued to accept a division of authority between the Lord and Baal in that fertility in Palestine remained the province of the lesser gods. The official religion remained Yahwism; but popular religion included Baal and Asherah as the active agents in the agricultural cycle and in human procreation.

THE JACOB AND ISAAC TRADITIONS An important reference point for Hosea and Amos is that of the patriarchal tradition (Hos. 12:3-5, 12). The Israelites identified more with the patriarch Jacob than with Abraham, since Jacob's stay in Palestine centered in the area later occupied by the ten Northern tribes.

Several places named in the Jacob story later became the possession of the Northern Kingdom: Succoth, Peniel, and the Jabbok east of the River Jordan; and Bethel, Shechem, and Dothan west of the river. Jacob's association with southern Palestine is limited to the description of the death of Rachel and his stay in Mamre when assuming the birthright after the death of Isaac (Gen. 35:16-29). Thus Jacob became the patriarch of promise and the model of faith for the Northern tribes. Bethel serves as Jacob's shrine center because there God met with him on two important occasions (28:10-22; 35:1-15). This historic connection with Bethel provided sanction for Bethel's role as the primary center of worship in the Northern Kingdom.

Amos quotes the priest Amaziah calling the Northern Kingdom "the house of Isaac" (7:16). Amos reports that the Lord is judging the "high places of Isaac" (7:9). Presumably, Israel identified itelf with Isaac because Isaac's ancestral home was Beersheba (Gen. 26:23-33; 28:10; 46:1, 5).

JUDAH AND DAVID, REFERENCES TO The assumption of most contemporary exegetes of Amos and Hosea is that the prophecies which mention Judah are not original to the ministry of these prophets. The usual interpretation has it that these Judean elements were added to make the books relevant for Southern readers and listeners of a later period. I have argued that both prophets were directing their words from the very first to Judah as well as Israel. They saw Judah bent on the same course as Israel, except not as far advanced in apostasy. In each case, the fulfillment of the prophecies against the Northern Kingdom was confirmation of the message directed against the South.

Hosea and Amos are agreed that the judgment forming against Israel will bring the Northern Kingdom to its end as a nation (Amos 9:9; Hos. 1:6-7). Judah, however, will be restored politically after her exile. That restoration will reunite the scattered remnants of both nations under the banner of one king, a descendant of David (Amos 9:8-12; Hos. 3:4-5).

JUSTICE AND RIGHTEOUSNESS Moderns tend to equate justice with the application of the legal system. Such a view is too narrow an understanding of biblical justice. There are those who distinguish universal justice (justice as virtue) from particular justice (such as commercial, remedial, and distributive justice; Nash: 74-76). Those categories are foreign to the biblical concept of justice, though some of the distinctions might be made. In Amos 5–6, for example, three references to justice appear in poetic parallels in which *righteousness* is the corresponding member in the pair (5:7, 24; 6:12). The parallel usage of these terms, *justice* and *righteousness*, suggests a large meaning overlap between them.

In a court or legal setting, the primary import of *justice* is "fair-ness." The judge(s) shall be evenhanded, treating all alike with regard to the law. The same law applies to king and commoner, rich and poor, slave and free, male and female alike (cf. Exod. 23:2-3, 6-8; Deut. 17:8-13; Lev. 19:15). Evildoers shall receive their due (Ps. 149:9); the innocent shall be exonerated and delivered (Ps. 76:9). In Amos 5:15, Israel is told to *hate evil and love good, and establish justice in the gate. They turn aside the way of the oppressed* (2:7; cf. 5:12); this appears to describe unjust practices current within the court or legal system. So God calls Israel to fairness in upholding and practicing the law of the land. That law consists largely of the "judgments" handed down or endorsed by God or godly rulers and judges (Deut. 5:1; 1 Kings 3:28). Yet it is always depicted as God's law.

The meaning of *justice* when paralleled with *righteousness* is not restricted to the role of the legal institutions. Such justice, Yoder observes, is concerned to restore harmony to the community. It consists of action for members of the community and against oppressors. It tries to change situations rather than meting out what people deserve. It struggles to create wholeness where currently there are pressing needs (Yoder: 27-37). An illustration of such justice appears in Job's concluding monologue (29:7-25). He describes how he "put on righteousness, and it clothed me; my justice was like a robe and a turban" (29:14). He did this by rescuing the poor and the fatherless, comforting the dying, supporting widows, helping the blind, lame, and needy, serving as an advocate of the stranger, and opposing those who would take advantage of others (29:12-13, 15-17).

In other words, biblical justice actively pursues the welfare of the community and the individuals in it. It is the responsibility of every member of the group, not merely the judiciary. It consists of concrete actions of caring. It moves beyond written codes to address weakness, poverty, and inequities of every kind. This is what it has in common with righteousness.

Righteousness appears three times in Amos (5:7, 24; 6:12). It could be described as virtue in action or the intent to do the right. It refers to the quality of relationships between individuals. Whereas *justice* in its parallel meaning addresses both the victim and the situation which created the need, *righteousness* draws attention to the character of the helper (Ps. 11:7) and (with only a few exceptions) the acts of mercy, caring, and rightness (Ezek. 33:12-20; Deut. 6:25). The ultimate expression of righteousness is God's saving words and deeds (Isa. 5:16; 46:13; 51:5, 7-8). He acts in accordance with his name to preserve and display his glory (Ps. 43:1; Dan. 9:7, 13-19; Piper, 1980a: 2-32; 1980b: 3-14). Human righteousness consists of those virtues and acts which reflect the righteousness of God.

Amos 5:7 and its parallel 5:10-13 illustrate the range of meaning present in the two words, *justice* and *righteousness*. Both are reflected in the gracious (5:8a-c) as well as the judgmental acts of God (5:9). Justice and righteousness are here set within the judicial context in which community life is regulated (5:10, 12d, 15a). Injustice and unrighteousness take the forms of resentment against those who promote the public morality (5:10), eagerness to take advantage of the poor (5:11), and perverting the judicial process (5:12). Justice and righteousness are the very opposite. They ensure the welfare of the members of the entire community.

God calls individuals as well as society to practice justice and righteousness. Amos points to failures in both domains. At the personal level, Israelites have practiced injustice and unrighteousness by defrauding the righteous, grinding the poor into deeper poverty, misusing people, extorting and bribing, and by being insensitive to the plight of the nation. Collectively they are called to account for denying the poor equal access to the courts and for perverting the judicial process. These acts are equally hated by God. Both destroy the fabric of peoplehood.

LITERARY PATTERNS Patterns are common to all compositions, whether sung, spoken, or written. Composers use patterning to aid the memory, please the eye or ear, draw attention to certain elements of story or instruction, show completion or wholeness, or add a wealth of subtlety and shading to what at first appears straightforward or strange. Each society develops its own unique patterns.

The most common pattern in Hebrew literature is parallelism. Parallels may consist of similar or contrasting words, phrases, or other grammatical constructions. They vary greatly in length and character. The most common and obvious are parallels within or between clauses, but parallel members may be of virtually any length, or of unequal length. The observant reader will notice a wide variety of parallel constructions at the phrase or clause level. Some that may not be as obvious are highlighted in the notes. Others may not be evident in translation.

Chiastic structures are patterns in mirror image: A B C . . . C' B' A'. Chiasm, meaning X-shaped, may characterize a textual subunit (Hos. 4:7-12), an entire oracle (Amos 5:1-17), or a larger section (Hos. 6:4—11:11).

The accusation-judgment-salvation sequence is another common pattern in Hosea (1–3) and even shapes the flow of the entire book of Amos.

Other observed patterns:
- similar sounds (Amos 5:5).
- sequences of common introductory phrases, as in Amos 1-2: *For three transgressions and for four*; Amos 3-6: *Hear this word*; and Amos 7-9: *I saw, the Lord showed me.*
- similar or identical beginning and ending (Hos. 6:4; 11:8-11).
- balance between alternating or interacting speakers (cf. outlines of Amos 5:1-17; Hos. 8:1—11:11).

Parallels may also take the form of two or more of something, whether illustrations, metaphors, or examples from life. It is common to hear the positive and negative as pairs.

Some patterns are specific to a culture, others to a person. Both Hosea and Amos frequently quote direct speech (in addition to words from the Lord).

Hosea:
> *Say to your brother, "Ammi," and to your sister, "Ruḥamah." (2:1)*
> *She said, "I will go after my lovers; they gave me. . . . (2:5)*
> *Do not swear, "As the Lord lives." (4:15)*
> *They will say, "We have no king." (10:3)*

Amos:
> *You commanded the prophets, saying, "You shall not prophesy." (2:12)*
> *. . . Who say to their husbands, "Bring us to drink." (4:1)*
> *. . . Those who say, "As your god lives, O Dan." (8:14)*
> *. . . the sinners . . . who say, "Evil will not overtake us." (9:10)*

Both prophets also make effective use of the rhetorical question:

Hosea:
> *Can the Lord now feed them like a lamb in a broad pasture? (4:16)*
> *What shall I do with you, Ephraim? (6:4).*
> *What will you do on the day of the appointed festival,*
> *   and on the day of the festival of the Lord? (9:5)*

Amos:
> *Do two walk together unless they have made an appointment? (3:3-8)*
> *Did you bring to me sacrifices and offerings the forty years in the wilderness, O house of Israel? (5:25)*
> *Are you not like the Ethiopians to me, O people of Israel? (9:7)*

The quotations and rhetorical questions tend not to be used in the same oracle. This reserves their impact at critical points in the argument. Both literary devices draw the reader-listener emotionally into the thought process and inject dialogue into what is otherwise a monologue.

MARRIAGE LAWS AND CUSTOMS, ANCIENT NEAR EAST

Sources During the past 25 years, scholars have vigorously gathered, translated or retranslated, and studied ancient Near Eastern (ANE) texts on the subject of marriage and family life. The more recent collections and primary studies include those of Westbrook (1988), Roth (1989), and Porten and Yardeni (1987-89). To these we add the collections of marriage contracts from Egypt, on papyri, written in Greek, as previously gathered and translated by Hunt and Edgar (1970-).

Relevance for Hosea Studies These documents illuminate marriage and family structures and customs within the larger world of which ancient Israel was a part. They supplement one's reading and interpretation of Hosea, and thus influence this commentary, yet with certain limitations.

No extra-biblical marriage and family texts exist from the era and area of the Northern Kingdom during its separate existence. The published documents cannot, therefore, be said to "prove" any interpretation of the biblical text. However, they are still useful in that they correct some false conceptions and statements made by commentators of the past.

They indicate that every ANE society was concerned to regulate or order or describe marriage with regard to (1) the economic aspects of the marriage agreement, (2) the nature of the marriage relationship, (3) the conditions under which the marriage would be regarded as broken or severed, (4) the status of children, and their rights of inheritance, including the children of blended families, (5) exceptional or unusual aspects of a given marriage, (6) the consequences of severing the marriage relationship, and (7) the role of family or community in assuring justice and protecting the rights of the weaker parties, usually those of the women and children. The awareness that those seven factors are of vital concern to ANE cultures is in itself significant for the study of Hosea. Each of those factors figures prominently in Hosea 1–3.

The basic concerns of these marriage laws and contracts were the same as those of the Hebrews. We can confirm the validity of this sociological correspondence by comparing ANE sexual, marriage and family legislation with that of Israel (cf. Exod. 21–22; Lev. 18-21; Num. 27, 30, 36; Deut. 21-25).

PROSTITUTION AS SACRED ACT AND METAPHOR

The Problem Why the language of prostitution? Why not speak of infidelity or adultery or draw on some other imagery to identify God's concern and judgment? Indeed, how is it that so many spheres of Israel's life can be referred to using the imagery of prostitution? On a number of occasions in Hosea, the language of prostitution is purely metaphorical. Is it possible to distinguish and separate the metaphorical from the literal references? What are the nuances of the metaphor? The answers to these questions will shape our interpretation of the books of Hosea and Amos.

The single reference to prostitution in the book of Amos interprets the fate of Amaziah's wife (7:17). Only one other reference to a sexual sin receives mention in Amos (2:7). Hosea is replete with sexual language, including the language of prostitution.

Prostitution as Sacred Act Israel's legislation prohibited profane (everyday, common) prostitution as a family enterprise, in which the father would act as pimp: "Do not profane your daughter by making her a prostitute, that the land not become prostituted and full of depravity" (Lev. 19:29). It also prohibited prostitutes from bringing their wages in payment of a vow (Deut. 23:18). Israel's legislation prohibited sacred prostitution as well: "None of the daughters of Israel shall be a temple prostitute; none of the sons of Israel shall be a temple prostitute" (Deut. 23:17). Clearly, prostitution violated God's creation and moral order.

Sacred prostitution as literal prostitution is mentioned only once in connection with Northern Kingdom religious practice, in Hosea 4:14, where the prostitute is female. All the gender-specific references to sacred prostitutes in Judah are to males (1 Kings 14:24; 15:12; 22:46; 2 Kings 23:7). Yet sacred prostitution was common in fertility religions.

The precise function and significance of the sacred prostitute is not clear. The sex act between a profane prostitute and her client constitutes a fee for services rendered at her discretion. The sex act between sacred prostitute and worshiper constitutes the person's moral and religious obligation to ensure fertility and generate progeny. The worship of Baal and Asherah involved the worshiper in the procreative act to ensure the annual rebirth of Baal.

Some understanding of sacred prostitution can be gained from various biblical texts and extra-biblical data. A number of figurines of the nude female figure have been unearthed in Palestine, dating from the early period of Israel's occupation of the land (ANEP: figs. 464, 465, 469). They tend to focus attention toward the breasts and crotch, suggesting that these deities had a sexual function.

It is possible that Eli's sons were practicing a fertility ritual when they slept with the women who served at the entrance to the tent of meeting (1 Sam. 2:22). In any case, Eli recognized that this act represented a sin against God in some distinctive way (2:25).

Baal, Anat, and Asherah were worshiped in the high places, the hilltop shrines normally located within groves of trees, in connection with the cycles of nature and reproduction [Canaanite Fertility Myth, p. 376]. There, also, the rites of offering infants in sacrifice to gods, the practice of prostitution, and divination and sorcery took place (cf. 2 Kings 17; Hos. 4:13-14).

The incident with the Baal of Peor before entry into the Promised Land illustrates the nature and effects of Baal worship (Num. 25). Apparently, on Balaam's advice (31:16), the Moabites and Midianites undermined Israelite morale and promoted defection from God by encouraging the Israelites to worship in Moabite fashion. This worship included sexual immorality with Moabite women, sacrificing to their gods, eating in the presence of these gods, and worshiping the idols representing the gods of Moab (25:1-3). The sexual immorality was not confined to copulation in the shrines but spilled over into immoral living in the Israelite camp (25:6-8). All this agrees with what Hosea depicts of the sexual degradation which characterized Baal worship. It sets the backdrop for the attack by the Lord and Hosea against the unfaithfulness of their spouses and the rampant evil which physical and spiritual prostitution had introduced into the nation.

However, a survey of the criticisms leveled against the Northern Kingdom by the author(s) of the books of Kings (other than the summary statements of 2 Kings 17) produces no references to prostitution, no comments about their worship at high places, and no indication of Baal worship after the reforms of King Jehu (cf. 10:25-29). The sins in which they followed Jeroboam I are the worship of the golden calves at Bethel and Dan (10:29) and the use of the asherah poles in Samaria (13:6). Indeed, Jehu is described as rooting out official Baal worship *[Israelite Religion, p. 385]*.

How, then, are we to understand the book of Hosea with its frequent references to prostitution, the evident presence of Baal, the use of idols, and the prominent role of a fertility cult? How shall we understand the apparently genuine Yahwism represented in Israel's confessions, appeals for help, and oath formulas?

Hosea 4:14 suggests that the distinction between profane and sacred prostitution was not as great as we might suppose. The fathers were offended when their daughters and daughters-in-law had sex outside of marriage. Hosea points to the fathers' immoral behavior with profane (4:14a) and sacred prostitutes (4:14b) as the model their daughters and daughters-in-law are following. Such prostitution is always associated with high places; there is no linkage between prostitution and the worship of the Lord at Bethel, Gilgal, Dan, or Beersheba. This suggests that Yahweh and Baal had been assigned distinct spheres of influence. Israel had forgotten that the Lord was the Creator, the God of fertility (2:5, 8-13).

Prostitution as Metaphor The imagery of prostitution is more appropriate than that of adultery. Prostitution involves an exchange of goods and services. In the fertility cult, the worshiper expected a return on his/her investment. Furthermore, in the ANE, religion was the integrative center for society. Since the Sinai covenant was all-embracing, and since worship was as large as life itself, the language of prostitution became a broad metaphor involving any aspect of life in which Israel was taking guidance from Canaanite values and practices. In Hosea, the language of prostitution is definitely associated with the perversion of worship (Hos. 4). It is connected with the priests' failure to teach and with sacrifice, famine, drinking wine, consulting God, burning incense, and offerings at the high places. The sexual language begins as sexually explicit reality but quickly becomes imagery of the variety of forms which this perverted concept and practice entails. Sexual acts become a "spirit of prostitution."

Covenant breaking (Hos. 6:7-10) is spoken of as prostitution. Israel's national policy warrants the language of prostitution because the nation has *sold herself to lovers* (8:9); Israel was willing to pay tribute or make a contribution to Assyria for protective services rendered. The bull calves of Bethel and Dan or Samaria and the worship at high places become prostitution in the sense of breaking covenant with God.

Hosea does not hesitate to use sexual or fertility language to represent God's relationship to Israel. This is so in promise as well as in judgment (Hos. 2). The most sexually explicit word is *therefore I am now going to seduce her; I will lead her into the desert* (2:14). When the text says, *Know the Lord* (2:20) or *I know Ephraim* (5:3), it conveys the aura of the bedroom, since sexual intercourse in marriage is described as a husband "knowing" his wife. The Lord speaks openly about Israel's lovers, his betrothal to Israel leading up to the remarriage, and the platonic relationship which shall exist between himself and Israel until the full restoration of the Northern Kingdom (Hos. 3). He places a restriction on his redeemed betrothed bride/wife in that she shall not give herself to another man, nor will the Lord give himself to another woman (3:3).

The three salvation pericopes in part 2 (Hos. 6:1-3; 11:8-11; 14:1-8) are constructed with fertility vocabulary and concepts. Baal is said to be the one who provides children, rain, crops, and riches. Indeed, rain is Baal's stock in trade. The message of Elijah's Mt. Carmel encounter with the prophets of Baal was that the Lord and not Baal was the Giver of rain and dew, the One who blessed the earth and endowed nature with the ability to produce new life each year (14:1-8). The Lord bested Baal while using Baal's weapons (rain, the bull). Repentant Israel must recognize the Lord's supremacy over all other supposed gods of fertility and fecundity (6:1-3).

The further the topic moves from the cult, the less Hosea uses sexual imagery, though fertility language occurs throughout. In the concluding section (11:12—14:9), where social and economic aspects of national apostasy are in focus, there are no explicit references to prostitution, though fertility language abounds. Amos focuses on the social and economic sins of the Northern Kingdom. His prophecies, too, contain fertility language, but not the language of prostitution. In this respect, then, Amos and Hosea speak the same language when addressing issues of justice, whether of a social or economic nature. The difference between them is that Amos does not adopt the language of prostitution or use sexual imagery when he addresses cultic issues (Amos 4–6, 8) or matters concerning knowing God (Amos 5, 8).

TABERNACLES, SIGNIFICANCE OF THE FEAST OF The occasion for recalling the Lord's choice and creation of Israel was the Feast of Tabernacles or Booths. Traditionally, this festival commemorated several things: (1) Israel's rescue from Egypt so that the nation, God's "son," could worship him in the wilderness (Exod. 4:22-23; 5:1-3). (2) The covenant making and law giving at Mt. Sinai. (3) The Lord's role as King and his concern for the just administration of his people. (4) God's gracious provision during the forty years of wilderness wandering, marked by living in booths for seven days. (5) The harvest, representing the bounties flowing from the land which God gave his people.

This was the festival which Jeroboam I shifted from the seventh to the eighth month [*Israelite Religion, p. 385*]. In the Northern Kingdom, the harvest would have been completed a month previously. That change in dates of this great feast effectively separated the action of the Lord in redeeming the people, and the Lord's activity as the Guarantor of fertility. Or, it might be more accurate to say, "Fertility took precedence over redemption."

The change in date of this festival underlies the text of Hosea 9:1-5. In the interval between the harvest (9:1-2) in the seventh month and the Feast of Tabernacles in the eighth month, misfortune and judgment devour the produce, and the people have eaten the meager crop. When they come to celebrate the Festival of Tabernacles a month later (9:4-5), nothing will be left to commemorate the Lord's provision. This shift in time of the Feast of Tabernacles also underlies Israel's mistaken claim that the produce of the land (2:5, 8-9) is from Baal. He is given the credit for the Lord's generosity.

The reference to the *fallen booth of David* (Amos 9:11) and the word play on *Sikkuth your king* (5:26) point toward the Feast of Tabernacles/ Booths as the occasion in which Yahweh's kingship was celebrated.

The Feast of Tabernacles also marks the Lord's concern for compassion and justice. It becomes the occasion for the presentation of the tithe given every third year to the Levites, aliens, fatherless, and widows (cf. Amos 4:4; Deut. 26). It is also the occasion for the seventh-year cancellation of debts (31:10; cf. 15:1-11).

Amos's passionate concern for justice is linked with the tradition of the Feast of Tabernacles. He speaks of the enslavement and oppression of the poor and helpless (2:6-8; 5:7, 10-12; 8:5-6) and points to how the wealthy and powerful substitute tithes and offerings for justice (4:4; 5:14-15, 21-27). Indeed, it has been argued that Amos's ministry occurred during the festival of the eighth month. If that is the case, then his words represent a commentary on Israel's failure to fulfill the essential meanings of the Feast of Tabernacles.

An essential element of the exodus tradition and its commemoration in the Feast of Tabernacles is the emphasis on covenant and law giving. According to Deuteronomy, the book of the law was to be read every seventh year at this festival (31:9-13; cf. Neh. 8). Amos declares God as Israel's covenant Lord in the words: *You only of all the families of the earth have I known* (3:2). Hosea is saturated with covenant elements. Chapters 1–3 are built on the Lord's covenant history with Israel. Five of the Ten Commandments are listed in 4:1-3. The salvation oracle of 6:1-3 represents a covenant renewal. The priests fail to teach the law (4:6), and as a result the people have forgotten God (8:12). God called his son out of Egypt (11:1), but this child rejected the parental love (11:2-4, 8-11). The spoken judgments in both Hosea and Amos follow the patterns of covenant curses found in extra-biblical international treaties and recorded in Leviticus 26 and Deuteronomy 28. In the end, Amos declares, Israel's neglect of the law will result in *a famine* of the word of God (8:11-14).

Hosea also treats the exodus and the subsequent covenant making at Sinai as the ideal and shaping event of the nation. The new redemption following the current judgments will take the form of a new honeymoon experience (2:14-15) in the pattern of the earlier salvation event. Israel's current defection stands in stark contrast to the Lord's rescue from their Egyptian masters (12:9, 13; 13:4). Their recovery depends on the people of Israel acknowledging the Lord alone as their God (13:4).

THE YAHWEH-BAAL CONFLICT AND PROPHETIC POLEMIC

The Story of the Conflict   God forbade Israel to worship the gods of the
land they were claiming. Indeed, the contest for Canaan was a contest between the gods Yahweh and Ba'al.

All gods were worshiped at local mountaintop shrines, called high places
(*bamoth*, 1 Kings 13:32). In Palestine, the high places were already claimed
by other gods. So, prior to the construction of the temple, official Israelite
worship was centralized around the location of the ark and the tent of meeting. This location changed from time to time (cf. Josh. 3–4, 6, etc.; Judges
20:27; 1 Sam. 2:14; 3:3; 7:1; 21:1-6). Even after the Philistines returned the
ark to Israel, authentic worship of Yahweh occurred at sites other than the official cult center (1 Sam. 7:17; 10:8).

Israel, too, worshiped at high places such as Mt. Sinai and Mt. Zion. The
secession and Jeroboam's religious changes effectively cut Israel off from the
authorized high place, Mt. Zion. The Northerners were left with high places
such as Gilgal, Bethel, Mizpah, Ramah, Gerizim, and Mt. Carmel. These particular centers were blessed by the presence and ministry of prophets such as
Samuel, Elijah, and Elisha. It seemed only natural to continue to worship
Yahweh where he had revealed himself in the past and where his people had
a long tradition of serving the true God.

Some 35 politically tumultuous years had elapsed since the death of Jeroboam I (910/09 B.C., following Thiele's chronology). Four kings took the
throne between Jeroboam and Ahab; two died at an assassin's hand, and one
committed suicide. The Northern Kingdom was rife with dissent. Undoubtedly, religious conflict fed the undercurrent of unrest.

The accession of King Ahab marked a turning point in the religious life of
Israel. The new capital city, Samaria, built by his father, Omri (1 Kings 16:24),
did not have historic ties with Yahwism, as did Bethel (cf. Gen. 28:10-22).
King Ahab made Baal worship an official religion. He reinforced this religious
change and secured his northern borders by marrying Jezebel, daughter of
the Sidonian king (1 Kings 16:31). She was a devout worshiper and zealous
supporter of the Asherah and Baal cults (18:19). Though Bethel remained
the sanctuary of the realm, the presence of the king in Samaria gave the temple of Baal there the status of a national shrine (16:32). It continued to have
that status throughout the 32 years Ahab and his son Joram ruled Israel (cf.
2 Kings 10:18-27).

Religious, human, and social values were changing. During Ahab's reign,
a dignitary from Bethel, the center of Yahwism in the North, offered his eldest
and his youngest sons as sacrifices to induce the gods to bless his restoration
of Jericho (1 Kings 16:34). The account of Naboth's vineyard (1 Kings 21) illustrates the decay of long-standing social and cultural values. It also reflects
the increasing concentration of power in the monarchy, and the disregard for
equity and justice. King followed king in quick succession, and each struggled
to shore up alliances for purposes of self-preservation. Fertility, land ownership, political alliances—the things that held them together were the substance of the conflict between Yahweh and Baal.

When Jezebel turned to active proselytizing for Baal and Asherah [*Asherah, p. 372*], her zeal expressed itself in persecuting the prophets of Yahweh
(1 Kings 18:4, 13; 18:9-10) and in rooting out Yahwism in the cult centers at

the high places (18:30-32; 19:10, 14). When Elijah named Yahweh the victor at Mt. Carmel, the queen's prophetic supporters had to go. Elijah slaughtered the prophets of Baal. This so incensed Jezebel that she threatened to destroy him. Fearing her wrath, he fled for his life (18:40—19:9).

In this entire exchange, Ahab seems to have assumed a passive role. Officially, he acknowledged Yahweh as Lord (1 Kings 18:41—19:1), but privately he supported Jezebel. He had personally witnessed two convincing proofs of Yahweh's rule over nature. First, Yahweh had shown himself supreme over Baal in one blinding bolt of lightning, effectively establishing himself rather than Baal as the god of storm. Second, the downpour of rain should have been proof positive that Yahweh rather than Baal refreshed the earth and that the Lord alone was worthy of Ahab's allegiance. But Ahab continued to vacillate between God and Baal.

The stories of Elijah and Elisha depict the Lord active through his prophets. Later, numerous other prophets appear on the stage of national events. Though Israel's kings, even antagonistic Ahab, recognize the validity of the divine message brought by Yahweh's prophets (cf. 1 Kings 20:13—21:29), an underlying, negative attitude prevailed toward the prophets. Ahab described Elijah as "the troubler of Israel" (18:17) and "my enemy" (21:20). Confronting adversaries with unpleasant truth required sensitivity and boldness.

The Polemic of Hosea and Amos in Favor of Yahweh The challenge to prophets of Yahweh such as Hosea and Amos was to communicate to Israel in ways and with arguments which would convince them of the logical inconsistency and the moral consequences of deserting their covenant Lord. Merely denouncing Baal worship or contending that the Lord was in control of nature would not be convincing to the eighth-century Israelites. This commentary is in large measure an attempt to trace the rationale of the polemic against Baal and in favor of Yahweh as contained within the prophetic books of Hosea and Amos. It is a study of the hermeneutics of anti-syncretism. It probes the message of uncompromising opposition to "other gods" (Exod. 20:3) as well as to the inappropriate symbols of the true God which have distorted the knowledge of the Holy One of Israel.

In the polytheism in which Baal played a principal role, each god was assigned a specific status, role, and task. The people of surrounding societies believed in the coexistence (sometimes peaceful, sometimes adversarial) of the different deities. Moreover, one and the same God (El) could be worshiped under local manifestations such as God Most High (El Elyon, Gen. 14:18-24), God Who Sees Me (El Roi, 16:13-14), God of Bethel (El Bethel, 31:13; 35:7), and the God of Dan or of Beersheba (Amos 8:14). In this way, the people brought harmony and coherence to their faith.

The process by which Israel ultimately came to understand that Yahweh was not Baal, even though their functions overlapped, was long and slow. Israel's moral and theological purification depended largely on a teaching priesthood. However, the Northern Kingdom lacked such a priesthood—a deficiency which was one of the major criticisms leveled against the Israelite kings from Jeroboam I until the Assyrians destroyed Samaria in 722/1 B.C.

The primary argument for Yahweh and against Baal drew attention to

Yahweh as the God who had had a long and intimate history with his people (Hos. 1–3; Amos 2–3, 9). Throughout that history (Amos 3:1-2), Yahweh had been providing his people with every good thing Baal ever claimed to provide. Baal was said to be the source of fertility; yet Yahweh was capable of sustaining a whole nation for forty years in a barren wilderness (Hos. 2; Amos 2:10-11). Indeed, the very land was a gift from Yahweh, who drove out the Canaanites (Amos 2:9).

This same God was capable of withholding the good things of the earth. He was at one and the same time the God of fertility and sterility (Hos. 2:6-23; 9:1-6, 10-13; Amos 4:4-9; 8:1-3, 7-10; 9:11-15). He was also the God who ruled nature and the God who directed the affairs of the nations (Amos 1–2), the God who sets up kings and deposes them (Amos 7). He ruled in every realm attributed to Baal, Anat, Nahar, Yam, Mot, and all the other deities whom Israel had associated with the worship of Baal (Amos 9:2-10) [Asherah, p. 372]. This multiple task is why the books of Hosea and Amos contain numerous names for God: Baal (Hos. 2:16), Elohim (God), Glory (4:7; 9:11), God of Beersheba (Amos 8:14), Helper (Hos. 13:9), High God (11:7), Holy One (11:9), King (7:5), LORD God Almighty (Yahweh, God of Armies; 12:5; Amos 4:13; 5:14-16; 6:14), Most High (Hos. 7:16, NIV), Pride of Jacob (Amos 8:7), Savior (Hos. 13:4), and Sovereign LORD (Adonai Yahweh; Amos 1:8; 3:7-8, 11; 4:2, 5; 5:3; 6:8; 7:1-2, 4 [twice], 5-6; 8:1, 3, 9, 11; 9:8), Lord, LORD Almighty (Adonai, Yahweh of Armies; Amos 9:5).

As part of the polemic against the gods of Canaan, the attributes of the indigenous, pagan deities were gradually assumed by Yahweh. For example, he took on the role and name "Rider of the Clouds" (cf. Ps. 18:10; 45:4; 68:4, 33; 104:3; Isa. 19:1), a common designation for Baal in the mythological literature. That role was to bring rain in season and ensure the harvest.

History and fertility merged in the annual nature cycle. Israel's celebrative events as recorded in the Torah were linked to Yahweh as the God of both history and nature simultaneously. These connections are most clearly evident in the events and celebrations regarding the harvest and the exodus.

Harvesttime, whether at the threshing floor or winepresses, was a time of celebration in song and sacrifice (Hos. 4:8, 13; 5:6; 6:6; 8:13; 9:1-2; 10:1; Amos 4:4-5; 5:21-25; 8:3, 10). By changing the date of the Festival of Booths, which was traditionally also the harvest festival, Jeroboam I separated the two: harvest was celebrated in the seventh month, Yaweh's preserving care and kingship in the eighth month. The harvest, celebrated locally, became linked to Baal. The high places, increasingly associated with Baal and Asherah worship, provided every community with a convenient shrine. Formally, Yahweh ruled the nation from Bethel. In practice, a form of Baal worship dominated everyday religion.

As polemic in behalf of the Lord Yahweh, Amos especially stressed his rule over nature and history. The first four visions of Amos (chaps. 7–9) are connected to themes of harvest, kingship, and "Egypt" (9:1-10). The earthquake which will level Israel's cities produces motions comparable to the rising and the falling of the Nile (8:8; 9:5). In Amos 9:9, harvest and earthquake are brought together in the metaphor of grains shaken in a sieve.

On three separate occasions, Amos focuses on the Egypt—forty-year desert experience by means of rhetorical questions (2:10-11; 5:25-26; 9:7-

8). The line of argument goes as follows: If Yahweh could rescue you out of the fertility of Egypt, and care for you so fully those forty years in the wilderness, where Baal is dead or helpless, surely the Lord can ensure the fertility of Israel's land.

The Polemic of Hosea and Amos Against Baal Hosea and Amos agree that Israel's dependence on cultic activity, particularly on the multitude of sacrifices brought to Yahweh at Bethel and Gilgal (Amos 4:4; Hos. 4:15; 5:4-7; 8:11-13), will not appease Yahweh's anger at the people's perversions. Both prophets assume that the Israelites really believe they are worshiping Yahweh at those centers. They also speak with one voice concerning the bull calf of Bethel, which serves as the pedestal or footstool of Yahweh, their King (Amos 5:26; Hos. 8:5-6; 10:5). Both denounce the religious assemblies and festivals, and particularly label the fellowship meals as unacceptable (Amos 4:4-5; 5:21-23; 6:1-7; Hos. 7:14; 8:13; 9:1-5). Yahweh will not accept such worship from his people. His corrective examples, words, and acts have for so long gone unheeded (Hos. 9:8; 12:10; Amos 2:11-12; 3:1-8; 4:4-13). The only remaining message is one of silence (8:11-14).

Yet, Hosea and Amos take different approaches to the existing religious practices in the Northern Kingdom. Amos's approach is to denounce all worship at the traditional sites in the Northern Kingdom. In so doing, he issues a blanket statement of judgment on Israelite religion because it is carried out at centers other than Jerusalem (cf. 1:2). Bethel (3:14; 4:4; 5:5-6; cf. 7:8-9, 11-13), Gilgal (4:4; 5:5), and Beersheba (5:5) all receive the verdict of "profane." He offers no explicit criticism of the nature of worship at these centers. Amos does not identify these centers of worship as pagan or Baalistic; he merely singles them out for judgment. Since Israel's worship has become a substitute for ethical living, their destruction is warranted.

Implicit in the condemnation of their worship is the contention that the worship at these centers is uncharacteristic of their God. They have persisted in suppressing the truth about God (Amos 2:9-12; 3:8; 4:12-13; 5:4, 8-10, 18; 6:10; 7:14-15; 9:5-8). The Israelites have not understood his purposes nor his past actions regarding his people (3:1-2; 4:6-11; 6:1-2; 9:7-8). The hymn fragments serve his polemic well in demonstrating the nature of God. The rhetorical question conveys Amos's argument with beauty and power (2:11; 3:3-7; 5:25; 6:2-3; 6:12; 9:7).

Amos, however, is not unaware of the religious perversions in the Northern Kingdom. His opening attack against the people of Israel (2:6-8) includes reference to their incestuous practices, their worshiping at many altars. Bethel's *altars* will be destroyed (3:14). He addresses the women of Samaria as the cows of Bashan (4:1), reflecting their identification with Anat and their allegiance to Baal. The Lord is the God of fertility. The Lord is the One who has withheld bread and rain and has sent insects and diseases to destroy their crops (4:6-9). The Lord threatens, in fact, to intensify his judgments through nature (7:1-6; 8:13).

In the day of the consummate judgment, the Lord will search the domain of the "other gods" where Israelites have tried to hide themselves, to escape detection or protect themselves against the sweep of the Assyrian army. The Lord himself will invade the domains of these so-called gods and drive his people into exile (Amos 9:2-4). The Lord Almighty, not Baal, is the One who builds his palace in the heavens *[Ba'al, p. 373]* and controls the forces of nature in judgment as well as in blessing (9:5-6; 9:13-15). The polemic of the book shows an intimate acquaintance with the Baal myth, the fertility cycle, and the character of Israel's worship, though it does not mention any other gods by name.

Hosea challenges the Baal cult by demonstrating the consequences of defecting from the Lord and following Baal. The two go hand in hand. Since there is no knowledge of God, no covenant love, and no integrity, sins of all kinds break out among the people (Hos. 4:1-2). The end result is judgment on the land itself.

The accusation speeches of the three cycles of Hosea 4:4—14:8 follow this line of argument. The first progression, for example, follows this reasoning. Let Israel know that its present way of life issues from their submission to what is false—to priests who do not know nor teach God's truth (4:4-13a), values which result from following other gods (4:13b-14), and the ethical practices which flow from those values (4:17-19). Israel has absorbed the way of life characteristic of those who worship the gods of Canaan. Truly, Ephraim has joined herself to idols!

The cause-effect sequences usually contrast the will of the Lord as it has been revealed and the consequences of following the way of Baal. The implication in the second set of accusation oracles is that the nation is without excuse. The people of Israel have rejected the truth they have known; they have consciously pursued a way other than *ḥesed* (Hos. 6:6-7; 7:2, 13). They have consecrated themselves to the way of Baal from the time of Baal-peor. As a result, they have come to resemble Baal, the object of their love (9:10).

The third accusation section follows a historical line of thought. Israel's problems in the past grew out of a penchant for deception (Hos. 11:12; 12:1, 3). This led to self-deception and arrogance (12:8, 12) and finally to submitting themselves to Baal (13:1-2).

If the calling of these prophets, Hosea and Amos, was to turn Israel from her destructive course, they failed. They did, however, broadcast seeds of hope. Their message and words of hope were directed in written form to Judah, urging the rest of God's people to avoid a similar moral, spiritual, political, and social catastrophe. Judah survived a long century beyond the independent existence of the Northern Kingdom. The recorded messages of Hosea and Amos served Judah with dire warnings to induce the nation to return to God. Possibly the reforms of Hezekiah were nourished by the words and lived message of Hosea.

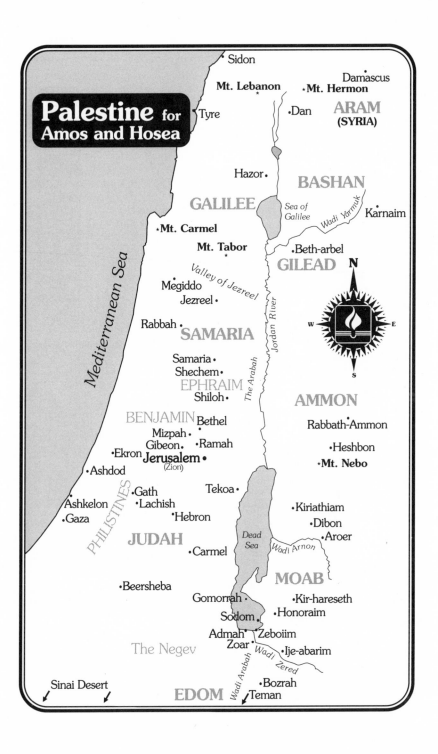

Palestine for Amos and Hosea

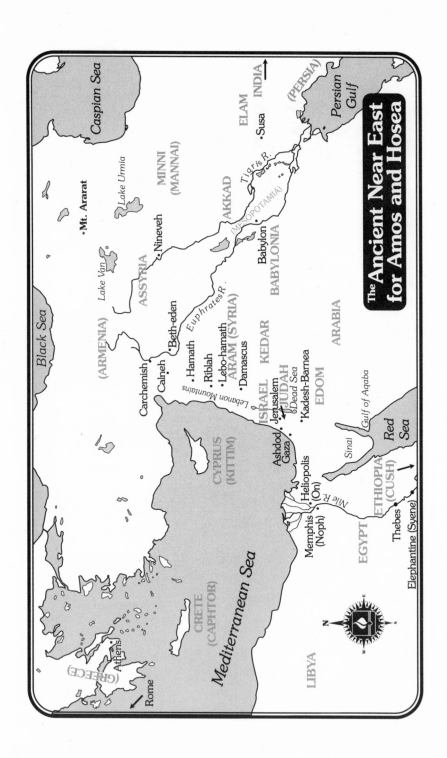

The **Ancient Near East** for Amos and Hosea

Bibliography

ABD   *The Anchor Bible Dictionary*
     1992   Freedman, D. N., et al., eds. 6 vols. New York: Doubleday.
Andersen, Francis I., and David Noel Freedman
     1980   *Hosea.* Anchor Bible, 24. Garden City, N.Y.: Doubleday.
     1989   *Amos.* Anchor Bible, 24A. New York: Doubleday.
ANEP   *The Ancient Near East in Pictures Relating to the Old Testament*
     1969   Ed. James B. Pritchard. 2d ed. with supplement. Princeton, N.J.: Princeton Univ. Press.
ANET   *The Ancient Near Eastern Texts Relating to the Old Testament*
     1955   Ed. James B. Pritchard. 2d ed. Princeton, N.J.: Princeton Univ. Press.
Barre, M. L.
     1978   "New Light on the Interpretation of Hosea VI. 2." *Vetus Testamentum* 28/2:129-141.
Barstad, Hans M.
     1984   *The Religious Polemics of Amos. Vetus Testamentum,* Suppl. 34. Leiden: E. J. Brill.
Beach, Eleanor Ferris
     1992   "The Samaria Ivories, Marzeah, and Biblical Texts." *Biblical Archaeologist* 55:130-139.
Block, Daniel Isaac
     1988   *The Gods of the Nations: Studies in Ancient Near Eastern National Theology.* ETS Monographs, 2. Jackson, Miss.: Evangelical Theological Society.
Bonhoeffer, Dietrich
     1959   *The Cost of Discipleship.* London: SCM.
Braun, Michael A.
     1977   "James's Use of Amos at the Jerusalem Council: Step Toward a Possible Solution of the Textual and Theological Problems." *Journal of the Evangelical Theological Society* 20:113-121.

Bright, John
1981 *A History of Israel.* 3d ed. Philadelphia: Westminster.
Bruce, F. F.
1958 *The Spreading Flame: The Rise and Progress of Christianity from Its First Beginnings to the Conversion of the English.* Grand Rapids: Eerdmans.
Buckley, Tom
1984 *Violent Neighbors: El Salvador, Central America, and the United States.* New York: Times Books.
CAH *Cambridge Ancient History*
1975 Ed. I. E. S. Edwards et al. 3d ed. Vol. 2/2: *History of the Middle East and the Aegean Region, c. 1380-1000 B.C.* New York: Cambridge Univ. Press.
1991 Ed. John Boardman et al. Vol. 3/2: *The Assyrian and Babylonian Empires and Other States of the Near East, from the Eighth to the Sixth Centuries B.C.* New York: Cambridge Univ. Press.
Cogan, Morton
1974 *Imperialism and Religion: Assyria, Judah and Israel in the Eighth and Seventh Centuries B.C.E.* Society of Biblical Literature (SBL) Monographs, 19. Missoula, Mont.: Scholars Press.
Craigie, Peter
1982 "Amos the *Noqed* in the Light of Ugaritic." *Studies in Religion* 11/1 (1982): 29-33.
Cripps, Richard S.
1960 *A Critical and Exegetical Commentary on the Book of Amos.* 2d ed. London: S.P.C.K.
De Moor, J. C.
1977 "Asherah." *TDOT*, 1:438-444. See *TDOT*
De Waard, Jan
1977 "The Chiastic Structure of Amos V. 1-17." *Vetus Testamentum* 27:170-177.
De Waard, Jan, and William A. Smalley
1979 *A Translator's Handbook on the Book of Amos.* "Helps for Translators." New York: United Bible Societies.
Dearman, John Andrew
1988 *Property Rights in the Eighth-Century Prophets: The Conflict and Its Background.* SBL Diss., 106. Atlanta: Scholars Press.
Deroche, Michael
1983 "Structure, Rhetoric, and Meaning in Hosea 4:4-10." *Vetus Testamentum* 33/2:185-198.
Earl, Richard
1982 "The Creative Use of Amos by the Author of Acts." *Novum Testamentum* 24/1:37-53.
Fleming, Daniel E.
1992 *The Installation of Baal's High Priestess at Emar: A Window on Ancient Syrian Religion.* Harvard Semitic Studies, 42. Atlanta: Scholars Press.
Freedman, David Noel. *See* Andersen; *ABD*

Friedman, Mordechai A.
1980 "Israel's Response in Hosea 2:17b: 'You are my husband.'" *Journal of Biblical Literature* 99/2:199-204.
Gardner, Richard B.
1991 *Matthew.* Believers Church Bible Commentary. Scottdale, Pa.: Herald Press.
Gordon, S. D.
1904 *Quiet Talks on Prayer.* New York: Fleming H. Revell.
Hasel, Gerhard F.
1972 *The Remnant.* Berrien Springs, Mich.: Andrews Univ. Press.
1991 *Understanding the Book of Amos: Basic Issues in Current Interpretations.* Grand Rapids: Baker Book House.
Hayes, John H.
1988 *Amos, His Times and His Preaching: The Eighth-Century Prophet.* Nashville: Abingdon.
Hayes, John H., and J. Maxwell Miller, eds.
1977 *Israelite and Judean History.* Philadelphia: Westminster.
L'Heureux, Conrad E.
1979 *Rank Among the Canaanite Gods: El, Ba'al, and the Rephaim.* Harvard Semitic Monographs, 21; Missoula: Scholars Press.
Hiebert, Paul
1980 "Conversion in Cross-Cultural Perspective." In *Conversion: Doorway to Discipleship,* 88-98. Ed. Henry J. Schmidt. Hillsboro, Kans.: Board of Christian Literature, Mennonite Brethren.
Hillers, Delbert
1964 "A Note on Some Treaty Terminology in the Old Testament." *Bulletin of the American Schools of Oriental Research* 176:46-47.
1964a *Treaty-Curses and the Old Testament Prophets.* Rome: Pontifical Biblical Institute.
Holladay, William L.
1970 "Once more, '*anak* = 'Tin,' Amos VII. 7-8." *Vetus Testamentum* 20:492-494.
Hubbard, David Allan
1989 *Joel and Amos: An Introduction and Commentary.* Tyndale Old Testament Commentaries. Downers Grove, Ill.: InterVarsity.
1990 *Hosea: An Introduction and Commentary.* Downers Grove, Ill.: InterVarsity.
Hunt, Arthur S., and C. C. Edgar
1970 *Select Papyri in Four Volumes.* Vol. 1. Loeb Classical Library. Cambridge: Harvard Univ. Press.
Jacobs, Paul F.
1985 " 'Cows of Bashan'—A Note on the Interpretation of Amos 4:1." *Journal of Biblical Literature* 104/1:109-110.
Janzen, Waldemar
1972 *Mourning Cry and Woe Oracle.* Berlin and New York: Walter de Gruyter.
Jepson, Alfred
1977 " '*Aman.*" *TDOT,* 1:292-323. See *TDOT*

Kaiser, Walter
   1977 "The Davidic Promise and the Inclusion of the Gentiles (Amos 9:9-15 and Acts 15:13-18): A Test Passage for Theological Systems." *Journal of the Evangelical Theological Society* 20:97-111.

Kalluveetil, Paul
   1982 *Declaration and Covenant: A Comprehensive Review of Covenant Formulae from the Old Testament and the Ancient Near East.* Analecta biblica, 88. Rome: Pontifical Biblical Institute.

King, Greg A.
   1995 "The Day of the Lord in Zephaniah." *Bibliotheca Sacra* 152:16-32.

King, Martin Luther Jr.
   1968 *The Trumpet of Conscience.* New York: Harper & Row.

King, Philip J.
   1988 *Amos, Hosea, Micah—An Archaeological Commentary.* Philadelphia: Westminster.

Klein, William W., Craig L. Blomberg, and Robert L. Hubbard Jr.
   1993 *Introduction to Biblical Interpretation.* Dallas: Word.

Kline, Meredith G.
   1961-2 "Divine Kingship and Genesis 6:1-4." *Westminster Theological Journal* 24:187-204.

Knierim, Rolf P.
   1977 " 'I Will Not Cause It to Return' in Amos 1 and 2." In *Canon and Authority: Essays in Old Testament Religion and Theology,* 163-175. Ed. George W. Coats and Burke O. Long. Philadelphia: Fortress.

Kugel, James L.
   1981 *The Idea of Biblical Poetry: Parallelism and Its History.* New Haven: Yale Univ. Press.

Latourette, Kenneth Scott
   1975 *A History of Christianity.* Rev. ed. 2 vols. New York: Harper & Row.

Limburg, James
   1988 *Hosea, Micah.* Interpretation. Atlanta: John Knox.

Lind, Millard C.
   1996 *Ezekiel.* Believers Church Bible Commentary. Scottdale, Pa.: Herald Press.

Martens, Elmer A.
   1981 *God's Design: A Focus on Old Testament Theology.* Grand Rapids: Baker.
   1986 *Jeremiah.* Believers Church Bible Commentary. Scottdale, Pa.: Herald Press.

Mattill, A. J. Jr.
   1964 "Representative Universalism and the Conquest of Canaan." *Concordia Theological Monthly* 35:8-11.

McCarter, P. Kyle Jr.
1987 "The Religion of the Israelite Monarchy: Biblical and Epigraphic Data." In *Ancient Israelite Religion: Essays in Honor of Frank Moore Cross*, 137-155. Ed. Patrick D. Miller Jr., Paul D. Hanson, and S. Dean McBride. Philadelphia: Fortress.

Menninger, Karl
1973 *Whatever Became of Sin?* New York: Hawthorne Books.

Mettinger, Tryggve N. D.
1982 *The Dethronement of Sabaoth: Studies in the Shem and Kabod Theologies*. Lund: Gleerup.

Miller, Perry
1956 *Errand into the Wilderness*. Cambridge, Mass.: Belknap.

Moran, William L.
1963 "The Ancient Near Eastern Background of the Love of God in Deuteronomy." *Catholic Biblical Quarterly* 25:76-87.

Mowvley, Harry
1991 *The Books of Amos and Hosea*. Epworth Commentaries. London: Epworth.

Mullen, E. Theodore Jr.
1980 *The Divine Council in Canaanite and Early Hebrew Literature*. Harvard Semitic Monographs, 24; Chico, Calif.: Scholars Press.

Murray, D. F.
1987 "The Rhetoric of Disputation: Re-examination of a Prophetic Genre." *Journal for the Study of the Old Testament* 38:95-121.

Nash, Roland H.
1983 *Social Justice and the Christian Church*. Milford, Mich.: Mott Media.

Newman, Albert Henry
1933 *A Manual of Church History*. 2 vols. Rev. ed. Philadelphia: American Baptist Publication Society.

Niebuhr, H. Richard
1951 *Christ and Culture*. New York: Harper & Brothers.

Paul, Shalom M.
1991 *Amos*. Heremeneia. Minneapolis: Fortress.

Piper, John.
1980a "The Righteousness of God in Romans." *Journal for the Study of the New Testament* 7:2-32.
1980b "The Righteousness of God in Romans 3:1-8." *Theologische Zeitschrift* 36:3-14.

Porten, Bezalel, and Ada Yardeni, eds. and trans.
1987-1989 *Textbook of Aramaic Documents from Ancient Egypt*. 2 vols. Jerusalem: Texts and Studies for Students.

Prichard, James B. *See ANEP; ANET*

Romero, Oscar A.
1984 *The Church Is All of You: Thoughts of Archbishop Oscar Romero*. Comp. and trans. James R. Brockman. Minneapolis: Winston.

Roth, Martha T.
1989 *Babylonian Marriage Agreements: 7th–3rd Centuries B.C.* Alter Orient und Altes Testament, Bd. 222. Neukirchen-Vluyn: Neukirchener Verlag.

Sakenfeld, Katharine Doob
1978 *The Meaning of Hesed in the Hebrew Bible: A New Inquiry*. Missoula, Mont.: Scholars Press.
Schneider, John
1994 *Godly Materialism: Rethinking Money and Possessions*. Downers Grove, Ill.: InterVarsity.
Smelik, K. A. D.
1986 "The Meaning of Amos V. 18-20." *Vetus Testamentum* 36/2: 246-248.
Smith, Gary V.
1989 *Amos: A Commentary*. Library of Biblical Interpretation. Grand Rapids: Regency Reference Library.
Starkes, M. Thomas
1984 *God's Commissioned People*. Nashville: Broadman.
Stuart, Douglas
1987 *Hosea-Jonah*. Word Bible Commentary, 31. Waco, Tex.: Word.
Talley, Jim
1985 *Reconcilable Differences: Mending Broken Relationships*. Nashville: Nelson.
Thiele, Edwin R.
1985 *The Mysterious Numbers of the Hebrew Kings: A Reconstruction of the Chronology of the Kingdoms of Israel and Judah*. 2nd ed. Grand Rapids: Eerdmans.
TDOT *Theological Dictionary of the Old Testament*
1977 Vol. 1. Ed. G. J. Botterweck and H. Ringgren. Trans. John T. Willis. Grand Rapids: Eerdmans. *See* De Moor; Jepson
Toews, Wesley Irwin
1990 "Monarchy and Religious Institution in Israel Under Jeroboam I." Doctoral diss. at Princeton Theological Seminary.
Wallerstein, Judith S., and Sandra Blakeslee
1990 *Second Chances: Men, Women and Children a Decade after Divorce*. New York: Ticknor & Fields.
Walls, Neal H.
1992 *The Goddess Anat in Ugaritic Myth*. SBL Diss., 135. Atlanta: Scholars Press.
Weippert, Helga
1985 "Amos." In *Beiträge zur prophetischen Bildsprache in Israel und Assyrien*, 1-29. Ed. Helga Weippert, Klaus Seybold, and Manfred Weippert. Orbis biblicus et orientalis. Fribourg, Switzerland: Universitätsverlag; Göttingen: Vandenhoek & Ruprecht.
Westbrook, Raymond
1988 *Old Babylonian Marriage Law*. Archiv für Orientforschung, Beiheft 23. Horn, Austria: Verlag Ferdinand Berger & Söhne.
Westermann, Claus
1967 *Basic Forms of Prophetic Speech*. Philadelphia: Westminster.
1991 *Prophetic Oracles of Salvation in the Old Testament*. Louisville: Westminster/John Knox.
White, John, and Ken Blue
1985 *Healing the Wounded: The Costly Love of Church Discipline*. Downer's Grove, Ill.: InterVarsity.

Wijngaards, J.
  1967 "Death and Resurrection in Covenantal Context (Hos. VI. 2)."
       Vetus Testamentum 17:226-239.
Wilberforce, William
  1958 *A Practical View of the Prevailing Religious System of Professed
       Christians in the Higher and Middle Classes in this Country Con-
       trasted with Real Christianity.* London: SCM.
Willis, Edward David
  1977 *Daring Prayer.* Atlanta: John Knox.
Wink, Walter
  1992 *Engaging the Powers: Discernment and Resistance in a World of
       Domination.* Minneapolis: Fortress.
Wolff, Hans Walter
  1977 *Joel and Amos.* Trans. Waldemar Janzen, S. Dean McBride Jr.,
       and Charles A. Muenchow. Hermeneia. Philadelphia: Fortress.
  1974 *Hosea.* Hermeneia. Philadelphia: Fortress.
Yoder, Perry B.
  1982 *From Word to Life: A Guide to the Art of Bible Study.* Scottdale,
       Pa: Herald Press.
  1987 *Shalom: The Bible's Word for Salvation, Justice, and Peace.*
       Newton, Kan.: Faith & Life.

Selected Resources

Andersen, Francis I., and David Noel Freedman. *Amos.* Anchor Bible, 24A. New York: Doubleday, 1989. Focuses on matters of translation, structure, and explanatory comments in 979 pages. Acquaintance with Hebrew is helpful but not essential.

Andersen, Francis I., and David Noel Freedman. *Hosea.* Anchor Bible, 24. Garden City, N.Y.: Doubleday, 1980. Massive and exhaustive treatment of issues of translation and interpretation. Technical and scholarly. Interacts with a range of alternative interpretations.

Hayes, John H. *Amos, His Times and His Preaching: The Eighth-Century Prophet.* Nashville: Abingdon, 1988. Superb introduction to prophetic literature and assumptions and conclusions in interpreting Amos. Aware of issues in Amos studies but focuses on setting out a considered and well-presented interpretation.

Hubbard, David Allan. *Hosea,* 1990. *Joel and Amos,* 1989. Tyndale Old Testament Commentaries. Downers Grove, Ill.: InterVarsity. Compact, informative, evangelical explanations of the text for the nonspecialist.

King, Philip J. *Amos, Hosea, Micah: An Archaeological Commentary.* Philadelphia: Westminster, 1988. A sourcebook of background information for the three prophets.

Mowvley, Harry. *The Books of Amos and Hosea.* Epworth Commentaries. London: Epworth, 1991. Primary attention given to the flow of thought in the book. These synthetic expositions are geared to the average reader and lay interpreter.

Paul, Shalom M. *Amos.* Heremeneia. Minneapolis: Fortress, 1991. An in-depth study of the language and structure of the book of

Amos. It assumes an understanding of Hebrew.

Smith, Gary V. *Amos: A Commentary.* Library of Biblical Interpretation. Grand Rapids: Regency Reference Library, 1989. Evangelical and thorough. Sensitive to literary features and theological implications, which receive explicit attention under separate headings. Valuable for teaching or preaching as well as personal study.

Stuart, Douglas. *Hosea–Jonah.* Word Bible Commentary, vol. 31. Waco, Tex.: Word Books, 1987. A detailed unit-by-unit analysis of the text, under headings: Bibliography, Translation, Notes, Form/Structure/Setting, Comment, Explanation.

Index of Ancient Sources

(Other than the book being interpreted)

The Author

Allen R. Guenther is known for his passion as a student and teacher of the Scriptures and his active concern for the vigor of the church. He relishes opportunities to interpret and communicate biblical insights for life situations. This reflects his pastoral experience and extensive life-oriented church and community ministries.

Currently Guenther is professor of Old Testament at the Mennonite Brethren Biblical Seminary, Fresno, California, where he has taught since 1981. From 1967–70 and 1975–81, he taught at Mennonite Brethren Bible College and College of Arts at Winnipeg. He pastored a new congregation in Lethbridge, Alberta, during 1963-65, and an inner-city congregation in Toronto in 1971-73.

Guenther was born in Manitoba and received his Th.B. from the Mennonite Brethren Bible College in Winnipeg, his B.A. from the University of British Columbia, an M.A. in New Testament from Wheaton Graduate School of Theology, an M.Div. from Gordon-Conwell Divinity School, an M.A. in Near Eastern Studies from the University of Toronto, and in 1978 his Ph.D. in Near Eastern Languages and Literature from the University of Toronto. He is a member of the Institute for Biblical Research, the Evangelical Theological Society, and the Society of Biblical Literature.

Guenther ministers to society at large in his volunteer work as a mediator between victims and offenders in the local reconciliation program (VORP) and in his service as founder and president of the Valley Parkinson's Support Group. He nurtures the life of the church in his many local church ministries and extensive writing in church publications. Internationally, Guenther has presented seminars at churches in Tulpengasse, Vienna, and Kiev, Ukraine.

Allen and Anne Guenther are active members of the Butler Avenue Mennonite Brethren Church in Fresno. They are the parents of three adult sons, Ron, Barry, and Michael.